# JAMES MADISON

*Father of the Constitution*

JAMES AND DOLLEY MADISON

PENCIL DRAWINGS ON IVORY BY T. C. LÜBBERS, AFTER OIL PORTRAITS BY GILBERT STUART. OWNED BY THE NEW YORK HIS-
TORICAL SOCIETY

# JAMES MADISON

*Father of the Constitution*

*1787-1800*

BY

## IRVING BRANT

AUTHOR OF

*Storm over the Constitution*
*James Madison: The Virginia Revolutionist*
*James Madison: The Nationalist*

ILLUSTRATED

## THE BOBBS-MERRILL COMPANY, INC.
*PUBLISHERS*

INDIANAPOLIS                    NEW YORK

# CONTENTS

# CONTENTS—*continued*

# LIST OF ILLUSTRATIONS

# JAMES MADISON

*Father of the Constitution*

# CHRONOLOGY

March 16, 1751. James Madison born.

1763-1772. Schooling under Donald Robertson and Thomas Martin, and at Princeton.

1776-1779. Revolutionary activities in Virginia Convention, House of Delegates and Governor's Council.

March 20, 1780, to October 25, 1783. Attends Continental Congress.

1784 to 1787. Member of Virginia House of Delegates.

September, October, 1784. Attends Fort Stanwix Indian Treaty with Lafayette and Marbois.

1784. Defeats public support of teachers of religion, secures passage of the Statute of Religious Liberty, sponsors Potomac and James River improvements.

1785-1787. Puts Jefferson-Pendleton-Wythe revisal of laws through legislature.

September 1786. Attends Annapolis Convention, sponsored by himself a year earlier.

November 1786. Sponsors Virginia's indorsement of convention to revise the Articles of Confederation and is named a delegate. Elected once more to Confederation Congress.

February through April 1787. Attends Congress in New York.

May 2, 1787. Leaves for Federal Convention in Philadelphia.

# CHAPTER I

## On the Threshold

JAMES MADISON was the first delegate to arrive in Philadelphia for the convention of 1787. He came in eleven days ahead of time to attend a meeting which opened eleven days behind time. Such eagerness was natural in one who had been devoting most of his thoughts to the remaking of government. However, there was a definite purpose in this forehandedness.

A full month earlier, while attending the old Congress in New York, Madison appealed to his close friend Governor Edmund Randolph to come early because Virginia ought to be prepared in advance with materials for the convention. Also, he needed to prepare the governor. It was axiomatic with Madison that Virginia would go no farther into federalism than Randolph would, but how far he would go sometimes depended more on Madison than on himself.

Randolph's opinion, at this time, was that alterations in government should be grafted onto the Articles of Confederation. Madison disagreed. Looking at the old articles and the federal government they established, this is what he saw:

A one-house Congress mixing executive and legislative powers.

Virginia sixteen times as populous as Delaware, but each state having one vote in Congress.

Seven or nine affirmative state votes required for every action, so that absent states in effect voted No.

Congressional delegates appointed and recalled by state legislatures, making the federal government subservient.

No money for federal purposes except by requisitions which the states ignored.

No federal power over commerce.

No federal judiciary except in maritime affairs.

All powers retained by the states unless expressly delegated.

No means of enforcing the powers expressly delegated.

11

No amendment without the unanimous consent of thirteen states.

Patching, Madison concluded, would not do. There must be a new form of government, a new relationship between states and nation, between the people and their institutions. In theory, the essential parts of sovereignty already were in the nation. Power must go with sovereignty.

Madison's preference was to enumerate the powers of the new Congress. But was this feasible? He was undecided between a government of specified and limited powers, or of general and virtually unlimited authority. Saying nothing of his doubts to Randolph or Washington, he wrote that in addition to its existing powers, "the national government should be armed with positive and complete authority in all cases which require uniformity; such as the regulation of trade, including the right of taxing both exports and imports, the fixing the terms and forms of naturalization, etc., etc."[1]

Individual independence of the states, Madison believed, was "utterly irreconcilable with their aggregate sovereignty." Ought they then to be consolidated into one simple republic? That neither should nor could be done. He sought therefore "for some middle ground, which may at once support a due supremacy of the national authority and not exclude the local authorities wherever they can be subordinately useful."

Beyond its positive powers, the federal government should have "a negative *in all cases whatsoever* on the legislative acts of the states, as heretofore exercised by the kingly prerogative." Without this, every positive power that could be given on paper would be evaded and defeated. Grant it, and the states would be restrained from thwarting and molesting one another, or from oppressing the minority by paper money and other unrighteous measures.

A legislature of two branches, one chosen by the people or the state legislatures; the other smaller, with a longer and rotating membership; a national executive; a judiciary to which national supremacy ought also to be extended—this was the structure Madison envisioned. Because of the way it would encroach on state sovereignty and override state constitutions, ratification must be obtained from the people, not from legislatures.[2]

It is imperative to recognize how completely Madison put the nation above the states in 1787. Not many years later, owing to changing political conditions, he sought to use the states as a makeweight against the federal government. Still later, vast political and social pressures growing out of slavery and other sectional issues forced him to bury his early nationalism from sight. The result has been a distortion, amazingly persistent, both of Madison's original purposes and of the concepts of sovereignty embedded in the Constitution.

State sovereignty had virtually no place in the scheme of government Madison outlined to Washington, Randolph and Jefferson on the eve of the Constitutional Convention. The state governments were to be regarded as "subordinately useful" local authorities subject to "a due supremacy of the national authority." Madison was led to this conclusion by his experience as a legislator—four years in Congress, three years in the Virginia Assembly—confirmed by the downward spinning of the Confederacy into chaos. What experience told him, study confirmed. Every confederation of states, from ancient Greece to modern Europe, made it plain that there could be no effective government when the members were not subject to central authority. With him, to enforce this lesson, he brought his "Study of Ancient and Modern Confederacies" and "Vices of the Political System of the United States."

At first, in 1781, Madison had sought to bring about the subjection of the states through armed coercion by the federal government. He thought now that the right of coercion should be expressly declared (not left to implication), but "the difficulty and awkwardness of operating by force on the collective will of a state" made it desirable to eliminate the need for it. That might be achieved, he thought, by the federal negative, which would cut off unconstitutional state laws and establish a mutuality of dependence between federal and state authorities. (That is, Congress would depend on the states for money above that raised from commerce and the states would furnish it from fear of having their laws vetoed.) Or, he finally suggested, "some defined objects of taxation might be submitted, along with commerce, to the general authority."

In the very course of writing these words, Madison's thinking jumped forward. Give Congress a power of internal taxation, in addition to the laying of duties on foreign trade, and all needed federal revenues would be drawn directly from the people. Change the structure too, and the states could be totally removed as buffers between the federal government and the people. Discarding the dominant aspect of the Confederation—a government operating chiefly on states instead of persons—he visualized the charter of a federal republic reaching directly to the people. Save for the retention of state influence in the Senate, the fundamentals of the future American government were in his mind when he stepped out of the New York-Philadelphia flier on May 3.

At thirty-six, Madison was in good shape for the heavy work that lay ahead. Incessant horseback riding and long rambles in the country didn't add any inches to his height, but the frailty and pallor of early youth were gone. The historian Grigsby, who drew part of his accounts from contemporaries, describes his appearance a year later—muscular, well-proportioned, ruddy complexioned. He probably was tending toward the habitual black which later ruled his dress, but Grigsby heard of him "handsomely arrayed in blue and buff," his coat single-breasted, ruffles at wrist and chest. His hair, combed low to conceal an early recession from the forehead, was dressed with powder and ended with a long queue. He walked with a bouncing step which was no less marked forty years later.[3]

It was by gradual steps that the framers of the Constitution moved toward their task. Calls for a convention had been heard for years before there was much thought of a basic change. Thomas Paine proposed such a gathering in 1776 and again in 1780, "for the purpose of forming a continental constitution defining and describing the powers of Congress." In the latter year Alexander Hamilton wrote that Congress should have complete sovereignty, "except as to that part of internal police which relates to the rights of property and life among individuals and to raising money by internal taxes." Even the national-minded Hamilton, by this exception, and by his limited concept of a federal judiciary, left the federal government hanging on the states.[4]

The movement for a constitutional convention received pamphlet support from William Barton in 1781 and from Pelatiah Webster in 1783. The latter struck into new ground by proposing that Congress be split into House and Senate, with executive power in a council of great ministers. But he left the choice of both houses to state legislatures. Noah Webster (not yet dehumanized by his dictionary) hit a more basic note in 1785. In all national affairs Congress should have the same power to enact laws and compel obedience as the state legislatures in their lesser jurisdictions. If any of these writings influenced Madison's plan of government, it was this last.[5]

In the Continental Congress, the suggestion of a constitutional convention was thrown out during the debate on Madison's 1783 revenue plan. Hamilton indorsed it. So did Stephen Higginson— as a means of killing the five-per-cent impost. Fathoming this purpose, Madison called on his colleagues to seek only what they had some chance of obtaining. He was not inclined to lose sight of reality while in quest of the ideal.[6]

In the demoralized years which followed the Revolution, Madison saw the battle against a common foe give place to trade wars among the states. He witnessed the creeping paralysis of federal power, the bankruptcy of the federal treasury. He observed the debauching of state money systems to wipe out debt, and fought the partisans of paper money in Virginia.

His own measures were suited to the moment. Alarm nobody by premature talk. Ask for little when there was little chance of obtaining that. Seek more and still more as the sense of disaster spread. That was the formula which caused him, in the beginning, to work for a simple power in Congress to tax imports; defeated in that, to strike for a general congressional power over commerce; beaten there, to secure Virginia's call for the Annapolis Convention; and, upon its failure, to ask for another with far broader objectives. That achieved, he undermined Patrick Henry's antifederal strength by re-entering Congress and striking down

John Jay's move to surrender the Mississippi to Spain. Madison was able to go on, from defeat to larger efforts, because the pace of national anarchy outran the rejected remedies. When, at last, the terror of Shays' Rebellion brought others to the point he had reached by analysis, he was ready for the bold course proposed to Washington:

"Temporizing applications will dishonor the councils which propose them, and may foment the malignity of the disease. . . . Radical attempts although unsuccessful will at least justify the authors of them."

Rhode Island would be absent—debauched by paper money and commercial predation upon its neighbors—but Madison saw little to worry about in that. Disagreement among those present was a far greater hazard. Add the need to win the approval of Congress and the final sanction of the states, and the prospect "would inspire despair in any case where the alternative was less formidable." That alternative, men were beginning to say, was to establish a monarchy or split the United States into three republican confederacies.[7]

For ten days not a delegate showed up. Madison was in his old quarters, with Mrs. Mary House at Fifth and Market. Her daughter Eliza Trist rejoiced at the impending political bustle. Home nearly two years from her tragic voyage to her husband's grave in Louisiana, she was still corresponding with Jefferson in Paris, about to tell him, in a letter which accompanied Madison's next, that the Trists in Devonshire had not yet sent her son Browse his inheritance, but her health, thank God, was much improved.

Madison plunged into a talk on tobacco with Merchant Samuel House, handler of the Montpelier crop, now slowly recouping his fortunes from the depression of the mid-eighties. It was not pleasing to learn that while old tobacco was worth $6.00 a hundred, or 40s., the new crop was unlikely to bring more than 32s. He was disappointed too in making purchases. Trade regulations by Pennsylvania and Virginia had raised the price of goods shipped by water to Fredericksburg.[8]

Time was spent attempting to unravel a mysterious tale told at

Montpelier by the runaway slave Anthony, who returned or was captured after being in too many places in an impossibly short time. Madison's servant John hinted at the complicity of his ex-runaway ex-servant Billey, whom he had set free under a seven-year indenture, five years before, because he would not punish a man for trying to obtain the liberty he heard members of Congress orating about. Billey's denials aroused suspicions as to John, but the latter's conduct was improving: "His misbehavior in Fredericksburg was followed by some serious reprehensions and threats from me which have never lost their effect." One of the lesser blessings of slavery was that it did not allow a slaveowner to stop thinking about slaves.[9]

For the first time, Madison came into personal contact with Benjamin Franklin, whom he had so ardently defended in the Continental Congress against the onslaughts of Arthur Lee and his anti-Gallic faction. Franklin, now president of Pennsylvania, was eighty-one years old, and (an English traveler reported) "much broke in his looks since I saw him last at Passy near Paris." On warm days, he received visitors under the large mulberry tree in his garden, set back in a deep courtyard off Market Street.[10]

On Sunday the thirteenth the City Light Dragoons and national officers of the Cincinnati rode down to Gray's Ferry on the Schuylkill, and came back amid the shouts of the people and the thunder of artillery with George Washington in tow. Apparently the general no longer had an ear for gunfire, for he wrote in his diary that on his arrival the bells were chimed. He "alighted through a crowd at Mrs. House's," intending to join Madison, but Robert Morris carried him off to his three-story brick mansion.[11]

Arrival of George Wythe and John Blair gave Virginia a quorum. That state and Pennsylvania, therefore, met at the State House on May 14 and adjourned. By the sixteenth, Governor Randolph and Dr. James McClurg were in from Virginia and took quarters with Madison. With them came John Beckley, aspiring clerk of the House of Delegates, whose desire to be secretary of the convention was not chilled by Randolph's observation that the office could have no lucre attached. He didn't get it, but stayed on in a confidential relationship with the Virginians. McClurg

was the stalking-horse candidate with whom Madison killed the
aspiration of Arthur Lee to be foreign secretary in 1781. He now
filled a vacancy caused by the ominous refusals of Patrick Henry,
General Nelson and Richard Henry Lee to take part in the convention's work—refusals which foretold their opposition to the
completed Constitution. A scratched-out footnote in Madison's
notes on the convention states that he actively promoted McClurg's
appointment. It would be useful to have so strong a nationalist on
hand, in case George Mason kicked over the traces.[12]

Scattered delegates were present now from seven states, but they
lacked a quorum for any business except to dine at Franklin's
house and broach a cask of "the best porter they have ever tasted."
Or so Franklin reported to the donor of it, while Washington recorded that he drank tea.[13]

The convention got a lift next day with the coming of South
Carolina's John Rutledge and precocious Charles Pinckney, who
afterward changed his birth date by four years to support his lifelong claim that he was the youngest member of a convention in
which three men were his juniors. The lagging of New England
caused Madison to suffer "a daily disappointment." But this left
time for a breakfast with General Mifflin, who then rode out with
Washington, Madison, Rutledge and others to visit country seats
across the Schuylkill. There was time, also, for all the Virginians
except Washington to attend mass at the Roman Catholic church
on Sunday the twentieth—"more out of compliment than religion,
and more out of curiosity than compliment," Anglican George
Mason explained apologetically. The general was at the Morris
farm, so a week later he too "went to the Romish church to high
mass"—a fact which led the newspapers to praise Father Beeston's
excellent sermon.[14]

With seven states able to vote on May 25, Washington was
unanimously elected chairman. The nomination, Madison commented, came with particular grace from Pennsylvania as Dr.
Franklin alone could have been thought of as a competitor. The
doctor himself was to have made the motion, but bad weather and
ill health confined him to his house. For secretary, Major William
Jackson, former assistant to the Secretary at War, defeated Wil-

liam Temple Franklin, Benjamin's grandson. His performance
heightened the reputation for incompetence made as a buyer of
war supplies in Holland.[15]

On May 29 the convention squared away for action. Among
the rules adopted, the most important was that seven states should
form a quorum, and decisions should be made by a majority of
the delegations possessing quorums of their own. This was a departure from the fatal "chaos clause" of the Articles of Confederation, which required the affirmative votes of either seven or nine
states to carry any legislative question. It put into practice the rule
which Madison argued for, on March 5, 1781, as the proper interpretation of the Articles themselves. Had he won then, there
might have been no need to write a new constitution.

Measured by visible historical impact, the outstanding order
was that nothing spoken in the house be printed or communicated
without leave. Jefferson thought this an abominable decision, but
Madison wrote that it not only would secure freedom of discussion, but would "save both the convention and the community
from a thousand erroneous and perhaps mischievous reports."
Years afterward he told Jared Sparks that no constitution would
have been adopted by the convention if the debates had been
public.[16]

Thanks to a further decision for secrecy on the closing day of
the convention, it was thirty years before even the journals became
known, while the complete debates were shrouded for a full half
century. But it was due to Madison that there was a record of
debates to shroud. During his research into ancient confederacies,
as he explained it, he was handicapped by ignorance of the purposes and principles which prevailed in their formation. This
determined him to preserve as far as he could an exact account
of what went on in the convention. Nor was he unaware of its
value to the history of a constitution on which would be staked
the happiness of the people and possibly the cause of liberty
throughout the world. He continued:

"In pursuance of the task I had assumed, I chose a seat in front
of the presiding member, with the other members on my right

and left hands. In this favorable position for hearing all that passed I noted, in terms legible and in abbreviations and marks intelligible to myself, what was read from the chair or spoken by the members; and losing not a moment unnecessarily between the adjournment and reassembling of the convention, I was enabled to write out my daily notes during the session or within a few finishing days after its close, in the extent and form preserved in my own hand on my files.

"In the labor and correctness of this I was not a little aided by practice, and by a familiarity with the style and the train of observation and reasoning which characterized the principal speakers. It happened, also, that I was not absent a single day, nor more than a casual fraction of an hour in any day, so that I could not have lost a single speech unless a very short one."[17]

With four specified exceptions, the speeches were neither furnished, nor revised, nor sanctioned by the speakers, but were written out from Madison's notes. The completeness, accuracy and lack of bias in this reporting would make it a lasting marvel even if Madison had done nothing else. It was, however, a chore voluntarily assumed in addition to his leading role in the convention. Other fragmentary records were kept, by McHenry of Maryland, King of Massachusetts, Pierce of Georgia, Paterson of New Jersey, Charles Pinckney of South Carolina, Hamilton, Lansing and Yates of New York. Of these men, only Judge Yates made more than a faint approach to Madison's thoroughness. His notes mixed the actual remarks of speakers with his own zipped-up condensations of them, and they ended with his and Lansing's early and disgusted departure from a convention they were unable to run or ruin.[18]

Madison recorded all speeches in the third person, a fact which the reader needs to bear in mind when the pronoun "he" smites him from a literal quotation.

The two leading note takers knew nothing of each other prior to the convention. Madison wrote that "a Mr. Yates" was to be there and Yates chronicled that "Mr. Matthewson" was a Virginia delegate.[19] During the first fortnight Madison recorded four times as many speeches and his notes were five times as long. However, Yates's technique improved as his temper worsened. In the final full week of their parallel work, Madison recorded seventy-three speeches, Yates sixty-five, with Madison's work only fifty per cent longer.

No less marked in Yates was his slow start and rapid improvement in estimating Madison's importance in the convention. He totally ignored the low-voiced Virginian's first ten participations in debate. But Yates was a partisan who paid more attention to adversaries than to friends. After he woke up he reported more Madison speeches than Madison did himself. In the whole period of his reporting, he gave more space to Madison than to any other delegate—nearly as much as to Yates's three leading allies combined.

The two weeks needed for Yates to recognize Madison's importance seem rather short, considering that it took thirty-four years for Madison to recognize Yates's. That recognition came in 1821, when publication of the Yates notes revealed Madison's long-buried nationalism and hostility to state sovereignty. If both sets of debates had been printed as soon as the Constitution was adopted, the public would merely have noted, thereafter, that Madison shifted his attitude as conditions changed. But by 1821 he had become an oracle of strict construction and a bulwark of state sovereignty. His contrary position, before and during the writing of the Constitution, was unsuspected. He could not admit the validity of what Yates had written without a shattering blow to his own prestige and an implied verification of the Marshall-Hamilton conception of national power. He combated it, therefore, by countercharge, avoidance and implied denial.

Yates, said Madison, "represented the strong prejudices in New York against the object of the convention," which was in part to take away that state's power to tax its neighbors' commerce. This warped his mind "to an unfavorable understanding of what was said in opposition to the prejudices felt." He then proceeded to restate his own position, not actually denying his previous hostility to the states, but toning it down far more than Yates had sharpened it.[20]

Knowledge that his own notes would verify Yates's probably helped Madison to the decision for posthumous publication. Urged in 1827 to publish them to refute Yates, he replied that only three of the framers were still living and it would be more delicate and more useful to wait until all were gone. No personal or party views could then be imputed. He did not explain (as he did to Jefferson in 1799) that publication would aid the opposing party.[21]

However, looking forward to publication after his death, Madison undertook to revise his notes. Here was a test of honesty—to let the record stand, with the certainty that it would someday rise to shatter his reputation for consistency and undermine the constitutional base of his fight against the money power in Congress, or doctor it and escape the consequences. Examining Madison's original manuscript today, one finds it marked through and through with changes, elisions and additions. Looked at, one by one, they fade away as evidence of distortion or become the contrary. The major part of the revision consists of corrections and additions made from the published journal and from Yates. A few state names are stricken out of harsh remarks. A few words are deleted to tone down nationalism. But the change is microscopic. The notes stand as an impressive example of integrity and impartiality, in the face of powerful motives for suppression. In one instance he struck out a word to fortify his condemnation of Yates, yet carried into his notes of that very speech a sentence from Yates which tore down state sovereignty.[22] Impelled to save face before Virginia friends and critics, he was willing to let future generations see him as he was in 1787—a champion of national power, and of national supremacy over subordinate states.

# CHAPTER II

## THE VIRGINIA PLAN

AMONG tardy delegates, to be less tardy was to be prompt. From the delay of others, the seven Virginians gained the opportunity Madison had sought for advance planning. Beginning May 17, they met every day for two or three hours "to form a proper correspondence of sentiment," as George Mason expressed it.

The delegation was to Madison's liking. Washington and McClurg would go as far as he would in strengthening the federal government and restraining the states. Like-minded George Wythe, the William and Mary legal scholar, was lost to them within a fortnight because of the fatal illness of his wife. Quiet Judge Blair leaned toward the federal side. So did Randolph, but could he be kept that way? With all his merits, George Bancroft wrote of him, "there was a strain of weakness in his character, so that he was like a soft metal which needs to be held in place by coils of a harder grain than its own. That support he found in Madison . . . and in Washington." Finally, what about Mason, who suffered from gout, stomach trouble, hatred of political gatherings and distrust of strong governments? Madison heard in advance that he was "renouncing his errors on the subject of the Confederation." Anyway, he was in better temper than usual. He would not, "upon pecuniary motives, serve in this convention for a thousand pounds a day," but was ready to help establish a wise and just government through the calm, sedate medium of reason. Quite a feat for this sixty-two-year-old Virginian, who had never been calm and sedate for a week in his life. On two points the delegation was a unit—devotion to government founded on the people, and belief in the need to check state assaults on property rights.[1]

Out of the consultations of these men came the Virginia Plan— the keystone of the Constitution—which Governor Randolph presented on May 29. The plan undoubtedly was written by Madison. In substance, it was a recasting of his April letters to Randolph and

23

Washington into fifteen resolutions on the form, powers and principles of the new government, with some proposals toned down a
trifle and others added. The opening paragraph was a concession
to win Randolph:

"Resolved that the Articles of Confederation ought to be so
corrected and enlarged as to accomplish the objects proposed by
their institution; namely, 'common defense, security of liberty and
general welfare.' "

This was not in the plan as originally written. Here it was followed, and reduced to an absurdity, by the whole Madison program of specific action—changes so great that they would require
the scrapping of the old articles entirely. Suffrage in the national
legislature was to be proportioned to state financial contributions
(that is, to population including three fifths of the slaves) or to
free inhabitants—no more state equality. The legislature should
consist of a first branch elected by the people and a second branch
elected by the first out of persons nominated by state legislatures.
    The plan provided "that a national executive be instituted; to
be chosen by the national legislature." It called for a national
judiciary of supreme and inferior tribunals with jurisdiction in
all questions "which may involve the national peace and harmony." State officials—legislative, executive and judicial—were to
be bound by oath to support the articles of union.
    As to the powers of that union:

"Resolved . . . that the national legislature ought to be empowered to enjoy the legislative rights vested in Congress by the
Confederation and moreover to legislate in all cases to which
the separate states are incompetent, or in which the harmony
of the United States may be interrupted by the exercise of individual legislation; to negative all laws passed by the several
states, contravening in the opinion of the national legislature the
articles of union; and to call forth the force of the Union against
any member of the Union failing to fulfill its duty under the
articles thereof."

This cut down Madison's previous demand for a federal negative
of state laws in all cases whatsoever, but gave greater sweep to his

desire for national legislation in all matters requiring uniformity. There was to be a council of revision, consisting of the national executive and part of the judiciary, but the national legislature could repass bills over its veto. The United States was to guarantee republican government in the states. Federal taxation and regulation of commerce were implied both in the sweeping description of legislative power and in a proviso that the national judiciary should deal with cases involving collection of the national revenue. The new system was to be submitted to Congress for approval, then to special assemblies chosen by the people of the several states. That would place it above state constitutions.

Owing to its early drafting, the Virginia Plan became known to some nondelegates before the convention met. It is easily recognizable in a description of the proposed reforms which Chargé d'Affaires Otto sent to his government on June 10, but there is no indication that the secrecy rule was violated. Otto's information had a preconvention flavor. He included provisions talked of but omitted from the plan and recorded none of the changes made after it was introduced. This well-informed French observer divided the American people into four groups:

1. Those who desired to establish a government on the model he described (the Virginia Plan).

2. Those who believed it impossible, under existing conditions, to reunite all the members of the Confederation under a single head. With the North devoted to fisheries and commerce, the Middle States to farming and the South to great plantations, they would break the country into three independent confederacies, allied for defense.

3. The Cincinnati. These old army officers, despairing of any other means of giving value to their defaulted pay certificates, were said to favor throwing the states into one mass under the rule of General Washington.

4. Those who wanted nothing done at all. This strong party, which included Governor Clinton and Samuel Adams, pointed to the steady increase of population, the clearing of vast forests, the growth of commerce and industry, as evidence that political evils were overstressed. Why risk subjecting the people to a despotism?

Otto erred in placing all the constructive reformers of govern-

ment in one group. However, the almost incredible fact is that
the other groups he described either had no advocates at all, or
only microscopic support, inside the convention. Madison testified
a few months later to the total absence of disunionism:

"It appeared to be the sincere and unanimous wish of the convention to cherish and preserve the Union of the states. No
proposition was made, no suggestion was thrown out, in favor of
a partition of the empire into two or more confederacies."

Many delegates belonged to the Cincinnati, but not to the ex-
tremist element in it. Few if any would have written as Secretary-
General Henry Knox did to Delegate Rufus King:

"The state systems are the accursed things which will prevent
our being a nation. The democracy might be managed, nay it
would remedy itself after being sufficiently fermented; but the
vile state governments are sources of pollution which will con-
taminate the American name for ages—machines that must produce ill, but cannot produce good. Smite them, in the name of
God and the people."[2]

Yates and Lansing were the only delegates who wanted no
action at all. Their party was a risk in ratification, not in the
framing of the Constitution, though in the risk there was a warning to be careful.

Governor Randolph supported the Virginia Plan in a long
speech. Warning of the prospect of anarchy, he itemized the
properties needed in a federal government and denied that the
Confederation had them. It could neither repel invasion nor check
rebellion. It could not levy duties, or push or protect commerce.
It was unable to establish great public works, improve inland
navigation, promote agriculture or manufactures—blessings of
which the states were singly incapable.

The authors of the articles, he would grant, had done all that
patriots could do, acting before financial and commercial evils had
arisen, before rebellion appeared in Massachusetts, before treaties
were violated and the havoc of paper money began. "Perhaps
nothing better could be obtained from the jealousy of the states

with regard to their sovereignty." According to Yates, Randolph candidly confessed that the resolutions "were not intended for a federal government—he meant a strong *consolidated* union, in which the idea of states should be nearly annihilated."[3]

Randolph was willing to go so far, he explained later, because a free communication with the best-informed delegates persuaded him "that the Confederation was destitute of every energy which a Constitution of the United States ought to possess." A man thus pulled into a plan could not have originated it, and his conversion did not prevent him from turning against some of its most vital provisions. Madison never asserted or admitted his own authorship of the Virginia Plan. To have done so, after its text became known in 1819, would have invited too many State Rights brickbats. But he did say, when people began to attack him for aiding Randolph in this monstrous assault on the now sacred states, that the governor had merely acted as the organ of the whole seven-man delegation, which thus absorbed and divided the blame.[4]

As soon as Randolph sat down, Charles Pinckney submitted and read a plan "grounded on the same principle," and it was referred along with the other to the committee of the whole. No action was taken on it in that body, and it has served chiefly to furnish historians with a great mystery. When John Quincy Adams, in 1818, was preparing the journals of the convention for publication, he asked Pinckney for a copy of his plan and received what its author *believed* was the original, among four or five almost identical versions. What he sent was a skillfully blended compound of his own plan and the August 6 report of the main drafting committee, which contained nearly all the features and much of the wording of the completed Constitution. Publication of it by Adams made Pinckney look like the almost unaided author of the charter of government.[5]

After this draft was printed—Madison told Jared Sparks in 1830—he intended to write to Pinckney, "asking, and even requiring, an explanation," but Pinckney died and the opportunity was lost. Aided by Madison, who showed that Pinckney was claiming credit for things he had opposed in convention, Sparks easily demolished the spurious draft. Historians then began an effort to reconstruct the genuine Pinckney plan, using a pamphlet of *Observations* on it which he had published in the fall of 1787. The title page referred to them as made at different times in convention, but a year later he said this was a single speech (as it was in form) delivered when he presented his plan. There is nothing in the convention debates to support either claim. Shortly after 1900, an outline of the genuine plan, and extensive extracts from it, were found by Professors Jameson and McLaughlin among the convention papers of Delegate James Wilson. These documents partially rebuilt Pinckney's reputation, for they included many features of the Constitution—Jameson counted about thirty—and several bits of its wording. Other writers, notably Hannis Taylor and Judge Nott, began to exalt him once more as the mastermind of the convention.[6]

The truth is that young Pinckney was both a sponger and a plagiarist, not only of plans of government but of speeches. In July 1787, *The American Museum* reprinted a speech, first published in the *New Jersey Gazette,* which Pinckney delivered before the New Jersey legislature in March of '86. Numerous changes in wording reveal the use of a fresh manuscript. In the reprint there are three interpolated paragraphs. On comparison, they are found to be rewritings of important speeches delivered in the Federal Convention by Wilson on June 20, and by Madison on June 19 and 21, 1787. For what reason, except to steal credit, did Pinckney insert them in the reprint of his 1786 address?[7]

When Pinckney's October *Observations* are examined, the same thing is found on a grander scale. He spoke many times in convention, yet only two passages in his entire pamphlet can be traced back to anything recorded from him in the notes of Madison and Yates. But it is full of paraphrases from the speeches of Madison, Wilson, Hamilton, Randolph, King, Franklin, Sherman, and he picked up verbatim the plagiarisms in *The American Museum*.

The purpose to deceive was as strong in Pinckney in 1787 as when he sent the final fictitious paper to Adams in 1818. With this fact known, it becomes easy enough to account for his genuine plan. A chance remark by Madison helps. Trying to account for its general resemblance to the Constitution, he observed that the division of government into three branches was "familiar in conversation when Mr. Pinckney was preparing his plan. I lodged in the same house with him and he was fond of conversing on the subject."[8] Pinckney arrived on May 17, the day Madison laid his own plan before the Virginia delegation. What Pinckney placed before the convention at the end of the month was a system compounded of the Virginia Plan and the Articles of Confederation, with incidental features from the New York state constitution and from a report which he made to Congress in 1786. That Pinckney actually used the Virginia Plan in writing his own is indicated by the resemblances in their provisions for amending the Constitution. Late in the convention, Madison rewrote his own clause, leaving Pinckney only the chagrin of having copied an abandoned proposal. Nothing daunted, he discussed the new clause in his *Observations,* saying that it was precisely the same in principle as his own. In reality, not only was it different, but here he was, in a speech which he claimed to have delivered on May 29, discussing an action which took place on September 10.

Pinckney's genuine plan was a useful instrument for picking up details, but embodied no consistent basic principle. It thrust the structure of government and specific powers called for by the Virginia Plan into a confederation of sovereign states, with no assimilation of the new features, no national supremacy. If Pinckney had been honest and blessed with modesty, he would have deserved something better than his Charleston nickname of "Constitution Charley," but the Constitution would be the same if his plan had never been presented. Had it been the only one presented, the convention would have had to struggle out of chaos—if it got out at all—to reach the final composite of form, power and sovereignty which was the natural outgrowth of the Virginia Plan, on which it based its deliberations.

The symmetry of the Virginia Plan was completed, or rather restored, after it was taken up clause by clause on May 30. Why, asked sharp-minded Gouverneur Morris of Pennsylvania, adopt an opening resolve that the Articles of Confederation be corrected and enlarged when the subsequent resolutions would not agree with

it? That was enough for Randolph. He immediately withdrew
the first resolve and offered a trio directly contrary to it:

"1. Resolved, That a union of the states merely federal will not
accomplish the objects proposed by the Articles of Confederation,
namely common defense, security of liberty and general welfare.

"2. Resolved, That no treaty or treaties among the whole or part
of the states, as individual sovereignties, would be sufficient.

"3. Resolved, That a *national* government ought to be established, consisting of a *supreme* legislative, executive and judiciary."

When these three highly nationalistic resolves are read in connection with the one which follows them, it becomes plain that
they were in the Virginia Plan as Madison wrote it, were eliminated because of Randolph's alarm, and were restored when he
surrendered. For the next one opens with these words: "Resolved
therefore . . . that the national legislature"—an utter *non sequitur*
when the proposal was to correct a confederation, but perfectly
fitting a resolve to establish a supreme national government. The
incident furnishes final evidence that the Virginia Plan was drafted
by Madison as a complete entity.

Confusion and some alarm greeted the substitute proposals. Did
the convention have power to discard the federal articles? The
question was sidetracked by taking up the third resolve. Asked
whether this was intended to abolish the states, Randolph said
No, they would merely yield when there was a clash with the
powers of the new government. Morris then "explained the distinction between a *federal* and *national, supreme* government;
the former being a mere compact resting on the good faith of the
parties; the latter having a complete and *compulsive* operation."
To propose such a change, he declared, was within the power of
the convention, for a *supreme* government was essential to the
ends they were charged with securing. "We had better take a
supreme government now, than a despot twenty years hence—
for come he must," the tall Pennsylvanian asserted.[9]

Scores of years later, State Righters seeking to disprove early
American nationhood took this definition as evidence that the
ordinary meaning of "national"—pertaining to a nation—was not

applied to the United States in 1787. In reality it had been commonly used since 1776—dozens of times by Madison. The Morris definition was a useful afterthought. The one in Madison's mind when he wrote the Virginia Plan can be judged from the words he used in 1833, in drafting a controversial letter (never sent) to John Tyler:

"But what alone would justify and account for the application of the term National to the proposed government is that it would possess, exclusively, all the attributes of a national government in its relations with other nations. . . . Even under the Confederacy the states in their united character were considered and called a nation, although their treaties and transactions with foreign nations depended for their execution on the will of the several states, and although the regulation of foreign commerce even remained with the states."[10]

With eight states present, the convention split four to four on a move to drop the words "national" and "supreme" and base the new government on "the design of the states in forming this convention." Madison opposed this deference to their credentials, though granting that it still allowed them to say "whether the states shall be governed by one power." The decisive vote against it was cast by Yates, who wished the wording to be as obnoxious to his faction as possible. The strongly phrased Virginia resolution was then adopted, with Connecticut opposed for strategic reasons and New York divided.

Up to this point no true cleavages had appeared, except that of Yates against everybody. Old Ben Franklin was made so enthusiastic by "the most august and respectable assembly he ever was in" that he looked to an early harmonious finish. There were no prejudices to overcome, no errors to refute. He was deceived by the fact that only Madison's group was organized for action, and many delegates were still to come. Those present were almost solid for a supreme national government. The real question had not yet come up: Who was to control that government?[11]

# CHAPTER III

## CORE OF THE CONSTITUTION

THE struggle for power began with deceptive gentleness when the next Virginia resolution was taken up in committee of the whole. Madison had given this a peculiar wording:

"Resolved therefore that the rights of suffrage in the national legislature ought to be proportioned to the quotas of contribution, or to the number of free inhabitants, as the one or the other rule may seem best in different cases."

Under a Confederation amendment drafted by Madison in 1783 and ratified by eleven states, quotas of contributions were to be proportionate to free inhabitants plus three fifths of the slaves. He was proposing now that in one house or on some questions, slave population should increase the strength of the South in Congress.

Fearing a digression over slavery, Madison recast his resolution into a plain motion that state equality ought not to prevail in the national legislature, but should give place to equitable representation. This was generally relished, he wrote in his notes, but the Delaware delegates pointed out that they were instructed not to agree to any change in suffrage. Adopt this, and it might become their duty to retire. Soft language, with a threat in it.

Madison argued strongly for his motion. Whatever reason there might have been for state equality in a federal union of sovereign states, it must cease when a national government should be set up. In the former case, acts of Congress were of little effect without state co-operation, so the states had influence nearly in proportion to their extent and importance. But a national government would enforce its own acts. Consequently a small state's vote would have the same efficacy as that of a large one.

In this mild fashion, the fierce battle between large and small states got under way. Madison was engaging in power politics—trying to fuse two groups of delegates, those from populous states

DECLARATION CHAMBER. MEETING PLACE OF THE CONTINENTAL CONGRESS AND THE FEDERAL CONVENTION OF 1787

JAMES WILSON

and from states which expected to become populous, into a common front for the abolition of state equality. In April he thought this would be easy. "To the northern states," he wrote to Washington, "it will be recommended by their present populousness; to the southern by their expected advantage in this respect. The lesser states must in every event yield to the predominant will." But the great argument for it was that it would reconcile the larger states to the necessary concessions of power. It did indeed work that way, but every word Madison spoke to win the medium-sized states repelled the small ones. With their instruction as a lever, the Delaware delegates put off the decision.[1]

The convention agreed that the legislature should have two branches but ran into a fight on May 31 over the resolve that the first branch be elected by the people. Madison and Mason of Virginia, Wilson of Pennsylvania carried the democratic banner. The opposition stemmed from strange and diverse sources. Elbridge Gerry of Massachusetts—he who afterward put "gerrymander" into the language—was sure that the country's troubles flowed from an excess of democracy. He was still republican but Shays' Rebellion had taught him the danger of the leveling spirit. The South Carolinians, representing a slave-holding oligarchy, came by the same opinion more naturally. With them stood Roger Sherman of Connecticut, but who knew what that wily old man was after? "He is as cunning as the devil," a resident of his state wrote about him just three days after this, and "if he suspects you are trying to take him in, you may as well catch an eel by the tail." Sherman talked of the people's liability to be misled, but probably was thinking that a vote for popular elections, at this moment, would make it harder to maintain state equality.[2]

Regard for the people was to be expected from George Mason, author of the Virginia Declaration of Rights. The larger house, he argued, was to be the grand depository of the democratic principle of the government, to which he thought the superior classes of society had better pay a little attention, since their own posterity was certain to drop into the lowest classes. Wilson and Madison mixed national policy and principle in their support of popular suffrage. The Pennsylvanian contended strenuously for election by the people, without whose confidence no government could long subsist. "He was for raising the federal pyramid to a considerable altitude, and for that reason wished to give it as broad a basis as possible."

Madison had the same double approach. He "considered the popular election of one branch of the national legislature as essential to every plan of free government." The popular will could be filtered in a Senate but if this were pushed too far the people would be lost sight of altogether. Then, in line with Wilson's position: "He thought too that the great fabric to be raised would be more stable and durable, if it should rest on the solid foundation of the people themselves, than if it should stand merely on the pillars of the legislatures."

Behind all this was an unvoiced thought. This great fabric, this high pyramid of federal power, would be safer to the large states if reared on popular suffrage, linked with proportionate representation. The vital fact, however, is that these convention leaders had both a nationalistic approach to self-government and a democratic approach to nationalism. They were seeking a durable, safe basis for a supreme government of high powers, in a system to which state governments were absolutely necessary, but only (in the combined words of Madison and Wilson) as "subordinately useful . . . lesser jurisdictions." There could be no safety or durability unless the people ruled.[3]

The large states were now piling up consistent majorities. Popular elections carried six to two, with two states divided. It was a significant vote. Sherman, captain of the opposition, lost his colleague Ellsworth but won New Jersey—the first step in creating a small-state bloc. The convention then deadlocked on Madison's proposal that senators be chosen by the first branch out of persons nominated by state legislatures. This had three objectives:

1. It would reduce state influence in Congress both by removing senatorial elections from state control and by choosing senators from a general pool.

2. It would make the Senate more conservative than the House.

3. It would make it possible to keep the Senate small and therefore vigorous.

From South Carolina came the objection that taking so many

powers out of state hands would upset the balance and security of interests among the states. That is, the South would be unable to defend slavery. Election by state legislatures was called for next. But that would mean either state equality or too many senators. A proposal to elect by popular vote in interstate districts was opposed by Madison. The larger states would monopolize the places. The whole proposition was then defeated and the convention turned to the Virginia resolve on the powers of the new government.

Written into the Constitution, this would constitute a sweeping "general welfare" clause giving Congress power "to legislate in all cases to which the separate states are incompetent, or in which the harmony of the United States may be interrupted by the exercise of individual legislation." Three South Carolinians got up, demanding an enumeration of powers, and protesting that too much was being taken from the states. Madison, a large-power man, had written this resolve, but Randolph, a medium-power man, was called on to explain its meaning. He "disclaimed any intention to give indefinite powers to the national legislature, declaring that he was entirely opposed to such an inroad on the state jurisdictions."

Forty-six years later Madison gave the same explanation. "It cannot be supposed," he wrote in reply to an attack on him by John Tyler, "that these descriptive phrases were to be left in their indefinite extent to legislative discretion. A selection and definition of the cases embraced by them was to be the task of the convention." No such conviction was in his mind on May 31, 1787. Randolph's statement put him in a hole. He did not wish either to challenge it or see it accepted, so he climbed out on a slant:

"Mr. Madison said that he had brought with him into the convention a strong bias in favor of an enumeration and definition of the powers necessary to be exercised by the national legislature; but had also brought grave doubts concerning its practicability. His wishes remained unaltered, but his doubts had become stronger. What his opinion might ultimately be he could not yet tell. But he should shrink from nothing which should be found essential to such a form of government as would provide for the safety, liberty and happiness of the community. This being the end of all our deliberations, all the necessary means for attaining it must, however reluctantly, be submitted to."

When he came to revise his notes, Madison was disturbed by the word "grave." For if he had brought grave doubts into the convention, and these had become stronger, it meant that he scarcely differed from Wilson, who said it was impossible to make an enumeration. Indeed, Pierce recorded Madison as saying: "At present he was convinced it could not be done." But to have such evidence presented in his own notes was a little too much. He scratched out "grave"—the one really important elision he made of his original views.[4]

Madison's whole statement was a strategic masterpiece. It let the resolution stand as a sweeping definition of power which might or might not be carried into the Constitution, with himself disliking such action, yet a determined supporter of it should it be found necessary. By leaving the way open to an enumeration, it invited the support of those who objected to a general grant. Unanimous approval followed, save for a split in Connecticut.

Next came Madison's cherished formula for restraining the states and insuring national supremacy: that the national legislature should have power "to negative all laws passed by the several states, contravening in the opinion of the national legislature the articles of union." Benjamin Franklin added treaties. This extraordinary resolve was adopted without a dissenting vote. Still left was a clause authorizing armed coercion of recalcitrant states. This (though he was its author) Madison induced the convention to drop. It was too akin to civil war and needless if state laws could be negatived.[5]

To some delegates, the heavy emphasis on national supremacy sounded like an indorsement of an assertion by Read of Delaware that the states ought to be abolished. Dickinson of the same state replied that to do away with them altogether would be ruinous. "He compared the proposed national system to the solar system, in which the states were the planets, and ought to be left to move freely in their proper orbits." In these words the sedate Madison, who confined his merriment to dinner tables, recorded the astronomical comparison for the pages of history. It was a different tale that Rufus King told, as a friend recalled:

"You may remember that you told me about Dickinson's imagery or phantasy when the new Constitution was under consideration. If I recollect right it was that the general government was to be likened to the sun, the center, and the state governments to the other planets revolving round it. Virginia was the Earth and Kentucky her moon. Connecticut from her fondness for *bundling* was Venus, and thievish little Rhode Island was Mercury, etc."

Dickinson's remarks drew a denial from Wilson that he wanted to extinguish the planets. Neither did he believe they would warm or enlighten the sun. Within their proper orbits the states "must still be suffered to act for subordinate purposes for which their existence is made essential by the great extent of our country." The significant fact about this colloquy is the total exclusion of state sovereignty from either concept. Both Dickinson and Wilson saw them as satellites of the federal sun.[6]

To enable the national government to coerce the states, Madison clung to his original thought of a federal negative "in all cases whatsoever." Charles Pinckney felt the same way, so they joined forces on June 8 to back the Carolinian's motion for an unlimited negative. The states, said Pinckney, "must be kept in due subordination to the nation." Madison termed this indefinite power absolutely necessary. Nothing milder would check the "constant tendency in the states to encroach on the federal authority; to violate national treaties; to infringe the rights and interests of each other; to oppress the weaker party within their respective jurisdictions." But to be effective the negative must extend to all cases. To reshape Dickinson's metaphor, the federal sun must control the centrifugal tendencies of the states. Otherwise the planets "will continually fly out of their proper orbits."

Wilson came to the support of the motion in principle. He contrasted the sentiments expressed in Congress before the states were organized—we are now one nation of brethren—with that which came later:

"No sooner were the state governments formed than their jealousy and ambition began to display themselves. Each endeavored to cut a slice from the common loaf, to add to its own morsel, till at length the Confederation became frittered down to the impotent condition in which it now stands. . . . To correct its vices is the business of this convention. One of its vices is the want of an effectual control in the whole over its parts."

The limitless scope of the proposed negative created panic. The large states would use their enormous and monstrous influence to crush the commerce of the small ones. Madison replied that such an attitude threatened to break up the Union. "If the large states possessed the avarice and ambition with which they were charged, would the small ones in their neighborhood be more secure when all control of a general government was withdrawn?" The warning didn't impress the little fellows. Massachusetts, Pennsylvania and Virginia alone voted Aye, and two Virginians were on the other side. This did not impair Madison's original negative, which had tremendous sweep, even though limited to state laws contravening the articles of union. Indeed, the discretionary words "in the opinion of the national legislature" would allow them to veto almost anything.[7]

The convention's unity on this point reflected the terrific impact of agrarian revolt upon men of property, also the less personal alarm of those who put order above liberty and looked on good faith as the cornerstone of social relations. Tax and debt moratoriums, the blotting out of private debt with worthless paper money, destruction of state and federal public securities by refusal of states to lay taxes or meet requisitions, antitax riots in the South and Shays' Rebellion in Massachusetts, produced a community of thought among the delegates which transcended all their differences. Madison's method of halting these practices was open to dispute, but the delegates who disagreed with the purpose could be counted on one man's thumbs.

Madison's course continued to be affected by the need to keep Randolph from getting out of line. Opinionated, impulsive and exceedingly sensitive, the governor needed to be gently led or urged, never sharply opposed. The problem became visible when Wilson moved, on June 1, that the national executive consist of a single person. Madison (Pierce records) indorsed the proposal, suggesting that he be aided by a council with power to advise but not to control him. No council, Randolph replied, could check an ambitious man. Unity was the fetus of monarchy. Wilson retorted that it would be the best safeguard against tyranny. To stop the clash, Madison moved that they proceed first to fix the extent of the executive authority. Then they could determine how far these powers might be entrusted to a single officer. To further this, he moved to strike out of his own plan the proviso that all the executive powers of Congress be vested in the national executive, then helped to narrow those powers to the execution of national laws and appointing of officers. His purpose was to make it plain that the powers of war and peace were legislative, though classed in England as executive. This would make it easier to give the office to one man.

The convention then swung to the mode of electing the executive and the duration of his service. The Virginia Plan, following the system of choosing state governors, called for election by the national legislature. Wilson was "almost unwilling to declare the mode which he wished to take place, being apprehensive that it might appear chimerical." However, out came his breath-taking proposal. In theory at least, he was for an election by the people. To Roger Sherman, this was the very essence of tyranny. At the suggestion of George Mason, Wilson was given time to digest the idea into his own form.

The Pennsylvanian needed but twenty-four hours. Let the people choose electors and the electors choose the executive. This too-sudden approach to democracy gave the convention indigestion. All states except his own and Maryland voted No. Then, by an exactly reversed vote, they decided (but not for all time) that the national executive should be chosen by the national legislature for a seven-year term. An effort to make him (or them) removable by the legislature was beaten down by Madison, Wilson and Mason, re-election was banned, and the convention took up once more the question of unity or plurality in the office.

Still hostile to the one-man system, Randolph shifted from his own fear of monarchy to the adverse temper of the people. Wilson floored him by pointing out that every one of the thirteen states was headed by a single magistrate. A plural system in national affairs would bring violent animosities which would spread poison through government and people. Madison, Washington and McClurg outvoted Randolph and Blair; the convention stood seven to three for unity.[8]

What power should this one man have to veto acts of Congress? Madison had proposed, in the Virginia Plan, that part of the judiciary be joined with the executive in a council of revision. Protests arose now against bringing in the judges. It was improper, urged Gerry and King, to give them a voice as to the policy of laws which might come before them later in a test of constitutionality. Wilson wanted an absolute veto. From Delaware came a protest against any check on the legislature whatsoever.

Madison guided the way to the basic decision. Saying no more about the judiciary, he argued strongly for a qualified veto power in the executive. If a proper proportion were required to override a veto, it would answer the same purpose as an absolute negative. The executive would rarely if ever oppose a unanimous legislature, but to give one man the power to do so would certainly be obnoxious to the present temper of the country. By unanimous action, the absolute veto was rejected and a proviso adopted for repassing vetoed bills by a two-thirds majority.

This left out the judges. Wilson and Madison undertook to bring them back. In a republic, Madison argued, no individual citizen could have "that settled pre-eminence in the eyes of the rest, that weight of property, that personal interest against betraying the national interest, which appertain to an hereditary magistrate." The executive would be envied and assailed by disappointed competitors. His small salary would not place him beyond the danger of foreign corruption. He must therefore be controlled as well as supported. Unite the judges with him in his revisionary function and it would both double the advantage and diminish the danger.

Other delegates seemed to have a better opinion of executives and a poorer one of judges, for the convention defeated the proposal seven states to three. Judge Ellsworth, Judge Sherman, Judge Yates, Judge Blair and future Judge Lansing were on the losing side.[9]

On the selection of federal judges themselves, Madison abandoned his own plan of appointment by the national legislature. He agreed with Wilson that to avoid intrigue and partiality they should not be chosen by a large body, but was rather inclined to give the power to the Senate instead of the executive—a body numerous enough to be confided in. However, he thought the matter should be left to maturer reflection. On a resumption of the subject, Pinckney and Sherman undertook to put through the original proposal. Thoroughly persuaded, now, that he had been wrong in this, Madison defeated it by picturing a judiciary appointed by incompetents and filled with unqualified men "who had perhaps assisted ignorant members in business of their own." The motion was withdrawn and appointment by the Senate, a body which would be actuated by lofty, disinterested motives, was agreed to without opposition.[10]

On the subject of inferior courts, the Virginia Plan ran into belated trouble. The whole clause was first rewritten to correct Madison's odd provision for one *or more* supreme tribunals, then agreed to on June 5. Before the day was over, Rutledge secured a reconsideration and moved to strike out lower courts. The right of appeal from state courts to the supreme national tribunal, he contended, was sufficient to secure national rights and uniformity of judgments.

Madison saw it differently:

"Unless inferior tribunals were dispersed throughout the republic with *final* jurisdiction in *many* cases, appeals would be multiplied to a most oppressive degree. . . . What was to be done after improper verdicts in state tribunals obtained under the biased directions of a dependent judge, or the local prejudices of an undirected jury? To remand the cause for a new trial would answer no purpose. . . . An effective judiciary establishment commensurate to the legislative authority was essential. A government without a proper executive and judiciary would be the mere trunk of a body, without arms or legs to act or move."

Southern fear and New England economy struck out the inferior courts, whereupon Wilson and Madison dropped the mandatory feature and moved for a simple power in Congress to establish such courts. "The people will not bear such innovations," cried Butler of South Carolina. But only Connecticut (with New York divided) joined the Carolinians when the vote was taken. Here was visible the slave states' fear of governmental agencies on the local level not subject to their own control. Here too was evidence of greater willingness to confer power than to set up bodies capable of wielding it. Madison and Wilson ran ahead of their fellows in seeing that the substance of government was more important than its theoretical authority. Their victory destroyed the ability of the states to sabotage the Union through their judiciary systems.[11]

During the fight over the courts, Madison's proposal of popular ratification of the new Constitution was taken up. Sherman, whose general strategy was to support the Articles of Confederation for the sake of state equality, objected to this departure from their provisions. Madison replied that the Articles themselves had been defectively ratified, resting on legislative sanction only. Hence state tribunals were reluctant to look on acts of Congress as superior to state laws conflicting with them. He thought it indispensable that the new Constitution should be ratified by the supreme authority of the people themselves.

Gerry remarked that the wildest ideas of government were prevalent among the people of the Eastern states. "He seemed afraid," wrote Madison, "of referring the new system to them." Fortunately Rufus King of Gerry's state had Daniel Shays less on the brain. He came to Madison's support with the logical statement that it would be easier to win the approval of a one-house convention than a two-house legislature, the more so as the new charter would take powers away from state legislatures. Postponed a week, the resolve for ratification by the people was adopted six to three—New York, New Jersey and Connecticut opposed.[12]

Madison's and Wilson's contention that power should reside

primarily in the whole people was challenged on June 6 by Charles
Pinckney. The young Carolinian moved that members of the first
branch of the national legislature be elected by the state legislatures, and not by the people, whose fitness he denied. Sherman
came to his support with a hint that popular elections were a device for abolishing state governments. These must elect the national legislature or there could be no harmony. Wilson replied
that the people of the states would support federal authority, but
the state governments would oppose it. The government should
possess not only the *force* but the *mind* of the people at large.
"The legislature ought to be the most exact transcript of the whole
society," and popular elections would make it so.

Madison followed with the most significant speech of the convention—one into which he threw his whole philosophy of government. He considered an election by the people, of at least one
branch of the legislature, as a clear principle of free government—
besides which, it would secure better representatives and avoid too
great an agency of the state governments in the general one. He
disagreed with Sherman's list of the objects which made a national
government necessary—national defense, internal peace, treaties,
regulation and taxing of foreign commerce. These were certainly
important, but it was necessary also to provide for the security of
private rights, and the steady dispensation of justice. Interferences
with these had more perhaps than anything else produced this
convention. Picking up an admission by Sherman that faction and
oppression would prevail in a very small state, he drew the inference that wherever these prevailed the state was too small.

"Were we not thence admonished to enlarge the sphere as far
as the nature of government would admit? This was the only
defense against the inconveniences of democracy consistent with
the democratic form of government."

That statement of principle forms the invisible core of the Constitution. Addressing himself to those delegates—Gerry, Hamilton, Dickinson, Read, the Pinckneys and others—who were
smitten with fear of democracy, Madison pointed the way to
stability and justice in a representative government founded on

democracy. His words were the more persuasive because he spoke
not as an enemy of property rights, but as a defender of them. In
phrases foreshadowed in his "Vices of the Political System of the
United States," he set forth the inevitable human conflicts:

"All civilized societies would be divided into different sects,
factions and interests, as they happened to consist of rich and poor,
debtors and creditors, the landed, the manufacturing, the commercial interests, the inhabitants of this district or that district,
the followers of this political leader or that political leader, the disciples of this religious sect or that religious sect. In all cases where
a majority are united by a common interest or passion, the rights of
the minority are in danger. What motives are to restrain them?"

He took up, one after another, the ordinary restraints upon
wrongdoing—honesty as the best policy, respect for reputation,
conscience. Inadequate in their effect on individuals, they were
even less regarded by bodies of men. In Greece and Rome, the
rich and poor alternately oppressed each other. In America, a
mere distinction of color was made a ground of the most oppressive dominion ever exercised by man over man. What was the
source of the unjust state laws currently complained of?

"Has it not been the real or supposed interest of the major number? Debtors have defrauded their creditors. The landed interest
has borne hard on the mercantile interest. The holders of one
species of property have thrown a disproportion of taxes on the
holders of another species. The lesson we are to draw from the
whole is that where a majority are united by a common sentiment,
and have an opportunity, the rights of the minor party become
insecure."

At this point, had he chosen to align himself with the latent
monarchists and panicky fearers of democracy, Madison could
have produced a powerful swing toward aristocratic government.
He pulled the other way:

"In a republican government the majority if united have always
an opportunity. The only remedy is to enlarge the sphere, and

thereby divide the community into so great a number of interests and parties, that in the first place a majority will not be likely at the same moment to have a common interest separate from that of the whole or of the minority; and in the second place, that in case they should have such an interest, they may not be apt to unite in the pursuit of it. It was incumbent on us then to try this remedy, and with that view to frame a republican system on such a scale and in such a form as will control all the evils which have been experienced."[13]

Madison's description of clashing interests, and the need to protect minorities, is often used as an argument against democracy, and as evidence of his hostility to it. That is to overlook his emphasis upon the paramount remedy for democratic ills—the only remedy, he called it—enlargement of the sphere of government. On this occasion he used it persuasively for direct election of representatives. It carried him also toward the election of President and Vice President by the people, and he used it finally to promote moderate conservatism in the Senate. Faction and oppression in the states, stability and justice in the national government—these, as he saw it, were the contrasting fruits of the same political system, the difference in expected results being due to the difference in the sphere. Acceptance of this principle brought three consequences of transcendant importance to the American people:

1. A convention dominated by devotees of property rights was able to write a democratic Constitution.

2. A democratic government in the large sphere—the nation—was held to be a safe depository of high positive powers.

3. The government in the large sphere was empowered to restrain the excesses of the states. But, being itself less subject to factionalism and having greater responsibilities, it was not placed under similar constitutional restraints.

In the vote on Pinckney's motion, South Carolina and New Jersey kept up their hostility to popular elections. Eight states stood by the people, holding with Madison that democratic self-government in a large area was safe.

# CHAPTER IV

## THE NEW JERSEY PLAN

PROCEEDING on June 7 to the mode of electing senators, the convention split in a manner which pointed to deeper cleavages. John Dickinson, though a citizen and delegate of Delaware, was a Philadelphia lawyer and former president of Pennsylvania—leader there of what French Minister Luzerne called the patrician party. From him came a motion that members of the second branch be chosen by state legislatures. The Senate should be a body of "the most distinguished characters, distinguished for their rank in life and their weight of property, and bearing as strong a likeness to the British House of Lords as possible." Such characters were more likely to be selected by legislatures than by the people.

This was a double-motived maneuver. Pennsylvania Dickinson was working for government by the rich, wise and good. Delaware Dickinson was jockeying for state equality. Madison and Wilson counterattacked from different directions. Wilson urged the same system as in the House. "If we are to establish a national government, that government ought to flow from the people at large." Good democratic doctrine, but useful too as an obstacle to state equality. Said Madison: If state legislatures were to choose the senators, it would be necessary either to drop proportional representation or make the Senate very large. The first was unjust, the second inexpedient.

"The use of the Senate is to consist in its proceeding with more coolness, with more system, and with more wisdom, than the popular branch. Enlarge their number and you communicate to them the vices which they are meant to correct."

All this was logical, but the two men were arguing at cross-purposes. Wilson's call for election by the people ran counter to Madison's appeal for a small Senate. There was no common ground that would save proportional representation, unless state lines were ignored in choosing the Senate. Madison already had

46

proposed that senators be chosen from interstate districts by the lower house of Congress, but this had died at birth. Wilson now made a kindred suggestion with a more popular base. "He was for an election by the people in large districts which would be most likely to obtain men of intelligence and uprightness." Interstate senators popularly elected—here was Madison's doctrine of the enlarged sphere as the stabilizer of republican government. But the purpose was to knock out state equality. The Virginian, swinging to his ally's support, made Wilson's plan a reply to Dickinson. There was no need to go to the state legislatures if "an election by the people, or through any other channel," would produce as meritorious a choice.

"The great evils complained of were that the state legislatures run into schemes of paper money, etc., whenever solicited by the people, and sometimes without even the sanction of the people. Their influence then, instead of checking a like propensity in the national legislature, may be expected to promote it."

This argument threw the shadow of Daniel Shays across the floor. Gerry insisted that the commercial and moneyed interest would be more secure in the hands of state legislatures than of the people. As for interstate elections, small states joined to large ones in such districts would have no chance of gaining seats. A cross fire came from Mason, who demanded legislative election of senators to defend the states against federal encroachments.

The combination of forces was too great for Madison. On this point, his effort to weld the large states and the South into a solid bloc failed. It fell before a tripartite fusion of small-state delegates, Southerners seeking to promote state power in the federal government, and defenders of property interests menaced by paper money. Pennsylvania cast the only vote for election by the people, then joined in unanimous approval of a choice by legislatures.[1]

Contrary to an almost universal assumption, the desire for a conservative Senate played a minor role in this decision for indirect election. Massachusetts was probably the only state dominated by that motive. Madison himself wrote in a footnote to this debate that the real issue was the principle of proportional representation, involved in the size of the Senate. Every delegate was governed by some economic consideration. The small states were maneuvering to promote state equality, for purposes not yet disclosed. The South was pushing state influence as a protection to commerce and slavery. Madison and Wilson, in urging election by the people, were thinking less of popular rights than of putting the large states in a position to defend their interests.

The next question: How long should men serve in Congress? "Instability," said Madison, "is one of the great vices of our republics." Let there be a three-year term in the House, seven years in the Senate. Gerry objected. Annual elections were the only defense of the people against tyranny. New Englanders never would give them up. Madison challenged that line of thought. No man present could say what the opinions of his constituents were, still less what they would be in six months. The convention should consider what was right and necessary in itself. Base a government on that idea and all the most enlightened and respectable citizens would be its advocates. Fall short, and this influential class would turn against the plan, while "little support in opposition to them can be gained to it from the unreflecting multitude." As for the Senate, even with a seven-year term his fear was that the popular branch would still overmatch it.

The convention agreed (for the time) to these terms of office and took up the compensation of members. Madison won a decision to end the old system of state pay for congressmen—a system which resulted in improper dependence on the states. He asked too that their pay be fixed in the Constitution. It might be made flexible, going up or down with the average price of wheat or some other article, but in any event it was indecent and might in time prove dangerous to let them regulate their own salaries. The convention ignored the wheat-price plan, nor did anybody mention that it would make Congress unanimous, through all eternity, for federal aid to agriculture. Temporarily, the rule for fixed salaries was approved without their being tied to the value of money—an unworkable proposal. Sensing that this would be dropped, Franklin moved to strike out Madison's word "liberal" before "compensation." He followed with a comparison, related very pleasantly (Madison said), between the probable course of congressional salaries and the growth of ecclesiastical stipends from

St. Peter to the Pope. The vote was taken and "liberal" went out.[2]

In two weeks the convention went through article after article of the Virginia Plan, accepting most, changing some, but always producing a majority favorable to the big purposes of the plan. Always, that is, except for the flash of small-state strength in deciding who should elect senators. In general the South was standing with the large states. A sweeping victory seemed in sight for Madison, Wilson, King, Gouverneur Morris and their allies. Yet, even as events took this course, a challenge was developing which threatened not only their victory but the life of the convention. Three entries reveal personal factors:

Notes of Dr. James McHenry, June 1: "Received an express from home that my brother lay dangerously sick, in consequence of which I set out immediately for Baltimore."

Madison's notes, June 5: "Governor Livingston from New Jersey took his seat." June 9: "Mr. Luther Martin from Maryland took his seat."

Governor Livingston brought the prestige of state leadership and personal standing to the entire small-state bloc. Its members in general had more ability than reputation (notably William Paterson of Jersey) though some had both and others neither. The governor added luster, though he twinkled faintly compared with the galaxy from Pennsylvania, Virginia and South Carolina.

Luther Martin furnished driving fanaticism and strategic voting strength. With McHenry gone, he was able to deadlock Maryland and carry it out of the large-state bloc, if not into the other.

On the day Martin took his seat, Paterson moved that the convention take up the rule of suffrage in the national legislature. This was Madison's resolve, postponed on May 30 out of deference to Delaware. It was understood then (Madison wrote) that when resumed it "would certainly be agreed to, no objection or difficulty being started from any other quarter." He did not know that the Delaware delegates themselves had asked for the instruction from the legislature, to be used as a weapon.

Opening the debate on Paterson's motion, his colleague Judge Brearly pictured the terrors of large-state tyranny if equality should be given up. Virginia, with sixteen times the population of Georgia (citing Georgia was an artful move to break Madison's coalition), would be a formidable phalanx indeed. The three large states would sweep all before them. He had come prepared to give energy and stability to the federal government. Confronted with the proposition for destroying state equality in that government, he was astonished, he was alarmed. On the other hand, he would not say that equality was fair to the large states. What remedy then?

"One only, that a map of the United States be spread out, that all the existing boundaries be erased, and that a new partition of the whole be made into thirteen equal parts."

Paterson then took over. He was a squat, mouselike man whose quiet manner belied his oratorical and legal talents. From him came an assault on the basic decisions of the convention. Every law and commission under which they were to act limited them to amendment of the Articles of Confederation. Go beyond them and they would be charged with usurpation, for the American people were sharp-sighted and not to be deceived. The commissions of the delegates were not only the measure of their power, they denoted also the sentiments of the states:

"The idea of a national government as contradistinguished from a federal one never entered into the mind of any of them. . . . We have no power to go beyond the federal scheme, and if we had the people are not ripe for any other."

Paterson renewed the alarms thrown out by his colleague. "Give the large states an influence in proportion to their magnitude, and what will be the consequence? Their ambition will be proportionally increased, and the small states will have everything to fear." He made a sophistical comparison between men and states: it was as wrong to give a great state more votes than a little one, as it was to give a rich man more votes than an indigent one. He pierced a sophistry of the opposition—that a government operating directly on the people must be chosen by them directly. Why should not one chosen by state legislatures act on the people who choose the legislatures? The alternatives of confederal and national government presented Paterson with no dilemma—he seized both horns and twisted them to his purpose:

"A confederacy supposes sovereignty in the members composing it and sovereignty supposes equality. If we are to be considered as a nation, all state distinctions must be abolished, the whole must be thrown into hotchpot, and when an equal division is made, then there may be fairly an equality of representation."

These alternatives had been in Paterson's mind from the very moment the Virginia Plan was disclosed. Taking skeleton notes of it as it was read, he interjected after the clause for proportional representation: "Objn—sovereignty is an integral thing— We ought to be one nation—" Paterson was a high nationalist, as his later career on the Supreme Court revealed, but just now he was making parochial threats, and he had others to offer. Squaring up to a hint by Wilson that the large states might be forced to confederate among themselves, he threw back this challenge:

"Let them unite if they please, but let them remember that they have no authority to compel the others to unite. New Jersey will never confederate on the plan before the committee. She would be swallowed up. He had rather submit to a monarch, to a despot, than to such a fate. He would not only oppose the plan here but on his return home do everything in his power to defeat it there."[3]

Pennsylvania's stubborn Scotchman, James Wilson, promptly gave a warning:

"If New Jersey will not part with her sovereignty it is in vain to talk of government. A new partition of the states is desirable, but evidently and totally impracticable."

As a further notice of small-state seriousness, Paterson held up the vote on his motion—which was merely to take up the subject— with a request that as so much depended on it, the decision be postponed. The delegates at once adjourned. There was plenty to talk about that Saturday night at the Coffee House, the Indian Queen and Mrs. House's.

The Paterson-Brearly proposal of hotchpot and redivision was about as practicable as a motion to carve up the moon. Because of the fantastic impossibility of carrying it out, it has been almost ignored by historians. Yet without taking account of the desires behind it, without sensing its emotional supercharge from twelve years of jealousy, ambition and fear, one cannot fathom the significance of the principal struggle in the Federal Convention. It was the final, bitter, almost post-mortem flare-up of the great battle for ownership of the western lands. It was by no means the only basis of the small-state position, but was the one which gave it intransigence, and was the only one that could make it critical by winning support from Maryland. Behind it was a broad and formidable public opinion. "It is much to be lamented," wrote Congressional Delegate William Grayson just three days after this debate, "that the desire of dismembering states prevails in so great a degree among the citizens of the Union."

"Hotchpot" was a façade set up to cover realities which could not be debated without the probability of wrecking the convention. Madison, the master strategist against New Jersey and Maryland land speculators in the Continental Congress, knew well that Western landownership was a subject to keep silent on when harmony was being sought. He could not have forgotten how the mere mention of it in debate killed a report on peace terms which he was trying to steer through Congress in 1782. The weight he attached to this phase of the convention struggle may be judged from his summary to Jefferson after adjournment. Hotchpot was the only thing he mentioned in connection with the small states:

"The remaining object created more embarrassment, and greater alarm for the issue of the convention than all the rest put together. The little states insisted on retaining their equality in both branches, unless a complete abolition of the state governments should take place; and made equality in the Senate a *sine qua non*."[4]

So too it was the only aspect of the small-state position belatedly reported by Chargé d'Affaires Otto to his government. The little states, to whom representation according to population would be very prejudicial, "offer to consent to it today, provided that all the states are divided into equal parts."[5]

When the convention reconvened on Monday, poker-faced Roger Sherman played the next card. Let suffrage in the first branch be proportionate to free inhabitants, but give each state one vote in the Senate. This put Connecticut in the apparent role of peacemaker, but aided the small states by putting their *sine qua non* in the form of a compromise. Lurking in the words "free inhabitants" was the sharp issue of slave representation, on which the large states and the South might conceivably split. Rutledge fell back on the Virginia Plan—suffrage according to quotas of contribution, which meant free inhabitants plus three fifths of the slaves. Wilson converted this into a straight motion to use the five-three ratio itself. New Jersey and Delaware cast the only opposing votes. By a strange coincidence, Madison had proposed the five-three compromise on contributions in 1783 to end just such a controversy, and carried the day by winning Wilson and Rutledge to its support.

Then came the question of questions. "Everything," said Sherman in moving for state equality in the Senate, "depended on this. The small states would never agree to the plan on any other principle." Defying this threat, the convention voted down the motion six to five. By the same margin it decreed that suffrage in the Senate should be the same as in the House.

On this crucial test, Martin carried Maryland into the small-state bloc. Yates and Lansing, hostile to all the work of the convention, put New York there too. The large states held their Carolina and Georgia allies. Swollen in prospects of congressional power by counting slaves, and looking to further growth through settlement of empty acres, they stood with the Big Three for both House and Senate based on population.

For three days the committee of the whole went on with its work—torrid, sultry days outside, and smoldering fires within the chamber. The revised Virginia Plan was reported to the convention—a victory, from end to end, for the large-state nationalists, a victory also for government by the majority. But everybody knew that the main struggle lay ahead. There was no objection when Paterson asked for a day's recess to allow the small-state delegates to contemplate the plan reported and prepare one of their own.[6]

The New Jersey Plan[7] put before the convention on June 15 served only to present an issue and lay motives bare. The Articles of Confederation were to be revised, corrected and enlarged. Familiar words! Madison's original concession to Randolph was picked from the wastebasket and used against him. In addition to the powers already in the Confederation, Congress was to raise a revenue by import duties and a stamp tax, regulate interstate and foreign commerce and compel the states to meet federal requisitions for money. The existing one-house Congress, in which the states voted equally, was to be supplemented by a plural federal executive and a supreme court. Lacking only direct taxes, these were great powers in a weak structure. The new plan carried this carefully worded declaration of federal supremacy:

"Resolved that all acts of the United States in Congress made by virtue and in pursuance of the powers hereby and by the Articles of Confederation vested in them, and all treaties made and ratified under the authority of the United States, shall be the supreme law of the respective states so far forth as those acts or treaties shall relate to the said states or their citizens, and that the judiciary of the several states shall be bound thereby in their decisions, anything in the respective laws of the individual states to the contrary notwithstanding."

In a footnote to his notes of debates, Madison reported that the New Jersey Plan was concerted among the members from Connecticut, New York, New Jersey, Delaware and perhaps Mr. Martin from Maryland "who made with them a common cause on different principles." Preliminary drafts stamp it as a composite production. The powers of Congress were written by Lansing, with insertions from a similar draft by Sherman. The executive and judiciary articles were taken by Paterson from the Virginia Plan, later modified to exclude inferior courts and pluralize the executive. Martin wrote the national supremacy proposal.[8]

The New Jersey Plan was in truth a hodgepodge of diverse objectives, put together to consolidate the supporters of one objective common to all. On the surface, the two plans gave the convention a choice to amend the Articles of Confederation or discard them entirely, to preserve or reject state sovereignty, to follow their credentials or go beyond them. All this was spangled rhetoric to cover one real question—whether the large or small states should control the new government. That would be answered by the decision on state equality in Congress.

# CHAPTER V

## The Men and Their Motives

The fortnight which brought the convention to its great cleavage also made it ready for battle. Only six delegates were yet to arrive. All states were able to vote except New Hampshire—whose deputies were trying to scrape coach fare out of an empty treasury—and "infamous Rhode Island," which named none. In two weeks the delegates had sized one another up, tested the worth of friends and the skill and stamina of foes. As Abraham Baldwin looked back on this gathering, it brought together the oldest and most venerable statesmen of the country. But he was only thirty-two, many were younger and only six were over sixty. Their average age was but forty-three.[1]

William Pierce of Georgia, who etched thumbnail sketches of his fellows, mixed more sugar than acid in his ink. The nearest he came to the economic basis of politics was to identify a dozen delegates as respectable gentlemen of family and fortune. Nevertheless, he left a comparative index of reasoning power, scholarship and public address which seldom went astray. Of Madison he wrote:

"Mr. Maddison is a character who has long been in public life; and what is very remarkable every person seems to acknowledge his greatness. He blends together the profound politician with the scholar. In the management of every great question he evidently took the lead in the convention, and though he cannot be called an orator, he is a most agreeable, eloquent and convincing speaker. From a spirit of industry and application which he possesses in a most eminent degree, he always comes forward the best informed man of any point in debate. The affairs of the United States, he perhaps has the most correct knowledge of, of any man in the Union. He has been twice a member of Congress, and was always thought one of the ablest members that ever sat in that council.

Mr. Maddison is about thirty-seven years of age, a gentleman of great modesty—with a remarkable sweet temper. He is easy and unreserved among his acquaintance, and has a most agreeable style of conversation."[2]

Convention Secretary Jackson told John Quincy Adams that Madison was by far the most efficient member of the convention. Delegate William Blount of North Carolina wrote in July that his fellows "were in sentiment with Virginia who seemed to take the lead. Madison at their head though Randolph and Mason are also great." In the Continental Congress, where Madison was given first place by French Minister Luzerne, he had shone against the background of its declining eminence. In the convention he was still at the top, amid the finest talent of America.[3]

Madison had a world-wide reputation in 1787 because of the credit given him in France for Virginia's pre-eminence in liberty and stability. So many Frenchmen asked Minister Jefferson for letters of introduction to him that they arranged a code system to appraise the visitors. When French Consul Crèvecoeur told Legation Secretary William Short in May of '87 that he would not leave for New York without credentials to Madison, Short wrote to the latter:

"If you have read the article *Etats Unis* in the new Encyclopedia, you will not be surprised either at Mr. Crevecoeur's earnestness to cultivate your acquaintance or my unwillingness not to contribute to it."

This article (which Jefferson had a hand in preparing) mentioned Virginia's failure to abolish slavery when the laws were being revised. This, the *Encyclopédie Méthodique* explained, was not due solely to the absence of Jefferson and Wythe when the revisal was taken up in the legislature:

"In the assembly one could find men courageous and honest enough to ask for it, and sufficiently enlightened to support the proposition with all the eloquence of which they were capable, (we shall cite but one, Mr. Maddisson, who at the age of 30 astonished the new republics with his eloquence, his wisdom and his genius);

but they saw that most of the members of the legislative body were not yet ready for such a striking social change. They feared that a futile effort would only clamp down the chains of slavery and would not hasten the day when the Negroes would be set free."

The acclaim was increased by Madison's sponsorship of other policies which had raised the reputation of Virginia while that of the Confederation was sinking. Wrote Short:

"It is but just to mention it to you, sir, who have contributed so much by your exertions in the legislature to the fame she has acquired in every part of Europe. . . . The act [of voluntary separation] respecting Kentucky—that on religion and the almost unanimous refusal either to emit a paper currency or meddle with the certificates of public credit—have acquired our state sir a degree of eclat and of honor of which it is difficult to form an idea. The *philosophical legislation* of Virginia is in the mouths of all the learned of this place, and quoted by all the advocates of the *lumière de la philosophie*."[4]

Scotch-born James Wilson of Pennsylvania, who shared the nationalist leadership with Madison, was hardly an adjective behind him in the estimation of Delegate Pierce. Ranking among the foremost in legal and political knowledge, he knew all the political institutions of the world in detail, and drew attention not by the charm of eloquence but the force of reasoning. Quite different was Gouverneur Morris, another Pennsylvanian and third member of the large-state triumvirate. He was a genius in debate, charming away the senses—yet fickle and inconstant, never pursuing one train of thinking. Thrown from a phaeton in 1780, Morris had suffered the amputation of a crushed foot and ankle, and his right arm was scalded fleshless in boyhood.

These were the large-state generals, Madison and Wilson working closely together, Morris going his erratic way but usually aiding with a strategic talent more important than his oratory. On a lower level of leadership were Rufus King and Nathaniel Gorham of Massachusetts—King distinguished for eloquence and parliamentary talents, Gorham (says Pierce) a merchant with more sense than education, whom Madison always called "Mr. Ghorum." In this same group, but not taking the leadership which might have been expected, were the octogenarian philosopher Benjamin Franklin, the "deservedly celebrated" Alexander Hamilton, and financier Robert Morris. Reputed overlord of Congress during the Revolution, Morris spoke not once in the convention. Thirty-year-old Hamilton's strong judgment and convincing eloquence offset a feeble voice, but Pierce found his manners tinctured with stiffness, and sometimes with disagreeable vanity.

Franklin impressed Pierce more with his storytelling than his political finesse, but Madison saw the latter in the former. As when, after a day of jangling disagreement, the old man related that once with him on shipboard, a passenger who had been from birth without a sense of smell listened to his table companions argue endlessly whether the meat did or did not stink, and finally remarked: "Now, gentlemen, I am satisfied of what I have long suspected, that what you call smelling has no existence, and that it is nothing but mere fancy and prejudice."[5]

Describing the Virginians, Pierce presented General Washington as a blend of Gustavus Vasa, Peter the Great and Cincinnatus. Governor Randolph, scholar and statesman, had a most harmonious voice, a fine person and striking manners. George Mason won praise for his clear and copious understanding, firm principles and extraordinary debating power. (Madison called him the clearest reasoner he ever heard.)

Southern talents were concentrated in South Carolina, whose Revolutionary governor, John Rutledge, was too rapid a speaker to justify his oratorical fame but undoubtedly an able man and a gentleman of distinction and fortune. In Charles Pinckney, Pierce saw a young gentleman of the most promising talents. Government, law, history and philosophy were his favorite studies. His cousin Charles Cotesworth Pinckney had extensive legal knowledge and a fortune to match. Williamson of North Carolina and Baldwin of Georgia were placed well above the convention cellar.

Among the small-state delegates Pierce gave first place to William Paterson, "one of those kind of men whose powers break in upon you, and create wonder and astonishment. He is a man of great modesty, with looks that bespeak talents of no great extent— but he is a classic, a lawyer, and an orator." The fact that he termed Paterson of very low stature, but said nothing about Madison's physical equipment, corrects the too great emphasis often placed on the latter's unimpressive height. Jersey's Governor Livingston showed more sportiveness of wit than strength of thinking, while his colleague Brearly was an esteemed and virtuous non-orator. The pre-Revolutionary pamphleteer, John Dickinson, now chronically ill, made no such impression with his tongue as with his pen. "With an affected air of wisdom he labors to produce a trifle." George Read, likewise of Delaware, was a great lawyer and feeble, fatiguing orator; corpulent Gunning Bedford a bold and nervous speaker, warm and impetuous in his temper, precipitate in his judgment.

Luther Martin of Maryland possessed a good deal of information, which he imparted with a bad delivery and at such vast length that he tired everybody out. Oliver Ellsworth pulled up the small-state average with his deep and copious understanding. Judge Sherman's strange New England cant made him grotesque and laughable, but no man had a better heart or a clearer head. This ex-shoemaker was "extremely artful in accomplishing any particular object—it is remarked that he seldom fails."

Pierce's sketches are especially useful to those who believe that the delegates performed their work in the cerulean atmosphere of pure statesmanship, unclouded by thoughts of class or group, local or personal economic interest. Jefferson, who knew their earthiness, called them a group of demigods, and even the superrealistic Madison, in after years, exaggerated their merits through the incompleteness of his true appraisal:

"But whatever may be the judgment pronounced on the competency of the architects of the Constitution, or whatever may be the destiny of the edifice prepared by them, I feel it a duty to express my profound and solemn conviction, derived from my intimate opportunity of observing and appreciating the views of the convention, collectively and individually, that there never was an assembly of men, charged with a great and arduous trust, who were more pure in their motives, or more exclusively or anxiously devoted to the object committed to them."[6]

It was Madison, with his everlasting insistence on conflicting property interests as the basis of political division, who inspired Charles A. Beard to his iconoclastic *Economic Interpretation of the Constitution of the United States.* Beard in 1913 produced case histories of the framers—their main business interests, investments, speculations, slaveholdings—every element of self-interest that might (whether it did or not) influence the thirty lawyers, thirteen commercial men and ten plantation owners who were among the fifty-five men at Philadelphia. The Constitution, he made clear, was drafted by men drawn almost entirely from the property-owning classes whose interests it protected. He put far too much emphasis on ownership of public securities, but having made no comparable study of the convention itself, wisely refrained from drawing conclusions as to personal self-interest. This restraint was immediately construed as failure, by those who write history to mummify the social order. They fought desperately (and still do) to perpetuate what Beard destroyed forever—the myth of a Constitution written by moral supermen in an economic vacuum.

It is Madison who should have written the story of the Constitution, not by setting down speeches and motions, but in hard cold analysis like that which marked his 1782 study of Vermont statehood and western land speculation as ruling factors in Congress. He should have done so by applying the principles which he himself put into words a few weeks after the constitutional convention adjourned:

"Those who hold and those who are without property have ever formed distinct interests in society. Those who are creditors, and those who are debtors, fall under a like discrimination. A landed interest, a manufacturing interest, a mercantile interest, a moneyed interest, with many lesser interests, grow up of necessity in civilized nations and divide them into different classes, actuated by different sentiments and views. The regulation of these various and interfering interests forms the principal task of modern legislation, and involves the spirit of party and faction in the necessary and ordinary operations of the government."[7]

It would have been fatal to the Constitution to analyze it by such rules before ratification. By the time Madison had leisure for it, his own change of views on federal power forbade the attempt. Yet even his meager preface to the debates has been called an economic interpretation.[8] And it is from Madison that the full story can be learned—by applying his theory of class division to the record of debates, illuminated by the ten-year background of interstate struggle and the clash of contending groups. When this is done, the fears, prejudices and personal interests of nearly all delegates drop into place as a natural part of group and sectional interests. And there is still plenty of patriotic statesmanship.

Applying Madison's doctrine that government is bent to the will of contending groups, the first conclusion is inescapable. On the greatest potential issue of all, only one side was present at Philadelphia. Save for two or three delegates, the whole convention desired to protect property rights by the strength and form of the federal government, and to strike down state laws designed to wipe out debt or impair financial contracts. The effect of this is to eliminate, at one swoop, the whole conflict between rich and poor, creditors and debtors, as a direct source of contention between factions in the convention. The poor were not represented, though they had friends. The great struggles lay between the owners of different kinds of property, between sections with different economic interests, between those who stood for and against the aims and ambitions of states, groups and individuals.

When the convention came to its choice between the Virginia and New Jersey plans, two composite groups faced each other. The maritime, mercantile and manufacturing interests of Massachusetts and Pennsylvania were linked with the planters of Virginia and the South in a demand for representation according to population. Each big state, with proportionate voting in prospect, saw federal power as its own power and ceased to fear it. Commerce was to be regulated, land policies to be determined. The great commercial and landed states, with their huge populations,

must not be reduced to the voting level of Delaware and Connecticut. The states south of Virginia had slavery to defend and
foreign trade to safeguard. With enormous vacant hinterlands to
develop they saw future strength in proportional representation.

On the once convulsive issue of western lands, the large states
felt virtuous but not tranquil. Cessions to the nation by Virginia,
New York and Massachusetts had ended the rivalry among themselves produced by their overlapping claims north of the Ohio.
They had given the small states a stake in the West and reduced
their clamor. Virginia ended another crisis by offering independence to Kentucky, subject to her admission to the Union. But they
were worried as they saw how Vermont's escape from the sovereignty of New Hampshire and New York whetted the western
appetite for statehood and the craze for speculative fortunes.

On the discordant side, states of the deeper South were ignoring
congressional appeals to transfer their western lands to the nation.
North Carolina did so, then revoked the cession and had to spend
the next two years (1785-1787) putting down a speculators' rebellion in the "State of Franklin." Georgia was robbing Indians
and starting land sales along the Mississippi, both in defiance of
national policy. Maine was agitating independence from Massachusetts. Vermont rifles furnished a warning against any military
invasion to validate New York land warrants. Pennsylvania, vic-
torious in a congressional court, faced an insurrection of settlers
holding Connecticut titles in the Wyoming Valley.

Within the old charter limits of Virginia, the great speculative
schemes of Marylanders, Jerseyites and Pennsylvanians were dead
or dormant—struck down by Madison, Joseph Jones and Mason
in their skillful handling of the Virginia cession. But there was
a suspicion in that state that the Indiana Company, which once
ruled Congress through its ability to boss New Jersey, was sleeping
with one eye open. It still held an Indian deed to Vandalia (the
State of West Virginia) which was not transferred to Congress in
the deed of 1784. Other speculators were asking Congress to bite
a hole out of southwestern Virginia and North Carolina. The Old
Dominion, even after disgorging the 265,878 square miles of the
Northwest Territory, still exceeded the combined areas of seven
of the states, with enough left over to count five of them twice, and

there were plenty of covetous fingers on which to do the counting.[9]

The large states had no need of a strong federal government to protect their lands against their neighbors. On that score, the weaker it was, the safer they were. But if the government was strong, they must control it lest it be used against them. The large states, like the small ones, felt the need of a strong government for other reasons—to control commerce, suppress insurrections, protect public credit and private creditors, promote the country's development, solidify its union, repel foreign commercial aggressions, and—by displaying strength and stability—make the United States secure against military attack and respectable in the eyes of the world. Measuring the future government by the magnitude of these aims, the large-state delegates came to a dual conclusion. Power should go to the powerful, but was dangerous in multiple Lilliputian hands. The landed states would not let this great new instrument pass into the custody of those who wanted to carve away the West.

On the positive side, the large-state bloc was not fully cohesive. Southern delegates feared the North because of its ship monopoly, its small need for European imports and its hostility to slavery. Wealthy Elbridge Gerry, Massachusetts merchant, had a horror of federal taxes, commercial regulations and centralized military power. George Mason, sincere devotee of personal liberty, had purchased thousands of acres of British-owned lands, confiscated by Virginia in violation of the treaty of peace. No tyrannous federal court should compel him to pay quitrents.[10]

If the large-state bloc gaped a little, it was unity itself compared with the polyglot group behind the New Jersey Plan. Thanks to the rule that ancient utterances shall always be taken at face value, this group of delegates appears in history as defenders of state sovereignty and opponents of a strong government. Delaware's instruction to defend equality has been seen as a symbol of fervent devotion to the state. But George Read, who obtained that order to relieve the delegation "from disagreeable argumentation," was the same man who proclaimed in convention on June 6:

"Too much attachment is betrayed to the state governments. We must look beyond their continuance. A national government must

soon of necessity swallow all of them up. They will soon be reduced to the mere office of electing the national Senate."

Devotion to state sovereignty didn't explain why a tiny asteroid
like Delaware should have the same political weight as the huge
planet Virginia. Delegate Read told Dickinson why Delaware
must have equality:

"I conceive our existence as a state will depend upon our preserving such rights, for I consider the acts of Congress hitherto as to
the ungranted lands in most of the larger states, as sacrificing the
just claims of the smaller and bounded states to a proportional
share therein, for the purpose of discharging the national debt
incurred during the war; and such is my jealousy of most of the
larger states that I would trust nothing to their candor, generosity
or ideas of public justice in behalf of this state."

Land, debt, cash—these were the synonyms of Delaware's devotion to state sovereignty. Read was perfectly willing to see his
state vanish in a consolidated government, but until then it must
have an equal vote in order to get a fair share of the public lands.
With equality lost, he concluded, the state "would at once become
a cipher in the Union and have no chance of an accession of district or even citizens."[11]

With Read's attitude in the background, it becomes easy to
understand the alternatives offered by Paterson and Brearly—state
equality or territorial "hotchpot" and redivision. It was a continuance, partially emotional, of the New Jersey-Maryland-Dela-
ware campaign to cut down the large states and establish federal
title to the West, from mingled motives of general welfare, aid to
land speculators and plain envy. For two years after Virginia
offered to cede the Northwest to Congress, New Jersey and allied
delegates declaimed about the territory as a heritage won by common expenditures of blood and treasure—and blocked Madison's
effort to exclude the piratical claims of land companies holding
Indian deeds. New groups were now trying to buy vast areas—
among them Symmes and Dayton of New Jersey, the latter the
youngest delegate to the convention, notorious a decade later for

MADISON DECRIES STATE SOVEREIGNTY. MADISON'S NOTES OF SPEECH BY HIMSELF, SHOWING INSERTION OF SENTENCE FROM YATES'S NOTES AND ELIMINATION OF "EQUAL" AND "THEIR CHARACTER." SPEECH AT TOP IS BY READ

GOUVERNEUR MORRIS. AFTER A PAINTING BY CHAPPEL

his speculations in public-land warrants while serving as speaker of the national House of Representatives. Nothing done in Philadelphia was likely to aid or retard these sales, but it was easy to see that the states with the most votes in Congress would be best able to get what they wanted.

Connecticut had an approach of her own to public lands. Deprived by a special federal court of her weak claim to part of Pennsylvania, she had refused to honor the judgment until given a vast western area—the Connecticut Reserve—with which to satisfy the clamors of her disappointed land companies. In Connecticut lay the strength and the weakness of the small-state bloc. Unhelped by her, the other small states had not even pressure power. Having accomplished an incredible territorial coup, she needed no power of offense in Congress, but with a reversal of her land grab still possible, defensive strength was imperative. She would neither accept the Virginia Plan nor strain a tendon wielding the New Jersey carving knife. State equality in one house of Congress was all she needed.

In the angry trade wars of the states the small ones were both victims and victimizers. New Jersey and Connecticut had identical grievances, arising from lack of seaports. Placed between New York and Philadelphia, said Madison, the former state "was likened to a cask tapped at both ends." The latter, drained by the import duties of Massachusetts, Rhode Island and New York, was striking back with discriminatory imposts against the Bay State.[12] New York, in her determination to tax her neighbors' imports, "had inflexibly refused [said Madison] to grant even a duty of five per cent on imports for the urgent debts of the Revolution."[13] Yates and Lansing stood for state equality not because it would aid their state, but because insistence on it might wreck the convention.

Four states and a man made up the small-state bloc. Luther Martin, attorney general of Maryland, was listed by Madison as "representing the party of Mr. [Samuel] Chase opposed to federal restraints on state legislation."[14] That is, he wanted the states to have a free hand to wipe out debts with paper money. Martin, ultraconservative in later life, has been pictured as the poor man's advocate in the convention. Before that is taken for granted, it should be noted that he came from Harford County, of which a Baltimorean wrote a few months later: "Baltimore and Harford counties alone are clearly anti-federal in which are many powerful and popular men who have speculated deeply in British confiscated property and for that reason are alarmed at shutting the door against paper money." The same men and their friends had paid off British debts in depreciated continental currency and were fearful that the Constitution might "bring about a due execution of the treaty between Great Britain and America to their loss."[15]

Martin's backers, under this analysis, were "wealthy debtors" with a two-way interest in paper money. In debt to the state for confiscated property, they wanted the state to issue paper money whose depreciation would make payment easy. Also, acting under state law, they had discharged pre-Revolutionary debts to British merchants by depositing the face amount of the debts in the state treasury. At the average depreciation, they got rid of a $5,000 debt for $10. The peace treaty threatened them with payment in full.

Debt-ridden speculators did not give the Chase faction all its political strength. The forcible closing of Maryland courts by tumultuous mobs furnished evidence of wider backing. However, Martin and his still absent colleague, John Francis Mercer (owing a large defaulted debt to George Washington), represented a Maryland minority. The whole original slate of delegates chose to stay in the legislature and wage battle against Chase's money bill. Three out of the five substitutes chosen on May 26 were opposed to paper money. Of these five only Martin and Jenifer were present in convention, and were dividing on every crucial vote at the time the New Jersey Plan was framed.

It was not to protect fiat money that Martin went into the small-state bloc, whose members included the most violent enemies of paper currency. His tie with the small states was on western lands. Maryland's historic demand for common ownership of British crown lands—or, to state it another way, to tear Virginia to pieces—still lived in him with undiminished heat. On this issue his fellow delegates stood with him, but their hearts were not in it. Six years earlier, Daniel of St. Thomas Jenifer had been the toughest fighter in Congress against Virginia's title to the Northwest, and against Madison's effort to transfer it to Congress unclouded by the claims of land speculators. Now the Maryland-sponsored Illinois-Wabash Company was as dead as Pocahontas. Its disappearance left full play to Jenifer's paramount interest as agent of the British-owned House of Baltimore, in behalf of whose minor heir (according to Luzerne) he had vainly exerted his influence as wartime president of the Maryland Senate. He needed a strong treaty power and a strong legislative power to enforce treaties. So (like two of his absent colleagues) he was allied with ex-enemy Madison in support of the Virginia Plan, except when Martin's blustering threats forced him to make a contrary record for the Maryland legislature. "He sits silent in the Senate, and seems to be conscious that he is no politician," wrote Pierce, who didn't know that politics compelled his silence.[16]

In the framing of the New Jersey Plan, Martin saw a chance for a triple killing. To carve up Virginia, protect paper money and leave contracts unprotected he needed a federal government weak in some respects, strong in others. The workings of his mind can be seen in his national-supremacy provision. It made acts of Congress and treaties "the supreme law of the respective states," and binding on their judges, anything in the laws of the individual states to the contrary notwithstanding. Nothing was said about constitutions. The way this was written, the United States Constitution was not binding on state judges. Neither was a federal law or treaty binding on the judges if it conflicted with a state constitution.

Under Martin's wording, a constitutional ban on paper money or on laws impairing contracts would not of itself bind state judges. A federal law to enforce the ban would not bind them if it was in conflict with a state constitution. The same was true of treaties. Since, under his system, there were to be no inferior federal courts, this meant that such laws and treaties would be utterly unenforceable by judicial process.

But suppose Congress had constitutional power to cut a state in two without its consent. A law doing so would not bind state judges, but it would be binding on the state itself. For Martin's article provided further that "if any state or any body of men in any state" should prevent the execution of "such acts or treaties," the federal executive should have power to enforce them by military action. It was only in cases in court that federal power was to be subordinate to state constitutions. Laws of a political nature, directed against the state itself, had the full executive authority and military force of the general government behind them. Did Martin plan that Congress should have constitutional power to subdivide states against their will? One need but read the clause he subsequently offered on the floor of the convention:

"The legislature of the United States shall have power to erect new states within as well as without the territory claimed by the several states or either of them, and admit the same into the Union; provided that nothing in this Constitution shall be construed to affect the claim of the United States to vacant lands ceded to them by the late treaty of peace."[17]

This was the refined and final form of "hotchpot"—the real desire of Martin and the New Jerseyites who formed a bloc within a bloc. The crude beginnings of it, curiously mixed with a nationalism which the Marylander did not share, can be seen in the final section of Paterson's preliminary draft of the New Jersey Plan:

"Whereas it is necessary in order to form the people of the U. S. into a nation, that the states should be consolidated, by which means all the citizens thereof will become equally entitled to and will equally participate in the same privileges and rights, and in all waste, uncultivated, and back territory and lands; it is therefore resolved, that all the lands contained within the limits of each state individually, and of the U. S. generally be considered as constituting one body or mass, and be divided into thirteen or more integral parts."

One historian comments on this seldom published article: "To account for such a proposition as this in connection with the New Jersey Plan is a matter of some difficulty."[18] To be sure it is, if one accepts the old assumption that the small-state delegates were governed by devotion to state sovereignty. But not if Hamilton knew what he was talking about when he said in convention: "The truth is, it is a contest for power, not for liberty." And vibrating in all his more than 200 pounds, Bedford of Delaware verified that assertion with these impetuous words:

"If political societies possess ambition, avarice and all the other passions which render them formidable to each other, ought we not to view them in this light here? . . . Are not the large states evidently seeking to aggrandize themselves at the expense of the small? . . . Can it be expected that the small states will act from pure disinterestedness?"

He described the large-state alliance—Georgia and the Carolinas, puffed up with lands and Negroes and prospects of future greatness; Virginia, Pennsylvania and Massachusetts, all having a direct and palpable, present and future interest in the course they were following. Shouted Bedford:

"I do not, gentlemen, trust you. If you possess the power, the abuse of it could not be checked; and what then would prevent you from exercising it to our destruction?"[19]

This was no spasm of abstract fear. Madison had built the large-state bloc on the very lines Bedford described. To the Virginian, who had no aggressive aims, these elements of strength furnished legitimate reason for ceasing to fear high federal power; to Bedford they were evidences of a purpose of aggrandizement, which he confessed the small states also possessed.

What was the aggrandizement which the small states feared from the large? Not commercial, for big North Carolina was a victim on that score, and absent Rhode Island one of the worst offenders. Little Delaware, too, had nullified the nation's wartime embargo and was a center of smuggling into Pennsylvania. The threatened aggrandizement was exclusion of the small states from western lands desired for revenue and soldiers' bonuses; a sucking of small-state farmers into western territories favored by low taxation made possible by land sales; a possible squeezing out of small-state land companies by rival speculators.

In part, the small states were seeking to retain excessive power out of sheer unwillingness to give it up. Delaware, swollen to equality with Virginia, had no desire to shrink to one sixteenth of her neighbor's political bulk. Beyond this, and beyond and above its fears, the small-state bloc was engaged in active aggression. The large states were seeking to defend their possessions, but these possessions were so enormous that the mere holding of them constituted a form of passive aggression.

Again and again, during that crucial summer, Madison sought to guide the small-state delegates away from their obsession, arguing that the real and lasting clash of interests was between North and South. His words were largely wasted, but there was a truer corrective in the convention's work. The need of new powers, combined with the fear of them, forced the delegates to decide first who should wield those powers. They would come then to the greater question: whether, after a decision which could not be satisfactory to all, they would be united enough to frame a government on the broad principles of general welfare to which they all subscribed.

# CHAPTER VI

## BATTLING FOR POWER

To PUT them on a par, both the revised Virginia Plan and the New Jersey Plan were sent to the committee of the whole on June 15. After denying the powers of the convention, Paterson got down to cases. The large states acceded readily to the Confederacy, he recalled.

"It was the small ones that came in reluctantly and slowly. New Jersey and Maryland were the two last, the former objecting to the want of power in Congress over trade: both of them to the want of power to appropriate the vacant territory to the benefit of the whole."

He reverted to his former theme: State sovereignty required equal sovereignty. The only cure for that was throwing the states into hotchpot. To say that this was impracticable would not make it so. He argued for continuance of the present Congress. The people did not complain of it. What they wished was that Congress have more power.

Wilson replied with a point-by-point comparison which showed that the Virginia Plan went far beyond the other in giving effective powers to the general government and in checking the states. Challenging the supposition that the people were devoted to state governments, he asked:

"Where do the people look at present for relief from the evils of which they complain? Is it from an internal reform of their governments? No, sir. It is from the national councils that relief is expected."

Yet he would be reluctant to add to the authority of a body not resting on the people. Equal representation by states produced unequal representation of the people, a poison contaminating every branch of government. To which Charles Pinckney added:

71

"Give New Jersey an equal vote, and she will dismiss her scruples and concur in the national system." The situation was paradoxical. The highest powers were in the large-state proposals, but the small states complained most bitterly about the weakness of the existing government.[1]

Hamilton liked neither plan. Outvoted by Yates and Lansing, he had kept silent, but now, on June 18, he delivered one of the most brilliant and ineffective speeches of the convention. Rejecting the New Jersey Plan for its preservation of state sovereignty, he declared that if the powers were made adequate, they would give rise to a tyranny built on local prejudices. Except for the shock to public opinion, he would propose to extinguish the state governments and retain only subordinate authorities. Yet he almost despaired that republican government could be established over so vast a country. His private opinion, supported by "so many of the wise and good," was that the British government was the best in the world and he doubted much whether anything short if it would do in America.

"Their House of Lords is a most noble institution. Having nothing to hope for by a change, and a sufficient interest by means of their property, in being faithful to the national interest, they form a permanent barrier against every pernicious innovation, whether attempted on the part of the Crown or of the Commons."

So, in the United States, let one branch of the legislature hold their places for life or during good behavior. "Let the executive also be for life." At present the people would not adopt this nor even the Virginia Plan, but he saw the Union dissolving and evils operating which must soon cure this fondness for democracies. Hamilton then read, but did not offer, a plan of government in accord with his ideas.[2]

This speech was at bottom a challenge of Madison's doctrine that in a large federal republic the diverging interests of sections and classes made popular government safe. Hamilton held to the ancient belief of Aristotle that rich and poor must have mutual checks on each other—with the rich doing about four fifths of the checking. The convention's total disregard of Hamilton's views was due in part to knowledge that the people would reject them, but it measured also the influence of Madison's reasoning, which sustained republican principles against the fears aroused by current assaults on debts and mortgages. Hamilton and Madison were still able to work together for a strong government, but their future antagonism was plainly in view.

The small-state forces now made a neat maneuver. Proposing a slight change of wording in the first article of the New Jersey Plan, they offered a substitute instead of an amendment to it. Had that been adopted, the second article could have been called up and the Virginia Plan would have been sidetracked. The Madison-Wilson forces defeated Dickinson's substitute, and (said Madison) "Mr. Paterson's plan was again at large before the committee."[3]

There remained but to give it the knockout blow. Madison did that. Answering the claim that the convention lacked power to propose any other than a *federal* plan, he pointed out that in dealing with piracies, captures, etc., the existing government operated directly on the people, and in Connecticut and Rhode Island delegates to Congress were elected by the people. Thus, in part, it already was a national government. Considering it as a federal body (as the other side did) unanimous consent was not necessary to its dissolution, since under the law of nations a breach of any one article by one party left the others free to dissolve the compact or repair the breach by force. He then examined the New Jersey Plan by two tests: Would it preserve the Union? Would it remedy the evils felt by the states collectively and individually? Item by item, he showed its weaknesses.

It provided no means of enforcing treaties. The states could go on threatening the country with foreign wars.

Would it prevent encroachments on the federal authority? That was an evil inherent in all confederated republics, ancient and modern. Witness the illegal interstate commercial compacts, the unlawful raising of troops by Massachusetts, the refusal of New Jersey to comply with requisitions, the bribery of Connecticut to accept the territorial decree against her, the Indian wars and treaties entered into by Georgia.

Not only did Paterson's plan omit a control over the states as a general defense of federal prerogatives, but it failed in specific measures of supremacy. There was to be no ratification by the people, therefore no supremacy over state constitutions. It gave nothing but appellate jurisdiction to the federal judiciary. The absence of a federal negative on state laws left the way open to interstate aggressions.

Would the New Jersey Plan halt the Massachusetts insurrections? The nation must have authority to override minorities which obtain power by military conquest, by seditious aid from the disfranchised poor, or by force drawn from slavery. Would Paterson's plan insure against the multiplicity, the mutability, the injustice, the impotence of the laws of the states—factors which had a full share in producing the present convention? It contained no remedy for this dreadful class of evils.

Madison then did some down-to-earth talking to the small-state delegates. They relied on coercion of the states to uphold federal power. Coercion could never be exerted but on themselves. The larger states would be impregnable. He begged them to consider what would happen in case their stubbornness led to dissolution of the Union. The states must then either remain individually independent, or form two or more confederacies. In the first event would the small states be more secure against their larger neighbors than they would be under a general government pervading every part of the empire? If the United States were split up, would the small states in each confederacy be granted equal suffrage by their larger neighbors?

Having planted these corroding doubts, Madison turned to the hotchpot proposal. Paterson and Brearly admitted, he said, that state equality was *unjust* to Virginia, sixteen times the size of Delaware, but claimed it was *unsafe* to Delaware to allow Virginia sixteen times as many votes. So they proposed that all the states be thrown into one mass and a new partition be made into thirteen equal parts. Would this be practicable? Dissimilar rules of property, differences in manners, habits and prejudices amounted to a prohibition of the attempt. But granting that it was practicable, would not a voluntary coalition of the small states with their neighbors be just as effectual for their safety? One thing more—

state equality would put disproportionate power in the hands of the new states forming in the West. Let them vote according to population and all would be safe and right. Give them an equal vote, and a more objectionable minority than ever might give law to the whole.

That ended the debate. On a motion to postpone Paterson's plan, New Jersey and New York alone clung to it. The revised Virginia Plan was reported back to the convention. The vote was a deathblow to the old Confederation and a final decision for a more effective form of government.[4]

This overwhelming defeat of the New Jersey Plan reflected the inability of the small-state delegates to agree on anything except their basic drive for control. Most of them wanted a stronger government than would win the support of *all* who wanted state equality. That doomed the New Jersey Plan. But it also meant that the small-state bloc would regain solidity and strength as soon as the question of state equality came up in the Virginia Plan. The battle for power still lay ahead.

Skirmishing for position, Rufus King minimized the extent of the change in going to a supreme national government. The so-called sovereign states were not sovereigns at all. They could not make war, nor peace, nor alliances nor treaties. They were deaf and dumb, for they could neither listen to nor speak to any foreign sovereign. A union of the states was a union of the people composing them, "from whence a *national* character results to the whole." The mere fact of union gave the convention power to propose consolidation. "He doubted much the practicability of annihilating the states; but thought that much of their power ought to be taken away from them."

Luther Martin made the challenging remark that when the states cast off their allegiance to Great Britain, they were thrown into a state of nature and became individually independent. Wilson denied that doctrine. "He read the Declaration of Independence, observing thereon that the *United Colonies* were declared to be free and independent states, and inferring that they were independent, not *individually* but *unitedly* and that they were confederated as they were independent, states." Hamilton agreed with Wilson and invited the small states to forget their fears. They should note that the large states were far apart, diverse in interests, wherefore any ambitious combination of a few states was bound to be counteracted by the others.[5]

At this jockeying stage, the words "a national government" in the first Virginia resolve were changed to "the government of the United States." This was done, Madison explained to jubilant State Righters who discovered it in 1819, not to change the meaning, but merely to get rid of a term which might be liable to mistake or misrepresentation.[6]

On the next resolution, the small-state delegates argued (but without meaning it) against a two-house legislature. Nearly all the states, Sherman pointed out, had agreed to give the present Congress power to draw a revenue from trade. If the people would trust Congress with the all-important money power, they would trust them with any other necessary powers. Finally he got to his real position—a compromise. If the difficulty on representation could not be otherwise got over, "he would agree to have two branches, and a proportional representation in one of them; provided each state had an equal voice in the other."

Suave Dr. Johnson of Connecticut then made a suggestion. Advocates of the Virginia Plan, he remarked, proclaimed a desire to leave considerable subordinate jurisdiction in the states. How could this jurisdiction be made secure without giving the states an equal vote in the national government? If this could be shown to the satisfaction of the small-state delegates, many of their objections would be removed.

Wilson undertook to reply. He assured them that since national and state legislators both represented the same people, the former would be certain to leave the latter in possession of what the people wished them to retain. Madison took over and laid down two propositions which would have caused Patrick Henry or Samuel Adams to burst an artery.

1. There was less danger of encroachment from the general government on the states than from the states on the federal government.

2. Federal encroachments, if they occurred, would work less fatal mischiefs than encroachments by the states.

All confederacies, he observed, showed a greater tendency to anarchy among the members than tyranny in the federal head. Would this be altered by the greater powers of the new government and its direct link with the people? Suppose for a moment that indefinite power should be given to the general legislature, and the states be reduced to dependent corporations. "Why should it follow that the general government would take from the states any branch of their power as far as its operation was beneficial, and its continuance desirable to the people?" As far as local authority was convenient to the people they were attached to it, and their representatives would respect their attachment. The objection made against general power lay not against its probable abuse, but the imperfect use that could be made of it over so vast a country.

"As far as its operation would be practicable it could not in this view be improper; as far as it would be impracticable, the conveniency of the general government itself would concur with that of the people in the maintenance of subordinate governments. Were it practicable for the general government to extend its care to every requisite object without the cooperation of the state governments, the people would not be less free as members of one great republic than as members of thirteen small ones. A citizen of Delaware was not more free than a citizen of Virginia: nor would either be more free than a citizen of America."

This led him to his ultimate conclusion:

"Supposing therefore a tendency in the general government to absorb the state governments, no fatal consequence could result. Taking the reverse of the supposition, that a tendency should be left in the state governments towards an independence on the general government, and the gloomy consequences need not be pointed out."

One can imagine the political earthquake that would have shaken Virginia had Madison made this speech publicly in 1830 instead of behind silent walls in 1787. His words did not seem to shock his associates, and closed the debate. The convention,

Connecticut again joining the large states, approved a two-branch legislature seven to three.[7]

South Carolina now made a final effort to do away with elections by the people, by letting state legislatures direct the manner of choosing representatives. In the debate, Rutledge and C. C. Pinckney let the cat out. Legislatures could express the sense of the people better than the people themselves. The state governments should be a part of the general system in order to insure its benefits to the Southern states. In other words, the federal government must be responsive to big slaveowners, not to the people. On the vote, six states stood by popular elections. Three small states joined South Carolina, but they were merely maneuvering for state equality.

A revival of the effort to have the states pay congressmen brought Madison and Randolph together again, both decrying a dependence on the states which would vitiate the whole system. Madison then took up a North Carolina argument (a reflex of the "State of Franklin" rebellion) that old states ought not to pay the expenses of men who would be sent from poverty-stricken new states for no purpose but to thwart the older ones.

"He disliked particularly the policy suggested by Mr. Williamson of leaving the members from the poor states beyond the mountains to the precarious and parsimonious support of their constituents. If the western states hereafter arising should be admitted into the Union, they ought to be considered as equals and as brethren."

A decision for congressional pay from the Treasury brought back the question of who should say how much. Madison wanted a liberal salary fixed in the Constitution. He didn't want congressmen to be able "to put their hands into the public purse for the sake of their own pockets." His victory on this point was temporary, but on a kindred issue, by offering a compromise, he planted a clause that stuck—the one forbidding appointment of senators and representatives to executive offices which had been created during their terms, or whose emoluments had been increased. Neither he nor Mason, who wanted a stronger restriction, has ever received the Congressional Medal of Honor for this ban on building nests for lame ducks.[8]

Next came the composition of the Senate. Charles Pinckney took this occasion (on June 25) to urge his special plan for that body—states to have one, two, three or four senators, according to their standing in the Union. All these were to be elected by the lower federal house—Madison's original idea in the Virginia Plan. Pinckney's proposal was supported, or rather accompanied, by a remarkable speech.

The people of the United States, said the young Carolinian, had fewer distinctions of fortune and less of rank than the inhabitants of any other nation. With vast empty lands in the West this equality was likely to continue. There would be few poor, few dependent, and hardly a hundred men with the great riches needed to support a nobility. The people could be divided into three classes—professional men, commercial men, the landed interest, all mutually dependent and forming but one order of citizens, the order of commons. To their interests the government must be suited—a republican government sufficiently active and energetic to rescue the country from foreign contempt and preserve our domestic happiness and security.

Ringing words! Spoken by a man who so feared the people that he fought their right to vote from the beginning to the end of the convention. The derivation of the speech explains its incoherence. Pinckney was taking over the thought expressed by Wilson on June 7: "The British government cannot be our model. We have no materials for a similar one. Our manners, our laws . . . the whole genius of the people, are opposed to it." From this the Carolinian moved to a dream-picture of equality by classifying the people as professional, commercial and landed. But these were not the people of the United States. They were the people who were people in the eyes of a planter aristocracy.

It is one of the ironies of history that Madison's recording of Pinckney's speech has given the convention's leading opponent of political rights a lasting reputation for equalitarianism. Unfortunately, Madison relied on Pinckney for a text which was cut off a few sentences before the end. Only from Yates does one learn that the Carolinian was arguing for an ultraconservative Senate to protect the three groups which he regarded as the people. The Virginian too believed in a conservative Senate, but his fundamental attitude was utterly different. The difference made Madison the architect of a stable government harmonizing with the genius of a free people, Pinckney an ineffective advocate of the law-enforced supremacy of wealth.[9]

Election of senators by state legislatures was carried (said Madison) by a combination of small states seeking power through state equality, and large-state delegates most anxious to secure the importance of the state governments. Virginia and Pennsylvania cast the only opposing votes. They were influenced, Madison intimated in a later footnote, by a feeling that election by legislatures would interfere with representation according to population. He himself had other objections, as shown by his remark immediately after the decision:

"By the vote already taken, will not the temper of the state legislatures transfuse itself into the Senate? Do we create a free government?"[10]

This was a double argument. A conservative Senate could not be obtained through legislatures tainted with paper money, etc. And such an election would subject the Senate to state control. At first, Madison had wanted the lower house to elect senators. His switch from that to election by the people is proof that he gave first thought to the independence of the Senate from state control. For its conservatism he looked elsewhere—to a lengthened term and staggered elections.

The choice in terms was four, six, seven or nine years, with a few delegates favoring life. On this issue Madison brought forward his favorite theme of political warfare between economic classes. To guard against this danger, divide the trust between different bodies of men, who might watch and check each other. The people and their short-term representatives were liable to temporary error, through want of information, fickleness and passion. Select, then, a portion of enlightened citizens whose limited number and firmness might check impetuous councils. It was true that the United States had not the hereditary distinctions

or extremes of wealth and poverty found in Europe. But, Madison
continued:

"An increase of population will of necessity increase the proportion of those who will labor under all the hardships of life, and
secretly sigh for a more equal distribution of its blessings. These
may in time outnumber those who are placed above the feelings
of indigence. According to the equal laws of suffrage the power
will slide into the hands of the former. No agrarian attempts
have yet been made in this country, but symptoms of a leveling
spirit, as we have understood, have sufficiently appeared in certain
quarters to give notice of the future danger."

How was this danger to be guarded against on republican principles? By the counterweight of wisdom and virtue. That being
the object of the Senate, considerable duration should be given to
it. Madison "did not conceive that the term of nine years could
threaten any real danger" (he had voted for six the day before),
but he would couple with it a perpetual disqualification to be
re-elected. Since the plan they were digesting probably would
decide forever the fate of republican government, they ought not
only to provide every guard to liberty, but be equally careful to
supply the defects which experience had pointed out.

The nine-year proposal collapsed under Gerry's warning that
the people would reject it, and Sherman's remark that frequent
elections were necessary to preserve the good behavior of rulers.
Six years was decided on.

Madison then helped to defeat, by a narrow margin, a South
Carolina motion that senators be paid no salaries. The majority
rejected C. C. Pinckney's contention that a body meant to represent the wealth of the country ought to be composed of persons
of wealth. Once more Madison had to fight a proposal for state
pay. Such a system would make senators, like the old Congress,
"the mere agents and advocates of state interests and views, instead
of being the impartial umpires and guardians of justice and general good." Delaware's high nationalism broke the small-state and
Southern combination for this motion and brought it to a five-to-
six defeat.[11]

Next in the Virginia Plan came the powers of Congress. It was futile to discuss them, so they jumped to the question of questions—state equality or proportional representation in Congress. Luther Martin took the floor and almost wore it out under a desultory two-day harangue. He might have continued two months, his then ally and later critic Oliver Ellsworth wrote during the ratification fight, "but for those marks of fatigue and disgust you saw strongly expressed on whichever side of the house you turned your mortified eyes."[12]

It really wasn't such a bad speech, compared with senatorial filibusters, for in the five-hour talk Madison found 700 words worth recording. Martin contended that the general government was meant only to preserve the state governments, and its powers ought to be kept within narrow limits. The states were created by a compact of the people in them, the Confederation by a compact of the independent states. To resort to the people at large for their sanction of a new government would violate both compacts and dissolve the state governments as well as the Confederation, throwing everybody into a state of nature. Shifting to more realistic nonsense, he declared that if the states were to vote in proportion to numbers, nine smaller states would be enslaved by three large ones plus one smaller ally. Instead of the small states forming a junction, as Madison had suggested, he thought a division of the large states would be more eligible.

Two days of such talk, in his stumbling manner, put nerves on edge. The calmness of Madison's reply was offset by the sharp scalpel he applied to state sovereignty. Martin, he pointed out, had been discussing the Confederation as if it were a mere treaty, whereas in some respects it set up a government paramount to the states, making laws by which they were bound. Federal laws already operated in some degree directly on people and properties; the same would be true in a far greater degree under the new government. This called for a federal legislature built on the same lines as those of the states.

Was a combination of the large states dreaded? That could result, said Madison, only from some common interest or from the mere fact of size. What were their staples? Massachusetts, fish; Pennsylvania, flour; Virginia, tobacco—as dissimiliar as any three

states in the Union. Would mere equality of size hold them together? The *Journals of Congress* revealed no peculiar association
of these three states. Large counties in a state showed no tendency
to cling together. Carthage and Rome tore each other to pieces
instead of uniting to devour the weaker nations. In every stage of
civilization the weak suffered most when there was no efficient
government to control the strong. The two extremes, Madison
went on, were separation and consolidation. In the first case the
states would be independent nations; in the last, mere counties
of one entire republic, subject to one common law.

"In the first case the smaller states would have everything to
fear from the larger. In the last they would have nothing to fear.
The true policy of the small states therefore lies in promoting those
principles and that form of government which most approximate
the states of the condition of counties."

This might be convincing, but it was not persuasive to delegates whose talk of danger from the large states covered a quest
for power to carve them up. He shifted to that underlying reality.
If the general government was feeble, the security of the large
states would depend on their own size and strength. They would
never submit to a partition. However——

"Give to the general government sufficient energy and perma-
nency, and you remove the objection. Gradual partitions of the
large, and junctions of the small states will be facilitated, and time
may effect that equalization which is wished for by the small states
now, but can never be accomplished at once."

These counterproposals had no effect on skeptical small-state
delegates. But the hint as to federal power was a forceful one. It
stimulated both the desire for a strong government and the determination to control it—factors which tended to hold the delegates to their task, but intensified their strife. Wilson compared
the small states to the rotten boroughs of England. Sherman
replied that grading state votes by population was the same as
giving a rich man more votes than a poor one. At this point
Benjamin Franklin, recalling that during the Revolution "we had

daily prayer in this room for the divine protection," and that these appeals were graciously answered, asked why they had sought no illumination from the Father of Lights.

"I have lived, sir, a long time, and the longer I live, the more convincing proofs I see of this truth—*that God governs in the affairs of men.* And if a sparrow cannot fall to the ground without his notice, is it probable that an empire can rise without his aid?"

He moved, and Roger Sherman seconded him, that prayers be held every morning, with the clergy of the city called in. Madison records that Hamilton took the lead in opposition, but says nothing of his "impatient and impious" remark (as it seemed to Jonathan Dayton) that he saw no necessity of calling in *foreign* aid. The motion was side-stepped by adjournment, following arguments that belated adoption of prayers would spread rumors of dissension.[13]

Franklin's reference to prayer "in this room"—that is, where the Continental Congress used to meet—locates the convention in the east room of the first floor. The passage is commended to those (or the survivors among them) who have been lamenting for a hundred years that there is nothing in the convention records to clear up the uncertainty on this point. In mid-July, the Reverend Manasseh Cutler found the convention on the second floor. In September, the Pennsylvania legislature found it on the first floor. Franklin's remark supports the supposition that the delegates moved upstairs in July to escape the crowds attending the session of the Pennsylvania Supreme Court.[14]

Old Ben's maneuver probably tempered the heat, but next day's debate was still more torrid—Massachusetts warning Delaware of the danger to her in disunion, Read taunting the Bay State with Shaysian weakness and calling once more for nationalization of land:

"These jealousies are inseparable from the scheme of leaving the states in existence. They must be done away with. The ungranted lands also which have been assumed by particular states must also be given up."

Madison rebuked Ellsworth for setting up plighted faith as a bar to departing from the federal compact. Any party putting up such a claim ought to be guiltless itself, but what state had a worse record than Connecticut? Witness her transmittal to Congress of a vote refusing to comply with a federal requisition. He warned the small states once more against letting the Confederacy go to pieces. If, as some said, lack of energy in the large states was a protection to the small, that condition would disappear when each state was forced to depend on itself for its own security. Then, he greatly feared, all their governments would have too much power, with results dangerous to the small states and fatal to the internal liberty of all. Once this point of representation was fixed, Madison believed, both groups would see the necessity of circumscribing the state governments and enlarging the general one. As Yates records his next words:

"Some contend that states are sovereign, when, in fact, they are only political societies. There is a gradation of power in all societies, from the lowest corporation to the highest sovereign. The states never possessed the essential rights of sovereignty. These were always vested in Congress. Their voting, as states, in Congress, is no evidence of sovereignty. The State of Maryland voted by counties—did this make the counties sovereign? The states, at present, are only great corporations, having the power of making by-laws, and these are effectual only if they are not contradictory to the general confederation. The states ought to be placed under the control of the general government—at least as much so as they formerly were under the king and British Parliament."

Paterson recorded the same denial of sovereignty: "Mr. Madison. Will have the states considered as so many great corporations and not otherwise."[15]

When the Yates version was published in 1821, Madison could not face the critical blasts. "Who can believe," he wrote to a friendly inquirer, "that so palpable a misstatement was made on the floor of the convention, as that the several states were political societies, *varying* from the *lowest* corporation to the *highest sovereign;* or that the states had vested *all* the essential rights of sovereignty in the old Congress?" The New York delegate, he said, did not willfully misrepresent, but his notes were crude and desultory, full of egregious errors, and sprang from prejudices which gave "every tincture and warp to his mind of which an honest one could be susceptible."[16]

Well, what did Madison say according to his own original notes?

"Too much stress was laid on the equal rank of the states as political societies. There was a gradation, he observed, from the smallest corporation, with the most limited powers, to the largest empire with the most perfect sovereignty. He pointed out the limitations on the sovereignty of the states. Under the proposed government their character will be much farther reduced. According to the views of every member, the general government will have powers far beyond those exercised by the British Parliament, when the states were part of the British Empire."

Practically everything Yates ascribed to Madison was in his own version, except the remark about bylaws. His denial validly covered only his inaccurate paraphrase of the Yates notes. To support the denial, he scratched the word "equal" out of his own notes of debates, and also made them read that "the powers of the states," instead of "their character," would be much farther reduced. Perfectly willing, however, to let future generations know his general views, he wrote into his notes the sharp attack on the states which Yates had ascribed to him: "As now confederated their laws in relation to the paramount law of the confederacy were analogous to that of by-laws to the supreme law within a state."

This incident—so foreign to Madison's customary conduct—has a significance going far beyond personal unwillingness to acknowledge utterances made forty years earlier. It shows the terrific pressure, in the third and fourth decades of the nineteenth century, toward a State Rights interpretation of the formation of the Constitution. This helped to conceal the nationalism which actually governed Madison and others in the framing of it, and has played a powerful role, since his death, in the unceasing effort to use state sovereignty as a curb upon the legitimate powers of Congress.

Hamilton, Pierce and Gerry reinforced Madison's criticism of state sovereignty and equality, leading Luther Martin to the rejoinder that "the language of the states being *sovereign and independent* was once familiar and understood; though it seemed now so strange and obscure." The convention, six to four, then voted down the motion for equality in the lower house and approved a contrary one.[17]

This opened the way for Connecticut to push its compromise. Proportional representation in the House, equality in the Senate— this would make the government partly national, partly federal. Proportional voting in one house would safeguard the large states, equality in the other would give security to the small. On this ground and no other, asserted Ellsworth, a compromise could take place. Try to exclude state equality from both houses, he warned, and the Union would be chopped in two at the Delaware. Let a strong executive, a judiciary and national legislature be established, to preserve peace and harmony, but attempt no more lest all be lost.

Madison refused to budge. Don't, he begged, implant defects to be cured by future amendments of a kind that cannot be obtained. Wilson analyzed the vote just taken on suffrage in the first house, showing that the six-to-four division by states would have been 90 to 22 on the basis of population. He deplored the small-state threat of disunion, but, to prevent less than one fourth of the people from going, "shall more than three fourths renounce the inherent, indisputable and unalienable rights of man, in favor of the artificial systems of states?" No answer, he observed, had yet been given to the observations of Mr. Madison on the impossibility of a combination of three states against the others. "It is all a mere illusion of names. We talk of states, till we forget what they are composed of."

Under Ellsworth's plan, the Pennsylvanian asserted, the smaller number of people would govern the greater. Not true, retorted Ellsworth. As in the British House of Lords, power was given to the few to save them from being destroyed by the many. This brought a sarcastic protest from Madison. On one occasion, Ellsworth had pictured the large states as aristocracies, ready to oppress the small. "Now the small [states] are the House of Lords requiring a negative to defend them against the numerous commons." With state equality in the Senate, asserted the Virginian, the minority could *obstruct* the interests of the majority, *extort* measures repugnant to it, and *impose* adverse measures by using powers not shared by the first branch. He then attempted to undermine the opposing bloc by challenging the whole idea of a conflict between large and small states.

"The states were divided into different interests not by their difference of size, but by other circumstances; the most material of which resulted partly from climate, but principally from the effects of their having or not having slaves. These two causes concurred in forming the great division of interests in the United States. It did not lie between the large and small states; it lay between the northern and southern, and if any defensive power were necessary, it ought to be mutually given to these two interests."

Madison said he had some thought of suggesting a compromise on this very point, that slaves be counted in the proportional representation in one branch but not in the other, but he had dropped the idea because he was unwilling to urge a diversity of interests which was all too likely to arise of itself. At this hint of compromise by its chief opponent, the large-state front began to crack. Davie of North Carolina said he would not vote for any plan yet proposed. Wilson suggested a temporary concession to the smaller states—one senator for each 100,000 souls, and one for each state having less. When the smallest reached that population there would be full proportional representation. Madison offered to accept it on condition that the Senate be kept independent.

"The plan in its present shape [*i.e.* with election by legislatures] makes the Senate absolutely dependent on the states. The Senate therefore is only another edition of Congress. He knew the faults of that body and had used a bold language against it. Still he would preserve the state rights as carefully as the trials by jury."

That last sentence has been cited again and again as evidence of Madison's great concern for state sovereignty—something off-setting or overriding the general nationalism of his convention utterances. In reality it was not in his original notes, but was transferred from Yates's, where the context made it even more trivial. To make room for it, Madison blotted an antistate utterance out of his own notes, taking great care—but not quite enough—that it should never be read. Putting the original text of the Madison and Yates notes together, the speech is found to end as follows:

"Make it [the Senate] properly independent and it is of little consequence from what states the members may be taken. I mean, however, to preserve the state rights with the same care as I would trials by jury; and I am willing to go as far as my honorable colleague."

Thus he was merely contending that state rights were fully cared for in a Wilson compromise which was to do away with individual state lines in the Senate. It didn't look that way to the small-state delegates. "Mr. Madison has animadverted on the delinquency of the states," said Sherman, when all that was needed was power in Congress to make right measures effectual. To young Dayton, the plan before the convention was an amphibious monster. Bedford of Delaware shook the pillars with his combined denunciation of avarice in the large states and confession of it in the small. "The large states dare not dissolve the Confederation," he shouted. "If they do the small ones will find some foreign ally of more honor and good faith, who will take them by the hand and do them justice."

King, who had been accused of using dictatorial language, now threw the charge back at Bedford, "who, with a vehemence unprecedented in that house, had declared himself ready to turn his hopes from our common country, and court the protection of some foreign hand." He was grieved that such a thought, to be excused only on the score of passion, could have entered into his heart or fallen from his lips.[18]

So the debate ended on the last day of June, with tempers raw, the small states adamant, the large states slightly conciliatory, the realities of interstate strife hidden under generalities about tyranny, oppression, sovereignty, safety and self-defense. Facing the scene of wordy battle, Chairman Washington felt neither despair nor optimism. The one thing he was sure of, as he penned his thoughts to a friend in the next day's Sunday leisure, was the toughness of the obstacle:

"Persuaded I am that the primary cause of all our disorders lies in the different state governments, and in the tenacity of that power which pervades the whole of their systems. . . . To please all is impossible, and to attempt it would be vain. The only way, therefore, is . . . to form such a government as will bear the scrutinizing eye of criticism, and trust it to the good sense and patriotism of the people to carry it into effect."[19]

By a tie vote, five to five, on July 2, Ellsworth's motion for state equality in the Senate failed of adoption. Ordinarily, on a test of this kind, Maryland would have been divided and Georgia with the large states, giving the latter a six-to-four majority against the motion. But Jenifer got up late that Monday morning and Pierce had gone to New York to fight a duel which didn't come off. As a result, Martin swung Maryland into the small-state bloc and Baldwin (a recent migrant from Connecticut) reversed his position and split Georgia's vote. These two absences have been treated, by some writers, as the decisive event of the convention—a vital working of chance on American history. In reality they did not even decide the fate of the motion, which was beaten by the tie vote.

As soon as Jenifer came in, the large states possessed a five-to-four majority. Why did they not proceed to vote on the business before the house—the resolve for proportional representation in the Senate? Because the large states, though able to defeat a motion for equality, lacked the nerve to force adoption of their own proposition. All knew that the small states would not surrender. The tie vote, left unbroken, created a technical balance which opened the way to compromise at the very moment underlying conditions made it imperative. During this whole fortnight, Luther Martin reported to his legislature, the convention was "on the verge of dissolution, scarce held together by the strength of a hair."[20]

General Pinckney asked for a committee from each of the states. With the convention "now at a full stop," as Sherman put it, support for this came from everybody who spoke except Wilson and Madison. The former objected to a committee so formed as to vote by states. Madison said the convention could propose a compromise as easily as such a committee could, and avoid delay.

In the choice of a grand committee, another gain was made for compromise. Madison and Wilson were left off, Mason and Franklin representing their states. Davie and Baldwin, the men who broke the large-state front, both went on, and so did Martin from divided Maryland. The others—Gerry, Ellsworth, Yates, Paterson and Rutledge—consisted of large-state men who were ready to compromise, and small-state men who would not yield on the basic issue. It was a loaded body, but the convention loaded it.

"That time might be given to the committee [wrote Madison], and to such as chose to attend to the celebrations on the anniversary of independence, the convention adjourned till Thursday."

The delegates who listened to James Campbell's Fourth of July oration at the German Lutheran church heard a cheerful forecast and a prayer. "Methinks I already see the stately fabric of a free and vigorous government rising out of the wisdom of the federal convention." In the framing of it let every proposition for kingly power be regarded as treason to the liberties of the country.[21]

# CHAPTER VII

## COMPROMISE

ON JULY 5 the grand committee reported its compromise: In the first branch, one representative to each 40,000 inhabitants, with five slaves reckoned as three persons; in the second branch, each state to have an equal vote. As a concession to the large states, all money bills were to originate in the first branch, to be accepted or rejected without alteration in the second.

This report, Madison recorded, was founded on a motion in committee by Dr. Franklin. The large-state delegates barely agreed to it, and the other side looked on it as a victory. Taking the floor, Madison said the money-bill provision was no concession at all. The Senate would defeat bills to force a revision of them. Obstinate altercations would be produced. The convention must either depart from justice in order to conciliate the smaller states and a minority of the people, or adhere to justice and gratify the majority. He himself could not hesitate. If the principal states comprehending a majority of the people should concur in a just and judicious plan, "he had the firmest hopes that all the other states would by degrees accede to it."

By degrees? That meant outside the convention. Madison was inviting the three large states and any allies they might have to submit a plan to the country and let automatic pressures do the rest. A more belligerent statement was crossed out when he revised his notes: "He was not only fixed in his opposition to the report of the committee but was prepared for any event that might follow a negative of it." As Lansing summarized the speech: "He would rather have a system received by three or four states than none." This was not a threat of disunion, but of political and economic coercion, which Gouverneur Morris straightway amplified with some oratorical bloodletting:

"This country must be united. If persuasion does not unite it, the sword will . . . and the gallows and halter will finish the work of the sword. . . . State attachments and state importance have been the bane of this country. We cannot annihilate; but we may perhaps take out the teeth of the serpents."

The goriness of this language might be discounted, but not the threat of force. An armed revolution was but four years past. Rumors were current in New England that the people were to be called on to take arms to impose the new government. Even Madison's nonmilitary compulsion had armed power behind it. The reaction was a protest by Paterson against "sword and gallows" arguments and a complaint "of the manner in which Mr. Madison and Mr. Gouverneur Morris had treated the small states." What held them back, however, was lack of support from delegates unwilling to take chances.

Madison's contention that the money-bill proviso was worthless fell on stuffed ears. Mason and Gerry, who thought it valuable, talked vaguely of a spirit of accommodation. The small-state leaders shrewdly declined to say whether their gift was gold or brass. They had made a full and sufficient concession in agreeing to proportional representation in the House. The money-bill proviso was just thrown in.[1]

For two delegates, any compromise was a defeat. Yates stopped taking notes, foreshadowing his and Lansing's departure from the convention five days later. They had defeated themselves by helping to bring about the small-state victory. It held the convention together and insured the termination of New York's power to rob her neighbors through control of their overseas commerce.[2]

The compromise was taken up item by item. So many shared Madison's disgust over the alleged concession on money bills that not one of the large states voted to retain it. It was held in the report by four small states and North Carolina, lest the compromise fall to pieces.

Next came the critical question of Senate equality. If those words fell, the convention might fall with them. Massachusetts and Georgia divided, cleaving head and foot of the large-state bloc. North Carolina went over entirely. Pennsylvania, Virginia and South Carolina alone answered No, but Madison refused to confess defeat. Several states, he recorded, voted Aye because another question was to be taken on the full report. He was deeply unsettled, however, as shown by his protest when it was proposed to consider the powers of Congress while waiting for a committee to revise a portion of the compromise:

"It would be impossible to say what powers could be safely and properly vested in the government before it was known in what manner the states were to be represented in it. He was apprehensive that if a just representation were not the basis of the government it would happen, as it did when the Articles of Confederation were depending, that every effectual prerogative would be withdrawn or withheld, and the new government would be rendered as impotent and as shortlived as the old."

As a warning against Senate equality, this was weakened by its wording. Nobody *threatening* to withhold power would paint consequences which he himself most abhorred. But the gloom was deep, and Washington wrote to the absent Hamilton that things were worse, if possible, than when he left on June 29:

"In a word, I *almost* despair of seeing a favorable issue to the proceedings of the convention, and do therefore repent having had any agency in the business. The men who oppose a strong and energetic government are, in my opinion, narrowminded politicians, or are under the influence of local views."[3]

The convention president did not see that the same factor which now caused Madison to hold back on high government power would swing the small states to it. A new battle, this time in relation to slavery, was touched off on July 9 by a committee report apportioning representatives and leaving future changes to Congress. The apportionment of fifty-six members, it was admitted, was little more than a guess at population and wealth. Reckoning on that basis had been proposed on July 5 by Morris, who, after some generalities, disclosed his real purpose—to cut down the representation of poor new western states and prevent them from outvoting the maritime states. Rutledge instantly moved that state representation be proportioned to future sums paid into the federal

treasury. Since those sums were to be based on population including three fifths of the slaves, this was a device to give the South
an unbreakable position in future apportionments. The motion
was defeated, but the principle of it—a counting of slaves—was
used by a committee which revised the apportionment. Protests
followed at once. Slaves, said Paterson, were property. Why should
they be represented in Congress and not in state legislatures?

This brought Madison up. Instead of defending the South, he
turned the argument against its author. Paterson's doctrine, sound
in principle, "must forever silence the pretensions of the small
states to an equality of votes with the large ones." Logically, that
was irrefutable, but Paterson was bidding for power. Now that
the small states had gained the Senate, he was trying to give them
a larger voice in the House by whittling down Southern membership. Madison next sought to scrap the whole compromise by
shifting to one he had hinted at before. He wanted free inhabitants
to be the measure of strength in one house; total population, including slaves, in the other. This maneuver to build up Southern
strength and escape state equality got nowhere.[4]

New protests came from the South when a grand committee
proposed to enlarge the lower house by nine members, and to give
all of them to states from Virginia northward. Nobody objected
to the increase, which would raise the membership of the House
and Senate to ninety-one, the exact authorized size of the old
Congress. Being familiar with this number, the people would not
die of fright over a costly horde of federal despots.

The allocation was what caused trouble. The Carolinas were
still above their quota based on population, but their real demand,
voiced by General Pinckney, was that the South have equality with
the North, regardless of population. Otherwise, with regulation
of trade vested in Congress, the Southern states would be nothing
more than overseers for the Northern states which would monopolize their wealth.

Madison added a few tears of sympathy. He wished—believing
that main differences lay between North and South—that the
extra congressmen he got for his own state could be turned into
one apiece for North and South Carolina. But when motions
followed to add one to each of the Carolinas, Virginia stood with

the North and voted No. Madison then tried to double the total number of representatives, in order to bring them closer to the people by making the districts smaller. Too expensive, his fellows decided.

During this tussle, Randolph proposed a periodic census, with representation fixed according to population and wealth. Williamson reworded this to make it a census of free white inhabitants and three fifths of all others. South Carolina demanded a full count of slaves. This stirred the ire of Morris—or rather produced a facsimile of anger. He objected to a census because it would uplift the incoming western states and give them power to ruin the Atlantic interests. He didn't want Negroes counted either. "The people of Pennsylvania would revolt at the idea of being put on a footing with slaves." If representation was to be based on wealth, and slaves were to be included on that account, why was no other wealth but slaves brought in? The best course was to fix no rule of apportionment in the Constitution, but leave the interests of the people to the representatives of the people.

Madison realized instantly what this spokesman for seaboard commercial interests was up to. He would cut down the South in Congress by omitting slaves from the census, and exclude the West by giving Congress a discretionary power over reapportionment. His final remark gave Madison just the opening he needed. He was not a little surprised to hear this confidence in Congress urged by a member who, on all occasions, dwelt on the political depravity of men, and the necessity of pitting one vice against another. His reasoning was not only inconsistent with his former reasoning, but with itself.

"At the same time he recommended this implicit confidence to the southern states in the northern majority, he was still more zealous in exhorting all to a jealousy of western majority. To reconcile the gentleman with himself, it must be imagined that he determined the human character by the points of the compass."

Madison condemned both Pennsylvania and his own state for denying full political right to their western settlers, and likened

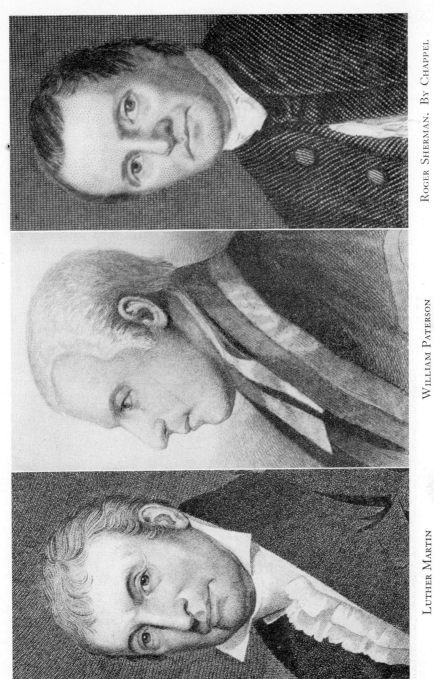

LUTHER MARTIN

WILLIAM PATERSON

ROGER SHERMAN. BY CHAPPEL

WILLIAM DUER

FISHER AMES. BY STUART

MANASSEH CUTLER

the seaboard to the rotten boroughs of England which had defeated every reform. With regard to the western states, no unfavorable distinctions were admissible. The West would contribute,
through land sales, to payment of the national debt, and pay its
share of imposts by importations through the Atlantic ports or the
Mississippi. Representation and wealth, it was agreed, should go
together, but it was contended that wealth and population were
not measures of each other. Perhaps not, under some conditions,
but in the United States similar laws and free intercourse tended
toward a constant equalization of the value of labor, which was
the principal criterion of wealth. People were constantly swarm-
ing to the less populated places, from Europe to America, from
Eastern America to the South and West, to all places where land
was cheap and labor dear. They kept going until competition
cheapened labor and destroyed the inequality. In this he saw a
warrant for making population the perpetual standard of representation.

The census was readily approved, thus taking care of the West,
but a torrent of protest met the effort to count three fifths of the
slaves. "Are they admitted as citizens?" asked Wilson. "Then
why are they not admitted on an equality with white citizens?"
As property? Then why was not other property brought into the
computation? South Carolina, which wanted all slaves counted,
joined the opposition and defeated the motion.[5]

Overnight, a brilliant idea came to Morris. The Southerners
wanted to include slaves in reckoning members of Congress, but
not in fixing their share of taxation. Link the two together. Give
them their option of paying more taxes to obtain more congressmen, or of taking fewer congressmen in order to pay less taxes.
Presumably expecting this to check their drive for federal power,
he moved that direct taxation be in proportion to representation.

The Carolinians chose power. It was a fair proposition, said
General Pinckney, but must be written into the Constitution. After
the attacks that had just been made on slavery he would take no
chances. Davie echoed him. If the Eastern states meant to exclude
slaves altogether the business of the convention was at an end.

Ellsworth, Randolph and Wilson united in making representation proportionate to direct taxation, and direct taxation proportionate to the 5-3 ratio of free men and slaves. Thus Madison's original proposal in the Virginia Plan was approved, but in such a form that the Northern delegates could say they didn't actually vote to count the slaves in the congressional apportionment—it just worked out that way.

By this time, Morris didn't like the results of his own strategy. Madison's North-South cleavage, he said, had struck him as heretical, but he saw now that the South was striving to secure a majority in Congress. The result would be such an oppression of commerce, from the transfer of political power to the South and West, that he should be obliged to vote for Senate equality in order to give the North some defense. His thought, presumably, was that the Senate would refuse to admit new states, but he got cold comfort on that. Whenever the interior acquired a majority, Wilson told him, it not only would have the right to rule, but would do so whether the East liked it or not. Pierce Butler interjected: "The security the southern states want is that their Negroes may not be taken from them, which some gentlemen within or without doors have a very good mind to do." Opposition collapsing, the compromise on slavery was put into the general compromise on the composition of Congress. The convention had jumped another hurdle—not an extra high one, but full of splinters.[6]

What of Senate equality? The advocates of it had lost a state when Yates and Lansing left. One delegate won back in Massachusetts, perhaps no more than one in North Carolina, would restore the large-state majority. On the evening of July 12 a traveler from Boston went to the Indian Queen quarters of Delegates Strong and Gorham of his state. He was introduced to Madison and Mason of Virginia, Charles Pinckney and Rutledge of South Carolina, Williamson and Alexander Martin of North Carolina, and Hamilton. Some of these men lived there, but what brought Madison and Pinckney?[7] It may have been mere coincidence, but two days later Pinckney made a proposal about the Senate, which Madison indorsed as a reasonable compromise and which depended for success on Massachusetts and North Carolina. It was that the states be allotted from one to five senators.

Pinckney had proposed something like that in June (from one to three), but Madison and Wilson were too sure of success to give it their support. Now the opposition refused to treat it as a real attempt at compromise. They saw it as the proposition Madison would like to put before the country, backed by the large states and any allies they could get. On that score, Gerry of Massachusetts rejected it. He was "utterly against a partial confederacy, leaving other states to accede or not accede." King supported it. Gorham was absent, so the state's vote depended on Strong, the man Madison had been trying to win. He stood with Gerry, fearing that if the small states did not accede—and he didn't believe they would—the Union would be dissolved.

Madison opened his rebuttal with what seems now a clairvoyant vision of wool and silver blocs. State equality would enable a Senate minority to extort measures as the price of their support of other measures. He cut to pieces the argument that state equality was imperative in one branch of Congress because the new government would be partly national, partly federal. Let the Senate vote by states in all cases where it was to act on the states as such. Were there any such cases? "He called for a single instance in which the general government was not to operate on the people individually." At last came a final bid for victory by frightening his slaveholding associates.

"It seemed now to be pretty well understood that the real difference of interests lay, not between the large and small, but between the northern and southern states. The institution of slavery and its consequences formed the line of discrimination."

There were five states on the Southern, eight on the Northern side of this line. State equality would give perpetual predominance to the Northern scale. With proportional voting, said the Virginian, the Northern side would still have a moderate advantage but every day would tend toward an equilibrium. This was a powerful appeal, but it came a month too late. Four to six, the convention voted down the Pinckney-Madison motion. When a vote was taken on the full compromise, Madison's slavery alarum jolted Georgia back into line against state equality but made no impression on North Carolina—the less so as Williamson was an abolitionist in principle. Five states to four, with Massachusetts again divided, the convention approved the complete report. Pennsylvania, Virginia, South Carolina and Georgia were all that was left of the once all-powerful large-state bloc. Thus the small states won their victory, by virtue of which, in the middle of the twentieth century, the 100,000 inhabitants of Nevada came to possess the same voting strength in the Senate as the 13,000,000 of New York.[8]

Even after the adoption of the great compromise on July 16, Madison refused to concede defeat. On the following morning, he records, a number of large-state delegates held a caucus. Some urged (and his past utterances identify him as the leader of this group) that the principal states hold firmly to their scheme of government and present it separately to the states if the small states would not agree to it. Others seemed inclined to yield and "the time was wasted in vague conversation." As several small-state delegates had been graciously allowed to attend the caucus, the effect was to notify them (wrote the disgusted Virginian) "that they had nothing to apprehend from a union of the larger." That disclosure, more effective than a dozen roll calls, ended his resistance.[9]

# CHAPTER VIII

## Small-State Nationalism

Controlling the Senate, the small states had nothing to fear and much to gain from a high-powered government. How would they react now to Madison's proposal that Congress be empowered "to legislate in all cases to which the separate states are incompetent; or in which the harmony of the United States may be interrupted by the exercise of individual legislation"? Should those words go into the Constitution? These questions arose the instant the issue of state equality was decided on July 16. South Carolinians complained that the word "incompetent" was vague. Following Gorham's statement that this merely established general principles, Rutledge moved that the clause be committed, so that specified powers might be reported. The motion lost by a tie vote, five states to five.

It is self-evident that all who voted for this motion desired an enumeration, though some might wish a general power added to it. The presumption is strong that those in the negative were for a general grant, although some might have voted as they did for other reasons. This was the line-up:

For enumeration: Connecticut, Maryland, Virginia, South Carolina, Georgia.

Against enumeration: Massachusetts, New Jersey, Pennsylvania, Delaware, North Carolina.

To the extent that leading delegates can be classified by this vote, it went like this:

For enumeration: Madison, Randolph, Mason, Rutledge, Butler, the Pinckneys, Sherman, Ellsworth, Luther Martin.

For general power: Wilson, Morris, Franklin, King, Livingston, Paterson, Bedford, Dickinson.

Madison here took his stand—in line with his desires but contrary to his earlier expectations—against general power. If his decision was not made earlier, it was a reaction to small-state capture of the Senate. On the other side, in favor of sweeping power, New Jersey and Delaware stood now as partners of their recent bulky enemies, Pennsylvania and Massachusetts. And the whole convention was in a dead tie. Developments came fast on the following day, when Sherman offered a substitute for Madison's resolve. Congress should have power:

"To make laws binding on the people of the United States in all cases which may concern the common interests of the Union; but not to interfere with the government of the individual states in any matters of internal police which respect the government of such states only, and wherein the general welfare of the United States is not concerned."

This was both a curtailment and expansion of the Virginia resolve. Wilson, a large-power leader, quickly seconded the motion. Morris objected to the police-power clause. Sherman read an explanatory enumeration of powers, including the levying of taxes on trade but not direct taxation—an omission which, he admitted, called for some kind of supplement. The motion was voted down almost unanimously by those who thought it either too strong or too weak. Another small-state delegate, Bedford of Delaware, then sought to stiffen the Virginia resolve by making it read as follows (his insertion italicized):

"Resolved that the national legislature ought to be empowered to enjoy the legislative rights vested in Congress by the Confederation, and moreover to legislate in all cases *for the general interests of the Union, and also in those* to which the states are separately incompetent, or in which the harmony of the United States may be interrupted by the exercise of individual legislation."

Morris seconded him, but Randolph cried out that this was a formidable idea indeed. "It involves the power of violating all the laws and constitutions of the states, and of intermeddling with their police." Formidable as it was, Bedford's amendment was adopted six to four. For it—Massachusetts, New Jersey, Pennsylvania, Delaware, Maryland, North Carolina—the same states which had voted against an enumeration, plus Maryland. Against

it—Connecticut, Virginia, South Carolina, Georgia. The stiffened
resolution was then adopted, with all states for it except South
Carolina and Georgia.[1]

It is evident that both the Sherman and Bedford powers were
designed to go into the Constitution. In Sherman's manuscript[2]
(probably written for the New Jersey planners) the clause on
general power stands as the final item of his enumeration, and
late in the convention he moved to insert the police-power proviso
in the Constitution by itself. Randolph's outcry against the Bedford resolve leaves no doubt that he construed it as a literal grant
of power. There would be no invasion of state constitutions or
police power in a mere declaration of purpose to draft an enumeration reaching to all the general interests of the Union. Madison
opposed Bedford's motion to strengthen the Virginia resolve, but
voted for its adoption after the stiffening. He could do so, to show
his continuing desire for a strong government, even though he
intended to oppose the incorporation of such a clause in the charter.

Over the convention as a whole, a profound change had come.
Small-state delegates had become leaders in the building of national power. Now that each major group was sure of defensive
strength in one branch of Congress, a strong government was safe
to both. Only the southernmost slave states—henceforth an isolated minority—presented delegations of a different mind. Failure
to recognize this basic fact is more responsible than anything else
for the persistent myth of a Constitution framed by men who
cherished state sovereignty and feared high federal power. Madison knew the truth. To Martin Van Buren he wrote in 1828:

"The *threatening contest* in the convention of 1787 did not, as
you supposed, turn on the degree of power to be granted to the
federal government, but on the rule by which the states should
be represented and vote in the government."

Bancroft recorded:

"From the day when every doubt of the right of the smaller
states to an equal vote in the Senate was quieted they—so I received it from the lips of Madison and so it appears from the

records—exceeded all others in zeal for granting powers to the general government."[3]

The fight over the Bedford resolution did not dissolve the tie vote by which an enumeration was defeated the day before. On the specific issue of general power or enumeration, there remained an even division of states and a close division of talents. But the convention was unperturbed. There was no longer a struggle for power to make the cleavage dangerous. Both groups were free now to stand for strength in government. The question of limits upon it was pushed into the future.

A bit of celebration was in order after these strenuous events. Washington noted in his diary that he dined at Mrs. House's on July 17, which meant with Madison and other delegates living there. He then made an excursion with a party to Gray's Ferry for tea. If Madison was of that party, when did he write out the 5,000 words found in his notes of that day's debates? Delegate Johnson of Connecticut took it easier. He wrote three words in his diary on the seventeenth: "Cool. In convention."

Next came Madison's cherished scheme of a power in Congress to veto state laws. This was attacked, surprisingly enough, by Morris, who thought it would "be terrible to the states, and not necessary, if sufficient legislative authority should be given to the general government." Sherman came to the same conclusion from another angle. Any state law contravening the authority of the Union should be treated as invalid by the state courts.

Madison rebutted these arguments with energy. The federal negative was essential to the efficacy and security of the general government. State courts could not be relied on as guardians of the national authority and interests, and the damage would be done before federal courts could set the laws aside. The British system proved the utility of this method:

"Nothing could maintain the harmony and subordination of the various parts of the empire, but the prerogative by which the crown stifles in the birth every act of every part tending to discord or encroachment."

Faced with the problem of giving quick effect to emergency legislation, he hinted at the appointment of federal governors in each state. This threw him far onto the defensive and the federal negative was rejected, eight states to three. Martin then reoffered the federal supremacy clause of the New Jersey Plan, which was unanimously adopted.[4]

Thus, on the very day following the compromise on voting in Congress, the small-state delegates swept into the lead in granting powers to the federal government, the convention stood for power in Congress "to legislate in all cases for the general interests of the Union," and for the enforceable supremacy of national laws and treaties over the laws of the states—though not yet over their constitutions.

Taking up the election of the executive, the delegates proceeded to chase him and themselves around the barn. First they reaffirmed the naming of the President by Congress. No state but Pennsylvania supported strong pleas by Morris and Wilson for popular elections to make the executive independent. Next, the convention reversed an earlier action and made him eligible to re-election. That made him a mere creature of the congressmen who were to re-elect him.

McClurg of Virginia promptly moved that the President hold office during good behavior. His purpose, stated in his speech and confirmed by Madison, was merely to emphasize the folly of the last vote by showing that this was the only mode left to keep the executive independent. However, a rhapsodic indorsement by Morris stirred up protests against monarchism and forced Madison to attempt to rescue his inexperienced friend.

A monarchic revolution, he warned, was most likely to follow the throwing of all power into the legislative vortex. Whether McClurg's plan was a proper one was another question, as it depended on setting up adequate means of impeachment. But they should either give this proposition a fair hearing or provide a less objectionable means of guarding against a dangerous union of the two branches.

Madison's excessive concern for McClurg's feelings heightens the likelihood that the doctor was acting as his agent in offering this motion. That is a near certainty because on June 1, when a seven-year motion was before the convention, "Madison proposed good behavior or seven years with exclusion forever afterwards." Madison's notes omit his own proposal, which is recorded by King. The omission suggests that, like the McClurg motion, this was a strategic move to keep the executive independent of Congress, and if recorded would have required an explanation.

Madison's vote for the McClurg motion, which was beaten four to six, became highly embarrassing some years later. Alexander Hamilton, denying Jefferson's charge that he had stood for life tenure in the presidency, said that he had favored tenure during good behavior but his final opinion was against it. He then cited McClurg's motion and commented: "Thus, if I have sinned against *republicanism,* Mr. Madison was not less guilty." Even without Madison's footnote explanation, his speech and McClurg's would offer sufficient proof that they did not actually favor this proposition. He was more generous to Hamilton, observing in his footnote that in the entire convention there were not more than three or four avowed friends of an executive during good behavior, "nor is it certain they would finally have adhered to such a tenure."[5]

Whatever the origin of this Madison-McClurg strategy, its effect was helpful. First the convention reconsidered the vote allowing a re-election. With that subject once more before them, Randolph argued against re-election, in order to free the executive of legislative domination. Morris, plugging for Wilson's electoral system, saw no evil in re-election provided the people did the electing. Wilson carried on:

"It seems to be the unanimous sense that the executive should not be appointed by the legislature, unless he be rendered ineligible a second time: he perceived with pleasure that the idea was gaining ground, of an election mediately or immediately by the people."

Madison came to his support. Independence of the departments was the only guarantee that they would remain separate. Independence was impossible if the executive was to be appointed by the legislature. Even with a one-term limit the connection would give rise to intrigues and contentions.

"He was disposed for these reasons to refer the appointment to some other source. The people at large was in his opinion the fittest in itself. . . . [Negroes could not vote but] the substitution of electors obviated this difficulty and seemed on the whole to be liable to fewest objections."

The result was a Northern vote for electors, the Carolinas and Georgia opposed. All except Virginia and South Carolina then voted that state legislatures choose the electors. Virginia wanted them chosen by the people. South Carolina, presumably, just didn't want them chosen.

An attempt by Charles Pinckney to build up the executive by eliminating impeachment was knocked on the head by Franklin's protest: Would they leave no way out except assassination? Madison helped to bury the proposal by drawing a distinction between governmental servants in such a matter. Mere numbers guaranteed a legislative majority against disability, bribery or betrayal to foreign powers, but in a one-man executive, loss of capacity or corruption was more probable and either might be fatal to the Republic. The arguments were so effective that Morris, who had seconded Pinckney's motion, announced that he was converted.[6]

Wilson next revived Madison's idea that the judiciary be united with the executive in a Council of Revision. Laws, he said, might be unjust, or dangerous, yet not "so unconstitutional as to justify the judges in refusing to give them effect." Let their weight be thrown against such laws by a share in the right to veto them.

Madison seconded the motion. It would be an added check against "those unwise and unjust measures which constituted so great a portion of our calamities." Even with this co-operation of the two departments, he feared that the legislature would still be an overmatch for them. Their union would be no violation of the principle of separation of powers. Separation on paper was not the test. To ward off legislative supremacy, there must be such a balance of powers and interests as would guarantee the provisions on paper.

The convention thought otherwise. The judges as judges, said Martin, will pass on the constitutionality of laws. Join them in the revision and they will have a double negative. Three states to four, with two divided, the Council of Revision was voted down.[7]

Madison now pushed a motion he had made some days before that judges be nominated by the executive, subject to confirmation by the Senate. This would fix responsibility in the executive and make it impossible for selections to be made by senators representing a minority of the people. It was no use. Fearful of such an extension of presidential power, all but three states clung to the previous decision that judges be chosen by the Senate.[8]

The convention then renewed its "ring around the rosy" game on presidential election. Fearing that capable men would not serve as electors, the convention flopped back, seven states to four, to a choice by Congress. (New Hampshire's belated delegation was one of the seven.) A chain of motions followed—to limit the executive to one term, to stretch out that term to eleven years, fifteen—and finally a sarcastic call for twenty years, "the medium life of princes."

Wilson pointed out that they had run into all this trouble by going back to election by the legislature. Gerry, who wanted a fifteen-year executive independent of Congress so that he would furnish a sure defense to public creditors, proposed a choice by state executives. That brought Madison to his feet for one of his penetrating analyses. First repeating his objections to an election by Congress, he told the convention that a choice by state legislatures would infect the national government with the pernicious tendencies complained of in the states (paper money and stay laws) while a choice by state executives would open the way to intrigues by candidates and foreign powers. There were but two systems free from these evils:

"An appointment by electors chosen by the people."

"An election by the people, or rather by the qualified part of them, at large. With all its imperfections, he liked this best."

Ellsworth instantly picked up an admission by Madison that the tendency to vote for home-state candidates would put the smaller states at a disadvantage—an unanswerable objection, said the Connecticut judge. Williamson and Morris answered it. Let each man vote for two candidates, only one of these to be from his own state. Madison quickly indorsed the plan, but his effort to bring it before the house was met by Gerry's cry that a popular election in this case was radically vicious. The ignorance of the people would cause them to be deluded by some set of men like the Order of the Cincinnati. Gerry was afraid of army officers, but the argument had deeper roots—fear of a President elected by the kind of people who followed Daniel Shays.

Madison was defeated in his effort to bring the new electoral plan to a vote, but it received backing of high strategic importance for the future. This came from Pennsylvania, Virginia, New Jersey and Connecticut, which contained powerful members of the vanishing large and small-state factions. The convention as a whole was now in such a stalemate that, to clear the way for the work of a drafting committee, it restored the seven-year term for the executive, made him ineligible to re-election and voted that he be chosen by Congress. That left them almost where they started. They adhered to the *principle* laid down by Madison, that if Congress was to elect the President, he should have a long term and be ineligible to succeed himself. They discarded the *policy* which both Wilson and Madison urged, that he be chosen by the people, for a short term, and be indefinitely re-eligible.[9]

In this period of hasty decision, Mason moved that the Committee of Detail provide qualifications of landed property and citizenship in members of the national legislature. This impressed Morris as "a scheme of the landed against the moneyed interest."

Madison responded with a motion to strike out the word "landed." Many landed men, he observed, were in debt for more than they were worth and the unjust laws of the states had proceeded more from them than any others. Moreover, every class of citizens should have the opportunity of making their rights felt and understood in the public councils. With a large landed class set off against small commercial and manufacturing (artisan) classes, and none understanding the others well, the interests of one or two should not be left to the third. A small land requirement would be useless, a large one improper, so some other criterion should be devised. In effect, this was an argument against any property test at all. The convention struck out everything

except a call for "qualifications of property and citizenship." It
was a restrictive attitude, yet showed the decay of the old tenet of
political philosophers that safe and free government must be a
government of landowners.[10]

The time had come now when the convention must answer a
critical question: Was it a constitutional or a revolutionary body?
If the former, its work must be unanimously ratified by thirteen
state legislatures. The Virginia Plan called for ratification by state
conventions—an act of revolution, regardless of unanimity.

Debating a motion by Ellsworth for action by legislatures, not
one delegate declared himself bound by the Articles of Confederation. State lawmakers were accused of incompetence and demagogy, and were defended, but the convention treated its course as
optional. Madison as usual summed up and closed the debate.
Singling out the issue of authority to ratify as the crucial one, he
thought it clear that the legislatures were incompetent.

"These changes would make essential inroads on the state constitutions, and it would be a novel and dangerous doctrine that a
legislature could change the constitution under which it held its
existence. . . . He considered the difference between a system
founded on the legislatures only and one founded on the people
to be the true difference between a *league* or *treaty,* and a *constitution.*"

In *moral obligation* these might be on a par, but in *political
obligation* there were two distinct advantages in favor of a constitution:

"1. A law violating a treaty ratified by a pre-existing law might
be respected by the judges as a law, though an unwise or perfidious
one. A law violating a constitution established by the people themselves would be considered by the judges as null and void.

"2. The doctrine laid down by the law of nations in the case
of treaties is that a breach of any one article by any of the parties
frees the other parties from their engagements. In the case of a
union of people under one constitution, the nature of the pact has
always been understood to exclude such an interpretation."[11]

Had that speech been blazoned over the country, during the half century it lay buried in manuscript, it might have altered history. The first conclusion puts Madison behind the power of the Supreme Court to invalidate state laws. The second is a complete denial of the right to secede from the Union, after a ratification of the Constitution by state conventions elected by the people.

Connecticut, Delaware and Maryland cast the only votes for ratification by legislatures. All but Delaware then approved submission to state conventions. That done, thoughts turned to the actual drafting of the Constitution. On a motion to name a drafting committee, General Pinckney cut in with a sharp warning. If the committee should fail to insert some security to the Southern states against an emancipation of slaves, and taxes on exports, he would be compelled to vote against their report. South Carolina was telling them, not asking, and the convention took it so well that a former governor of that state was elected chairman of the Committee of Detail.

During this time no effort was made to break the tie vote on an enumeration of powers. That question was left to depend on the personnel of this new committee, and no doubt was a factor in the choice of it. These were its members, chosen by ballot: Rutledge of South Carolina, Randolph of Virginia, Gorham of Massachusetts, Ellsworth of Connecticut, Wilson of Pennsylvania.[12]

On the straight drafting job, this might be called a committee of Wilson and four others. With Wilson on, it mattered little that Madison was off. Less gifted than the latter in synthesizing the principles of government, he was the Virginian's only rival as a student of public law and surpassed him as a translator of principles into constitutional clause and section. Madison, a republican by deepest feeling and conviction, furnished the reasoning which bound property-minded men to broad principles of self-government. Wilson, devoted to republicanism for unshakable reasons of public policy, was particularly adept in shaping the instruments for its expression.

Three variable majorities, each one settling a matter of major import, were visible in the make-up of the drafting committee. In defense of slavery, the South not only had Rutledge and Randolph, but could count on Ellsworth for the sake of continental harmony. Wilson, Ellsworth and Gorham bound the committee to a strong course in mapping the form and powers of government.

The vital choice between a general grant and an enumeration was made in effect when the committee was chosen. Randolph and Rutledge would not sign a report conferring general power. They could count on support from Gorham, who indicated on July 16 that he expected an enumeration. Wilson was all-out for general power. Ellsworth probably agreed in principle. (His course as chief justice suggests it.) But he would be held to an enumeration by his desire to get results through compromise. In drafting specific powers and in fashioning the instruments of their use, this committee was in full sympathy with the dominant desires of the convention. There was certain to be effective national strength in its draft of a constitution.

To allow plenty of time for this work, the convention on July 26 unanimously adjourned to the sixth of August.

# CHAPTER IX

## Struggles behind Closed Doors

DURING the early weeks of the convention, a cheerful optimism about its work pervaded the country. Newspapers eulogized its personnel. These gentlemen, said a widely copied communication to the Philadelphia *Independent Gazetteer* of June 27, were assembled at a most fortunate period, with leisure to examine all the governments that ever existed, with passions uncontrolled by the resentments of the late war, and with evidence before them of the feebleness, tyranny and licentiousness of the American forms of government. It should not be difficult for them to frame a suitable federal constitution.

Going to New York for a long stay about this time, Hamilton wrote to Washington that men of information reported an astonishing revolution in the minds of the people. The prevailing fear was that the convention would not go far enough. Some gentlemen, Edward Carrington of the Virginia congressional delegation told Madison, "think of a total surrender of the state sovereignties," though he would be content with a federal veto.[1]

Outside, guesswork took the place of knowledge. The armed sentries at the inner doors sealed them hardly more effectively than the delegates did their lips. Benjamin Franklin, showing a pickled two-headed snake to a caller, asked what would happen if the two heads insisted on passing on opposite sides of the stem of a bush. When he said it reminded him of the day's proceedings in convention, another delegate warned him into silence. At the very summit of discord the *Pennsylvania Packet* reported: "So great is the unanimity we hear that prevails in the convention upon all great federal subjects that it has been proposed to call the room in which they assemble Unanimity Hall."

Congressmen and governors were well informed of preparatory discussions, but later knowledge was limited to the broadest matters—consideration of the Virginia Plan, the small-state move for territorial redivision, ratification by conventions. Chargé d'Affaires Otto claimed to have daily information of what was going on, yet a bare statement of these three things made up the only dispatch that revealed a violation of the secrecy rule.[2]

"If you cannot tell us what you are doing," the Reverend James Madison pleaded to his cousin, "you might at least give us some information of what you are not doing." Madison's father received information of this sort: "We have till within a few days had very cool weather. It is now pleasant after a fine rain."[3]

The little that seeped out emphasized the nationalism of the convention and its devotion to protection of property. General Knox of the Cincinnati, who seemed better posted than anybody else, wrote to Washington in mid-August that he no longer feared leakage and misuse of earlier stages of the convention's business. Although persuaded that the existence of the state governments was an insuperable evil, he did not "see how in this stage of the business they could be annihilated."

The *Independent Gazetteer,* mouthpiece of Philadelphia conservatives, heard that one of the first objects of the new government would be to provide for the national debt. "Every holder of a public security of any kind is therefore deeply interested in the cordial reception and speedy establishment of a vigorous continental government." Across the Atlantic, according to this same newspaper, the oppressed and persecuted in every country were looking eagerly to the United States. Should the new federal government be adopted thousands would embark immediately. From "A Foreign Spectator" (the likely pseudonym of any native American) came this domestic-sounding comment: "The federal allegiance is supreme and obligates every person to be an enemy of his own state if it should prove treacherous to the Union."[4]

In England rose an American voice—that of Minister John Adams. In form his 1787 *Defense of the Constitutions of Government of the United States of America* was a reply to a French attack on the state systems. Its real purpose, he wrote to a friend, was to put Americans on guard against any wild schemes of government growing out of the disturbances in New England. Madison predicted that the book would revive New England predilections for the British Constitution.

"Men of learning find nothing new in it. Men of taste, many things to criticize. And men without either, not a few things which they will not understand. It will, nevertheless, be read and praised, and become a powerful engine in forming the public opinion."

The book also had merit, he conceded, and he hoped that the remarks in it unfriendly to republicanism would not receive fresh weight from the operation of American governments. He did not seem to think that people would see how Adams built kingly characteristics into the presidency and molded the Senate into the shape of a House of Lords. Yet one word, "well-born," used in relation to a proper Senate, aroused fury against its aristocratic tenor. Denunciations hit the press. But the book undoubtedly helped to draw people toward a three-branch government even though Adams himself confined that recommendation to state governments and advocated a one-house Congress.[5]

In Congress, midsummer brought adoption of the Ordinance of 1787 and approval of a huge Ohio land sale to the Cutler-Sargeant-Putnam syndicate. The effect was to stimulate the vision of empire and bring western statehood more acutely before the convention. The Reverend Manasseh Cutler came over from New York to see the Massachusetts delegates (it was he who found Madison and Pinckney with them at the Indian Queen) just before he made the final push for his land concession. He may have told them that he planted the now-famous clause on religion and morality in the great ordinance. He could not tell them—for it was a few days too early—how he got six million acres by agreeing to resell two million to William Duer of the Treasury Board and his political partners, and by pledging his congressional bloc to the President of Congress, General St. Clair, for first governor of the Northwest Territory. Congress behaved beautifully at the finish, except for "that stubborn mule of a Kearney" who seemed to think that two thirds of a dollar per acre, payable in public securities worth twenty cents on the dollar, was a trifle low.

During his brief stay in Philadelphia, the Reverend Mr. Cutler joined Strong (of his own state), Madison, Hamilton and a few

other delegates in an early-morning trip to the famous Bartram
botanical gardens on the Schuylkill, followed by breakfast at
Gray's Ferry on a high piazza overlooking the river. William
Bartram, embarrassed that "so large and gay a company" should
catch him barefoot, showed them exotic trees and the results of
his father's experiments in hybridization. But what were Madison's feelings when he saw that Cutler had arrived in company
with Dr. Geraldus Clarkson and his newly ordained son Joseph?
They were the father and brother of the young medical student,
now Dr. William Clarkson, who four years earlier smashed Madison's romance with Kitty Floyd. In 1789, when General Floyd
employed a Clarkson to carry papers to Madison from New York,
he arranged that somebody else should actually deliver them.[6]

With leaks and rumors all pointing to a strong government, and
secrecy continuing month after month, it was inevitable that a
countermovement should set in. Late in July a circular letter
spread word that the Bishop of Osnaburgh, second son of King
George, was slated for American sovereign. The wording marked
it as a satirical hoax, but malice and fear converted the jest into a
Philadelphia plot. For the first and only time in their deliberations, the delegates inspired an unofficial statement in the press:
"Though we cannot affirmatively tell you what we are doing—we
never once thought of a king."

In Virginia, Madison heard, there were revolts against taxes and
talk of paper money. Sheriffs would not or could not put up
collection bonds. "In several counties the prisons and court houses
and clerk's offices have been wilfully burnt," he reported to Jefferson. "In Green Brier the course of justice has been mutinously
stopped and associations entered into against the payment of
taxes." If this inspired caution, it also increased his desire for
federal curbs on the power of the state legislatures. He saw too
(so he wrote later) that some people were working to delay a
reform in the hope that popular government would be disgraced,
paving the way to a monarchical or aristocratic form. The result
was a disposition to give the new system "all the vigor consistent
with republican principles."[7]

It was in this spirit that the Committee of Detail did its work.
Its papers disclose a first draft by Randolph, based on the revised

Virginia Plan, with numerous and far-reaching alterations presumably made in committee. Wilson then rewrote parts of the Randolph draft, made extracts from the New Jersey and Pinckney plans, and, with these as working materials, drew up a full and nearly final report. A few changes in committee and the work was done. Basically, the five men expanded the Virginia Plan into a complete system of government. They carried over, as directed, the powers of Congress contained in the Articles of Confederation, added many other specific powers and brought in various guaranties, requirements and prohibitions contained in the old Articles. Federal taxing power was unlimited, save for the requirement that direct taxes be in proportion to population, and two other restrictions put in to satisfy the South. One prohibited the taxing of exports. The other protected slavery by forbidding a capitation tax unless in proportion to a census.

Totally omitted was the Bedford proposal of power to legislate for the general interests of the Union. In place of it the committee followed seventeen specific powers with the "necessary and proper" clause—a broad power to "make all laws which shall be necessary and proper for carrying into execution the foregoing powers, and all other powers vested by this Constitution in the government of the United States, or in any department or officer thereof." This was written into Randolph's first draft by Chairman Rutledge, indicating that it originated in a committee discussion.

The desire for a strong executive was evident in the listed duties of the President, but two vital omissions were in obedience to convention orders. The Senate was to make treaties and appoint judges. In place of Madison's general definition of federal judicial power, the report spelled out the original and appellate jurisdiction of the Supreme Court.

In dealing with elections, the Committee of Detail made two decisions of the utmost importance: Implementing the requirement that members of the lower house be chosen by the people, it provided that the qualifications of the electors in each state should be the same as those of the electors of the most numerous branch of the state legislature. The times, places and manner of holding elections were to be prescribed by state legislatures, but Congress could make or alter the regulations at any time. The effect was to make elections of members of Congress a federal function, and to endow Congress with plenary power to regulate them except that it could not set up qualifications for voters.

Hardly was the draft of the Constitution taken up on August 7 when Morris sought to restrict the suffrage to freeholders. Protests came quickly from Wilson, Ellsworth, Mason, Butler, Rutledge. The people would not accept the Constitution if it subjected them to disfranchisement. Abridgments of suffrage tended to a rank aristocracy. Morris defended his position. He had learned "not to be the dupe of words." Aristocracy would grow out of a suffrage which allowed people without property to sell their votes to the rich. He denied that his proposed limitation would be unpopular. Nine tenths of the people were freeholders and they would be pleased. Dickinson had the same view. Restriction to freeholders was a necessary defense against "those multitudes without property and without principle with which our country like all others, will in time abound." Old Benjamin Franklin (said McHenry) "opposed to this the natural rights of man—their rights to an immediate voice in the general assemblage of the whole nation, or to a right of suffrage and representation." As Madison records that warning appeal:

"It is of great consequence that we should not depress the virtue and public spirit of our common people. . . . He did not think the elected had any right in any case to narrow the privileges of the electors."

Madison's notes make it clear that the purpose of the clause adopting state qualifications for federal elections was to insure a broad suffrage, not to invite restrictions. He himself was pulled by conflicting thoughts . The right of suffrage, he observed, was a fundamental article of republican government, and ought not to be left to legislative discretion. "A gradual abridgement of this right has been the mode in which aristocracies have been built on the ruins of popular forms." As to a constitutional restriction:

"Viewing the subject in its merits alone, the freeholders of the country would be the safest depositories of republican liberty. In future times a great majority of the people will not only be without landed, but any other sort of property. These will either combine under the influence of their common situation; in which case, the rights of property and the public liberty will not be secure in their hands: or what is more probable, they will become the tools of opulence and ambition, in which case there will be equal danger on another side."

On the actual question of a freehold qualification, Madison said his position would depend much on the attitude of the people in states with a broader suffrage. He joined in defeating it, Delaware alone voting Aye.[8]

This limited indorsement of a freehold qualification disturbed Madison greatly in later years. His observations, he commented, did not convey his more full and matured view of the subject. Such a limitation "violates the vital principle of free government that those who are to be bound by laws ought to have a voice in making them. And the violation would be more strikingly unjust as the lawmakers become the minority." If there was no other choice, he would rather weaken property rights than take away personal rights.[9]

When the regulation of elections came up, Charles Pinckney and Rutledge tried to strike out federal power over the times, places and manner of holding them. Madison affirmed and defended the sweeping nature of the control. "These were words of great latitude," made necessary by inability to foresee all the abuses of the discretionary power vested in the states. Gorham, King, Morris and Sherman helped to beat down the Pinckney motion. In this debate and in the Virginia ratifying convention, Madison set forth three major evils to be reached by this power over the times, places and manner of electing representatives:

1. The federal government must have authority over elections to enable it to produce uniformity, and prevent its own dissolution.

2. When the states had favorite measures to promote, they would so mold their regulations as to favor the candidate they wished to succeed.

3. "Should the people of any state, by any means be deprived of the right of suffrage, it was judged proper that it should be remedied by the general government."[10]

No sooner was this settled than Franklin and Madison attacked a clause giving Congress power to establish property qualifications for its members. Charles Pinckney, raising the issue from the opposite direction, proposed an unincumbered estate of $100,000 for the President, $50,000 for judges and congressmen. Franklin once more told them not to debase the spirit of the common people, adding that some of the greatest rogues he ever knew were the richest rogues. The delegates shouted down Pinckney's proposition and Madison proceeded to attack the "improper and dangerous power" of the legislature to fix the qualifications either of its own members or of the electors. Such things were fundamental and ought to be fixed by the Constitution.

"If the legislature could regulate those of either it can by degrees subvert the Constitution. A republic may be converted into an aristocracy or oligarchy as well by limiting the number capable of being elected, as the number authorized to elect."

Following this speech, three of the five committeemen who produced the article turned against it. As in the contest over qualifications of voters, the concern of the convention was to protect the democratic basis of government.[11]

Madison carried the issue of republicanism into the question of the eligibility to office of foreign-born citizens. Seconding a motion by Hamilton (born in the West Indies) that no fixed term of citizenship be required for election to Congress, he said that he wished to invite foreigners of merit and republican principles among us. That part of America which had encouraged them most had advanced most rapidly. He saw no danger in their political activities and wished to maintain the liberality which had been professed in all the constitutions and publications of America.

New England and Southern delegates united to put over a seven-year requirement for the House, nine for the Senate. An effort to exempt foreigners already citizens led Sherman to say that only the individual states were morally barred from discrimination. Madison denounced this as a subtlety by which every national engagement might be evaded. Any restriction whatever would point the finger of mortifying suspicion at men who love liberty and wish to partake of its blessings. It was brought out that three Pennsylvania delegates—Robert Morris, Fitzsimons and Wilson—were foreign born, and so were almost all the general officers of the Pennsylvania line in the Revolution. But the New England-Southern combination voted down the exemption.[12]

Madison asked that a clause calling for one member of Congress to each 40,000 inhabitants be changed to "not exceeding" that number. Otherwise future increases of population would render the number of representatives excessive. Gorham answered that the government would not last long enough to produce this effect. "Can it be supposed that this vast country including the western territory will 150 years hence remain one nation?" Had Madison's effort failed, the House of Representatives at the end of that period would have numbered about 3,500 members—enough, surely, to fulfill Gorham's gloomy prediction.[13]

Next came that alleged concession to the large states—denial to the Senate of the right to originate or amend money bills. One after another, spokesmen for the states it was supposed to benefit stood up and repudiated it. Madison helped knock it out, seven states to four, but this agitated a few delegates so greatly that the vote was reconsidered. Randolph suggested that they allow Senate amendments which did not increase or diminish the sum to be raised. Madison assailed the revision. Why should the Senate be restrained from checking the extravagance of the other house? Who could tell whether changing a duty would increase or diminish the revenue? Of the five large states to which this provision had been conceded, only North Carolina favored it. Why then should the small states support it against their judgments? The convention voted against the whole clause, but when the same question came up in another section a decision was postponed.[14]

Within the Virginia delegation, on this issue, Convention President Washington broke a deadlock by joining Mason and Randolph against Madison and Blair. The general, Madison wrote in a footnote, gave up his judgment to prevent others from becoming hostile on more essential points. The Virginia group was becoming deeply factionalized. Madison had seen the danger, two weeks earlier, of a persistent cleavage with him and Washington on one side, Mason, Randolph and Blair on the other. He wrote to Dr. McClurg, who had gone home, urging him to return to Philadelphia. There wasn't much hope of this. McClurg's original departure for Philadelphia had set his friends to ribald speculation on how soon he would be drawn back by his well-known uxoriousness. Rejecting Madison's appeal, he said his vote would only produce a three-to-three division and might create bad feeling. Rumors of the Virginia dissension spread over the state, reflecting the ominous fact that Mason and Randolph were shying away from the cumulative decisions of the convention.[15]

Some problems, too knotty for immediate solution, or tied up with others lying ahead, were either postponed or referred to committees. The method of electing a President, his powers and duties and those of the Senate, were thus thrown forward, while tough controversies over the powers of Congress were dealt with by the committee method.[16]

On Madison's motion, Congress was given power to "declare" instead of "make" war. The intention was to enable the President to repel sudden attacks and to place military operations in his hands. The unintended effect was to enable him to carry on undeclared wars.[17]

The more extreme enemies of paper money struck out a power to emit bills of credit. Madison finally acquiesced because he believed it still existed by implication. The clause denying Congress power to tax exports was upheld in spite of pleas by Madison, Wilson, Morris, Dickinson and others that such taxes might someday be necessary for revenue or to secure concessions from foreign states. Mason made a veiled thrust at Madison: "If he [Mason] were for reducing the states to mere corporations, as seemed to be the tendency of some arguments, he should be for subjecting their exports as well as imports to a power of general taxation." The fear was that the Northern commercial states would levy federal export taxes on Southern staples.[18]

The Committee of Detail had proposed a two-thirds requirement for passage of navigation acts, which meant that a Southern minority could block any bill regulating foreign commerce. Other clauses forbade interference with the importation of slaves either by prohibition or taxation. The navigation restriction favored the whole South, because of its reliance on foreign shipping to hold down freight rates. The other aided only the deep South, which relied on African importations to offset the three-year span of life among slaves clearing tidewater plantations.

When this last clause was reached, Martin of Maryland and Mason of Virginia opened a powerful drive for destruction of the slave trade. Morris, Wilson and King joined them. Perhaps their indignation against "this infernal traffic" was not based entirely on morality. Maryland and Virginia, it was pointed out, bred a surplus of slaves which they sold into the "sickly rice swamps" of the deep South. The Northern big-state delegates wished to create such a threat to slavery that the South would give up the two-thirds requirement for navigation acts. Ellsworth warned that the attempt might drive Georgia and South Carolina into bloodshed or secession. His fears were disregarded. With Morris managing the risk, a grand committee produced on August 24 one of the major compromises of the convention—the slave trade to be subject to abolition after 1800 (changed next day to 1808) and navigation acts to be passed by a simple majority. The last was the great objective of New England shipping interests.

Madison was the only delegate to protest the change to 1808. "Twenty years," he said with prophetic vision, "will produce all the mischief that can be apprehended from the liberty to import slaves." He and Sherman objected to a clause allowing slaves to be taxed like other imports. It was wrong, said Madison, to admit in the Constitution that there could be property in men. They secured a change to a straight tax of ten dollars for each person. But there was no effort to abolish slavery. That would have split off five states, not two.[19]

To the Marylanders the whole compromise was anathema. They (like Virginia) were on the paying side of both concessions—one of them destroying the minority veto of commercial regulations, the other damaging the market for home-bred slaves. Martin convoked a night session with Gerry, Mason, Charles Pinckney, a

Georgian and members of the old New Jersey bloc. Postponement of the navigation clause gave time to work for an alliance.[20]

On a motion and committee report giving Congress power to organize, arm and discipline the militia, and control parts of it called into federal service, Madison argued strenuously for complete national control. The states already neglected their militia, and the more they were consolidated into one nation, the less each would rely on its own forces for its safety. Thwarted by the claim that the states needed the militia for domestic security, he made a final effort to allow the federal government to name its general officers. Such a threat of destruction of the states, Sherman and Gerry warned, would arouse the people everywhere and might produce civil war. Madison's reply won him no victory, but it carries the principle of compulsory union back to 1787:

"As the greatest danger is that of disunion of the states, it is necessary to guard against it by sufficient powers to the common government, and as the greatest danger to liberty is from large standing armies, it is best to prevent them by an effectual provision for a good militia."

Here was notice that no state had a right to withdraw from the Union, that attempts at secession would be countered with military force. The decision was for partial federal control.[21]

Madison found the definition of treason too indefinite. The words "giving them aid and comfort" were added from the Statute of Edward III to show what was meant by adhering to the country's enemies. Franklin secured the requirement of two witnesses to the same overt act. Madison revised a wording which might have led to double punishment for treason against state and nation. By such microscopic work the Constitution was kept from becoming the arsenal of tyranny.[22]

On August 29, Martin's nocturnal sessions bore fruit. Pinckney, Martin and Mason attempted to break up the North-South compromise on navigation and the slave trade by a motion to require a two-thirds vote for regulation of either foreign or interstate commerce. Mason declaimed upon government founded in the affections of the people, but took his real stand on sectional self-interest:

"The southern states are the *minority* in both houses. Is it to be expected that they will deliver themselves bound hand and foot to the eastern states, and enable them to exclaim, in the words of Cromwell on a certain occasion—'the Lord hath delivered them into our hands'?"

The pugnacious Wilson retorted that it was better to bind the minority hand and foot than the majority, but Madison used calm analysis. A navigation act might bring about a temporary rise of freight rates, due to exclusion of foreign shipping. But that would increase shipbuilding in both North and South, and bring a southward migration of seamen and merchants. Existing retaliations among the states would be eliminated. A simple majority rule would reduce the danger of corruption by foreign interests. All these good results would follow even if the power should be abused. But abuse was made improbable by the independence of the Senate and the great and growing strength of the agricultural regions. The Southern states themselves would derive security from American maritime strength. It would offset the vulnerability of their coasts, especially Virginia's. Coastwise navigation would increase the consumption of Southern produce. And if the East gained a still greater proportion of wealth, who would be harmed? That wealth would be a national benefit.

Here was the perfect blend of logical analysis, continental outlook and disinterest which gave Madison such weight in the national councils. Disregarding Virginia's self-interest, he was working to save a compromise whose breakdown would imperil the whole work of the convention. His own colleagues were not persuaded. As the Constitution now stood, Governor Randolph announced, it contained features so odious that he doubted whether he could agree to it. Rejection of the two-thirds majority for navigation laws would complete its deformity. In spite of this threat, three South Carolina delegates joined the solid North in defeating the Pinckney-Martin motion. Then came a postscript to the compromise—unanimous approval of Butler's motion for a clause requiring the return of fugitive slaves.

The effect of these decisions ran far beyond their contents. The

South, by definitely winning two points and definitely losing another, was freed of uncertainties. It need no longer resist government power in general from fear of a hostile use of it. Next, this spelled the failure of Martin's effort to unite the small states and the South. He was suffering other blows, too. Rutledge amended the Marylander's national supremacy clause by making the *Constitution* and laws of the United States supreme over the *constitutions* or laws of the states. That upset the scheme of using state constitutions as a bar to enforcement of federal constitutional restraints upon the states. Those restraints followed quickly.

Responding to Sherman's suggestion that this was a favorable crisis for crushing paper money, the convention on August 28 voted an absolute ban on issuance of it by the states. A motion followed to forbid the states to interfere in private contracts. Morris and Mason protested that this was too sweeping—it would upset a thousand laws. The judicial power would be a sufficient protection. Madison disagreed. A negative on the state laws alone could cope with the ingenuity of legislatures. A remark by Wilson that only *retrospective* interferences with contracts were to be prohibited led Madison to ask:

"Is not that already done by the prohibition of *ex post facto* laws, which will oblige the judges to declare such interferences null and void?"

It was an important query, though based on errors. The ex post facto prohibition as it stood then applied only to Congress, not yet to the states. Delegates dug into law books and discovered that the term "ex post facto" was confined by Blackstone to criminal law. The result was a permanent rule of interpretation. Retrospective civil laws—noncriminal laws bearing on past actions—are not forbidden to either Congress or the states, in the absence of a specific restraint in the Constitution. The convention proceeded to impose such a restraint by forbidding the states to pass laws "impairing the obligation of contracts." Gerry tried to extend the prohibition to Congress, but was not seconded.[23]

This was the second time in the convention that Madison affirmed the power of the federal judiciary to hold state laws unconstitutional and void. He did not indicate whether he thought they had similar power over acts of Congress. His view a year later was that Congress, the President and the courts had equal and independent power to determine questions of constitutionality within the province of their own duties, but he saw no present method of settling a conflict between them. To John Brown of Kentucky he wrote in 1788:

"In the state constitutions and indeed in the federal one also, no provision is made for the case of a disagreement in expounding them; and as the courts are generally the last in making the decision, it results to them by refusing or not refusing to execute a law, to stamp it with its final character. This makes the Judiciary Department paramount in fact to the legislature, which was never intended and can never be proper."[24]

While state power to impair contracts was being taken away, Madison asked for a clause barring the states from laying embargoes. Morris remarked that the matter came within the federal power over interstate commerce. Madison then tried to secure a complete prohibition of state import and export duties, instead of forbidding them without the consent of Congress. Mason protested that some states might need import duties to encourage manufactures. A system of that sort, Madison replied, would require duties on imports from all the other states and would revive all the mischiefs experienced from the want of a general government over commerce.

Four states which were subjected to taxation by their neighbors—New Hampshire, New Jersey, Delaware and North Carolina—supported Madison's motion. His own state and Connecticut helped to beat it, but a few hours of reflection made the Nutmeggers feel less safe. Sherman moved that all state import duties be for the use of the United States, a change which Madison rightly hailed as preventing all state imposts.[25]

All through the framing of these restrictions, Madison chafed against his defeat on the power of Congress to negative state laws. One might have thought he would be satisfied with the expansion of the national supremacy clause, which gave full effectiveness to

the Supreme Court's power to review state laws. Instead, he joined
Charles Pinckney in asking for a power in Congress to negative,
by a two-thirds vote, all state laws which were thought to interfere
with the general interests and harmony of the Union. Wilson
called this the needed keystone of the wide arch of government.
To Sherman's protest that federal laws already were supreme and
paramount, the Pennsylvanian replied that the federal government
needed defensive power and the firmness of judges would not
suffice. To which Rutledge offered the smashing comment:

"If nothing else, this alone would damn and ought to damn
the Constitution. Will any state ever agree to be bound hand and
foot in this manner? It is worse than making mere corporations
of them whose bylaws would not be subject to this shackle."[26]

Madison's motion to commit was defeated, but the amazing fact
is that New Hampshire, Pennsylvania, Delaware, Maryland and
Virginia voted for it. One more state would have carried it. This
illustrates a little-recognized fact. Except where special interests
were involved, such as slavery, or deep emotional prejudices, which
pitted the militia against standing armies, there was no *dominating*
defensive force for State Rights in the convention. Almost at the
close of the convention, a bare majority could be mustered against
such an atrocious, clumsy and unworkable scheme as a congressional veto of state laws. Its chief opponent, Rutledge, could be
counted among the dozen delegates most devoted to the states, yet
he had just stiffened federal supremacy with an amendment which
drove the last vestige of genuine state sovereignty out of existence.

Late in his life, Madison attempted to dismiss the federal veto
as something he abandoned early in the convention. This plan,
he wrote to N. P. Trist in 1831, "though extensively favored at the
outset, was found on discussion liable to insuperable objections
arising from the extent of country and the multiplicity of state
laws." That was true, but it was the convention's attitude, not
Madison's. Who would suspect from this letter that he still
favored the plan five days before the convention adjourned? The
Supreme Court, he said then, must be the source of redress against
unlawful levying of state duties, though it was his opinion that "a

FARMING BY REMOTE CONTROL. MADISON SENDS INSTRUCTIONS TO HIS FATHER FOR HIS FARM MANAGER, THE SLAVE SAWNEY. NOTE HIS SPELLING OF "DOLLEY"

HAREWOOD

negative on the state laws alone could meet all the shapes which these could assume." The completed Constitution failed to wean him, for on October 24 he wrote to Jefferson:

"It may be said that the judicial authority under our new system will keep the states within their proper limits, and supply the place of a negative on their laws. The answer is that it is more convenient to prevent the passage of a law than to declare it void after it is passed. . . . Injustice may be effected by such an infinitude of legislative expedients, that when the disposition exists it can only be controlled by some provision which reaches all cases whatsoever."

Here is conclusive evidence that Madison's desire to handcuff the states to a federal custodian was carried completely through the Constitutional Convention. His later efforts to produce a contrary impression have been a potent influence in putting history out of focus. Most remarkable of all, in so realistic a student of politics, was his failure to realize that if his idea had prevailed, the Constitution never would have been ratified.

Following Martin's double defeat on paper money and navigation acts, the Marylander made one last effort to achieve his territorial objective. On August 29 Morris and Madison were engaged in one of their periodic fights over equal rights for western states. Yielding to Madison's protest against attempts to degrade the West, Morris reworded a clumsy committee clause to provide that no state should be erected within the limits of any state without the consent of its legislature and of Congress. Martin jumped onto this at once. "Nothing he said would so alarm the limited states as to make the consent of the large states claiming the western lands necessary to the establishment of new states within their limits." Was Vermont to be turned over by force to the states claiming it? Was Virginia to be given a guarantee of Franklin and its other western country?

By the closest of votes—six states to five—the Morris clause was substituted. Still to be adopted, it faced a dangerous resurrection of the New Jersey bloc, with New Hampshire taking the place of absent New York. Maryland, Delaware and New Jersey proceeded to attack. Why should the small states secure the large ones in their vast territorial claims? Morris hit back with a threat. "If the forced division of states is the object of the new system, and is to be pointed against one or two states, he expected the gentlemen from these would pretty soon leave us." The Virginians, knowing Maryland tempers, said nothing. Let Pennsylvania fight the battle for them. Pushed into the open, the landless state delegates avowed their objective. As Madison tells it:

"Mr. Carroll [of Maryland] moved to strike out so much of the article as requires the consent of the state to its being divided. He was aware that the object of this prerequisite might be to prevent domestic disturbances, but such was our situation with regard to the crown lands, and the sentiments of Maryland on that subject, that he perceived we should again be at sea, if no guard was provided for the right of the United States to the back lands. . . . Should this point be disregarded, he believed that all risks would be run by a considerable minority sooner than give their concurrence."

Here was a counterthreat that Maryland, Delaware and New Jersey would leave the convention if the federal government failed to obtain power to cut up the large states. Coming from a solid conservative like Carroll, it was not to be ignored. Nor yielded to. North Carolina, Williamson proclaimed, was well disposed to give up her western lands, but compulsion was no proper policy. The Virginians still kept mum, while Wilson came once more to their aid.

"Unanimity was of great importance, but not to be purchased by the majority's yielding to the minority. . . . He knew of nothing that would give greater or juster alarm than the doctrine that a political society is to be torn asunder without its own consent."

During the debate it developed that New Hampshire and Connecticut were opposed to the Morris clause only because they believed its wording would prevent the admission of Vermont. They wanted statehood for that unruly district in order to halt the migration of their citizens to a region exempt from federal taxes.

A change of wording took care of this. Carroll's amendment was then voted down, eight to three.

Bulldog Martin kept right on fighting. It was unreasonable to force the western populations of Virginia, North Carolina and Georgia, and the people of Maine, to continue under the states now governing them. Wilson, he said, treated the states as phantoms when the rights of the small states were in question, but of a sacred nature when the large states were to be affected. There came a new threat of secession:

"It was said yesterday by Mr. Gouverneur Morris that if the large states were to be split to pieces without their consent, their representatives here would take their leave. If the small states are to be required to guarantee them in this manner, it will be found that the representatives of other states will with equal firmness take their leave of the Constitution on the table."

He then offered a substitute giving Congress power to erect new states "within as well as without" the territory claimed by any state. On this Maryland, New Jersey and Delaware were outvoted by eight states. Thus vanished, at last, the contention over western lands, which earlier had locked the states in desperate battle and led to state equality in the Senate. With it vanished Luther Martin, who packed his bag and went back to Baltimore to work for rejection of the Constitution.[27]

Nobody left with him. The small states were too well pleased with control of the Senate, they had too great need for federal power over commerce, their opposition to paper money was too keen, to let them risk their gains. Under the Constitution, they could hope to obtain a territorial revision in time; if the Union was broken, never.

# CHAPTER X

## General Power or Enumeration

Reflecting on the responsibilities of the national government, Madison saw gaps in its enumerated powers. In mid-August he prepared an additional list. Congress should have specific power to dispose of public lands, institute temporary governments in new states, regulate Indian affairs, exercise exclusive jurisdiction over the seat of government, grant charters of incorporation, issue copyrights, establish a university, subsidize useful knowledge and discoveries and acquire land for national defense. Nearly all of these proposals had a background in his prior work and studies. In 1780 he induced Congress to authorize new states. In 1783 he proposed exclusive federal jurisdiction over a capital on the Potomac. Other measures stemmed from his Virginia legislation. John Fitch, for whose steamboat he had sought a Virginia patent in 1785, was now preparing for a trial run on the Delaware River. Within a few days the whole convention saw twelve steam-driven canoe paddles send a boat against the tide—a fitting prelude to federal sponsorship of useful discoveries.[1]

Just as Madison was about to offer his proposals on August 18, "Me Too Charley" Pinckney jumped in ahead of him with a virtually identical list—the fruit undoubtedly of their evening conversations at Mrs. House's. Both sets, together with several motions by Gerry and others, were unanimously turned over to the Committee of Detail. In the published Madison notes, the Pinckney list comes second and is much longer. That is due to the fact that in revising his notes, Madison followed the *Journal,* which lumped together all the referred motions without indicating authorship. Madison credited Pinckney with everything that followed his own set. The parasitic nature of the Pinckney list would have been self-evident if Madison had not inadvertently added the other proposals to it.

The Committee of Detail now had on its hands nine specific new powers offered by Madison, four by Gerry, one (excluding

duplicates) from Pinckney, a Rutledge-Mason prohibition of perpetual revenues and diversion of funds, a short list of civil rights
offered later by Pinckney and a motion by Morris for a council
of state. Gerry's motions covered power to secure payment of the
public debt, pledge public faith to creditors, grant letters of marque
and reprisal and regulate stages on post roads.[2]

Faced with such a lengthening of the specific powers, the Committee of Detail came to a conclusion which, if held to, would
have revolutionized the Constitution. It abandoned the thought
of relying on an enumeration and turned to indefinite power. One
item from Madison's list—power to regulate commerce with the
Indians—was reported separately because other objects of the
commercial power were already specified. Similarly, from the
Gerry list, a provision for payment of debts and necessary expenses
was added to the taxing power. The committee then offered a
sweeping "general welfare" clause for addition to the sixteenth
and final clause of the specific powers of Congress:

"... and to provide, as may become necessary, from time to time,
for the well managing and securing the common property and
general interests and welfare of the United States in such manner
as shall not interfere with the governments of individual states, in
matters which respect only their internal police, or for which their
individual authorities may be competent."[3]

This grant of almost unlimited federal power blended the
wording of three prior proposals by Madison, Sherman and Bedford, to which the committee added "well managing and securing
the common property." These words covered Madison's August
18 request for power to dispose of unappropriated lands and institute temporary governments for new states. The core of the
whole proposition was in the Virginia Plan.

There is no record of the vote in committee on this reversal of
position. Wilson, Ellsworth and Gorham were high nationalists.
Chairman Rutledge presented the report, which does not suggest
that he disagreed with it. Possibly the special protection given to
slavery had removed his hostility to a general grant. Randolph
undoubtedly was opposed.

The convention took action on this "general welfare" clause without identifying it—a fact which has caused it to be ignored by historians. Yet without an understanding of what happened to it, it is impossible to appraise the work of the two main committees of the convention or to realize the close balance in the choice between a limited and an unlimited government.

The new clause was included in the big, tough problems which on August 31 were referred to a new and all-important Committee on Unfinished Parts. To this grand committee went all postponed clauses of the August 6 draft of the Constitution, and all parts of committee reports that had not been acted on. Appointed by ballot, it was made up of powerful leaders. Madison, Morris and King went on from the three big states. Sherman, Brearly and Dickinson came from the small-state bloc, with Gilman of New Hampshire unallied. Carroll reflected Maryland's mixed interests, and Williamson, Butler and Baldwin represented the deep South. These men would make the ultimate decisions on the structure, strength and energy of the national government.

To understand what was before this committee, it is necessary to run through some complicated moves, late in August, connected with debts and taxes. On August 21, a grand committee headed by Governor Livingston reported on assumption of state debts. Congress should have power to "discharge as well the debts of the United States as the debts incurred by the several states during the late war, for the common defense and general welfare." The convention, on the twenty-third, cut out state debts, converted the rest into a positive command and made it part of the taxing clause, thus: "The legislature shall fulfill the engagements and discharge the debts of the United States and shall have the power to lay and collect taxes duties imposts and excises."

On a protest by Butler and Mason against paying money "to the bloodsuckers who had speculated on the distresses of others," this mandatory clause was reconsidered two days later. Sherman then moved that the power to tax be followed by the words: "for the payment of said debts and for the defraying the expenses that shall be incurred for the common defense and general welfare." That, said Madison in his notes, was rejected as unnecessary. No further vote was taken, so the reconsidered tax clause went to the Committee on Unfinished Parts.[4]

For more than a hundred years, the proceedings of this committee have been a cause of high controversy and bafflement. From it came constitutional provisions of profound importance. Yet the knowledge of its work has been limited to a statement by Morris that the origin of revenue bills was one of the bases of a new compromise, and a footnote by Madison saying that one of the purposes of the compromise was "the elevation of the government." Nobody looked to see what was actually before the committee, though every postponement was by vote and every action on a committee report was recorded.

A search of Madison's debates shows that the committee had eleven proposals before it. Six of these were incidental—a section on the eligibility of congressmen to appointive office; two sections on impeachment; and committee reports limiting the duration of revenue acts, adding commerce with Indians to the commerce power, setting up a council of revision and fixing presidential qualifications. The remainder were vitally interconnected. Three of them dealt with the powers of Congress:

Article VI, section 12 of the August 6 draft: "Each house shall possess the right of originating bills, except in the cases before-mentioned." (But the earlier exceptions had been defeated.)

Article VII, section 1, clause 1, revised on August 23 to read: "The legislature shall fulfill the engagements and discharge the debts of the United States and shall have the power to lay and collect taxes duties imposts and excises."

Report of Committee of Detail, giving Congress power: to provide ... for the well managing and securing the common property and general interests and welfare of the United States."[5]

Two were concerned with the machinery of government:

Article IX, section 1: Giving the Senate power to make treaties and appoint ambassadors and judges of the Supreme Court.

Article X, section 1, amended: Providing for election of President by Congress for seven years and forbidding re-election.[6]

From the Committee on Unfinished Parts came three decisions of far-reaching import:

1. The President was made elective by the people, through the electoral college, to serve four years and be eligible to re-election. If no one received a clear majority, the Senate was to make the final choice from five high candidates.

2. Power to make treaties and appoint ambassadors and judges was transferred from the Senate to the President, subject to senatorial approval.

3. The all-inclusive "general welfare" clause was rejected. In place of it the committee reported four specific powers from the Madison and Gerry lists (only one clause of which had been referred to it)[7] and established a "general welfare" spending power in these words: "The legislature shall have power to lay and collect taxes duties imposts and excises, to pay the debts and provide for the common defense and general welfare of the United States."

Added to these, and forming part of the compromise, was a decision that the Senate might amend but could not originate revenue bills. The committee also set up qualifications for the President, established the office of Vice President, and dealt with all the minor matters referred to it.[8]

The second of three reports, submitted on September 4, was the hot one. Morris secured a postponement of the clause on origin of revenue bills to make sure that its advocates would hold to their bargain. Mason and Randolph saw aristocracy and intrigue in the final choice of President and Vice President by the Senate, in case the electoral college failed to elect. Wilson sought a shift to the whole Congress, which would give the large states a greater voice in the selection.

Sherman, Madison, Morris and King thereupon came to the support of the committee plan. King observed that the influence of the small states in the Senate was balanced by that of the large states in bringing forward the candidates. Recording this, Madison said in a footnote that it explained the compromise.

"Colonel Mason, Mr. Gerry and other members from large states set great value on this privilege of originating money bills. Of this the members from the small states, with some from the large states who wished a high mounted government endeavored to avail themselves, by making that privilege the price of arrangements in the Constitution favorable to the small states, and to the elevation of the government."[9]

That shows what Mason, Gerry and the small states got. Who were the large-state delegates who wished a high-mounted government? What did they win for its elevation? On these points Madison was silent, but the facts are discoverable. Mason and Gerry were not members of the committee. Madison, Morris and King, its large-state members, were hostile to the money-bill provision. They disliked the small-state advantage in choosing a President. Yet these three bore the brunt of the fight for these provisions in the ensuing debate. Why? Obviously because Madison, Morris and King were the large-state delegates who placated Mason and Gerry, and made concessions to the small states, in exchange for "arrangements in the Constitution favorable . . . to the elevation of the government."

What were these arrangements? The report of the committee contains two provisions which did in fact elevate the government: (1) The transfer of treaty-making and appointive powers from the Senate to a President chosen by the people. (2) The power to spend for the general welfare. The former (proposed by Madison on August 23) was the controversial point, because it took power away from the small states. The "general welfare" clause involved no contention between large and small states, and, when cut down to money matters, probably stirred no opposition.

Nevertheless, it is with reference to the "general welfare" clause that the record of what was before the committee becomes important. After his shift to strict construction, Madison challenged Hamilton's contention (afterward approved by the Supreme Court) that the power to spend for the general welfare covered everything that was for the general welfare. The phrase, he said, was copied from the Articles of Confederation, where it was always understood as nothing more than a general caption to the specified powers. Many years later, combating a contention that the clause carried an indefinite power of legislation, he undertook to trace the use of the words in the Constitutional Convention.

Writing in 1830 to Andrew Stevenson, speaker of the House of Representatives, he said they first appeared in the Virginia resolve (written by himself) calling for a revision of government adequate to the objects of "common defense, security of liberty and general welfare." They reappeared on August 21 in a committee report for payment of debts incurred "for the common defense and general welfare." Four days later they cropped up in a defeated motion for payment of debts and "defraying the expenses that shall be incurred for the common defense and general welfare."

After this, said Madison, came the report of the Committee on Unfinished Parts, giving Congress power to lay taxes, "to pay the debts and provide for the common defense and general welfare." His conclusion was that these latter words never would have gone into the Constitution, except for their connection with the debt-paying clause of the Articles of Confederation. Inattention to phraseology probably accounted for the failure to make it plain that spending for the general welfare was limited by the other enumerated powers.[10]

This chronicle omits the whole chain of "general welfare" legislative clauses in the 1787 Convention. It omits the dynamic part of his own proposal that, to make the government adequate to "common defense, security of liberty and general welfare," Congress have power "to legislate in all cases to which the separate states are incompetent." It omits the Sherman proposal of power to make laws "in all cases which may concern the common interests of the Union." It omits the Bedford request for power "to legislate in all cases for the general interests of the Union." It omits the Committee of Detail's revolutionary reversal of August 22, when it proposed a power to provide "for the well managing and securing the common property and general interests and welfare of the United States." Finally, it omits the fact that this last proposal, formally recommended for inclusion in the Constitution, was the one and only clause relating to the general welfare that was referred to the committee which drafted the final clause.

Madison's 1830 account totally ignores the fact that the principal decision to be made by the Committee on Unfinished Parts was whether to complete the powers of Congress by means of an enumeration, or by means of the sweeping "general welfare" clause reported by the Committee of Detail. The decision was for an enumeration. But the fact that this choice had to be made renders it utterly impossible to dismiss the narrower clause as the accidental product of language drawn from the Articles of Confederation without thought of its meaning. Furthermore, a convention which hovered so close to a general power to *legislate* for the general welfare would not have been likely to set sharp limits, or to think of sharp limits, on the less inclusive power to *spend* for this purpose. During all but two weeks (August 6 to 22) of its more than three months' session, an unrestricted power to spend for the general welfare was included in the vastly broader legislative proposals lying before the convention, two of them approved by it. The final spending power was submitted to the convention in the very act of dropping the broader power.

Madison did not go into the subject until his original nationalism had been swept out of existence by concern over misuse of federal power. Having sincerity of purpose, he felt no insincerity of position. For more than a hundred years his inaccurate account of the "general welfare" clause lived on, furnishing fallacious arguments against the Supreme Court's interpretation of it—an interpretation required by the necessities of the nation, but squarely in line with the history of a provision whose true paternity runs back to Madison himself.

# CHAPTER XI

## Perfecting the Constitution

A sense of fulfillment was in the air as the framers worked through the report of the Committee on Unfinished Parts. From mid-August the convention had been holding sessions from ten o'clock until three—till four, in fact, until complaint was made that it interfered with dinner. On September 6, free of committee service, Madison wrote to Jefferson in Paris:

"Nothing can exceed the universal anxiety for the event of the meeting here. Reports and conjectures abound concerning the nature of the plan which is to be proposed. The public however is certainly in the dark with regard to it. The convention is equally in the dark as to the reception which may be given to it on its publication. All the prepossessions are on the right side but ... certain characters will wage war against any reform whatever. My own idea is that the public mind will now or in a very little time receive anything that promises stability to the public councils and security to private rights, and that no regard ought to be had to local prejudices or temporary considerations. If the present moment be lost it is hard to say what may be our fate."

Every enterprise, the *Pennsylvania Gazette* reported on August 29, was suspended till it was known what kind of government was in prospect.

"The states neglect their roads and canals till they see whether those necessary improvements will not become the objects of a national government. Trading and manufacturing companies suspend their voyages and manufactures till they see how far their commerce will be protected and promoted by a national system of commercial regulations. The lawful usurer locks up or buries his specie till he sees whether the new frame of government will deliver him from the curse or fear of paper money and the tender laws."

With secrecy nearing an end, only lack of time to use more cipher prevented Madison from amplifying the brief outline he sent to Jefferson. The extent of the powers might surprise his friend, yet he would hazard the opinion that the new plan would neither achieve its national object nor prevent the mischiefs which inspired such disgust against the state governments. This belief, he made plain later, was based solely on the absence of federal power to veto state laws. Except for this, and except for state equality in the Senate, the Constitution embodied every principle of power and sovereignty he had advanced, explained and fought for during the summer.

The long-delayed question of ratification came up on August 30. How many conventions must approve the Constitution to make it effective? Wilson suggested seven—a majority. Randolph preferred nine, that number being familiar as a requirement for acts of Congress. Madison remarked that if the blank were filled with seven, eight or nine, "the Constitution as it stands might be put in force over the whole body of the people, though less than a majority of them should ratify it." He suggested seven or more that were entitled to a majority in the House of Representatives.

Madison's comment showed that he expected the entire nation to be bound by the affirmative action of states containing a majority of the people. Wilson thought that only the states which ratified would be bound. Not that he had any qualms. "We must he said in this case go to the original powers of society. The house on fire must be extinguished, without a scrupulous regard to ordinary rights." On a motion by King, the Constitution was made effective among the states ratifying it.

Then came an effort to strike out ratification by conventions because Maryland's constitution could not be altered in such fashion. The people, Madison answered, were the fountain of all power, and could alter constitutions as they pleased. A six-to-four vote upheld conventions and the alluring number nine was adopted.

Morris called for speedy action in the states, lest their officers intrigue to turn the popular current. His motion brought into full view the revolt of a quartet of delegates. Luther Martin (about to go home) agreed that delay would be fatal, but for a different reason. The people would not ratify unless hurried into it by surprise. Gerry represented the system as full of vices, and insisted that unanimous consent was needed to destroy the existing Confederation. Mason declared "that he would sooner chop off his right hand than put it to the Constitution as it now stands." Randolph announced that if the final form of the Constitution did not permit his signature, he would like to have the state conventions submit amendments to a second national gathering.

Here were four men with four sets of reasons for acting alike. Martin was a low-power man when it came to federal restraints on state money, a high-power man when it came to subdividing the large states. Defeated on both points, he had nothing to live for in Philadelphia, and an uncertain prospect at home. As Mc-Henry records a parting colloquy on the Constitution:

Martin: "I'll be hanged if ever the people of Maryland agree to it."

Jenifer: "I advise you to stay in Philadelphia lest you should be hanged."[1]

The key to Randolph's course was temperamental indecision which he rationalized into moral scruples. Time and again, in previous teamwork with Madison, he had shown a fear of specific measures adequate to his own avowed objectives. He could present Madison's Virginia Plan as if it were his own, but faltered at the steps needed to put it into effect.

Three weeks before his revolt, Mason had said the Constitution was founded on sound principles and he was disposed to put extensive powers into it. What happened in the interval? During it he won a partial victory over the slave trade, defeated the federal power to tax exports, defeated mandatory payment of the war debt, sponsored federal regulation of the militia and was on the winning side of almost every roll call. The convention, to be sure, turned down his motion for a federal power to pass sumptuary laws—that is, to regulate eating, drinking and purchase of luxuries—but that merely excluded a tremendous express power. Barring gout and dyspepsia, only the elimination of the two-thirds rule for navigation acts, added to his fear of the treaty power, will account for his change of front.[2]

And what of Elbridge Gerry? Some unknown person described him as "a man of sense, but a Grumbletonian. He was of service by objecting to everything he did not propose." Gerry and Randolph, said the writer, "sink in the general opinion. No wonder they were opposed to a Washington and Madison."[3] Such an estimate does less than justice to Gerry's complex personality. He combined democratic impulses with such a concern for his own property interests that he was incapable of consistent thought or policy. Shays' Rebellion made him see democracy as a raging demon, but he still felt a fear of intrigue and cabal, of infrequent elections, of strongly organized government and of the military.

In June and July, as Gerry described it, the states were intoxicated with the idea of their sovereignty; the Confederation was dissolving. The delegates must reach an agreement or some foreign sword would do it for them. By September he was ready to destroy the country by standing on the letter of a dissolving law. Why? As sweet-spoken Oliver Ellsworth explained it later, Gerry tried to place the old continental currency on a par with other securities. Since he was supposed to hold large quantities of this paper, "his motion appeared to be founded in such bare-faced selfishness and injustice that it at once accounted for all his former plausibility and concession, while the rejection of it by the convention inspired its author with the utmost rage and intemperate opposition to the whole system he had formerly praised."[4]

Ellsworth's charge was incorrect. What Gerry did was to put such emphasis on an absolute mandate for payment of the old securities in general that he had to make a public defense against convention whispers about his speculations in them. His move for a mandate to pay, instead of mere power to do so, went down under a volley of remarks from Butler and Mason about bloodsucking speculators, fraudulent purchases from soldiers and the pestilent practice of stockjobbing. Gerry retorted that he had no interest in the question, "being not possessed of more of the securities than would, by the interest, pay his taxes." The practice being common, it did no harm to admit that he evaded four fifths to nine tenths of his taxes by paying in defaulted indents. But why did this Massachusetts merchant not see that a solvent new government *empowered* to pay its debts was a better risk than a bankrupt one *obligated* to do so? To understand Gerry one must note that he was the only man in the convention to vote against a general power of taxation in Congress. If this twin stand for public debt payment and against taxation was not exactly logical, it is nevertheless a paradox conspicuous in American history.[5]

The Gerry episode throws light on other delegates. The adverse reaction to his rumored speculations offers the strongest evidence that the framers of the Constitution, in general, were not swayed by similar interests of their own. They refused to compel payment of their own securities, though opening the way to it.

On September 5, the Pennsylvania Assembly reconvened from its March recess and found its meeting room occupied. Ten days, the state assemblymen were told when they graciously went upstairs, would wind up the work of the convention. That confidence was felt because every remaining nut appeared to be cracked by the report of the Committee on Unfinished Parts. The item most likely to cause trouble was the presidency. Nearly everybody now accepted the electoral-college principle. But only the small states wanted the Senate to elect the President if the college failed to do so. Eight senators—a majority of a quorum—might make the choice. Mason and Randolph attacked that as a bold stroke for aristocracy. The natural cure was a shift to the whole Congress or to the House of Representatives, but that would transfer power from the small to the large states.

Madison attempted to keep the election out of Congress entirely. Only two states supported his proposal that one third of the college be enough to elect a President. Delegates sat up when Wilson echoed Mason's fear that Senate participation would produce "an aristocracy worse than absolute monarchy." Sensing an undercover maneuver for large-state control, Sherman suggested a choice by the whole Congress *voting equally by states*. Instead, the convention voted for election by the Senate. Madison then moved that at least two thirds of the Senate be present at the choosing of a President. That might prevent any choice, warned Gorham, thinking of low attendance in the old Congress. But it went through, and left so much dissatisfaction that Sherman's proposal was revived. He revamped it to refer the election to the

House of Representatives, each state delegation having one vote, and the matter was settled.

The debate revealed Alexander Hamilton's till then unknown attitude toward the Constitution. Absent from June 29 to September 6, save for a few silent days in July and a pop-in on August 13, he had kept out of the discussion because of "his dislike of the scheme of government in general." But as he meant to support it as better than nothing, he wished to say that he liked the new arrangement on President better than the old, which made the executive a seven-year congressional monster who would seek to subvert the government to stay in power. In effect, Hamilton indorsed the four-year term. This no doubt was the basis of his faulty recollection, sixteen years later, that a three-year term was in his plan of government, as could be proved (he said) by the copy he handed to Madison near the close of the convention. The latter, informed in 1830 of this assertion, ascribed it to forgetfulness. It was impossible, he told Jared Sparks, that Hamilton could make such a statement with intent to deceive, and refer it to the only source where it could be confuted. But when John C. Hamilton discovered after Madison's death that his copy of the Hamilton plan included life tenure for President and senators, he accused Madison of palming off Hamilton's June sketch as the September plan, to leave an impression that Hamilton favored a monarchy. At the time Biographer Hamilton emitted this slander, he had in his possession the text of the plan in his father's handwriting, word for word the same as Madison's copy of it, and containing unmistakable evidence that it was written after September 12.[6]

Madison settled one question, or thought he did, during this discussion of the executive. Under the Constitution, if President and Vice President both leave office through death or disability, the presidency passes to whatever officer Congress may designate by law "and such officer shall act accordingly, until the disability be removed, or a President shall be elected." Statesmen and editors sometimes timidly suggest that this appears to allow a special election, though the mere hint of breaking the four-year cycle seems sacrilegious. They should take note of the original wording: "such officer shall act accordingly until the time of electing a President shall arrive." And of this entry in the debates:

"Mr. Madison observed that this, as worded, would prevent a supply of the vacancy by an intermediate election of the President, and moved to substitute—'until such disability shall be removed, or a President shall be elected.'"

The convention worriers, Mason and Gerry, concluded that it was too hard to impeach a President. He should be removable for maladministration. Madison protested that so vague a term would be equivalent to a tenure during pleasure of the Senate. A little later, he rescued the presidency from a crippling proposal that persons impeached by the House be suspended from office until tried and acquitted by the Senate. Said the Virginian:

"The President is made too dependent already on the legislature, by the power of one branch to try him in consequence of an impeachment by the other. This intermediate suspension will put him in the power of one branch only. They can at any moment, in order to make way for the functions of another who will be more favorable to their views, vote a temporary removal of the existing magistrate."[7]

By such quick and clear analyses, Madison saved the country from ills whose effects can only be guessed at. Had he lost on these two points, easy impeachment and automatic suspension might have become a debauching instrument of congressional cabal, or a routine method of getting rid of a President whenever Congress showed up with a hostile majority.

The clause on money bills was held back until every other part of the Constitution was disposed of. Then, on September 8, a Committee of Style and Arrangement was elected—Dr. Johnson of Connecticut, Hamilton, Morris, Madison and King. All these men were known for exactness of expression. Morris was a verbose orator, but with pen and ink he let one word do the work of three. "The finish given to the style and arrangement of the Constitution," Madison wrote in 1831, "fairly belongs to the pen of Mr. Morris.... A better choice could not have been made."[8]

Madison himself probably took little part in the work of the committee, although its covering letter from Washington to Congress is so much in his style that it may be ascribed to him. Since August 23 he had been struggling against illness added to fatigue. Beginning on that day, his notes dropped thirty per cent and his share in debate became scanty. The work and confinement, he told his later secretary Edward Coles, almost killed him. But he refused to give way and missed not a single session.[9]

Combining and reshaping the twenty-three articles of the Constitution, the Committee of Style cut their number to seven. Morris converted a colorless preamble into a noble declaration of national and individual dignity. In the original introduction the thirteen states had been named, after the fashion set in national treaties and the Articles of Confederation. Here it was "We the people of the United States." Legally it meant the same—the people of thirteen distinct states united in a common national sovereignty. But the way was opening for disappearance of the sense of component parts in the nation. The phrase "in order to form a more perfect union" set up an implication against secession, for the old Articles provided that the Union should be perpetual. Many people have seen a positive grant of power in "to promote the general welfare." That was a purpose, not a power, but the tonal breadth of it forbids a narrow definition of the specific powers set up for its achievement.

While style and arrangement were being revamped, Gerry, Mason and Randolph appointed themselves a Committee of Fear and Apprehension. With Gerry thinking it was too easy to amend the Constitution, Hamilton that it was too hard, Madison rewrote the article both for clarity and utility. The old wording directed Congress to call a convention on the application of two thirds of the states. He failed in an effort to get rid of that, but implanted a workable alternative—Congress, by a two-thirds vote, should submit amendments either to state legislatures or state conventions, to be effective when ratified by three fourths of them.[10]

The revised Constitution came back from Morris and company on September 12. There remained only swift approval of the changes in wording, a glance at the adequacy of the powers of

Congress, and some incidental wooing of the three rebels. Madison
supported Mason's request that a warning against standing armies
be placed in the Constitution. The Gunston Hall moralist was
further humored by appointment of a committee on sumptuary
laws, but it made no report. The convention might have won
Mason and Randolph, perhaps even Gerry, had it given heed to
a Mason-Gerry appeal for a bill of rights in the Constitution. The
proposal drew a single comment that it was unnecessary and
every state voted No. A specific motion by Pinckney and Gerry,
to guarantee liberty of the press, was voted down on Sherman's
objection that the power of Congress did not extend to the press.
Four states, including Virginia, answered Aye. In the haste and
fatigue of the closing days, Madison observed later, the delegates
were less considerate of Mason's desires than they would have
been had he raised the issue earlier.[11]

Discussing a proposed ban on state tonnage duties, Madison and
Sherman offered divergent interpretations of the power to regulate
commerce. Their disagreement has been carried on in conflicting
Supreme Court opinions ever since. From Madison came this:

"Whether the states are now restrained from laying tonnage
duties depends on the extent of the power 'to regulate commerce.'
These terms are vague, but seem to exclude this power of the
states. They may certainly be restrained by treaty. He observed
that there were other objects [than harbor work] for tonnage
duties as the support of seamen etc. He was more and more
convinced that the regulation of commerce was in its nature indivisible and ought to be wholly under one authority."

Sherman put it this way:

"The power of the United States to regulate trade being supreme
can control interferences of the state regulations when such interferences happen; so that there is no danger to be apprehended
from a concurrent jurisdiction."[12]

Madison's interpretation foreshadowed Chief Justice Marshall's
conclusion that the power of Congress over interstate and foreign
commerce is supreme and exclusive. Sherman saw federal power

as supreme but not exclusive unless Congress made it so by exercising its power to regulate. The great problem, still unsettled, is to fix the dividing line between exclusive and concurrent jurisdictions. Madison's statement had more in it. With the regulation of commerce looked on as indivisible, local commerce comes into the federal orbit wherever it impinges upon interstate activities. Also, Congress could restrain the states by treaty when it had no other power to do so. Here is an empire of powers by implication.

When the Committee on Unfinished Parts offered new powers drawn from Madison's August 18 list, it made no report on his request for authority to issue charters of incorporation. He saw an opening for this when Franklin, on September 14, moved a power for cutting canals. To Sherman, this meant spending general funds for local purposes. To Wilson, canals were a probable source of federal revenue. Madison tried to enlarge the motion into a power "to grant charters of incorporation where the interest of the United States might require and the legislative provisions of individual states may be incompetent." His primary object, he said, was to secure an easy communication among the states, following the removal of political obstacles. In other words, he wanted a national program of inland waterways and road development, modeled on the Potomac and James River charters which he put through the Virginia legislature in 1784-1785. But his motion took in much more and ran into trouble.

King protested that the power was unnecessary. The states would be prejudiced and divided into parties by it. In Philadelphia and New York it would be referred to the establishment of a bank, in other places to mercantile monopolies. Wilson insisted that it was necessary to prevent a *state* from obstructing the *general* welfare. He feared no stirring of prejudices against banks, while "as to mercantile monopolies they are already included in the power to regulate trade." This stirred up Colonel Mason. He was afraid of monopolies of every sort, which he did not think were authorized by the commerce clause. (He and Gerry charged afterward that they were.) The motion was limited to canals, and was defeated, Pennsylvania, Virginia and Georgia voting Aye. Madison and Pinckney then tried to secure a power to establish

a university. That was defeated after Morris said it was not necessary. The exclusive power at the seat of government would reach
the object.

It is evident from Madison's action that he thought specific
power necessary for the granting of federal charters. Throughout
his life he cited the defeat of these motions as evidence that Congress had no power to establish national banks or to make internal
improvements. But it was not so clear-cut as that. King (who
voted later in Congress to set up a bank) was merely objecting
to a specific clause which would stir up enmity. Wilson's remarks
about mercantile monoplies and general welfare create an impression that he thought banks and canals would require specific
authorization. But only two years before he had written that the
federal charter of the Bank of North America, granted in 1781,
was lawfully granted because the old Congress had inherent power
in the national field. The Articles of Confederation, this future
Supreme Court justice continued, only reserved to the individual
states those undelegated powers which they were capable of exercising individually. Said he:

"To many purposes, the United States are to be considered as
one undivided, independent nation, and as possessed of all the
rights and powers and properties, by the law of nations incident
to such. Whenever an object occurs, to the direction of which no
particular state is competent, the management of it must, of necessity, belong to the United States in Congress Assembled."[13]

It is easy to disagree with that doctrine, but absurd to contend
that the man who held it would think the new Congress had no
implied power to set up a national bank or dig interstate canals.
He wanted the power spelled out because others might question its
existence.

On a cloudy, cool September 15, following terrific heat, the
delegates moved rapidly toward the end. When Article V on
amendments was reached, canny Sherman made a final drive for
small-state security. Expressing fear that three fourths of the states
might abolish all of them or upset senatorial equality, he offered
a motion "that no state shall without its consent be affected in its
internal police, or deprived of its equal suffrage in the Senate."

Madison protested. Begin with these special provisos, and every state will insist on them. All but three small states voted No, whereupon Sherman moved to strike out Article V altogether. Brearly seconded him. The warning came like a clap of thunder from a small, unnoticed cloud. Morris broke up the storm with the final concession in the Constitution, making it impossible to deprive a state of equality in the Senate without its consent. In his notes Madison wrote:

"This motion being dictated by the circulating murmurs of the small states was agreed to without debate, no one opposing it, or on the question, saying no."

Mason failed in a last effort to secure a two-thirds requirement on navigation acts, and announced that he would give no support to a structure leading either to monarchy or tyrannical aristocracy. Both he and Randolph would sign if another convention were provided for. Gerry offered all but his real reasons for refusing assent.

To Charles Pinckney these declarations "from members so respectable" gave a peculiar solemnity to the close of this important scene. He too had objections, but he would support this plan rather than invite an ultimate decision by the sword. On the question for a second convention all the states answered No. Madison recorded the final steps:

"On the question to agree to the Constitution, as amended. All the states aye.

"The Constitution was then ordered to be engrossed.

"And the House adjourned."

On Monday the seventeenth, aged Benjamin Franklin "rose with a speech in his hand" which Wilson read for him. Once more the great conciliator made an appeal for harmony. There were several parts of the Constitution of which he did not approve, but he was not sure that he should never approve them. In his long life, he had been obliged many times to change opinions even on important subjects. He urged the delegates to accept the Constitution with all its faults, and expressed his own surprise that they were so few.

"For when you assemble a number of men to have the advantage of their joint wisdom, you inevitably assemble with those men all their prejudices, their passions, their errors of opinion, their local interests, and their selfish views. From such an assembly can a perfect production be expected? It therefore astonishes me, Sir, to find this system approaching so near to perfection as it does, and I think it will astonish our enemies, who are waiting with confidence to hear that our councils are confounded like those of the Builders of Babel."

Franklin moved the adoption of a signature form which testified to the unanimous consent of *the states* present. "This ambiguous form," Madison commented, "had been drawn up by Mr. G. M[orris] in order to gain the dissenting members and put into the hands of Dr. Franklin that it might have the better chance of success."

In a final effort to gain Randolph's adherence, a motion was made to allow one member to every 30,000 persons instead of 40,000. Chairman Washington made his only speech of the convention in support of the motion, and it was agreed to unanimously. This did not win the Virginia governor, but seemed to mellow him. Apologizing for his refusal to sign the charter "notwithstanding the vast majority and venerable names that would give sanction to its wisdom and its worth," he said this was not a decision to oppose ratification of the Constitution. He meant only to keep himself free. Hamilton begged all to sign, lest they kindle latent opposition among a part of the people. "No man's ideas were more remote from the plan than his were known to be," but was it possible to deliberate between anarchy and the chance of good?

Gerry then let slip a little of his real attitude. In Massachusetts there were two parties, "one devoted to democracy, the worst he thought of all political evils, the other as violent in the opposite extreme." Instead of taking a mediating shape, to abate the heat and opposition of parties, the Constitution would drive the country toward civil war. Gerry had tried to prevent the election of Congress by the people. He wanted a President chosen for fifteen years by state governors. That was his idea of a middle course, contrasted with a war-breeding surrender to democracy.

The last decision of the convention followed. King suggested that the Journals of the convention either be destroyed or deposited with the President and kept secret. The decision was that Washington take charge of them, subject to the orders of the new Congress, if it should ever be formed. Madison's vastly more important papers remained in his own possession.

The members proceeded to sign the document—first "George Washington, President and deputy from Virginia," then the delegations from New Hampshire southward. Gerry, Mason and Randolph fulfilled their threats. Out of thirteen delegates who had left the convention, two from New York and either one or two from Maryland would have withheld their signatures. Six or seven lost out of fifty-five—that was an astonishing approach to unanimity among purposeful, powerful, determined men. Summarizing conflicting objects, Madison described the whole task to Jefferson as something more difficult than could be conceived by those not concerned in the execution of it. Add the natural diversity of human opinions on new and complicated subjects, and it was impossible to consider the ultimate concord as less than a miracle.[14] That too was the feeling of the convention's great conciliator. In the notes taken with such tireless devotion for three and a half months, Madison made this final entry:

"Whilst the last members were signing it, Dr. Franklin looking toward the President's chair, at the back of which a rising sun happened to be painted, observed to a few members near him that painters had found it difficult to distinguish in their art a rising from a setting sun. I have, said he, often and often in the course of the session, and the vicissitudes of my hopes and fears as to its issue, looked at that behind the President without being able to tell whether it was rising or setting: but now at length I have the happiness to know that it is a rising and not a setting sun."

On this hopeful note "the convention dissolved itself by an adjournment *sine die.*"

# CHAPTER XII

## Appraisals

THE signing of the Constitution on September 17 was completed at four o'clock, the Philadelphia dinner hour. Differences cast aside, two score delegates hastened to the City Tavern, where a farewell feast was timed to allow evening departures. Through three months of summer heat these men worked and fought, until, from a composite of their wisdom and desires, their harmonies and conflicts, the national charter of government took shape. From the written record, perhaps half of the fifty-five who attended the convention can be put down as active builders of the Constitution. The silent ones knew how they were voting. Of deliberate obstructors or self-promoters there were few indeed, of marplots not one.

What would have been the verdict of these men on one another, had they undertaken to apportion credit for their achievement during the final festivities at the City Tavern? There is enough in the writings of the period to indicate that they would have given first place to Madison. The contemporary verdict on his work can be found in the statement of a North Carolina delegate that Virginia took the lead and Madison led Virginia, of the Georgian who found him the best prepared man in every debate, of the anonymous Philadelphian who linked Washington and Madison as the chief winners of public esteem.

None of the delegates would have thought of calling Madison the "Father of the Constitution." Not, at any rate, with the mythical implications of authorship which that title carries. Madison himself disclaimed this, writing to a casual correspondent in 1834:

"You give me a credit to which I have no claim, in calling me 'The writer of the Constitution of the U. S.' This was not like the fabled goddess of wisdom the offspring of a single brain. It

154

ought to be regarded as the work of many heads and many hands."

Madison richly deserved to be called the "Father of the Constitution," but few of those who fixed the title on him would have helped to do so had they known what he put into that document, and what his purposes were. His fundamental gift to the Constitution was the concept of national supremacy and local autonomy in a federal republic ruled by the people, with checks and balances to guard against legislative or executive tyranny and against impetuous legislation. He proposed, supported and helped to secure such a government, organized for energy, and freed of dependence on the jealous and ambitious state political systems. He outlined the mechanisms by which the states were stripped *in fact* of those sovereign powers which *in theory* had already been transferred to the Confederation, and he took the lead in a huge additional transfer both in theory and fact. The states were left in sole control of a myriad of local matters, dignified with the name of state sovereignty, but with no sovereignty behind the name. For the general government, besides being declared supreme, was given judicial power to decide what was left to the states and what was not.

The framers of the Constitution were able to do this with confidence because they knew that the real sovereignty was in the people, who were both states and nation, and they themselves were part of the people. When the people, organized as states, transferred sovereignty from states to nation, they merely moved it from thirteen small pockets into one large pocket, and it was still theirs. State officeholders, on the other hand, looked on sovereignty as Blackstone defined it—as a supreme attribute *of government*. When it was transferred from states to nation, the states lost it. This was the reason for Wilson's repeated statements that the people would support the new system but the state governments would fight it. Madison had this dual concept in mind when he insisted that the Constitution must be ratified by conventions of the people, not by state legislatures.

To apportion credit for the framing of the Constitution, one must give it to groups rather than individuals. There were several kinds of striving and achievement, each of which presented its own set of leaders. Some leaders won, others lost, and sometimes the losers shaped the course of the winners.

In setting forth principles accepted by the convention, the outstanding men were Madison, Wilson, Franklin, King, Paterson, Randolph and Mason.

Principles rejected by the convention came most notably from Luther Martin, Paterson, Hamilton, Charles Pinckney, Gouverneur Morris, Read and Gerry.

In actual construction of the government, the leaders were Madison, Wilson, Morris, Sherman, Rutledge and (in minor details) Pinckney.

In the solution of problems through compromise, leadership came from Franklin, Ellsworth, Sherman and Morris.

Madison and Wilson stand out as the constructive statesmen of the convention. Both had a profound knowledge of public law, drawn from the history of it. Both were high nationalists. Both were committed to rule by the people under moderate safeguards against the passions and impetuousness of democracy. They formed a mighty team against the veiled monarchism of Hamilton, the might-makes-right of Morris, the rule of propertied aristocracy sought by the two Pinckneys, the prostrating weakness (especially of the executive) which Mason and Randolph mistook for liberty. They won a fifty-per-cent victory in form, but far more than that in effect, in limiting small-state hegemony to state equality in the Senate. And they lost where they deserved to lose, in their effort to bring all state laws under the control of Congress and the federal executive.

Madison had a broader approach to public law than Wilson, and a better understanding of the stabilizing role of federalism in the American republic. Wilson showed more inventiveness—witness his electoral college device for the choice of a President. A faulty system, but it furnished the only path along which the convention could be carried toward an election by the people. The argument for such an election came from Madison—not to make the President what he has intermittently become, a tribune of the people, but to save the country from congressional tyranny by making the executive independent. This particular combination of Madison's principles and Wilson's inventiveness has given the American federal government the characteristic features by which it is set apart from the parliamentary governments of the world. At the same time Madison's doctrine of national supremacy in a federal republic has set the United States apart from consolidated republics, while rescuing it from the weaknesses of a confederacy.

The work of other men in setting principles was narrower but important. Franklin, when not hunting holes in deadlocks, concentrated on the need to base government on the common people and to check corruption. Rufus King rendered a service not easily appreciated. Never speaking at length and seldom suggesting a positive action, he had a gift, as Madison did, for discerning error. No man in the convention rivaled him in exposing a fallacy in two or three trenchant sentences. Paterson laid down one principle—state equality—in order to gain specific advantages for his own state. Having bludgeoned the convention into partial acceptance of it, he must be rated both winner and loser on the same issue.

Randolph deserves a place among the leaders in accepted principles, but not for the overrated services on which his reputation was built. His speech presenting the Virginia Plan was a mere echo of Madison's opinions. His preliminary draft of a constitution for the Committee of Detail was a wordy scaffolding around a cluttered mass of timbers. However, he was more responsible than any other delegate for the fact that the powers of Congress were itemized instead of general. George Mason's steady hammering for democratic principles helped to fix the policies of the convention, yet the rejection of specific proposals turned him against the Constitution.

In the field of actual construction, Madison's leadership began with the formulation of the Virginia Plan, followed by effective championship of its main provisions. He was quick to accept changes in it, most notably in relation to election of the President and an increase of his powers. As the work went on, he showed the utmost skill in judging what would achieve and what would upset the balance between the great departments of government. Finally, he was a swift detector of flaws in superficially plausible proposals, and never lacked a remedy.

Madison's original plan was modified from two sides. The changes which he indorsed, tending both to popularize and strengthen the government, came chiefly from Wilson, with Morris as their final architect. From the small-state group, with Paterson as the driving force but Sherman as the strategist, came the changes which were forced upon the Madison-Wilson-Morris leadership. Pinckney through his submitted plan furnished numerous details of construction, but was a failure on the floor. Rutledge planted the defenses of slavery in the Constitution and lifted the national supremacy clause to its ultimate height.

Among the harmonizers, Franklin carried on the art of conciliation with which he had eased the relations of revolutionary America and Bourbon France. Morris loved political manipulation. Ellsworth's effort was to hold North and South together, while Sherman used compromise to gain specific objectives.

All through the convention's work ran the compulsion and clashes of economic interests. Of necessity, virtually every decision related either to security, personal liberty, property interest or the general welfare. If one looks at the provisions of the Constitution to see where they land in these four categories, the most striking fact is the number of double, triple or even quadruple listings.

Congress was established from all four motives. Liberty governed the election and tenure of the House. Economic interest and security determined the character of the Senate. The veto power of the President is to give security to him, to the country, to liberty and property against legislative ambition or indiscretion. The power to override a veto aims at security and liberty. The taxing power is visibly related to security and the general welfare, but is also the basis of all protection of liberty and property. In the sections restraining Congress and the states, defense after defense is provided for personal liberty or economic interests. The judiciary was built for national security and to halt state encroachments on property rights, but a good part of the article creating it was designed to safeguard civil rights against courts and Congress.

When the Constitution is examined in this manner, the results do not diminish the economic motivation of the framers, but they build up the accompanying devotion to liberty. It becomes easier to understand why men intent on protecting property through government did not resort to a concealed monarch or produce an aristocracy. The Constitution was written by men who believed in liberty and in republican government—that is, in representative government based on the great body of the people. Madison became its foremost exponent not because he was more staunch than others in advocating it, but because, along with his advocacy, he had the clearest understanding of its nature, its elements of strength and weakness, and what to do about them.

The longer a believer in democracy studies the work of the framers of the Constitution, the higher his estimate of them is bound to become. That is due in part to the cumulative evidence of their integrity and ability, in part to the fact that, property-minded though they were, they accepted the people as the final custodians of public power. The convention opened on the note of the fury and follies of democracy. Safeguards against democratic excesses were planted in the Constitution, and local interests and selfishness crowded their way in. But the convention ended on a note of trust in the people. No greater error can be made than to say that the Constitution was written either in a spirit of blind self-interest or of hostility to democracy.

Madison and Franklin contributed more than any others to the trend of the convention toward popular self-government—the former by his exposition of the rational basis for a qualified trust in the people, the latter by his ability and readiness to portray their feelings. This veering toward democracy was unrelated to the shift of power inside the convention. It resulted, rather, from a continuing reappraisal of measures. To some extent it represented an evolution inside the men themselves.

Madison did more than contribute to this in others: he also changed. The Constitution to which he set his hand on September 17 established a more democratic as well as more powerful form of government (chiefly due to revisions in the presidency and the Senate) than the one whose outline he provided at the opening of the convention. These alterations were made with his active indorsement. Out of it all came a government high in positive powers, checked and balanced to prevent misuse of them, but fundamentally so much a government of the people that (as Franklin asserted) its ultimate character would be determined by theirs. It would either bring happiness to them, through the wisdom and integrity of those they chose to be their governors, or it would end in despotic rule when the people were too corrupted for anything but despotism.

Those final alternatives still lie ahead. Never out of sight, not always seeming far away, they have ever been pushed into the future. Perhaps that is the greatest tribute time has paid to the men who wrote the Constitution.

# CHAPTER XIII

## ANTIFEDERALISM

THE proposed Constitution had now to run the gantlet of Congress—a minor test, yet capable of affecting the vital decisions in the states. Madison remained in Philadelphia for some days, filling out his notes of debates. He was on his way to New York when Edward Carrington sent an urgent call for haste in spite of fatigue. The same schism which split the Virginians at Philadelphia was appearing in the congressional delegation. Richard Henry Lee wanted such drastic alterations in the Constitution that the effect would be to oppose it. Grayson would give it only a silent passage to the states. Henry Lee agreed that it ought to be warmly recommended. Madison's arrival broke the Virginia tie. The earlier coming of King and Gorham overrode hostile Nathan Dane of Massachusetts. Dr. Johnson, Few, Pierce (already there), Gilman, Langdon, Blount and Butler were other convention delegates who swelled the friendly forces.

R. H. Lee opened for the antis. Resolved, he wished it said, that the power of Congress does not extend to the creation of a new confederacy of nine states—but it is deemed respectful to submit the plan. Clark of New Jersey, Carrington and Dane played seesaw with substitute motions, but all died at adjournment. The constitutional arguments of Lee and Dane were by this time pretty well beaten down by Madison and others of the "fiery zealots" (as Lee called them) who rolled in from Philadelphia. They pointed out that the original resolve of Congress recommending the convention had called for a firm *national government*. Congressmen, by their credentials, had substantially the same powers as the convention delegates. Either the plan was within the powers of Congress, or, if beyond those powers, the same necessity which justified the convention would justify Congress. In several instances, said Madison, it had "exercised assumed powers of a very high and delicate nature, under motives infinitely less urgent than the present state of our affairs."

Giving up on this point, Lee attempted to amend the convention plan by putting in a bill of rights. The framers admitted the power of Congress to amend, but denied the expediency. If changes were made, some states might ratify the original plan, some the amended one, and dire evils would ensue.

There were only six antis in Congress. Of eleven states present, New York alone would oppose a vigorous indorsement. Madison preferred complete agreement on a mild resolution, especially since Virginia was touchy about advice from Congress. The contest was fortunately terminated, he wrote, by a unanimous resolve that the report "be transmitted to the several legislatures, in order to be submitted to a convention of delegates chosen in each state by the people thereof."[1]

To R. H. Lee this was the work of a coalition of monarchy men, military men, aristocrats, drones and rapacious anti-Southerners against whom the patriot voice was raised in vain. This reaction by Virginia's No. 2 orator promised little repose for Madison in coming months. And what of Orator No. 1? "Much will depend on Mr. Henry," Madison remarked. He welcomed reports that a few favorable words had fallen from those eloquent lips, but still thought that the verdict would be negative. Washington tried his hand with Henry but received only a polite regret at disagreement with a revered personage. More forthright was Benjamin Harrison, who told Washington that he saw in the Constitution the seeds of civil discord, Southern subjection and armed tyranny.[2]

Reports favorable to the Constitution were reaching Madison at the end of September. The seacoast (*i.e.,* the commercial interests) seemed everywhere fond of it. Both sides in Philadelphia's boiling politics had espoused it warmly, but a country party might spring up and turn the scale. In New York the general voice was friendly but the party in power would use every effort to defeat it. In Boston the reception was extremely favorable, but more would depend on the country (where the Shaysites were hostile) than the town. A favorable echo was heard from Connecticut and New Jersey. He had not yet learned of the "unlucky ferment" (as he called it later) in the Pennsylvania Assembly, where opponents boycotted an evening session and were forcibly brought back next day by the sergeant-at-arms, to restore the quorum needed for the calling of a convention.[3]

Before the end of October, Madison had a fair notion of the Virginia line-up and did not like it. A decided majority in the assembly was said to be zealous for the Constitution, but individuals of great weight were opposed and gaining ground. Joining Mason were Patrick Henry, R. H. and Arthur Lee, Theodorick Bland, Benjamin Harrison, the Nelsons and Cabells, St. George Tucker, John Taylor, John Page, William Ronald. The bench and bar, Randolph wrote, were generally against it. Supporting the plan, aside from its Virginia framers, were Edmund Pendleton, Archibald Stuart, John Marshall, Wilson C. Nicholas, Paul Carrington, James Innes and men of lesser repute. Joseph Jones and Madison of the College were undecided but extremely critical.

To Madison, this diversity among men of equal integrity and discernment was "a melancholy proof of the fallibility of the human judgment and of the imperfect progress yet made in the science of government." Luckily both sides agreed that the issue must go to the voters. The assembly rejected Henry's proposal that the state convention should adopt, reject, *or amend* the plan and submitted it for "full and free investigation, discussion, and decision." But the affirmative majority was shrinking.[4]

Just for exercise, Congress sent another requisition to the states for money. From 1782 onward, they had paid one sixth of the money asked for. Current costs of government were terrific. For 1787 the civil departments would need $124,000, the army (of 700 men) $176,000. Pensions and contingencies ran the operating costs to $418,883.12. The national debt was appalling. Domestic interest ran $1,700,000 a year (unpaid of course), while the interest and annual installment on the foreign debt were just under a million. Grand total, $3,010,798.64.

Congress could ask for such a gigantic sum. But get it? Madison was on the committee of five which dealt with the problem. Answering the cry for economy, they cut $1,000 off the contingent fund. The Board of Treasury advised that the "indent" system be dropped, and only gold and silver be received in taxes. Preferring to get something in paper to nothing in specie, the committee

tried to straighten out the use of indents, which nobody understood except the speculators.

These were promissory notes for interest on the domestic debt,
receivable for taxes. Soldiers and other small creditors sold their
indents to wealthy men for a small fraction of their face value.
They were then either held for a speculative profit, or used at face
value to reduce taxes or purchase western lands. However, there
was a time limit on their use for tax purposes. So most of the states
(Virginia and Pennsylvania being exceptions) did nothing at all
until the indents became worthless. Congress was then belabored
into restoring their validity, after which the states used current
federal funds to buy up old indents. They got rid of federal deficits
at a discount of from eighty to eighty-five per cent, while Congress
went into debt for pay rolls.

In Virginia, Madison had put federal revenues on so sound a
basis in 1784 that his state collected more 1785 indents than all
the rest of the country combined. But they never reached the
Treasury. They were held back to compel Congress to issue the
1786 indents, which had been withheld to compel the states to
make payments in specie. The result was that up to September
1787 not one penny had been received from any of the thirteen
states, either in cash or paper, on any requisition later than 1785.
By advice of its committee, Congress now issued the 1786 indents
and took off all time limits and other restrictions. This was done
because state laws to stabilize the indents merely caused speculators and tax evaders to sell their indents at home and buy them
back in states which did no stabilizing.[5]

Madison and the other Virginia delegates had no liking for this
system, which, they told the governor, enormously oppressed the
taxpayer who paid cash and created undue profits for speculators.
Instead of receiving indents for taxes, they advised, let Virginia lay
as great a tax in specie as the people could reasonably pay, and
apply it in the purchase of indents. With such a fund available
"the great speculators would be ready to enter into contracts for
supplying them at certain prices."

Out of this confusion and paralysis came a great part of the
driving desire for a federal government independent of the states

and strong enough to sustain itself. So desperate was the situation that Madison doubted whether the old government could be kept alive until the new one should take its place. Collapse appeared even closer when he wrote to Jefferson a few weeks later:

"The states seem to be either wholly omitting to provide for the federal Treasury or to be withdrawing the scanty appropriations made to it. The latter course has been taken up by Massachusetts, Virginia and Delaware. The Treasury Board seem to be in despair of maintaining the shadow of government much longer. Without money, the offices must be shut up, and the handful of troops on the frontier disbanded, which will probably bring on an Indian war, and make an impression to our disadvantage on the British garrisons within our limits."[6]

Though he did not know it, Madison was re-elected to Congress on October 25, getting 126 out of 140 votes, but the body supposed to convene in November did not achieve a quorum till late in January. Studying the country's reaction to the Constitution, he was aware of a double trend late in October. Except in Rhode Island and New York, there was a strong presumption that the northern and middle states were favorable. The South would be all right unless misled by Virginia. But the tone of the press was changing. Tench Coxe had led off in Philadelphia with a series of articles which Madison and Washington republished in Virginia. Soon Madison reported newspapers in the northern and middle states teeming with hostile publications.

"The attacks seem to be principally leveled against the organization of the government, and the omission of the provisions contended for in favor of the press and juries, etc. A new combatant, however . . . strikes at the foundation. He represents the situation of the United States to be such as to render any government improper and impracticable which forms the states into one nation, and is to operate directly on the people. Judging from the newspapers, one would suppose that the adversaries were the most numerous and the most in earnest. But there is no other evidence that it is the fact."[7]

Actually, the enemies of the Constitution were shooting their last heavy bolts. Mason's "paltry objections," as Madison termed them, backfired in New England when it was disclosed that the antis had deleted his criticism of the federal commerce power. Gerry's similar assaults netted him a defeat for election to the Massachusetts convention. Violating the secrecy rule, Luther Martin spilled several tons of convention beans, chaff and gravel on the floor of the Maryland legislature. His "Genuine Information," published in a two months' newspaper serial, presented the Constitution as a hellish conspiracy by Virginia and her wicked allies against virtuous Maryland and the small states. It was a thunderous attack, but everybody in Maryland recognized it as a Chase maneuver in defense of paper money. As for the small states, of all America they were best pleased with the Constitution.[8]

The biggest hostile shot was fired by Richard Henry Lee in his *Letters of the Federal Farmer,* which gained force from an air of impartial appraisal. He lamented the absence of eight or nine good republican characters, who, had they not refused to attend, might have restrained "the young, visionary men and the consolidating aristocracy" who accumulated too great powers in too few hands. Lee himself had rejected a convention appointment. Long before, in correspondence with Madison, he had shown himself obsessed with fear of federal power over commerce.[9]

It was a little singular, Madison remarked to Washington, that three of the most distinguished advocates of amendments were at sharp variance on the point they most criticized—the composition of the executive. If Lee, Mason and Randolph could not agree on that, it was pretty certain that other advocates of amendments would split up on other great points. He failed to realize that Lee's letters, appealing to emotion, had little need of logic.

In Virginia, affairs were going from dubious to bad. "Mr. Henry is the great adversary who will render the event precarious," commented Madison. This reflected a report to him that Henry was "loud on the distresses of the people and makes us tremble with apprehensions of a rebellion if they are driven to despair." To win the masses he sought a moratorium on debts and a shift of state taxation to foreign commerce. Bidding for the support of big planters and merchants, he opposed a bill (first sponsored by Madison in 1784) to repeal the laws which closed the courts to British creditors.

These British debts (which Randolph called the chief obstacle to ratification) gave many land-rich Virginians the same motive for opposing the Constitution as was felt by the mortgage-ridden Shaysites. The plight of one of them was described to Madison earlier in the year: "It is said that our friend Meriwether Smith is in the bounds for a debt due to Mr. William Lee, and that he has made over the whole of his property for a British debt." Smith might be no object of beauty (it was he whom Martha Bland described as having the grimace, face and figure of a baboon), but as a legislative legman for Patrick Henry he lacked nothing of agility or endurance.

Beaten on the moratorium, Henry secured a postponement of debt-law repeal until Great Britain should evacuate the western military posts—a step which delayed their evacuation for a decade. One of his bills prohibited the importation of foreign liquors, beef, candles and cheese, and (said Madison) "to enforce this despotic measure the most despotic means are resorted to"—confiscation of goods and fines for having them in possession even though lawfully acquired. "Mad freaks," Madison called these measures, but they were actually shrewd maneuvers. Henry's object was to create a feeling of dependence on laws which would be nullified by the new Constitution. To heighten the effect, he pictured federal courts as distant tribunals to which Virginia defendants in British debt suits would be ruthlessly dragged.[10]

To Madison, at the close of 1787, the assembly's policies furnished stronger proof than ever of the need of a constitutional anchor "against the fluctuations which threaten to shipwreck our liberty." He saw three parties developing. The first was for adopting without amendments. The second, led by Mason and Randolph, favored ratification with amendments to guard state and personal rights. The third concurred with Henry in seeking amendments which struck at the essence of the system. They would either lead back into the visionary principles of the Confederation or split the Union into several confederacies.[11]

Henry won Mason's co-operation by playing down his ultimate objectives and adopting the strategy of the middle group. Passing a bill to cover the expenses of the coming convention, they expanded it to include the expenses of delegates to a second general convention, should the state body find one necessary before ratification. The adverse majority, Madison saw, was obtained by a union of the enemies and dissatisfied friends of the Constitution. That union must be broken. Governor Randolph, weighty and wobbly, was the stone to be wedged out of line.

Madison had ignored his friend's arguments, sent personally, for a second convention. In January, however, a group of Antifederalists headed by Meriwether Smith persuaded the governor to let them publish an undelivered letter to the speaker of the House of Delegates. In this Randolph criticized the Constitution and advocated a second convention, but left his attitude toward ratification uncertain. Madison undertook to convert him with a subtle mixture of critical analysis and flattery. He had read the letter with attention and pleasure, "because the spirit of it does as much honor to your candor as the general reasoning does to your abilities." But not viewing the governor's objections in the same decisive light, he must own that he differed still more as to the proposed remedy. Then came an appeal to Randolph's vanity. Had the governor thrown his influence into the opposite scale, it would have given it such a preponderancy "that Mr. Henry would either have suppressed his enmity, or been baffled in the policy which it has dictated." Nothing could be further from Randolph's views, his friend assured him, than the principles of those men "who have carried on their opposition under the respectability of your name."

In New York, Madison continued, the adverse party notoriously meditated either a dissolution of the Union, or a protraction of it by patching the Articles of Confederation. In New England the opposition came from those who aimed at confusion. As for Virginia's antifederal leader:

"You are better acquainted with Mr. Henry's politics than I can be, but I have for some time considered him as driving at a southern confederacy and not farther concurring in the plan of amendments than as he hopes to render it subservient to his real designs."

A second convention would be futile, Madison told him, because the friends of a good constitution would differ among themselves, while the convention would be full of out-and-out opponents whose aim would be to frustrate. What was needed now was leadership. Had the new Constitution been framed by some obscure individual, it would have commanded little attention from most of its current admirers. But——

"Had yourself, Colonel Mason, Colonel R. H. L., Mr. Henry and a few others seen the Constitution in the same light with those who subscribed it, I have no doubt that Virginia would have been as zealous and unanimous as she is now divided on the subject."

This seductive appeal to Randolph's vanity was followed by an address to his fears. North Carolina had just postponed her convention to see what Virginia might do. Should that state fall into Henry's politics "it will endanger the Union more than any other circumstance that could happen. My apprehensions of this danger increase every day."[12]

In New England, Madison heard, there was heavy opposition in the Shays' Rebellion area, but affirmative zeal among men of letters, high officials, lawyers, clergy and men of property. In Virginia people of this type were split apart, with heavy opposition among judges and lawyers. Not less noteworthy, he remarked to Jefferson, was the fact that the mass of the people in Virginia, accustomed to being guided by their rulers on all new and intricate questions, were in this instance going contrary to their most popular leaders. "And the phenomenon is the more wonderful, as a popular ground is taken by all the adversaries to the new Constitution." His conclusion was "that the body of sober and steady people, even of the lower order, are tired of the vicissitudes, injustice and follies which have so much characterized public measures, and are impatient for some change which promises stability and repose." In other words, just as Patrick Henry's sway over the people represented the chief threat to ratification of the Constitution, so their reaction against his half-radical, half-reactionary demagoguery was its chief asset.[13]

Meanwhile, why was Madison himself staying so long in New York? All through the fall, friends clamored for him to come home, lead the fight and run for the convention. Washington told him that explanations of the Constitution would be needed and none could give them with more accuracy. Archibald Stuart supplicated him to become a delegate. "For God's sake do not disappoint the anxious expectations of your friends, and let me add, of your country." He was offered an election from the Borough of Norfolk, while, in Orange County, neighbors deluged the Madison family with inquiries and appeals.

On November 8 Madison told his brother Ambrose that he had wished a final decision on the Constitution to be made by men who had no hand in preparing it. But federal delegates were entering other conventions and much of the opposition in Virginia was based on misconceptions which he could help clear up. So he would not decline if the county saw fit to honor him. What would the opposition be?[14]

Following this decision, Madison left for Philadelphia under arrangements, he told Washington, for proceeding to Virginia or returning to New York. By the eighteenth, his books and papers packed, he was back in New York, ready for a long stay.

This decision followed a proposal made to Madison by Hamilton and Foreign Secretary John Jay. To cope with the flood of hostile propaganda, they were planning a series of newspaper articles (Hamilton's idea) which would explain the Constitution and defend it against every possible attack. For unity and anonymity all articles would be signed Publius. Would Madison join in the undertaking? His decision to do so established the most famous literary and political partnership in American history. From the three men, but chiefly from Hamilton and Madison, came the eighty-five papers of *The Federalist*—a cogent set of arguments for approval of the Constitution, but infinitely more significant as a light on its principles and a commentary on republican government.

For Madison this had a multiple appeal. Three men could cover the subject more adequately than one. With one partner cold and the other cool toward popular government, he could make sure of planting its principles in the most definitive discussion of the Constitution. Finally, the articles could be republished south of the Potomac with as great effect as if they had been written there. New York would be the base of his campaign for ratification in Virginia. Sending the first seven articles (all by Hamilton and Jay) to Washington for reprint in Richmond, Madison said his own connection with the publication restrained him from directly seeking republication elsewhere.

"You will recognize one of the pens concerned in the task. There are three in the whole. A fourth may possibly bear a part."

The last reference was to William Duer, whose output proved too poor for inclusion. Gouverneur Morris also was invited but declined. Madison suggested King, but was overruled. Hamilton disclosed his authorship to Washington, and Madison let Randolph know that he was in for a few numbers. Otherwise anonymity was maintained until the fight was over—and as far as the public was concerned, for years afterward. On August 1788, writing in cipher, Madison revealed the secret of *The Federalist* to Jefferson, and made an enlightening remark on the individual responsibilities:

"It was undertaken last fall by Jay, Hamilton and myself. The proposal came from the two former. The execution was thrown, by the sickness of Jay, mostly on the two others. Though carried on in concert, the writers are not mutually answerable for all the ideas of each other, there being seldom time for even a perusal of the pieces by any but the writer before they were wanted at the press, and sometimes hardly by the writer himself."[15]

Jay's illness in November piled the work on two men. The main effect was to admit a larger proportion of Madison's philosophy into a commentary destined to become a political guidebook.

# CHAPTER XIV

## THE FEDERALIST

THE first number of *The Federalist,* by Hamilton, outlined the whole project. The series was to cover the utility of the Union, the insufficiency of the Confederation, the necessity of an energetic government, the conformity of the proposed Constitution to republican principles, and the additional security it would bring to republican government, liberty and property.

Following this introduction in the New York *Independent Journal* of October 27, 1787, Jay carried on with four articles on the need of national union to cope with foreign menaces and sectional discord. Hamilton then made telling use of the commercial and territorial rivalries among the states. Threatening civil war even within the Confederation, they would be still more likely to produce a clash of arms between independent states or rival confederacies.

In No. 9 Hamilton laid the groundwork for more federal authority than he seemed to be claiming. The Union, he observed, would remain a confederacy of states as long as the members existed for local purposes, even though in perfect subordination to the general authority. He did not say their subordination was complete—on the contrary, they retained "very important portions of sovereign power"—but the net effect was to insinuate total federal supremacy into the concept of a confederacy. He then rebutted the cardinal position he had taken in convention—that a continental area could be safely ruled only by a near-monarchic concentration of national power. In place of it he adopted the Madison theory he had previously combated. Enlargement of the orbit of power offered no obstacle to republican government as long as it was federally organized. On this doctrine he placed a military stamp. Continental federalism gave assurance that the armed force of most of the country could be assembled to suppress popular insurrections in a lesser part.

Madison followed on November 23 with the most famous of all the articles signed Publius—*The Federalist* No. 10 on the sources of faction in government. This study of the origin of political parties put such emphasis on conflicts growing out of property interests that it has caused many people to call Madison the real author of the Marxian doctrine of economic determinism. Madison was a determinist all right. His rejection of free will, in theological debate with the Reverend Samuel Stanhope Smith in 1778, was the logical prelude to his conclusion that men respond to irresistible compulsions in politics. Observation told him that by far the most compelling force was economic self-interest. Political parties grew chiefly out of the struggle between rich and poor, debtors and creditors, and the conflicting interests of farmers, manufacturers, traders and financiers.

Had he stopped there, his doctrine would have been economic determinism. But he recognized the influence of differing opinions in religion, contrary theories of government, attachment to rival leaders and many other points which stir the human passions and drive men "into mutual animosities." Marx saw these same phenomena as mere by-products of economics in a society based on material self-interest. Madison saw them as independent motives which usually followed the economic groove but were capable of jumping out of it.

Quantitatively, this difference between the determinism of Madison and Marx is not great. Qualitatively, it puts them far apart in their attitudes toward democratic government and civil liberties. Marx, emerging from a background of European tyranny, produced the dictatorship of the proletariat as the way to the end he sought, and saw no human values that forbade its use. Madison thought far too much of liberty to sacrifice it to any economic goal. Having no desire to upset the social order, he would fight the harder for democratic self-government the more it was assailed, thus raising it in the scale of motives for political division, while Marx treated it as a destructible pawn in a campaign to destroy private property.

The principal effect of the tenth *Federalist* paper has been to promote the economic interpretation of history, and to stamp most historical writings as invalid or insufficient. It also has caused its author to be hailed as a property-defending conservative and a missionary of socialism. Daniel de Leon[1] achieved the latter goal by linking Madison's forecast (before Malthus) of general poverty through overpopulation and his contention that the right of the poor to vote was more fundamental than the right of the rich to defend their property. That interpretation ignores his belief that the rights of both were real, even though unequal. In truth, Madison was a pioneer advocate of controlled capitalism. Here is the core of what he said about the effect of property in producing political parties:

"The diversity in the faculties of men, from which the rights of property originate, is not less an insuperable obstacle to a uniformity of interests. The protection of these faculties is the first object of government. From the protection of different and unequal faculties of acquiring property, the possession of different degrees and kinds of property immediately results; and from the influence of these on the sentiments and views of the respective proprietors ensues a division of the society into different interests and parties."

It is easy and erroneous to simplify that into a mere statement that governments are set up to protect property rights. Madison's emphasis was on the protection of *different and unequal* faculties of acquiring property. Abstractly, that is equally a demand that the smallest acquisitive faculty be protected against the largest, and the largest against the smallest. But Madison was well aware that in a competitive society, with public order and private rights maintained, property would flow ceaselessly into the hands of those most able to gain and hold it. He was practically saying, therefore, that one of the first objects of government was to protect the poor and near-poor by laws restraining concentration of wealth and the power of its holders.

Conclusive evidence that this was his thought was furnished the next time he discussed the relationship of political parties to property, in the *National Gazette* of January 23, 1792. The evils of party strife should be combated, among other ways:

"1. By establishing political equality among all.

"2. By withholding *unnecessary* opportunities from a few to increase the inequality of property by an immoderate, and especially unmerited, accumulation of riches.

"3. By the silent operation of laws, which, without violating the rights of property, reduce extreme wealth towards a state of mediocrity, and raise extreme indigence towards a state of comfort."

Madison lived a century and a half too soon to be hauled before congressional committees as a subversive radical for talking like that, but one can only marvel at the historians who present him to modern generations as a conservative guarantor of the *status quo.* He saw no violation of property rights in taxation rising geometrically upon great fortunes (a system Jefferson recommended to him in 1785).[2] What he feared may be seen in his description, in the tenth *Federalist,* of the antidotes to the poisons of factional politics.

In a pure democracy, where the entire body of citizens assembled in person, there could be no check upon a common passion in the majority. In a republic, laws were made by a chosen body of citizens, whose wisdom, patriotism and love of justice furnished a safeguard. Also, representative government could operate over a larger area than was feasible for a pure democracy. Factious leaders, Madison concluded, might kindle a flame in their own states, but could not start a general conflagration. A religious sect might degenerate into a political faction in one region, but the variety of sects dispersed over the country would protect the national councils. The same principle would protect property rights.

"A rage for paper money, for an abolition of debts, for an equal division of property, or for any other improper or wicked project, will be less apt to pervade the whole body of the Union than a particular member of it."

There is the line of demarcation. It was wicked or improper to break down great fortunes by laws decreeing an equal division of property, or by discharge of debts in worthless paper. It was legitimate and desirable to do so by the silent force of taxation or inheritance laws. Madison was not assailing private property. He was seeking to protect men against property, and to protect property against the destructive effect of too great concentration in a country where the poor could outvote the rich.

Publius continued with three articles by Hamilton on the value of the Union to commerce and agriculture, and its utility as a taxing agency. Then, in No. 14, Madison returned to the last phase of his previous article—the advantage accruing to republican government from its exercise over a large area. This was no remote abstraction. Antifederalists, quoting Montesquieu, were crying out against a large republic with national powers. As Madison put it, they were resorting to the prevailing prejudice against a large republican sphere "in order to supply, by imaginary difficulties, the want of those solid objections which they endeavor in vain to find." Could it be said that the United States was too extensive for its representatives to meet whenever necessary? As western states were added, distances would be cut by improved roads, the opening of river navigation and canals. The most distant states would have greatest need of the Union and would be most devoted to its solidarity. He grew eloquent near the close:

"Hearken not to the unnatural voice which tells you that the people of America, knit together as they are by so many cords of affection, can no longer . . . be fellow-citizens of one great, respectable and flourishing empire. Hearken not to the voice which petulantly tells you that the form of government recommended for your adoption is a novelty in the political world. . . . If novelties are to be shunned, believe me, the most alarming of all novelties, the most wild of all projects, the most rash of all attempts, is that of rending us in pieces, in order to preserve our liberties and promote our happiness."

This article, published in the New York *Packet* of November 30, closed the first grand division of *The Federalist,* on the necessity of the Union. Hamilton then took up the insufficiency of the Confederation. The United States had reached almost the last stage of national humiliation. He laid the responsibility on the great vice of the federal system: that in the most essential matters, Congress passed laws binding on states instead of individuals.

"The consequence of this is that though in theory their resolutions concerning those objects are laws, constitutionally binding on the members of the Union, yet in practice they are mere recommendations which the states observe or disregard at their option."

That statement concisely disproves the careless assertion of latter-day writers that Congress during the Confederation was constitutionally limited to the making of recommendations. Many times before, Madison and Hamilton had lamented the impotence of the national lawmaking body. Then they were laboring to give reality to its powers. Now the emphasis was on the impossibility of doing so.

Hamilton had intended to discuss other confederacies, but turned the subject (and his notes) over to his partner when he found that the latter was already at work on it with far more extensive materials. Madison thereupon produced Nos. 18, 19 and 20 of the Publius series, essentially a rewriting of his 1786 "Notes of Ancient and Modern Confederacies." There was no need to set forth parallels: any American would know that the weaknesses he described were likewise those of the United States.

Two more articles by Hamilton completed the discussion of Confederation weaknesses. It was now mid-December. Twenty-two articles had been published, but so far the writers had only been laying the groundwork for discussion of the Constitution itself. Meanwhile the mills of the people were grinding. Between December 5 and 18, Delaware and New Jersey ratified unanimously, and Pennsylvania did so 46 to 23. Connecticut, as Madison saw things, was safe, Rhode Island hostile. In Massachusetts there was increased uncertainty. New York was divided but unlikely to resist united neighbors. In Maryland the opposition was stronger than expected. Virginia was most precarious of all.[3]

Here was a variant trend. Easy states were acting early, doubtful ones delaying. So, although the Publius project was stretching out, there was time for effect in the critical areas. A major division of labor was now in order: Hamilton and Madison each took a theme he could handle with competence and enthusiasm. Hamilton proved in seventeen successive articles (all but two on taxation and military matters) that the preservation of the Union required a constitution at least as energetic as the one proposed. While these were being published, Madison built up a backlog of articles designed to prove the fidelity of the Constitution to the true principles of republican government. Between January 15 and February 22, he furnished everything from No. 37 through No. 58—in bulk more than a quarter of the entire *Federalist,* and particularly notable for original thought and close reasoning.

First Madison sought to throw the opponents onto the defensive by pointing to their disagreements. They were like persons who, after a physician had given a prescription, offered half a dozen conflicting reasons why it would poison the patient, but produced no remedy of their own to keep him from dying. That done, he proceeded to his subject.

Only the republican form of government was compatible with the genius of the American people. But what was that form? If the usage of political writers were relied on, the term could be applied to aristocracies and mixtures of aristocracy and monarchy. Its true character lay in that principle which gave it validity in America—the determination of every votary of freedom to rely on the capacity of mankind for self-government. So he concluded:

"We may define a republic to be, or at least may bestow that name on, a government which derives all its powers directly or indirectly from the great body of the people, and is administered by persons holding their offices during pleasure, for a limited period, or during good behavior. It is *essential* to such a government that it be derived from the great body of the society, not from an inconsiderable proportion, or a favored class of it; otherwise a handful of tyrannical nobles, exercising their oppressions by a delegation of their powers, might aspire to the rank of republicans, and claim for their government the honorable title of republic."[4]

The new American government, Madison asserted, met the most rigid test of republicanism; also of federalism, since the people were to assent "not as individuals composing one entire nation, but as composing the distinct and independent states to which they respectively belong." The new government was federal in its origin, national and federal in the sources of its power, national in the operation of its powers and federal (because limited) in their extent—in fine, a composition of both forms.

He affirmed the power of the convention to do what it did. Congress had called for establishment of a firm national government. If there was usurpation of power, it was by Congress and the twelve states that heeded its call. In one respect only had the convention exceeded its powers—in making ratification by nine state conventions effective. This he compared with the revolutionary acts of the people in setting up the original state governments. In all great changes of established governments, forms ought to give way to substance. Otherwise the people would lose the precious right claimed for them in the Declaration of Independence, to abolish or alter their governments as they choose. As this new plan was to be submitted *to the people themselves,* they would either destroy it by disapproval, or, by their approval, blot out all prior errors and irregularities.[5]

Starting with No. 41, the powers of Congress were taken up. To the arguments of Hamilton for national military power, Madison added a general reason why this must be indefinite in scope: How could measures of defense be limited when there was no way of limiting the offensive force of other nations? He supplemented his colleague's defense of the congressional power of internal taxation. As population increased, domestic manufactures would take the place of foreign goods, imports would change from finished products to raw materials. Either these must be taxed more heavily, contrary to sound policy, or other forms of taxation must be resorted to. At this point Madison offered a reply to those who saw and feared an indefinite power of legislation in the general welfare clause. Had there been no other enumeration of powers that construction might be plausible.

"But what color can the objection have, when a specification of the objects alluded to by these general terms immediately follows,

"The powers delegated by the proposed Constitution to the federal government are few and defined. Those which are to remain in the state governments are numerous and indefinite. The former will be exercised principally on external objects, as war, peace, negotiation, and foreign commerce; with which last the power of taxation will, for the most part, be connected. The powers reserved to the several states will extend to all the objects which, in the ordinary course of affairs, concern the lives, liberties and properties of the people, and the internal order, improvement and prosperity of the state."[7]

Quoted out of context, as it has been many times, this appears to carry Madison's strict construction back to the *Federalist* Papers. In reality he was minimizing the sacrifice of state sovereignty in order to bulwark a doctrine of implied powers as broad as Marshall's. The strategic purpose is more evident when one contrasts these remarks with his position in the Philadelphia Convention. Here, the federal powers were few and defined, the state laws numerous and indefinite. There, the states were necessary only because "the general government could not extend its care to all the minute objects" of the local jurisdictions. Here, federal taxation was subordinate to regulation of foreign commerce; there it was "the highest prerogative of supremacy."[8]

This brought Madison to a string of twelve articles, Nos. 47 through 58, in which he discussed the structure of the federal government and the distribution of its powers. Refuting the claim that the Constitution violated the principle of separation of powers, he explained the need for a partial blending of the departments in order to make each one independent but subject to a check. If they were totally separate, the legislative department, being inherently stronger, would overwhelm the others and produce the same tyranny that was threatened by executive usurpations. In a hereditary monarchy the executive department is the source of danger. But in a representative republic, where the executive is carefully limited, it is against the enterprising ambition of the legislative department "that the people ought to indulge all their jealousy and exhaust all their precautions."[9]

Dealing with the House of Representatives, Madison emphasized the protection given the right of suffrage. The definition of this right being a fundamental article of republican government, it could not be left to the discretion either of Congress or of state legislatures. The convention therefore decided that the qualifications of those who were to vote for members of Congress should be the same as those of the electors of the most numerous branch of the state legislature. This would be safe because those qualifications were fixed in the state constitutions "and it cannot be feared that the people of the states will alter this part of their constitutions in such a manner as to abridge the rights secured to them by the federal Constitution."[10]

That was a bad guess, but only because he took no account of the people's inability to withstand force or deception. He did not foresee that in his own state, the poll-tax constitution of 1901 would be imposed on the people by the fiat of the convention that drafted it, without being submitted to the people. Failing to reckon with future antidemocratic forces, the Virginian grew lyrical in describing the constitutional guaranty of a broad suffrage:

"Who are to be the electors of the federal representatives? Not the rich more than the poor; not the learned more than the ignorant; not the haughty heirs of distinguished names more than the humble sons of obscurity and unpropitious fortune. The electors are to be the great body of the people of the United States. They are to be the same who exercise the right in every state of electing the corresponding branch of the legislature of the state."[11]

Hamilton, who had been attending court in Albany, resumed the Publius series at No. 59, with three articles on the power of Congress over election of its members. Madison came back with Nos. 62 and 63, presenting the Senate as a safeguard not only against the sudden and violent passions of large assemblies, but against that instability which gives advantage "to the sagacious, the enterprising and the moneyed few over the industrious and uninformed mass of the people." Jay inserted an article on the treaty power, and from that point Hamilton carried on alone.

Of the eighty-five *Federalist* articles, Madison wrote Nos. 10, 14,

18, 19, 20, 37 through 58, 62, 63—twenty-nine in all. Jay wrote five, Hamilton fifty-one. A list, made by Hamilton a few days before his death, credited Madison with only fourteen numbers and led to a 140-year controversy. During most of that period, partisans of each man gave credit according to their likes and dislikes. Later it became the custom to ascribe disputed articles to "Hamilton or Madison." It was not until 1944 that the studies of Douglass Adair, added to those made forty years earlier by E. G. Bourne, completely established Madison's authorship of every article he had said he wrote.[12]

# CHAPTER XV

## DIVIDED COUNSELS

MADISON's service in the Continental Congress came to a close when he set out for home on March 4, 1788, the day after his final *Federalist* article was published. He was then, an audit showed, overdrawn £100 for salary and expenses, which he refunded to the state. That ought to quash the ancient myth that he served in the old Congress without pay because of Virginia's poverty.[1]

The fate of the Constitution was far from clear at this time. From Massachusetts, late in January, he heard of a hostile combination of paper-money men, Shays insurgents and Maine delegates who were squatters on other people's land and feared ejection. Supporting the Constitution were Governors Hancock and Bowdoin (the former shaky with doubt and gout), and most professional people and merchants. Unluckily, Rufus King reported, this superiority of talents merely convinced the Shaysites that the Constitution was designed to split society into the opulent and great against the poor and illiterate.

Soon came the news that harmless amendments would mollify the opposition. The Bay State ratified, 187 to 168. Nobody told Madison of the psychological subtleties in the background—the suggestion to Hancock that he would be the country's first President if Virginia rejected the system, the decision to let him pose as author of the amendments Theophilus Parsons wrote. Two months earlier Samuel Adams protested to R. H. Lee: "I stumble at the threshold. I meet with a national government instead of a federal union of sovereign states." He stumbled across it when Paul Revere and a committee of merchants and mechanics (his political backers) told him the tradesmen of Boston wanted the Constitution for business reasons.[2]

The federal temple now had six pillars—Delaware, Pennsylvania, New Jersey, Georgia, Connecticut and Massachusetts. South Carolina was reported favorable. In North Carolina, as in Virginia, the body of the people were "better disposed than some of a superior order." Meanwhile the calls from home grew insistent. "Many have asked me with anxious solicitude," Washington wrote, "if you did not mean to get into the convention; conceiving it of indispensable necessity." Randolph was imperative:

"You must come in. Some people in Orange are opposed to your politics. Your election to the convention is I believe sure; but I beg you not to hazard it by being absent at the time."

From his father Madison heard that Thomas Barbour had become an antifederal candidate against himself and James Gordon for the county's two seats. Some of his friends were suspending their opinion till they saw him. "Others wish you not to come and will endeavor to shut you out of the convention." Even Chancellor Pendleton, favorable but not convinced, wanted help to resolve his uncertainties.

Madison was reluctant to serve in the convention at all. The undertaking, he told Washington, would involve him in laborious discussions and might jeopardize cherished friendships. But he had made up his mind, and if his presence at the election was thought indispensable, he would accept that condition too, little as he liked the appearance of soliciting votes.[3]

Patrick Henry, Madison's correspondents reported, was determined to amend the plan and let its fate depend on other states conforming to the will of Virginia. Should they stand out, Virginia could enter into foreign alliances. Among the counter influences: Publius. "His greatness is acknowledged universally." A hard jolt came in the news that New Hampshire's convention had adjourned until June. The move was actually useful, allowing converted delegates to seek release from their instructions, but it upset Madison's hope of confronting Henry and Mason with nine prior ratifications. He saw only one issue—"the simple one whether the Union shall or shall not be continued." Some opponents had disunion as their object; and with all of them that was its tendency. There was no middle ground.

Thus he wrote to Pendleton, old, ill and crippled, whose influence could still be decisive in Virginia, and it was an appeal to his

deepest feelings. During the Revolution, Madison had won Pendleton to the cession of Virginia's northwestern lands by a plea
that the resulting harmony would offset, in European eyes, the
military disaster at Camden. Now he found European object les-
sons for America. In France the spirit of liberty had made a
progress which must lead to some remarkable conclusion. But
in Holland, where a loose and weak government had just been
subverted by a Prussian army, the people were victims of their own
folly. That ought to be a very emphatic lesson to the United
States.[4]

Madison lingered a week in Philadelphia[5] and it was not until
March 18 that Washington wrote in his diary: "Mr. Madison on
his way from New York to Orange came in before dinner and
stayed all night." Washington had ridden over all his plantations
that day. He noted that slave women were clearing hedgerows
and preparing for fencing in the Neck. Elsewhere there was plowing of oats, sowing of barley, and in one field the plows struck
frozen ground only two inches below the surface. Madison's
arrival was something to break routine, as the next entries show:

"Wednesday 19th. Remained at home all day.
"Thursday 20th. Mr. Madison (in my carriage) went after
breakfast to Colchester to fall in with the stage."

Madison gave Washington a copy of the Pennsylvania convention debates and they sat down to a long discussion of news and
strategy. Presumably he repeated the daring suggestion ("I
barely drop the idea," he wrote in December) that Washington
publicly indorse the Constitution. And no doubt the latter repeated his complaint that his "hasty and indigested" comments on
it, included in a private letter on wolf dogs, had been published
all over the Continent. He had no objection to his views being
known, but felt injured that he should be quoted when no care
had been taken to dress the ideas. Actually, this lack of ornament
emphasized his hard conviction that there was no alternative between the Constitution and anarchy. Madison assured him (by
letter) that since this was a comment to a friend, the omission of
argumentative support would not seem improper. He felt sure

its publication was of service, notwithstanding the scandalous misinterpretations of it.[6]

At Fredericksburg, Madison picked up an urgent warning that he would be defeated unless he and his friends exerted themselves. On the way he should be sure to visit an influential Baptist leader and convert him from the idea that the Constitution menaced religious liberty. "There is nothing so vile but what the Constitution is charged with," his neighbor Joseph Spencer wrote. The election was one day off when he reached Orange on March 23. The county had but one polling place. Everybody came early and stood around, making it possible to conduct a last-minute campaign. Cousin Francis Taylor entered in his diary next day:

"Colonel Madison addressed himself in a speech to the people in defense of the new Constitution, and there appeared much satisfaction after the election was determined."

What the "colonel" said at the courthouse has never been recorded, but the effect of it can be read in the returns: Madison 202, Gordon 187, Barbour 56, Porter 34. The outcome surprised and delighted Federalist leaders. Carrington congratulated Madison on the success of his efforts "to turn the sinners of Orange from their wicked ways." Cyrus Griffin, President of Congress, rejoiced the more because "your being present, we are told, was absolutely necessary to counteract some unwarrantable proceedings."[7]

The Madison dinner table, stables and spare bedrooms were well filled during the next few days. In exchange for constitutional lore, the Piedmonters posted the newcomer on the effects of the severe winter which followed the 1787 drouth—planters forced to buy corn because of the short crop and heavy winter feeding, though luckily the price had not risen above $2.00 a barrel. Not so luckily, tobacco was bringing only eighteen shillings a hundred at tidewater. Like everybody else, the Madisons were finding it hard to pay or collect debts, but there is no indication that the double squeeze affected them as it did Washington. Forced to buy 800 barrels of corn, the father of his country had "put the sheriff of this county off three times" in a call for taxes, and had seen his lands in Greenbrier County posted for nonpayment.

These hard conditions had a direct bearing on ratification, especially in Maryland. When Washington called on Paper-Moneyite John Francis Mercer to fulfill a promise made at the Philadelphia Convention to pay enough of an old debt to meet the Mt. Vernon taxes, Mercer sent a bargeload of corn which froze up in the Potomac ice, and redoubled his opposition to the Constitution. What of the small farmer who faced a twenty-five-per-cent interest rate in refinancing his six-per-cent mortgage? "To save bread for his children he had better go to jail," exclaimed a correspondent of the Maryland *Journal*. But it was to the new Constitution that this exhorter looked for relief. All would be well as soon as stability in government brought reasonable loans from Europe "to pay workmen for improving our lands and houses that we may make the better crops." Also, the poor would be freed from tax gatherers because "taxes on imported goods which the Congress will lay can distress none but the rich."[8]

From George Nicholas, taker of Virginia's pulse, Madison received a briefing in early April. The Federalists appeared to have a slight majority in convention delegates, but this might be upset by returns from Kentucky or by the adverse effect on waverers if Maryland or South Carolina should postpone action. Opponents hoped to induce Pendleton to demand amendments before ratification, but Madison was expected to avert that danger. Patrick Henry, though talking of amendments, was "now almost avowedly an enemy to the Union." Mason had been seduced by the idea that he could dictate a constitution to Virginia and through her to the rest of the Union. Randolph talked of compromise. As in the great fight against Henry for religious freedom, young Nicholas urged Madison to prepare an address to the populace:

"Nine tenths of the people are strong friends to the Union, and such of them as are opposed to the proffered government are so upon suppositions not warranted by the thing itself. No person in the convention can so well prepare this address as yourself."

Madison replied that this could wait until the opponents disclosed their stand in convention. He sent a hurry call to Hamilton for copies of *The Federalist,* in response to another Nicholas suggestion. Apparently he thought better of the other advice too, for just as the delegates were assembling, the *Independent Chronicle* published two letters of "An American" to the members, precisely in Madison's style and full of thoughts he had been expressing. Reject the Constitution and thirteen jarring sovereignties, two or three contending confederacies, or a feeble union would be the miserable alternatives. Insult would follow, and then injuries abroad, while the dangers to liberty, property and peace at home would sink every American into despondency or drive him to despair. "The convention of Virginia will never be instrumental in bringing such evils on the United States."[9]

Agreeing that Kentucky, Maryland and South Carolina might govern the Virginia decision, Madison undertook "to counteract antifederal machinations" and work for speedy action. In Kentucky the first reaction had been favorable, he reported to Washington on April 10, but the torch of discord was thrown on materials only too inflammable. The torch was Patrick Henry's warning that a new federal government would surrender navigation of the Mississippi to Spain. To Daniel Carroll and James McHenry, Madison sent word that even the difference between postponement and quick adoption in Maryland might tilt the delicate balance in Virginia.

In Ann Arundel County the Carrolls had been defeated in a surprise move. The two Chases, Mercer and a fourth anti entered the race for the four convention seats four days before the election. They won by fifty votes, after a whirlwind campaign on such slogans as "No Excise," "No Poll Tax," "No Whipping of Militiamen," "No Direct Taxation without Previous Requisition." The swirl of leaflets was accompanied by furious oratory against a federal tax system said to have been proposed by Robert Morris and supported by the French minister. The frightened voters didn't know that Mercer was talking about a letter Morris had written during the Revolution, on state taxes for war purposes.[10]

Madison's letter to Carroll was sent through Washington and stirred him to a similar appeal to Thomas Johnson, his Potomac Canal partner. Adjournment of the Maryland convention would have such an effect on Virginia that it would be tantamount to rejection of the Constitution. Mercer, with a dunned debtor's love for Washington, spread a report that Johnson resented this "officiousness." Be that so or not, McHenry reacted strongly to Madison's warning, asked Washington for his opinion of it, and helped to kill the postponement. Informing Madison of Maryland's "sixty-odd to twelve" ratification, Washington described a debate shortened by the total silence of the affirmative:

"Mr. Chase, it is said, made a display of all his eloquence. Mr. Mercer discharged his whole artillery of inflammable matter; and Mr. Martin did something, I know not what, presume with vehemence, but no converts were made, no, not one. So business after a very short session ended; and if I mistake not will render yours less tiresome."[11]

On a straight yes or no, Maryland was made safe by the overwhelming defeat (outside of Ann Arundel) of the Chase-Mercer-Martin paper-money faction. After the ratification a committee majority offered to indorse clarifying amendments on civil rights. The minority insisted so strongly on its own defeated propositions that all were dropped. The antis rushed into print with a charge that they had been double-crossed—the majority had violated the pledge through which ratification was secured. This charge fooled nobody in Maryland, since the Antifederalists had voted against ratification. The purpose, a majority spokesman affirmed, was to mislead Virginia. A formal defense of the convention was rushed to Madison, while the antis flooded their neighbor state with leaflet accusations. Thus the Maryland struggle was a prologue to the one across the Potomac.[12]

Through the flowering season of the redbud which he loved so much, and on through the warmth of May, Madison recouped his strength by long walks and horseback rides. He applied himself also to two vital tasks—winning Governor Randolph and combating the hostility in Kentucky. "The governor is so temperate in his opposition and goes so far with the friends of the Constitution," he wrote to Jefferson, "that he cannot properly be classed with its enemies." To win him Madison employed a three-point formula. Agree with him wherever possible. In answering his objections, try to make him think the answers are his own. Play on his deep distrust of Patrick Henry.

After setting him right on minor points, Madison welcomed

Randolph's observation that only a coalition of high and low Federalists could save the Constitution. Welcomed it, and added that recommendatory amendments were the only ground for coalition. A conditional ratification or second convention ran contrary to the dictates of prudence and safety. If anything did come of such a move, it would be "more remote from your ideas" (not *my* ideas, but *yours*) than the present plan.

Randolph had been first to suggest a second convention, but now Madison was able to attack it as Henry's proposition. The opening was wide, for Henry had written to Randolph that he would keep on opposing the Constitution if only *one half* of one state should be against it. That is, if twelve states ratified, he would try to take southern Virginia out of the Union, or (as some reports put it) seek to carry the state into a Southern confederacy even though the Northern Neck should break away and enter Maryland. This threat enabled Madison to bring his warning to a climax. Secret plotters of disunion would carry on by demanding changes popular in some places but inadmissible in others:

"Every danger of this sort might be justly dreaded from such men as this state and New York only could furnish, playing for such a purpose into each other's hands. The declaration of H——y, mentioned in your letter, is a proof to me that desperate measures will be his game. If report does not more than usually exaggerate, Mason also is ripening fast for going every length."

Randolph in reply reserved his decision, but the thoughts Madison planted came right back with the governor's label on them:

"Two objections have always struck me as deserving consideration on the subject of previous amendments: one, that under their cover, a higher game might be played; the other, that the hope of obtaining them might be frustrated by the assent of too many states. The former I dread more and more daily, not knowing how far the schemes of those who *externally* patronize them may internally *extend*."[13]

Kentucky presented Madison with a tougher problem. George Nicholas planned to move there, so he was given elaborate evi-

Modern Bust of Madison in the New York University Hall of Fame.
By Charles Keck, 1929

CONGRESS HALL. BY BIRCH, 1799

dence that establishment of the new government would heighten the obstacles to sacrifice of Mississippi navigation. Highest of all would be the conversion of national impotence into national power in dealing with Spain:

"The present Congress if ever so well inspired is wholly and notoriously incompetent to this task. Their successors, if the new government take place, will be able to hold a language which no nation having possessions in America will think it prudent to disregard."[14]

In the rest of the state, Madison found the Northern Neck, Shenandoah Valley and Alleghany country to be federal. South of the James River the antis had control. The intermediate district was checkered. The greater abilities now seemed to be on the federal side—Pendleton, Wythe, Blair, Innes, Marshall, the Nicholas brothers, White, Stuart, young Bushrod Washington, possibly Monroe. Opposed to them: Henry, Mason, Harrison, Grayson, Tyler, Meriwether Smith, Ronald, Bland, Cabell. Luckily R. H. Lee had been beaten.[15]

The eyes of the continent were on Madison and Patrick Henry as the opening day approached. "We consider you as the main pillar of the business," the Virginian President of Congress wrote to the former. Appraising the other: "Henry is weighty and powerful but too interested—Mason too passionate—the Governor by nature too timid and undecided—Grayson too blustering."[16]

What did he mean by "too interested"? Henry is reported to have said that he refused to attend the Federal Convention because he "smelt a rat"—a statement usually construed to mean that he saw a conspiracy against the liberties of the people. What he certainly foresaw was the loss of the tax and debt moratoria by which he maintained his political supremacy. Outside of this he stood with the big planters and the "courthouse crowd"—an advocate of church establishment, an opponent of court or code reform, a confiscator of British lands and debts. It was not in relation to these, however, that known self-interest impaired his influence. Ever since Foreign Secretary Jay caved in to Gardoqui, Henry had been ridden with fear that the federal government would give up the river and thus damage or lose the Southwest. His most ambitious venture there, the Virginia-Yazoo Company, was to be launched some months later. His known attitude, however, was a foretaste of what he wrote to a Georgian when transfer of Creek Indian lands from state to nation was proposed in 1790:

"Our common interests as purchasers of western land, and also as American citizens, seems to be attacked by the proceedings of the general government—and I am not of a disposition to bow down before the threat of power, or the usurpations of those who from public servants are about to make themselves considered in another character."

The traits which made Henry powerful made him parochial. With independence achieved, self-interest was the only force strong enough to draw him beyond his state. Distrusting, in the realm of that self-interest, both the old and the projected federal governments, he was led an unknown distance along the road to a Southern confederacy. In sharp contrast, Madison's outlook was fundamentally national and totally unselfish. John Marshall, who was a delegate to the 1788 convention, is reputed to have said that of all the public men with whom he was acquainted, Henry had the greatest power to persuade, Madison to convince. On another occasion he combined these attributes:

"Eloquence has been defined to be the art of persuasion. If it includes persuasion by convincing, Mr. Madison was the most eloquent man I ever heard."[17]

The oratorical magic of voice, phrase and person cast a spell, temporary or permanent, over those who listened to Patrick Henry. Madison enjoyed no such gloss. To persuade, he had to convince by plain words. But unadorned logic, to convince the unwilling or the hesitant, had to be free of the slightest shadow of self-interest.

So David and Goliath, who had met often and indecisively in the Virginia Assembly, moved once more to the battlefield—the latter laden with the heaviest weapons of forensic war, the former carrying a verbal slingshot, light, plain, tough and flexible.

# CHAPTER XVI

## DAVID AND GOLIATH

ARRIVING in Richmond on Monday evening, June 2, Madison found to his surprise that a Virginia state gathering had made a quorum on the day it was supposed to. The accompanying news was pleasing. Edmund Pendleton, perennial chairman of conventions, had been chosen again, unanimously. The Henry-Mason forces did not want to start off with a visible defeat.

Richmond was overflowing with horses, men and boys. Farmers, lawyers, preachers, college students—so many rode in that the convention adjourned to the big New Academy on Shockoe Hill, just built by Frenchmen to house an international institute of arts and sciences.[1]

Next day, Mason informed the delegates that the curse of divine vengeance would be small compared with that which would smite them if they failed to discuss the whole Constitution, clause by clause, before propounding any question on it. John Tyler moved also that discussions be in committee of the whole.[2]

Madison at once concurred. He knew what they were aiming at—to prevent a repetition of the tactics in Maryland, where the majority confined the debate to general principles and forced an early vote. But such a course would be fatal in a seesaw convention, where a few men had to be won or held by placing facts against fears. The Antifederalists virtually commanded Madison to proceed in line with his greatest talent. Patrick Henry, on the contrary, needed to dwell on general principles or pick out scattered details to synthesize their terrors. So did Mason. They had hooked themselves and could tear loose only by violating their own rule.

Hardly less useful to the Federalists was the decision to hold all discussions in committee of the whole. That set up a parliamentary bar to any sudden decision under the spell of Henry's oratory. In addition, it placed the convention chairman on the floor, thus adding him to the federal team. Scarce had Pendleton called friendly, impartial George Wythe to the committee rostrum before the effect of the action became manifest. Patrick Henry moved a reading of all resolutions bearing on the Annapolis and Philadelphia conventions. Rising on his crutches, Pendleton said the order given them by the people was to decide whether the new system was a proper one, not whether the framers of it exceeded their powers. Henry withdrew his motion.

To start things off, on June 4 the convention took up the preamble and the first two sections of Article I, which deal with the House of Representatives. George Nicholas opened, but his speech might as well have been credited to Madison. It was a rewording of *The Federalist* 52 and 53. Patrick Henry made his usual cautious entry. His habit, pointed out by the admiring Grigsby, was to learn the facts in a controversy by listening, then turn loose his oratory. At this time he merely stirred two or three little whirlpools. A year before, the minds of citizens were at perfect repose. Now they were uneasy and disquieted. Whence had arisen this fearful jeopardy? To prove that it came from the Constitution, he picked three words out of the preamble and asked who authorized them. Who authorized the Philadelphia Convention to speak the language of "We the people" instead of "We the states"? The purpose was plain, to form a great consolidated government instead of a confederation.

Governor Randolph took the floor. Madison expected him to support the Constitution; others waited to hear him condemn it. He defended his refusal to sign and repeated his desire for amendments, but finally (as Madison reported to Washington) threw himself fully into the federal scale. His argument against amendments before ratification was almost a composite of Madison's letters weaning him from the opposite view. Randolph really took his stand when he suppressed a letter from Governor Clinton to him on joint action to secure a second general convention. But since the New York governor was known as a disunionist, it is doubtful if his advice would have turned any Virginia delegates who could not be swayed by Patrick Henry.

Elderly George Mason next took the floor. Ignoring his own

clause-by-clause rule, he made a long and slashing attack upon the federal taxing power. By destroying the concurrent taxing power of the states, it would lead to a consolidated government. This brought Madison up with a denial that consolidation would ensue. Under the rules of the convention, he would reply to Mason on direct taxes when they reached that subject. The delegate from Orange did not find the outlook too bad when he wrote to Washington that evening:

"Henry and Mason made a lame figure and appeared to take different and awkward ground. The Federalists are a good deal elated by the existing prospect. I dare not however speak with certainty as to the decision. Kentucky has been extremely tainted, is supposed to be generally adverse, and every piece of address is going on privately to work on the local interests and prejudices of that and other quarters."

Antifederal William Grayson, writing to a New England friend, lamented the unlucky loss of Randolph and the bad news that South Carolina had ratified. But he did not despond. "Kentucky is with us and if we can get over the four counties which lie on the Ohio between the Pennsylvania line and Big Sandy Creek, the day is our own."[3]

It was useless to discuss specific clauses until Henry had been answered. Pendleton and Henry Lee assumed that task next morning. If the public mind was at ease a year earlier, it was because national miseries had put the people in a stupor. "We the people" was proper language in a country where only the people have a right to form government. These speeches set the stage nicely for Henry. Ordinarily a half-hour orator, he held the floor all day, delivering what was probably the longest and most powerful address of his life.

The fate of America hung on that poor little expression, "We the people." By this alarming transition to a consolidated government, rights and privileges were endangered and the sovereignty of the states would be relinquished. "The rights of conscience, trial by jury, liberty of the press, all your communities and franchises, all pretensions to human rights and privileges, are rendered

insecure, if not lost, by this change." He repeated the threat of
secession by southern Virginia:

"It is said eight states have adopted this plan. I declare that if
twelve states and a half had adopted it, I would with manly firmness and in spite of an erring world reject it."

Against sedition, said Henry, the language of the Constitution
was clear and unequivocal, but when it spoke of the privileges of
citizens there was "an ambiguity, sir, a fatal ambiguity." Jury
trial in civil cases was gone—destroyed by the fact that it was
made mandatory in criminal cases. "Our glorious forefathers of
Great Britain made liberty the foundation of everything." Now
America was to become an empire, not on the foundation of liberty
but with the ropes and chains of consolidation. There was said to
be an easy way of getting amendments. Either those who said so
were mad, or he was. Virginia was no longer to be under a
Virginian but under an American government. Should the people
of Virginia wish to alter it, could they do so? A despicable
minority at the extremity of the United States could prevent it.

He went on to assail the new taxing power, picturing federal
sheriffs outdoing the barbarous ravages of those unfeeling bloodsuckers, the state sheriffs. (An echo of appeals for postponement
of state taxes.) Finally, this horribly frightful new government
had an awful squinting toward monarchy. Rules could be imposed on a king, but let the President once get in the field with
his army and it would puzzle any American to get his neck from
under the galling yoke. "The army will salute him monarch;
your militia will . . . fight against you, and . . . what will then
become of you and your rights?"

Following this, Henry rose to such oratorical heights that the
shorthand stenographer (a Federalist) was paralyzed and could
say only that he "strongly and pathetically expatiated on the probability of the President's enslaving America, and the horrid consequences that must result." Stay out, adjured the orator, and
notify the ratifying states of Virginia's unyielding demand for
prior amendments. The adopting states would doubtless yield, but
what would be the consequence if they were disunited? "I speak

the language of thousands. But, sir, I mean not to breathe the spirit nor utter the language of secession."

Here was a perfect repetition of the finale in his Stamp Act treason speech. Stories have come down in the Henry mythology of men actually feeling of their wrists to find whether there were iron rivets on them.[4] If the federal leaders were alarmed, they were also disgusted. "Mr. Chairman," said Governor Randolph, "if we go on in this irregular manner, contrary to our resolution, instead of three or six weeks it will take us six months to decide this question."

Randolph, Madison and Nicholas, the three big guns of federalism, devoted all of June 6 to answering Henry. Every distortion had to be set right. Randolph, big, handsome, eloquent, was able to follow him without a painful contrast of talents. The house could be put in a mood for Madison's calm reasoning, with Nicholas to make a hard-punching finish.

Challenging the portrayal of federal iniquity and state innocence, the governor recited a string of Virginia evils which every listener must recognize as a catalogue of Henry's legislative triumphs. Justice was strangled in the courts. Debts were uncollectible. In violation of the state constitution, the legislature had passed a bill of attainder against Josiah Phillips, accused of war crimes. "Was this arbitrary deprivation of life, the dearest gift of God to man, consistent with the genius of a republican government?" No need to remind this audience that Henry, as governor, had presented the Phillips case to the legislature, while Randolph, as attorney general, refused to act under the bill of attainder but convicted and executed the outlaw through a jury trial for robbery.

Madison, never strong-voiced, was doubly handicapped by the size of the convention and the packing in of hundreds of spectators. Grigsby gives an account of his manner, derived from men who observed him in the Virginia Assembly:

"He always rose to speak as if with a view of expressing some thought that had casually occurred to him, with his hat in his hand and with his notes in his hat; and the warmest excitement of debate was visible in him only by a more or less rapid and forward seesaw motion of his body."⁵

The Constitution, Madison said, should be examined through calm and rational investigation. It gave him pain to hear gentlemen distorting the natural construction of language, for it was sufficient if any human production could stand a fair discussion. He rebutted Henry's statement that loss of liberty usually resulted from the tyranny of rulers. Far more often, despotism was produced by the turbulence, violence and abuse of power by the majority trampling on the rights of the minority. He could not find Mr. Henry's usual consistency in his assertion that the people of the country had been safe, tranquil and at perfect repose. Why were deputies sent to the general convention? Why did complaints of national and individual distresses echo and re-echo throughout the continent? There was glaring inconsistency in the argument that it was too difficult to amend the Constitution. He argues for amendments by a bare majority, Madison commented, at the same time that he rejects any alteration in the inadequate, unsafe and pernicious Confederation without the absolute unanimity of all the states.

Against the pictured terror of a federal despotism protected by exclusive control of the ten-mile-square seat of its government, Madison asked what would happen if the safety of the Union were subjected to the control of some particular state. Had people forgotten the disgraceful insult which Congress received in Philadelphia in 1783?⁶ Was the power to raise a regular army a threat to liberty? If so, it was a lesser hazard than presenting a spectacle of weakness to powerful and avaricious nations. He challenged Henry's citation of the Swiss Confederation as a model for American imitation. Their government, at least in some cantons, formed one of the vilest aristocracies that ever was instituted.

Confining himself to the general nature of the new government, Madison explained it as he had in *The Federalist,* partly consolidated, partly federal, and emphasized that its legislative powers were defined and limited. Henry, he said, had satirized with peculiar acrimony the powers given to the general government. If those powers were necessary, the choice was to grant them or let the Union be dissolved. Consider the one most objected to— direct taxation. It would only be recurred to for great purposes. But could a war be carried on without it?

Replying to Mason, Madison undertook to prove that partial consolidation of government could not destroy the states. With the Senate elected by state legislatures and the House elected by the electors of state legislatures, there was no possibility that federal lawmakers would forget who chose them. Closing, he made a forecast contrary to his wishes but soothing to the opposition:

"I wish this government may answer the expectation of its friends, and foil the apprehension of its enemies. I hope the patriotism of the people will continue, and be a sufficient guard to their liberties. I believe its tendency will be that the state governments will counteract the general interest and ultimately prevail."

The final speaker of the trio, George Nicholas, was one of the most formidable debaters in Virginia. Short and grotesquely fat, blunt of speech and keen of wit, he could be more easily dealt with by cartoonists than by forensic adversaries. "A friend told me," Grigsby writes, "that he once saw Mr. Madison laugh till the tears came into his eyes at a caricature of George Nicholas, which represented him 'as a plum pudding with legs to it.' "[7] Nicholas ridiculed Henry's contention that taxation by a Congress in which Virginia had a minority voice would be taxation without consent. As well say that the state legislature had no right to impose taxes on a county if its representatives voted against them. He told Henry plainly that if Virginia looked to itself alone for security the Northern Neck would see greater security in annexation to Maryland. Bushrod Washington, writing to Uncle George, glowed with enthusiasm over all three speakers. But when it came to results, he spoke only of the quiet reasoner who came between the two powerful orators:

"Mr. Madison followed with such force and reasoning and a display of such irresistible truths that opposition seemed to have quitted the field. However, I am not so sanguine as to trust appearances or even to flatter myself that he made many converts. A few I have been confidently informed he did influence who were decidedly in the opposition."[8]

A swing of five votes, all polls indicated, would decide the result. It may have been decided by that speech. Holding back his detailed defense of the new government till Henry should complete his attack, Madison next day assailed the Confederation. From ancient and modern confederacies he turned to American experience. The wanton military seizures during the Revolution were due to inability to secure a regular revenue. The people tolerated such evils when the spirit of liberty overruled all else, but never would submit to them in peacetime. The country's foremost citizen had testified to the need of change when he laid down his military leadership, but "I did not introduce that great name to bias any gentleman here."

Foreign nations, Madison declared, were unwilling to form treaties which individual states would violate at pleasure. The United States had defaulted on its debts to a generous French ally. In the twelve months just past, the states had paid the miserable sum of $276,641 to meet all national expenses. "Suggestions and strong assertions dissipate before these facts." He cut off his speech with the abrupt remark that he would no longer fatigue the committee but would resume the subject as early as he could. For the next few days he was in bed with a "bilious indisposition."

Henry's bile was misbehaving too. Stung by citation of the Phillips attainder, he answered that the attainted man was not a Socrates. A pirate, an outlaw or a common enemy to all mankind could be put to death at any time without those beautiful legal ceremonies pointed out by the criminal laws. He then belabored the Constitution for its omission of a federal bill of rights.

Henry scoffed at the idea of danger to Virginia if she stood alone. He told of the immense sums which would be spent for the splendid maintenance of President and Congress while they were reducing independent citizens to abject slavery. Other speakers had called direct taxation the soul or the lungs of government.

Cried Patrick: "Must I give my soul—my lungs, to Congress?" Madison's portrayal of nationwide discontent was treated as a class appeal and smeared with a hated phrase: "The middle and lower ranks of people have not those illuminated ideas which *the well-born* are so happily possessed of."

The fight really got under way when the antifederal leader began bidding for Kentucky. Western territory, he said, was safe under the Confederation because it took nine states to make a treaty. Seven states in Congress had been willing to give up the Mississippi. Adopt the new Constitution and the navigation would be lost. Henry ridiculed the stir over paper money. That mighty federal convention had no business to deal with it, yet——

"I acknowledge that paper money would be the bane of this country. I detest it. Nothing can justify a people in resorting to it, but extreme necessity. It is at rest, however, in this commonwealth. It is no longer solicited or advocated."

One can only marvel at the nerve with which Henry uttered these words in a convention whose every delegate knew that he had attempted to ride to power on paper money in 1787, and dropped it barely in time to escape public discomfiture.[9] His next statement was on a par: "If we cannot be trusted with the private contracts of the citizens we must be depraved indeed." That from Virginia's chief destroyer of contracts of debt.

Once more Henry rejected the thought of disunion, but stirred his listeners to welcome it. Separate confederacies were evils never to be thought of till a people were driven by necessity. But compared with a consolidated government small confederacies were little evils. Virginia and North Carolina were despised, but "they could exist separated from the rest of America." He challenged the Madison thesis that republican government can exist over an extensive territory if it is judiciously organized and limited in powers. "Whoever will be bold to say that a continent can be governed by that system contradicts all the experience of the world." The new system would fail because the President, senators and representatives were to be the choice of the people. There were no checks founded on the irresistible stimulus of self-love, which induced the British House of Lords to protect the people from the king and the king from the Commons.

"Here is a consideration which prevails in my mind [thus spoke Patrick Henry] to pronounce the British government superior in this respect to any government that ever was in any country. Compare this with your congressional checks. . . . If you depend on your President's and senator's patriotism, you are gone."

Henry directed his withering sarcasm against Madison's description of a partly national, partly federal government. We could, if we chose, be deceived by this anatomical curiosity in which the brain is national, the stamina federal, this limb national, that limb federal—but what it really signified was that a great consolidated government would be pressing on the necks of the people. He pictured the simple and honest planter dragged hundreds of miles to a federal court, to be tried for treason if he resisted the attacks of federal tax collectors upon his person or property. Federal forts and garrisons would be planted in the state, with the legislature powerless to prevent the most dangerous insults to the people. There must be, Henry agreed, national credit and a national treasury in case of war. But did ever a republic fail to use its utmost resources when war was necessary? Under this plan Congress could both declare war and carry it on, "and levy your money as long as you have a shilling to pay."

Friends, we may assume, brought to Madison's sickroom an account of Light-Horse Harry Lee's answering condemnation of appeals to passion and fear. Jabbing at "that favorite system of the gentleman—king, lords and commons"—he challenged Henry to meet the issues with solid argument instead of those bolts which he had so peculiar a dexterity at discharging.

"Most feelingly does he dwell on the imaginary dangers of this pretended consolidation. I did suppose that an honorable gentleman whom I do not now see [Mr. Madison] had placed this in such a clear light that every man would have been satisfied with it."

The absentee heard too of Randolph's violent reaction to Henry's remarks. "I disdain his aspersions and his insinuations," cried the Governor, ". . . and if our friendship must fall—let it fall, like Lucifer, never to rise again." The recorded text of Henry's speech contains nothing offensive, but his personal assaults were delivered in mocking gesture and derisive intonation. The governor was more effective when he took up Henry's defense of the bill of attainder against Josiah Phillips:

"Because he was not a Socrates, is he to be attainted at pleasure? ... We all agree that he was an abandoned man. But if you can prepare a bill to attaint a man, and pass it through both houses in an instant, I ask you, who is safe?"

Henry's defense of the Phillips attainder, made worse by his Socrates remark, virtually destroyed the bill-of-rights issue as an argument against ratification. The fate of the Constitution turned on the power of direct taxation and navigation of the Mississippi. That was plain to Madison when, "extremely feeble," he returned to convention activity on June 11.[10] On the preceding day Monroe delivered a desultory speech against the Constitution and John Marshall spoke powerfully in its behalf. His name at this time carried no weight, but his arguments did. Repeatedly he used Henry's own position to knock down his case—hammering home the conflict between democratic maxims and the Phillips attainder, translating his "many eulogiums of the British constitution" into unpleasant American analogies (life terms for senators, the President can do no wrong), and demonstrating that denial of the need for direct taxes in peacetime was an admission of their propriety in war. Nicholas followed with the arguments Madison had furnished him a month earlier, to prove that the new government would defend the Mississippi more effectively than the old.

Madison on his return entreated the convention to steer away from vague discourses and sports of fancy. Let us stay in order, he urged, and confine ourselves to the clause under consideration— the same one that had been before them, but ignored, from the beginning. He then devoted his entire time to direct taxes, which had been treated, over his protest, as relevant to the pending clause.

The notes Madison used have been preserved.[11] They show that his speech was completely organized in advance, with single words or phrases set down as the basis of extended extemporaneous argument, and so newly prepared that they took account of Monroe's remarks the afternoon before.

The power of direct taxation, Madison undertook to prove, was necessary, practicable, safe and economical. Without it in time of war, regular troops could not be raised, militia must be relied on, with risk of national annihilation. He then forecast with uncanny accuracy the conditions which soon developed and plagued America for twenty years. France and Great Britain would shortly be at war again, with the United States a neutral nation.

"What is the situation of America? She is remote from Europe and ought not to engage in her politics or wars. The American vessels, if they can do it with advantage, may carry on the commerce of the contending nations. It is a source of wealth which we ought not to deny to our citizens. But, sir, is there not infinite danger, that in despite of all our caution we shall be drawn into the war? If American vessels have French property on board, Great Britain will seize them."

The choice then would be to give up neutral trade or go to war. The only preventive was to build up national strength before this should occur.

"A neutral nation ought to be respectable, or else it will be insulted and attacked. America in her present impotent situation would ... be insulted in our own ports and our vessels seized. But if we be in a respectable situation—if it be known that our government can command the whole resources of the Union, we shall be suffered to enjoy the great advantages of carrying on the commerce of the nations at war, for none of them would be willing to add us to the number of their enemies."

Taking up the system of requisitions which Henry eulogized, the federal leader gave many reasons why it never could succeed. As for federal taxes, if all expenses were thrown on commerce the burden would be heaviest on the South, which had the greatest dependence on foreign goods. The burden would increase as development of manufactures cut down imports in the North. Was it safe to give Congress power to levy taxes? Large electoral districts, he answered, were a protection against corruption. The people were devoted to their state governments and would not allow them to be swallowed up. Even in the early part of the Revolution, when Congress was the idol of America, the people were still attached to the states. Afterward they became wholly so, and still would be, were it not for the alarming situation of America.

"At one period of congressional history, they [Congress] had the power to trample on the states. When they had that fund of paper money in their hands [from 1775 to 1779], and could carry on all their measures without any dependence on the states, was there any disposition to debase the state governments?"

As in *The Federalist,* Madison argued that the powers of the general government were few and external in their objects, while the state powers related immediately to the prosperity of the people. The power of taxation was not really new; it was changed. "Now they tax states, and by this plan they will tax individuals"— one system ineffective, the other adequate to its purpose.

In closing he made one more appeal for a clause-by-clause advance. By sticking to it they could finish better in one week than in a month.[12] Henry and Mason were now thoroughly sick of their own rule, which allowed Madison to box up the Constitution a section at a time. They protested that so important a subject must be argued at large. Mason then borrowed a Maryland canard by reading Robert Morris' ancient letter advocating direct state taxes for federal purposes. Corruption would result from a Congress chosen "from the great, the wealthy—the *well-born*—the *well-born* . . . that flattering idea . . . lately imported from the ports of Great Britain." More dangerous was Mason's appeal to delegates from beyond the Blue Ridge. Adopt the Constitution without amendments and 20,000 families would be ousted by the Indiana Company. The story in circulation was that the clause on private contracts would compel Virginia to recognize a colonial grant outlawed by the legislature years earlier. The delegates at whom this was aimed could swing the convention.

Pendleton protested the setting apart, by Henry, of middling and lower classes of men. He was "a friend to the equal liberty of all men, from the palace to the cottage," distinguishing only between the good and the bad. Why drag in the whims of writers—the distinction of *well born* from others? "I consider every man *well born* who comes into the world with an intelligent mind and with all his parts perfect."

Madison analyzed Grayson's argument for requisitions, with direct taxes laid as a penalty if they failed. If requisitions were efficacious the people would give up the same amount as if taxed directly. If not efficacious, why resort to them at all? Grayson had called direct taxation chimerical. Would it be less so, used as a penalty? As to an assertion that the people would resist collectors, just as the states disregarded requisitions: "This goes against all government. It is as much as to urge that there should be no legislature." He pleaded for effectual measures to comply with solemn engagements for payment of the public debt.

A smoldering controversy over absent Virginians now burst into flame. To offset Washington's approval, at which Madison had hinted, Henry said he had information as to Jefferson: "This illustrious citizen advises you to reject this government till it be amended. His sentiments coincide entirely with ours." Pendleton protested against invoking the opinion of any private individual, but particularly when his views were presented inaccurately. From the very letter on which Henry's assertion was based, he read Jefferson's wish that the first nine conventions accept the Constitution, giving effect to the great and important good in it, and that the four others refuse to accede till amendments were secured. Henry swung to a technicality. "What is the substantial part of his counsel? It is, sir, that four states should *reject*." Gentlemen had insisted, when he denied it, that New Hampshire would ratify. If Virginia did likewise where would four states be found to reject?

This brought Madison in with a fresh allusion to Washington. "If the opinion of an important character were to weigh on this occasion, could we not adduce a character equally great on our side?" Protesting against reliance on the opinion of a citizen beyond the Atlantic, he nevertheless expressed his belief that if Jefferson were on the floor he would be for the adoption of the Constitution. Personal delicacy forbade a disclosure of what the illustrious citizen had written to him, but he would venture to assert that Jefferson approved the federal taxing power and was captivated with the equality of suffrage in the Senate, which Henry called the rotten part of the Constitution. No more was said about the minister to France, who soon afterward dropped his 9-4 idea, preferring later amendments, and offered his "hearty prayers" for universal ratification.[13]

Turning to the Mississippi, Madison denied that seven states in Congress were disposed to surrender its navigation. New Jersey, Pennsylvania and five Southern states were united in its defense. The North had defended it in 1780 when the South was impelled by a war crisis to give it up. (A reminder that a Virginia legislature ruled by Patrick Henry had forced Madison to drop his fight for the river in Congress.) Henry came back with the remark that he did not want to reflect on any private character, but he would like to have the transactions of Congress placed before the convention by past and present members of that body—a bid to Monroe and Grayson to violate the congressional rule of secrecy on foreign affairs.

Taking this as a slap at himself, Madison declared "that if the honorable gentleman thought that *he* had given an incorrect account of the transactions relative to the Mississippi, he would, on a thorough and complete investigation, find himself mistaken." He had always opposed the effort to give up the river and had no objection to having every light thrown on the subject. Monroe then told of Foreign Secretary Jay's proposal to surrender navigation for twenty-five or thirty years in exchange for a treaty of commerce. Grayson blamed this on New England's desire for a Spanish market for fish.

The convention was now at a crisis. Grayson had said nothing of the maneuvers by which Madison, after Monroe left Congress, discomfited Jay and wrecked the treaty beyond repair. Madison declared it to be dead, but cited the rule of secrecy. Seven states, he conceded, had once been ready to make a temporary cession, to avert a military coalition, but New Jersey delegates were now instructed on the other side. The real question was not whether the old Congress stood ready to defend the river, but whether the new Constitution would make it more or less secure. Neither government, in his opinion, had constitutional power to relinquish what belonged to the United States under the law of nations, though either might be forced to do so under the emergencies of war. Under the old charter, nine states in Congress could give it up. Under the new one, with a full Senate present, it would take nine states and the President, acting independently. As to the claim that ten senators could ratify a surrender, that assumed that all the Southern members would be absent. If ten senators could make a treaty, ten could prevent one. A weak system produced the project of temporary abandonment. A strong system would remove the inducement.

It was now or never with Patrick Henry and he turned on his eloquence. He was not merely "scuffling for Kentucky votes," as charged. He was defending both Virginia and Kentucky against a fatal policy which would throw their western brethren into the arms of Spain. The new Congress would offer no security because its members could not be recalled. "If you should see the Spanish ambassador bribing one of your senators with gold, can you punish him?" He challenged Madison's belief that the President would protect the West because of his direct responsibility to the people. "Sir, the President as distinguished from the Senate is nothing. They will combine and be as one." Every danger, Madison had said, must be judged by the rules of proportion, and he saw greater safety in President, Senate and House than in a one-house Congress. Henry dismissed this with a wave of his hand—an argument "I would not give a single pin for." As to the assurance that the project would not be revived in Congress, he would admit that the honorable gentleman could calculate as to future events, but not to that extent. A strong government, Henry argued finally, was not necessary to defense of sovereignty over the Mississippi. That was covered by the territorial guarantee of the treaty of 1778. He would lean on the strong arms of France, sustaining the present despised system, rather than trust to American strength, which might be employed to sacrifice it.[14]

If there was a French guarantee, George Nicholas asked, why had France not already acted on it? The American people "want a government which will force from Spain the navigation of that river." Kentucky could expect nothing from one state alone. Support and succor could come only from a government strong enough to command the resources of the Union.

Francis Corbin, like Nicholas, sustained Madison's contention that the House of Representatives would have an influence on treaties, especially of commerce. At this point the stenographer reported: "Here a storm arose, which was so violent as to compel Mr. Corbin to desist, and the committee to rise." On the following morning, June 14, Corbin moved that they adhere to the clause-by-clause rule, and the delegates agreed. In twelve days they had not moved beyond the two sections taken up at the outset. But the general issue of the Constitution had been threshed out at tremendous length and the outcome was unpredictable.

# CHAPTER XVII

## VICTORY IN VIRGINIA

No UNDUE optimism exuded from Madison as he reported to Washington on June 13. Appearances had become less favorable. Progress was slow and the delay was used to work on the local prejudices of particular sets of members.

"British debts, the Indiana claim and the Mississippi are the principal topics of private discussion and intrigue, as well as of public declamation."

Kentucky opposition, if solid, might be fatal, and the whole business was "in the most ticklish state that can be imagined." Antifederal Theodorick Bland recorded each side boasting of a majority running from three to eight.[1]

With the clause-by-clause rule enforced, the convention followed a new pattern. Opponents asked sensible questions, though Henry answered his own and challenged Madison to answer the answers. Some explanations were accepted without cavil. Others drew heavy fire, which brought Nicholas, Randolph, Marshall and Corbin to Madison's support.

Why did Congress have control over the times, places and manner of electing representatives? To prevent the dissolution of the general government, make elections uniform, insure equal representation of different parts of a state and protect the right of suffrage. Why did Congress have power to determine its own pay? Compensation, Madison agreed, ought to be fixed in the Constitution, but the diminishing value of all money made this impossible. It could not be left to state legislatures (as Henry wished) because that would enable the states to dominate or destroy the general government. However, Congress could not overpay itself without arousing universal indignation in the electorate. This swung Tyler and Grayson onto the opposite tack: Congress would convert the government into an aristocracy by fixing salaries so low that none but the rich could afford to serve. And who,

Madison came back, were to choose these aristocrats? "The rich? No, sir, the people." If one set of congressmen sought to give the rich a monopoly, another set would be put in to change the law.[2]

A storm came when Madison began to explain the power of Congress over the militia. Mason broke in with a denunciation of virtually every phase of federal control. By violating the Philadelphia secrecy agreement, Madison could have disclosed that Mason proposed a stronger militia clause.[3] Instead he relied on analysis. Suppose, as Mason wished, Congress could order a state's militia only into a contiguous state. The force available to repel an invasion would depend on the number of states contiguous to the invaded one. What if the enemy came through Georgia or New Hampshire?

Madison was asked whether use of the militia to execute the laws meant no enforcement through civil officers. His reply that military action was to be a last resort brought Henry to his feet with a twisting paraphrase. The civil power *might* act instead of the militia. So, it was the spirit of the Constitution that laws be enforced by military coercion. The civil power was not to be employed at all. Also, the strength of the state militia rested on a supposition that Congress would do its duty in organizing it. "Pardon me, if I am too jealous and suspicious to confide in this remote possibility." He paid another eulogy to his now beloved motherland:

"But how natural it is, when comparing deformities to beauty, to be struck with the superiority of the British government to that system.... Your President ... is but transient, and he will promote as much as possible his own private interests. . . . The King of England has a more permanent interest.... The sword and purse are not united in that government in the same hands, as in this system. Does not infinite security result from such a separation?"

Nicholas and Madison counterattacked on the same ground—a maxim against combining sword and purse in the same department was being treated as an argument against having them both in the same government. Such a division never had been and never could be. Said Madison:

"The means ought to be commensurate to the end. The end is general protection. This cannot be effected without a general power to use the strength of the Union."

Henry's rejoinder was swift:

"Mr. Chairman, it is now confessed that this is a national [*i.e.*, a consolidated] government. . . . Every essential requisite must be in Congress. . . . The means, says the gentleman, must be commensurate to the end. How does this apply? All things in common are left with this government. There being an infinitude in the government, there must be an infinitude of means to carry it on."[4]

Leaving it to Henry Lee to denounce Henry for "putting words into our mouths which we never uttered," Madison replied along another line:

"The honorable member expresses surprise . . . that I would risk the happiness of my country on an experiment. What is the situation of this country at this moment? Is it not rapidly approaching to anarchy? . . . Experiments must be made, and in that form . . . most to the interest of our country."

Over the week end, Henry came up with new and old alarms. Congress could billet armies on the public, to tyrannize, oppress and crush. Under the power to quell riots, the militia might be authorized to fire on a dozen men who failed to disperse. "It is a government of force, and the genius of despotism expressly."

Against this appeal to fear and ancient injuries, Madison had only quiet logic to offer. If there was any object which the general government ought to command, it was the national forces. The militia was the safest force. But was it wise to inform unfriendly nations that if they were to fall upon us, we should have no other defense? He agreed that a government of force was being set up. There never was a government without force. But the resort to the militia instead of a standing army, to execute resisted laws, proved that it was not a government of military force. Virginia used the militia to suppress smuggling fleets and deal with riots.

Why should not Congress do so too? As to ignominious punishment of the militia by Congress, Virginia herself inflicted punishments which were not lawful in any state north of Maryland. If any change was made by federal law, it would soften their rigor.

Henry disagreed with Madison's assertion that the states, as well as Congress, could use the militia to quell riots, etc. A *specific* federal power to call out the militia for these purposes must be an *exclusive* power. Concurrent jurisdiction was a political monster of absurdity. Madison proceeded to dissect this. The military power had to be in Congress, or in the states, or be concurrent. If division was a political monster and congressional control was oppressive, was all power to be vested in the states? If so, where was the provision for general defense? If America should be attacked, the states would fall successively, for each would retain its own militia for its own defense. He protested against nonsensical objections. Consume time in this fashion and "we shall never put an end to the business."

Suddenly it developed that the great danger was in the seat of national government, exclusively controlled by Congress. It would "become the sanctuary of the blackest crimes." For here, argued Mason and Grayson, the federal courts would sit, tyrants would be protected, felons and law-breaking federal officers would receive asylum. So another wearying task fell on Madison, while Henry Lee helped with the remark that if the place became filled up with rogues it wouldn't be very pleasant for Congress itself. Patrick Henry shifted ground. Even without this seat-of-government proviso, Congress under the "necessary and proper" clause could set apart ten miles square in which any man who acted contrary to their commands should be hanged without benefit of clergy. He would admit his inferiority in historical knowledge (sarcasm) but let any man show an instance where a part of the community was independent of the whole. Replied Madison:

"Was there ever a legislature in existence that held their sessions at a place where they had not jurisdiction? ... Does he mean that it should be under the control of any particular state that might at a critical moment seize it?"

If it was true that Congress could establish exclusive jurisdiction over a ten-mile area by virtue of the "necessary and proper" clause, what new terrors could arise from a specific power to do so? Madison denied however that the sweeping clause had any such effect: it only enabled them to execute the delegated powers.

Henry pointed out that Virginia reserved her rights in the old federal compact, but in the new one those rights were not reserved. "You have a Bill of Rights to defend you against the state government, which is bereaved of all power . . . and expose yourselves naked to the armed and powerful. Is not this a conduct of unexampled absurdity?" At this, Nicholas put forward the plan Madison had formulated in advance of the convention. Granting that a bill of rights ought to be in the Constitution, should they reject this government for its omission, dissolve the Union, and bring miseries on themselves and posterity? All the states wanted a bill of rights. Where then was the difficulty of securing it through subsequent amendments? "We shall find the other states willing to accord with their own favorite wish."

Thus the case for ratification was salvaged at its most vulnerable point. The twenty-year continuance of the slave trade led Mason into fresh denunciations. Much as he valued the Union, he would exclude the Southern states from it unless they would agree to give up this diabolical practice. To make it worse: "We have no security for the property of that kind which we have already." Slavery could be taxed out of existence.[5]

Delegates jibed at Mason for being both for and against slavery. Madison let them know that this paradox covered a double appeal to Virginian self-interest. But he undermined it in his method of explanation. At the Philadelphia Convention South Carolina and Georgia argued that their people had acquired lands to be improved by the labor of imported slaves. If the African trade were cut off, they said, "the slaves of Virginia would rise in value, and we would be obliged to go to your markets." The Southern states would not stay in the Union without a temporary continuance of the African trade. Great as the evil is, said Madison, a dismemberment would be worse. As to the present property in slaves, the new Constitution linked taxation with representation in such a way that no tax could force the freeing of them.

Henry replied that once Virginia's proportion of direct taxes was fixed, Congress could lay the whole tax on slaves—a grievous and enormous tax, compelling their emancipation. Luckily, he ruined this valid argument with a climactic shout, "They'll free your niggers!" which dissolved the tension in a roar of laughter.[6] Dodging the question of power, Madison answered that Congress would lay taxes most convenient for the people. Even the Carolinas and Georgia were perfectly satisfied and dreaded no danger to the property they held.

A terrible new peril was found in the prohibition of ex post facto laws. That meant, said Henry, that the old continental paper money which had depreciated a thousand for one, would have to be redeemed in gold and silver, shilling for shilling. Mason agreed: "We may be taxed for centuries, to give advantage to . . . rapacious speculators." It was true, replied Madison, that speculation had occurred. But the new Constitution provided that all claims against the United States should be *as valid* as under the Confederation. That was in accord with good faith, but meant also that they could not be made *more valid*. Consequently, the new rulers could not compel payment at an enhanced value without violating the Constitution.

That argument was fallacious, since the validity clause merely carried claims unchanged through a hiatus in government. However, the position Madison took throws a revealing light on his later course in Congress. It shows: (1) that he believed in good faith to public creditors; (2) that good faith did not require payment of a profit to speculators; (3) that he could easily discover a constitutional bar to doing what he did not want done.

Continuing the argument about old money, "Mr. Madison made some other observations which could not be heard." What he said (as indicated by Randolph) was that the prohibition of ex post facto laws related only to crimes. Ignoring this, if they heard it, Henry and Mason proceeded to ring the changes on ex post facto. The ban would prevent either states or Congress from scaling down the continental money, which would lie on their children to the tenth generation. A load of twenty million dollars might be dumped on Virginia, to be paid shilling for shilling or at the rate of forty for one. Madison seized on Mason's tacit admission that the old currency could not be raised above the forty-for-one devaluation of 1780. Suppose it were redeemed at that figure. Virginia's share would be no more than $500,000. This produced a forty-for-one devaluation of the debate.

Article II, dealing with the executive, doubled the initial scare. The President, said Mason on June 17, would be rechosen, term after term, as long as he lived. If the people wished to change him, the great powers in Europe would not allow it. The electoral college was a mere *ignis fatuus* thrown out to make the American people think they were to make the choice. Not once in fifty times would there be an election in the electoral college, because each of the ninety-one electors was to vote for two men, and a clear majority of the entire 182 votes must fall on one man in order to elect him. Madison explained that the high man needed only a majority of the electors—that is, forty-six out of ninety-one. He undertook to clear up other misconceptions. On the filling of presidential vacancies: "When the President and Vice President die, the election of another President will immediately take place." The reason for the electoral college: a direct election was difficult because of the extent and population of the states, but it was a democratic process because "the people chose the electors."

The treaty power brought Mason, Grayson and Henry into full-scale action once more. The President might get a treaty ratified in special session by failing to summon senators from states which would be injured by it. Replied Madison:

"Were the President to commit anything so atrocious . . . he would be impeached and convicted, as a majority of the states would be affected by his misdemeanor."

Treaties, said Henry, were to have more force in America than in any part of Christendom. Look in Blackstone, answered Madison, and read there that treaties made by the king are to be the supreme law. "They are so in every country." This led Henry into further declamation. British and French monarchs were subject to restrictions, but "you prostrate your rights to the President and Senate." It might be thought, he said, that he had cited Great Britain unfortunately for himself, but he could quote from Blackstone too. That learned judge says that a minister who sacrifices national interest is subject to impeachment. "I beg gentlemen to consider the American impeachment. What is it? It is a mere sham—a mere farce." In England they have blocks and gibbets; in America the guilty try themselves. If treaties are the supreme law they must be paramount to the Constitution. Those who exercised this enormous power could do so as they pleased: "there was no barrier to stop their mad career."[7]

Madison closed the debate. The treaty power was precisely the same in the new Constitution as in the Confederation. The old Congress had indefinite authority to make treaties which were recognized in many state laws to be the supreme law of the land. It did not follow, because this power was indefinite, that it was absolute and unlimited. He would not agree that it allowed the President and Senate to dismember the empire, or to alienate any great essential right. It would be impossible to define the scope of the treaty power and there was no danger in the failure to do so. Those who negotiated would feel the whole force of national attachment to their country. And if they proved false? In Britain, only the minister was subject to punishment. Here, the President himself could be impeached. He agreed with Corbin's assertion that the supremacy clause made treaties paramount only to the laws and constitutions of the states, not to the power of Congress. To allow state laws to counteract treaties "would bring on the Union the just charge of national perfidy, and involve us in war."

Each side was claiming a majority of three or four as the debate moved on to the judiciary department. Grayson on the evening before (June 18) counted eighty delegates as inflexibly opposed, eight undecided. Five were needed to defeat the Constitution. He thought two could be picked up by a masterly discussion of the court system. They had ten out of thirteen Kentucky members, but needed the whole. Madison believed the advantage still lay with the Federalists but it was too narrow for safety. He suspected the opposition of dragging out the debate in hope of hearing from the New York convention, or to weary the delegates into an adjournment to escape the intense June heat. The weather was the least of his own discomforts. He was still extremely feeble, he wrote to Washington and King, his illness continuing "in a degree which barely allows me to operate in the business."[8]

In a convention which contained Pendleton, Marshall and Randolph, Madison could hope for a little rest during the discussion of federal courts. He found himself, however, pulled into a personal controversy. Mason denounced the court system as an agency for the slow establishment of one great consolidated government. He knew many worthy men who had that desire, and he believed this was the purpose of the judiciary article.

"Here Mr. Madison interrupted Mr. Mason and demanded an unequivocal explanation. . . . He wished him to tell who the gentlemen were to whom he alluded."

It was notorious, Mason replied, that this principle prevailed at Philadelphia, but he could say with truth that the honorable gentleman, in private conversation, expressed himself against it. Madison declared himself satisfied.

As Mason described the federal courts, they would protect fedderal officers in "the most insolent and wanton brutality to a man's wife or daughter." The Supreme Court on appeal could hear new witnesses, suborned to perjury. Every British creditor could sue for his money in federal court. A thousand debtors who had paid once would have to pay again. (That is, pay in real money instead of worthless paper placed in escrow.) The Indiana Company would reassert its claim to the enormous area from the Alleghenies to the Ohio River. He had heard gentlemen of the the law say that this purchase was legally made and ought to be valid. (Patrick Henry gave the company a written opinion upholding the deed to *Virginia* lands given by *New York* Indians to *Pennsylvania* and *New Jersey* speculators, in exchange for a release from damages inflicted by unidentified Indians on the property of some of these speculators organized as a trading company.)[9] Finally, under the treaty power, the British heirs of Lord Fairfax would recover the vast properties confiscated by Virginia after the signing of the treaty of peace. Said Mason:

"I am personally endangered as an inhabitant of the Northern Neck. The people of that part will be obliged by the operation of this power to pay the quitrents of their lands."

That Mason's fear was genuine is suggested by his remedy: Eliminate inferior federal courts and confine the jurisdiction of the Supreme Court (except in certain instances) to cases arising after the Constitution was ratified. He was bidding strongly for the Federalist delegates of the Northern Neck and mountain country. Ill or not, Madison could not stay out. In Congress, he had defeated the Indiana Company's drive for a federal title, but that would mean little if the federal courts were as represented. So, after expressing belief that the fears were groundless, he undertook to justify the judiciary system. It was designed to avert disputes with foreign powers, prevent disputes between states and remedy improper decisions. Jurisdiction must extend to any case that could arise under the Constitution, therefore must be as extensive as the legislative power. It must extend to treaties to produce uniformity. No individual could call any state into court. (The Supreme Court held otherwise, and it took the Eleventh Amendment to make Madison's view effective.) In suits between citizens of different states, federal jurisdiction would protect Virginia merchants against prejudices in other states. As to Virginia's own tribunals: "We well know, sir, that foreigners cannot get justice done them in these courts."

The regulatory power of Congress, Madison contended, would make the judiciary safe and convenient to the whole country. Administering justice with celerity, it would help to establish that public and private confidence which was needed to give all men the rewards of their industry and economy. Thus debtors would be helped, not oppressed. Of actual lawsuits, ninety-nine in a hundred would remain in the state courts, whose annihilation was impossible. Why all this distrust?

"I have observed that gentlemen suppose that the general legislature will do everything mischief they possibly can, and that they will omit to do everything good which they are authorized to do. . . . I consider it reasonable to conclude that they will as readily do their duty as deviate from it. . . . I go on this great republican principle, that the people will have virtue and intelligence to select men of virtue and wisdom. . . . So that we do not depend on their virtue, or put confidence in our rulers, but in the people who are to choose them."

A sense of finality pervaded the hall as Henry rose to answer Pendleton and Madison. Lamentation was in his voice as he began: "The purse is gone, the sword is gone," and now the usurpations of Congress reached the last barrier, the Virginia judiciary. He centered on Madison's assertion that Congress would not make itself odious by abolishing jury trials in civil cases. "When Congress, in all the plenitude of their arrogance, magnificence and power, *can* take it from you, will you be satisfied?" For himself one comfort remained: As long as he lived his neighbors would protect him. "Old as I am, it is probable I may yet have the appellation of rebel.... As this government stands, I despise and abhor it."

Pendleton and Marshall replied to Henry. Would anyone suppose, listening to him, that the Constitution made trial by jury mandatory in all criminal trials and offered no bar to it in civil cases? They pointed out instance after instance in which civil cases were tried without juries in Virginia. Marshall rebutted Mason's warning about the effect of the treaty power on lands:

"He says that many poor men may be harassed and injured by the representatives of Lord Fairfax. If he has no right, this cannot be done. If he has this right, and comes to Virginia, what laws will his claims be determined by? By those of this state. By what tribunals will they be determined? By our state courts."

Perhaps this discussion gave Marshall an idea. Five years later he and his brother James bought, from the Fairfax heirs, 160,000 acres which had been confiscated by the state and sold in part to others. Instead of being determined under state law, by the state courts, the Fairfax-Marshall title was upheld by the United States Supreme Court, after twenty years of litigation—Chief Justice Marshall taking no part in the decision.[10]

On Monday, June 23, pressure arose for action and adjournment. The legislature was supposed to convene that day in special session, but its members flocked to the convention gallery. New voices came into the debate. General Adam Stephen had a word of advice for Patrick Henry: "If the gentleman does not like this government, let him go and live among the Indians." George Nicholas dipped close to the unspoken subject of self-interest. It could not be supposed that companies holding discredited Indian deeds would renew their claims, "But, sir, there are gentlemen who have come by large possessions, that it is not easy to account for." Jumping up, Henry hoped the honorable gentleman meant nothing personal. "I mean what I say, sir," rejoined Nicholas and went on with his speech. At its conclusion Henry protested again: "If the gentleman means personal insinuations—or to wound my private reputation—I think this an improper place to do so. . . . I can tell how I came by what I have. . . . I hold what I hold in right and in a just manner."

Nicholas replied, after the chairman appealed for peace, that he did not have Henry in mind, and would have said so earlier if the gentleman had not made some remarks which one gentleman should not make to another. The rest of the Constitution was run through before nightfall. The Federalists, Madison reported to Washington, would propose a ratification involving a few declaratory truths. The opposition would urge previous amendments.

"Their conversation today seemed to betray despair. Colonel Mason . . . held out the idea of civil convulsions as the effects of obtruding the government on the people. He was answered by several and concluded with declaring his determination for himself to acquiesce in the event whatever it might be. Mr. H——y endeavored to gloss what had fallen from his friend, declared his aversion to the Constitution to be such that he could not take the oath; but that he would remain in peaceable submission to the result. We calculate on a majority, but a bare one."[11]

George Wythe offered the motion for ratification, which opened with a statement that every power not granted remained with the people and could not be cancelled or modified by the federal government. "Among other essential rights," liberty of conscience and of the press were so protected. Henry attacked this at once. The specifying of three rights (he mentioned trial by jury as the third, but it does not appear in the published text) meant that those not enumerated were relinquished. Congress might make every slave a soldier and set him free. The declaration about reserved rights must be put into the Constitution before its adoption, or Virginia would be destroyed.

During his speech Henry placed his and Mason's proposals before the convention. They consisted of a bill of rights in twenty articles, founded on that of Virginia, and twenty other amendments to the Constitution. Randolph led off against them, asserting that the rights contended for already were secured in the Constitution or were outside the scope of congressional power. The other amendments were harmful, unneeded or unattainable in advance of ratification. The Confederation was gone.

"If in this situation we reject the Constitution the Union will be dissolved, the dogs of war will break loose, and anarchy and discord will complete the ruin of this country."

Grayson came back with a cynical assertion that by their position cutting the Union in two, Virginia and North Carolina could force the rest of the country to accept any changes in the Constitution they chose to demand. He pictured rich Virginia preyed upon by New England shipowners and by little states covetous to lay taxes on a bigger neighbor. Then he made a hopeless reference to the invisible influence which no argument could touch:

"I think that were it not for one great character in America, so many men would not be for this government. We have one ray of hope. We do not fear while he lives: but we can only expect his *fame* to be immortal. We wish to know, who besides him can concentrate the confidence and affections of all America?"

This recognition of a safe and popular national leadership formed a virtual prologue to Madison's last major speech of the convention. Nothing had excited more admiration in the world than the manner in which free governments were established in America—deliberately set up by free inhabitants in the midst of war and confusion. If that excited so much wonder, "how much more astonishment and admiration will be excited, should they be able, peaceably, freely and satisfactorily to establish one general

DOLLEY AND JAMES MADISON

SCOTCHTOWN. CHILDHOOD HOME OF DOLLEY MADISON, NEAR ASHLAND, VIRGINIA. PREVIOUSLY OWNED BY PATRICK HENRY

government, when there is such a diversity of opinions and interests, when not cemented or stimulated by any common danger?" The friends of the paper on the table did not deny that it had minor defects, but these could be removed when experience revealed them. What was the alternative? If nine states ratified, would they tread back their steps on the demand of a single state? Virginia would be listened to, when she spoke respectfully, but this was the language of neither confidence nor respect.

Madison referred to the difficulties in framing the Constitution—the mutual deference and concession that brought results where inflexible tenacity would have led to failure. If it was so difficult when men's minds were calm and dispassionate, what could be hoped for if the whole thing were thrown back upon the people? At every stage of the Virginia convention opponents of the Constitution had disagreed with one another. How much greater would be the discord among thirteen conventions?

The proposed bill of rights impressed him as dangerous. There was more safety in a general statement that every ungranted power remained with the people. He assailed the demand for a two-thirds vote to raise an army or to regulate commerce. Was it safe, especially for the weak Southern states, to say that national security might be frustrated by less than one third of the people of America? Those who contended for previous amendments, he felt sure, were not aware of the dangers that would result. Nine states might say with propriety:

"It is not proper, decent or right in you to demand that we should reverse what we have done. Do as we have done—place confidence in us, as we have done in one another—and then we shall freely, fairly and dispassionately consider and investigate your propositions and endeavor to gratify your wishes; but if you do not do this, it is more reasonable that you should yield to us than we to you. You cannot exist without us—you must be a member of the Union."

He would be willing to recommend some amendments to gratify the wishes of those who thought they were necessary. But previous amendments were pregnant with dreadful dangers. Henry saw a damaging admission in Madison's contention that forty amendments could not be obtained from the other states before adoption of the Constitution: "His arguments, great as that gentleman's abilities are, tend to prove that amendments cannot be obtained *after* adoption." Whatever defects there might be, Madison replied, could be removed by the mode set forth in the Constitution. He regarded a declaration of rights as unnecessary and dangerous—unnecessary because the general government had no power but what was given it, dangerous because an incomplete enumeration was unsafe. But he would be the last to oppose any amendment that would give satisfaction, unless it were dangerous.

On that statement the convention adjourned to the day of decision, June 25. It was the intention of those who had borne the brunt of the fight for the Constitution to stay out of the closing debate. They put their case into the ample custody of Attorney General James Innes. Reputed to be the largest man in Virginia, he was Patrick Henry's only near rival in eloquence, and some people thought him superior.[12] Innes said he came into the convention ready to recede from his favorable impression of the Constitution. Hoping to hear reasoning from its opponents, he had listened to horrors and chimeras. He observed with regret how jealousy of the North had supplanted the spirit of 1775. In that day men were not Virginians, Carolinians or Pennsylvanians, but the glorious name of an American extended from end to end of the continent. To his appeal for unconditional ratification the attorney general added a legal point—the people had sent them there to adopt or reject the document on the table. "It transcends the power of the convention to take it with previous amendments," thereby binding the people by what they knew not.

Adam Stephen and Zachariah Johnston wound up the federal argument. It mattered little what they said. An Indian fighter and a Shenandoah Valley Presbyterian were to steady western delegates against the Indiana Company bogey. Monroe, Tyler and Henry said the last words for the opposition, and Governor Randolph put in a few concluding sentences.

Eighty to eighty-eight, the convention refused to submit amendments to the other states. Then, eighty-nine to seventy-nine, it ratified the Constitution. As a Richmond newspaper described it, a crowded audience viewed the scene with awful reverence. A committee dominated by Federalists reported the Henry-Mason bill of rights and twenty other amendments. Madison and others attempted to strike out an article emasculating direct taxation, but nine Federalists changed sides. Without a roll call, all amendments were recommended to the consideration of Congress and the momentous meeting came to an end.

In guiding the Constitution to victory, Madison won the greatest forensic battle of his life, over the most formidable adversary he ever faced, for the greatest stakes in national welfare. His leadership was universally recognized. "Madison took the principal share in the debate for it," wrote one of Jefferson's correspondents—strongly assisted by Pendleton and somewhat by Innes, Lee, Marshall, Corbin, G. Nicholas and Randolph.[13] Patrick Henry knew who his adversary was. From June 11, the day Madison recovered from his illness, Henry made seventeen speeches in specific reply to him, fifteen in reply to all other delegates combined. The full extent of this leadership was not measured by his own work on the floor, extensive and effective as it was. Except for the arguments of Pendleton and Marshall on the judiciary, virtually every affirmative utterance from any source bore the stamp of Madison's thought, previously expressed in the convention, in letters or in *The Federalist*. Superior reasoning was not enough. He had to pile up an extraordinary margin of logic to cancel the opposing eloquence.

Madison told his later secretary, Edward Coles, that when Patrick Henry arose to reply to him, a pause, a shake of the head or a striking gesture would undo an hour's work before a word was uttered. Henry's oratory, young Spencer Roane wrote at the conclusion of the Virginia convention, contained touches of eloquence that would almost disgrace Cicero or Demosthenes. Madison was so weakened by illness that his normally low voice sank at times to an unheard whisper. Yet he won. He won by placing every disputed issue before the convention in terms so clear and logical,

"My opinion is that a reservation of a right to withdraw if amendments be not decided on . . . is a *conditional* ratification, that it does not make New York a member of the new Union and consequently that she would not be received on that plan. . . . The Constitution requires an adoption *in toto* and forever."[4]

The reading of that on the floor ended Clinton's scheme. By a margin of five votes, New York accepted the Constitution. The ratifying words were sandwiched between a bill of rights and thirty-two proposed amendments, but they stood alone in effect.

With ironic logic the people of New York celebrated Virginia's accession ahead of their own. On the twenty-third a grand procession of bakers, coopers, brewers and other Federalists marched from the plain before Bridewell out to the Federal Green. There, seated at ten tables set like the sticks of a fan, six or eight thousand people dined on whole roasted oxen, cows and sheep and took care of what the brewers brought along. Congressmen refused to march because New York had not ratified, but that didn't keep them from eating. To the honor of the city, wrote college boy John Randolph, aged 15, to his ever dear and affectionate papa, there was not a single drunken man or fight to be seen. He wrote before a Federalist mob, following New York's ratification, smashed the windows and threw away the types of the *Patriotic Register,* whose jeering comments on the festivities were not thought to register patriotism. As if to offer a virtuous alibi in a center of iniquity the future "John Randolph of Roanoke" added: "I saw Mr. Madison a few days since."[5]

It was fitting, though not in line with subsequent American custom, that Madison's revolutionary statesmanship should bring him an LL.D. from his own college. Forwarding the diploma, President Witherspoon wrote on August 11 that the Princeton trustees and faculty "were not barely willing but proud of the opportunity of paying some attention to and giving a testimony of their approbation of one of their own sons who has done them so much honor by his public conduct." Harking back to their service together in Congress, the old theologian added that there was none to whom it gave more satisfaction than to himself, who had the "peculiar happiness to know, perhaps more than any of them, your usefulness in an important station." He did indeed, having been Madison's toughest adversary in the latter's fight against the land companies.[6]

For more than a month Congress held back from steps to bring the new government into being. Those who wanted it located in New York "studiously promote delay," Madison reported to Washington. Others, including himself, were willing to let things run along so that newly elected legislatures, likely to be federal-minded, could choose the senators and pass election laws.[7]

Nobody opposed a resolve that presidential electors be appointed in January and cast their ballots a month later. March 4 was picked for the convening of Congress—but where? Philadelphia fell half a state short when Delaware divided to give Wilmington a chance. Madison's object was to take the temporary capital out of New York, because fixing it there would make it difficult to locate the permanent seat as far south as the Potomac. Thinking that Philadelphia might win after other trials failed, he voted on August 4 for Baltimore. To his astonishment the motion carried, South Carolina deserting New York. Such a vote, he commented to Randolph, could not stand, nor did he want it to. If Congress convened there, dissatisfied states to the north would form a coalition, remove the new government northward, and fix the permanent seat there too. Philadelphia was central enough to arouse no quick determination to leave, yet there would always be ten states, at the two extremities of the continent, who would take the permanent seat to a new location if they could agree on it.

"The only chance the Potomac has [said Madison to Washington] is to get things in such a train that a coalition may take place between the southern and eastern states on the subject, and still more that the final seat may be undecided for two or three years, with which period the western and southwestern population will enter more into the estimate."

Two days were enough to fulfill the prophecy about Baltimore, but on a final motion for New York, Congress found itself dead-locked by the refusal of Rhode Islanders to help set up a govern-

ment to which their state was opposed. Madison told his allies
that they must yield to New York or see the new government
strangled in its birth. Maryland and Delaware remained inflexible but all others at last consented.[8]

By this time a new danger had appeared—a circular letter from
the New York convention urging state legislatures to force a
second general convention. The object of this pestilent maneuver,
as Madison termed it, was to put the amending process in the
hands of men who would mutilate the system, particularly in the
all-important article of taxation. He thought it pretty clear that
a majority of the people were satisfied with the Constitution, but
management and menaces might produce dire results.

"An early convention [he wrote to Jefferson] is in every view
to be dreaded in the present temper of America. A very short
period of delay would produce the double advantage of diminishing the heat and increasing the light of all parties. A trial for one
year will probably suggest more real amendments than all the
antecedent speculations of our most sagacious politicians."[9]

As one means of reducing antifederal feeling, Madison joined
in securing a reaffirmation of the American right to the Mississippi.
The motion came from North Carolina, but while it was pending,
the convention in that state voted down the Constitution by a
hundred majority. The news arrived just as Madison was giving
a dinner for Brissot de Warville, who recorded the ensuing discussion in his *New Travels*. Madison believed that the refusal
was temporary (because of a paper-money faction) and would
have no weight in the minds of Americans. Brissot told him it
would be regarded in Europe as a germ of division and prevent
the resurrection of American credit. The French traveler added
to Madison's reputation by recording it:

"The name of Madison, celebrated in America, is well known in
Europe by the merited eulogium made of him by his countryman
and friend Mr. Jefferson. Though still young he has rendered the
greatest services to Virginia, to the American Confederation, and
to liberty and humanity in general. He contributed much, with

Mr. White, in reforming the civil and criminal codes of his country. He distinguished himself particularly in the conventions for ratification of a new federal system. Virginia balanced a long time before adhering. Mr. Madison won the members of the convention to it by his eloquence and his logic.

"This Republican appears to be about thirty-three years of age. He had, when I saw him, an air of fatigue; perhaps it was the effect of the immense labors to which he has devoted himself for some time past. His look announces a censor, his conversation discovers the man of learning, and his reserve was that of a man conscious of his talents and of his duties."[10]

Madison's French associations were rather close at this time. In the previous January the new minister, Count de Moustier, arrived from France, bringing a fine watch which Jefferson had ordered made at Madison's request. He brought also his sister-in-law, Madame de Brèhan, who, according to swiftly spreading report, deserved a more intimate appellation than official hostess of the legation. Moustier carried a letter from Jefferson introducing him to Madison as a sensible, well disposed, unostentatious man who (this in cipher) with adroitness could be pumped of anything. As to Madame de Brèhan:

"She is goodness itself. You must be well acquainted with her. You will find her well disposed to meet your acquaintance, and well worthy of it. . . . She hopes, by accompanying Monsieur de Moustier, to improve her health, which is very feeble, and still more, to improve her son in his education, and to remove him to a distance from the seductions of this country. . . . The husband of Madame de Brèhan is an officer, and obliged by the times to remain with the army."[11]

Apparently Madison made more of a hit with "the marchioness" than she did with the public, for President Cyrus Griffin showed unmistakable relish in forwarding inquiries and bits of information to Montpelier: "The marchioness . . . and the Count . . . entertain a very exalted [opinion] of you and talk much upon that subject." Again: "The marchioness is perfectly upon her feet—for she walks five miles every day—and with great pleasure I will execute your commands to her and the Count." Later: "A thousand inquiries concerning your health from the marchioness, etc." Madame's interest, it appears, extended to ethnology and eugenics. Early in the spring Griffin wrote:

"The marchioness . . . wants exceedingly to be present at the Indian treaty. I think the governor general [of the Northwest Territory] can do nothing less than take so sweet a companion in his train, but he seems to be averse from the plan."

And in March:

"The marchioness received your compliments with great pleasure. She and the Count most cordially return them. The lady has procured a Negro girl, and only wants a boy *in order that they may breed* to use her own language."[12]

Madison's return to New York enabled Madame Brèhan to make her wishes more directly known, and who was he to disoblige a lady? On August 18 he wrote to his father: "Tell my brother Ambrose if you please that he must draw on Mr. Shepherd for the price of the Negro boy for the French Marchioness."

Replying to a series of questions from Moustier, Madison outlined the opportunities for a larger trade between Virginia and France, but discouraged his hope of furnishing very cheap woolens *"pour l'habillement des nègres."* The price must be low indeed to create a market.

"The clothing of Negroes is made of the coarsest materials. It is at present supplied in part by family manufacture, especially where a few Negroes only belong to the same master, and this resource is daily increasing. Principal part however comes from Great Britain and if no foreign competition interferes this must be the case for a considerable time."[13]

Toward the end of the year Madison began to feel that the appointment of Moustier was a most unlucky one. Telling Jefferson so (in cipher) he continued:

"He is unsocial, proud and niggardly and betrays a sort of fastidiousness towards this country. He suffers also from his illicit connection with Madame de Brèhan which is universally known and offensive to American manners. She is perfectly soured toward this country. The ladies of New York (a few within the official circle excepted) have for some time withdrawn their attentions from her. She knows the cause, is deeply stung by it, views everything through the medium of rancor and conveys her impressions to her paramour over whom she exercises despotic sway."

In their travels the minister and his sister-in-law were said to "neglect the most obvious precautions for veiling their intimacy." Still, he thought part of the bad impression was due to the early hostility of French Consul de la Forest, a cunning disciple of Marbois' politics, who turned the French community against them. A few months later he was happy to report that Moustier was becoming more acceptable and "Madame Brèhan begins to be viewed in the light which I hope she merits."[14]

By mid-autumn of '88 the first national political campaign was showing precocious vigor. Washington, of course, was the only one thought of for President. Madison did no cheering when he heard that Hancock and John Adams were likely rivals for second place.

"Hancock is weak, ambitious, a courtier of popularity, given to low intrigue, and lately reunited by a factious friendship with Samuel Adams. John Adams has made himself obnoxious to many, particularly in the southern states, by the political principles avowed in his book. Others, recollecting his cabal during the war against General Washington, knowing his extravagant self-importance, and considering his preference of an unprofitable dignity to some place of emolument . . . as a proof of his having an eye to the presidency, conclude that he would not be a very cordial second to the General, and that an impatient ambition might even intrigue for a premature advancement."

All up and down the continent Federals and Antifederals were competing for control of the new Congress. The Clinton-Henry combine was working for the second convention. Friends of the Constitution were willing to put additional guards to liberty in it, without reducing the sum of power, but others Madison suspected had the insidious hope of throwing all into confusion and subverting the plan completely. "The articles relating to treaties, to paper money, and to contracts, created more enemies than all the errors in the system positive and negative put together." A declaration of rights probably would be added, though many thought it unnecessary in a federal constitution.

"My own opinion has always been in favor of a bill of rights; provided it be so framed as not to imply powers not meant to be included in the enumeration. At the same time I have never thought the omission a material defect, nor been anxious to supply it even by *subsequent* amendment, for any other reason than that it is anxiously desired by others."

To Patrick Henry's hope of a second convention was now added a vengeful desire to keep the man who had worsted him out of the new government. On October 31, he helped re-elect Madison to the old Congress—for the purpose, George Lee Turberville reported, of preventing his return to Virginia. Rejecting a place for himself, Henry's aim was to put Richard Henry Lee and Grayson in the Senate. Carrington, leaving Congress in October, was authorized to speak confidentially to Madison's friends concerning a Senate or House appointment for him. "I mean not to decline an agency in launching the new government," he stated to one of them, adding that he preferred the House. His long explanation silently included the fact that Henry was going to pick the senators.[16]

Washington urged Carrington to disregard Madison's wishes and press him for the upper chamber, where he would be more useful because of treaties and appointments. But of the powerful group which had upheld the Constitution in convention, only Corbin was in the legislature. The young and inexperienced friends of the new government, Richard Bland Lee reported, formed but a feeble band against the mighty Henry. As Washington described the situation to Madison:

"The edicts of Mr. Henry are enregistered with less opposition by the majority of that body than those of the Grand Monarch are in the parliaments of France. He has only to say let this be law, and it is law."[17]

The principal edict was for a second general convention. "To-morrow—'tis a fearful day," wrote Turberville on October 27. Henry had just brought in his firebrand which it was feared they could not withstand. "Would to heaven you were here." Two weeks later he forwarded a double dose of bad news:

"The triumph of antifederalism is complete. The resolution and preamble which I inclosed to you have passed by a majority of 85 to 39 . . . and to crown the whole R. H. Lee and William Grayson were yesterday elected to the Senate. The ballot for the first was 98, the second 86 and for you 77."

Had the election been delayed one day, Turberville commented, "I do religiously believe you would have been elected." He entreated Madison to come home before the election of federal representatives in February and furnish the aid so imminently needed by his native country:

"There is not a man upon earth so adequate as you are to her salvation and it would glad my very soul to see you in this city before the session rises. Your very presence would shrink into nonentity almost those now aspiring assassins who, triumphing in their calumnies of absent characters, have belittled themselves even in the estimation of their adherents."[18]

Patrick Henry's assault on Madison was reported to the victim of it by Henry Lee:

"Mr. Henry on the floor exclaimed against your political character, and pronounced you unworthy of the confidence of the people in the station of senator. That your election would terminate in producing rivulets of blood throughout the land."

Henry put his opposition on the basis of warrantable distrust. The friends of the system, he observed to R. H. Lee, were much displeased that Madison was left out. They urged the election of one Federalist as a sort of right, but how could Virginia secure amendments if one of her senators were averse to them? Madison was convinced that Henry was not genuinely seeking the safeguards to liberty which he talked about. "The destruction of the whole system I take to be still the secret wish of his heart and the real object of his pursuit." Otherwise why did he offer political help to persons less devoted to rational alterations than the men on whom he vented his hatred?[19]

Virginia's final action on the second convention—an address to Congress, a letter to Governor Clinton and one to all the states—showed quite a toning down of antifederal spirit. The hostile majority was cut in two. However, there was no falling off in the animus against Madison. It took the form of what should have become known as the Henrymander instead of the Gerrymander.

"The object of the majority of today [wrote Turberville on November 13] has been to prevent *your* election in the House of Representatives . . . first by forming a district (as they supposed) of counties most tainted with antifederalism in which Orange is included, and then by confining the choice of the people to the residents in the particular districts."

The residence requirement upset a plan to circumvent Henry by having Madison elected from tidewater counties. Needing both an opposing candidate and a hostile majority, Henry obtained the first (James Monroe) by taking in Spotsylvania County. He then carried the district far to the southwest to include big Amherst, the antifederal stronghold of the Cabell family. The district of eight counties (twelve on the modern map) was not misshapen, but violated regional alignments and was fashioned to control the election. According to the political writer "Decius," Henry would have put in Cumberland and Prince Edward had he thought them necessary.

Madison's friends quickly set to work to offset Henry's attack on him. Without waiting for his approval, they put in type a little pamphlet containing extracts from a letter he had written to Turberville—extracts, said Richard Bland Lee, which would "remove the slanderous imputation on you as an enemy to all amendments and in every form." Unwilling to appear active in his own defense, Madison asked that these be eliminated. Reluctantly agreeing, the pamphleteers insisted on a general allusion "to the impropriety of making a faithful and conspicuous public servant the victim of party rage." Lee urged him to hasten home:

"Your very presence probably would contribute much to dissipate the little plots which may be forming against you. If you were to visit the counties previous to the election and attend the Culpeper election yourself I think there would be little doubt of your success."[20]

Madison had gone to Philadelphia early in November, but hoped to spend the winter in New York attending to matters which required access to the papers of Congress. The trip his friends demanded had an unpleasant electioneering aspect. Nevertheless he set out and at Alexandria found himself invited to a week's stopover at Mt. Vernon.[21]

Washington noted in his diary that he spent all his time at the house from the day of Madison's arrival, December 18, until he left on the twenty-fifth. He wrote also about the ice in Occoquan Creek and the bad results of transplanting carrots, but said nothing of a superconfidential discussion of the presidency pointed to in their later correspondence.

At Fredericksburg Madison shifted from the stage to a two-wheeled chair sent from Montpelier. It was impossible to journey on horseback, he explained in advance, both because of his baggage and "some remains of the piles which for some weeks past have been very troublesome." There must be no delay in sending the carriage or he would be left on the road on Sunday. No candidate for office could let a wheel turn on that day. The campaign against him was already in full swing. Monroe was writing myriads of letters, Turberville reported, and Henry's insinuations were held forth to the people as sacred incontrovertible facts. His friends were not less active and grew more hopeful every day.

"The violence of the antifederals has begun to arouse suspicion and so soon as the people become acquainted with the conduct of their great high priest I have not a doubt but that they will take that direction which reason and moderation point out to them."[22]

At home Madison heard a story which changed all his plans. The Baptists were being told not only that he was opposed to any amendments whatever (Henry's story) but that he had "ceased to be a friend to the rights of conscience." Baptist Minister George Eve wanted a statement refuting the tales. Madison furnished it at once. As long as the Constitution remained unratified, he wished to avoid dangerous contentions. Now the situation was altered.

"It is my sincere opinion that the Constitution ought to be revised, and that the first Congress meeting under it ought to prepare and recommend to the states for ratification the most satisfactory provisions for all essential rights, particularly the rights of conscience in the fullest latitude, the freedom of the press, trials by jury, security against general warrants etc."

So Mr. Eve was all primed when on January 17, 1789, Messrs. Banks and Early converted his Saturday evening church service into an anti-Madison political meeting. They not only repeated Henry's canards but charged that the Virginia convention debates were being delayed in publication to conceal Madison's views. One of the latter's supporters told him of what followed:

"Mr. Eve . . . reminded them of the many important services which you had rendered their society, in particular the act for establishing religious liberty, also the bill for a general assessment, which was averted by your particular efforts. . . . I went with them [on Sunday] from the meeting house to the river, which gave me an opportunity [during the baptisms] of speaking to many of the people, and I think Mr. Eve has given a great wound to Mr. Early's cause."

A circular letter from Madison to T. M. Randolph and others was published over the country and inspired Hugh Williamson to remark that its sensible contents "might reconcile any moderate Antifed to supporting a good federal man." In the first test of strength in Madison's locality, General Edward Stevens, won by eighty-two votes over Colonel Cabell for presidential elector. Washington's secretary Tobias Lear thought this was largely due to Madison's personal appearance, and left little doubt that he too would triumph. Should he be left out the whole continent would feel the loss of his superior abilities.[23]

Madison himself was not so optimistic, since both candidates for elector were pledged to vote for Washington. Huge Culpeper County (Culpeper, Madison and Rappahannock on modern maps) appeared to be the critical spot, so he gave it continuous attention "to repel the multiplied falsehoods which circulated." This led to the most novel feature of his campaign—joint travels and debates by him and Monroe. Following Madison's first appearance in Culpeper, French Strother announced that Monroe would be there on the next court day (January 19) to "erase any false impressions." A hurry call was sent for Madison to come too. The two candidates were friends. Why shouldn't they explain the Constitution together, each in his own way, all over the district? For two weeks they traveled from county to county (at Orange Courthouse on the twenty-sixth) keeping political and personal views separate. This, Madison wrote after the February 2 election, "saved our friendship from the smallest diminution." Would it have done so if conditions had been reversed? What if Monroe, ever suspicious, had been subjected to the same kind of virulent falsehoods that his backers were leveling at Madison, without a word of public disavowal from their beneficiary?

Madison's later account of one of these meetings was written down by Nicholas P. Trist. It was before a gathering of Germans who usually voted together and were expected to turn the scale in Culpeper. "We met there at church," Madison began. (Evidently the Hebron Lutheran church in the present Madison County.)

"Service was performed and then they had music with two fiddles. They are remarkably fond of music. When it was all over we addressed these people and kept them standing in the snow listening to the discussion of constitutional subjects. They stood it out very patiently—seemed to consider it a sort of fight of which they were required to be spectators. I then had to ride in the night twelve miles to quarters; and got my nose frostbitten, of which I bear the mark now (touching the end of his nose on the left side)."[24]

After receiving this one scar of battle, as he called it, Madison carried Culpeper 256 to 103. Orange went for him 216 to 9, Albemarle 174 to 105, and he carried Louisa by 104. Monroe had a majority of but 74 in his own county, and only the solid Antifederalism of Amherst kept him from being swamped. Complete tabulation by eight sheriffs put Madison 336 ahead. The federal tide all over Virginia gave proof that the people were for the Constitution which their legislature opposed.[25]

Again Madison stopped at Mt. Vernon. A week after his December visit, Washington inquired for a safe and expeditious way of sending him a private and confidential letter which must not be subject to loss or inspection. Unluckily the inquiry was eleven days on the road and Washington was called to Seneca Falls. So he sent a rough draft of what he had in mind and pressed Madison to stop, and if necessary wait for him, on his way north. On the manuscript of the first inquiry Madison made this notation:

"The letter being peculiarly confidential was returned or rather left with its enclosure at Mt. Vernon on my way to New York. The return though not asked nor probably expected was suggested by a motive of delicacy, nor was any copy of my answer to the communication retained."[26]

A clue to the mystery can be found in a P. S. to Washington's letter covering the inclosure: "If it should be your *own* desire, I have not the smallest objection to your conversing freely with Colonel H—— on all matters respecting this business." Washington editors, thinking only of Virginians, have assumed that this referred to Benjamin Harrison, who was equally remote from Madison's politics and his line of travel. However, Madison was soon to be with Colonel Hamilton in New York. Plainly, the President-elect wanted advice concerning his new office. The inclosure to Madison probably was the sixty-five-page draft of an inaugural address, written by Washington but never delivered. Madison would have regarded it as inappropriate because of its lengthy recital of Washington's feelings and his too-quick plunge into legislative suggestions.

Already held back by the snow, the river at Fredericksburg and the unparalleled badness of the roads, Madison saw no reason for a hasty departure from Washington's wayside tavern. The continued foul weather would delay Congress anyway. On March 2, he set forth with John Page, one of the seven Federalists whom Virginia was sending to the lower house out of a total of ten. At Alexandria they were to pick up Richard Bland Lee. Following their departure, Washington borrowed £600 to pay pressing debts and traveling expenses and made one more effort to draw blood from a turnip—that is, to collect the money John Francis Mercer had so often promised him. Never until the last two years, he wrote, had he felt the want of money.[27]

On their way Madison, Page and Lee fell in with the bearer of the electoral vote of Georgia. He told of the scattering of southern "second votes" to avoid elevating John Adams into a tie for the presidency. At Philadelphia they met John Dawson of the old Congress, who had been in the death watch from December 1 to March 3—no quorum in all that time. When he left New York eighteen members of the new House were present. The number remained the same until the three Virginians presented their credentials, and April came in before a quorum did. During this time it was impossible to count electoral votes and notify Washington of what he and everybody knew. Madison no longer had any fear as to the attitude of House or Senate toward the Constitution, but he foresaw extra work in the fact that Congress seemed to contain "a very scanty proportion who will share in the drudgery of business."[28]

On April 6 the Senate achieved a quorum and electoral ballots were counted—sixty-nine for Washington, thirty-four for John Adams, thirty-five scattering. New York, squabbling over senators, had failed to elect either them or presidential electors, and Rhode Island and North Carolina held aloof. Following the joint session, the House addressed a message to the Senate—the most gracious, perhaps, that ever passed from one legislative branch to the other. The representatives desired that the President and Vice President be notified of their election "by such persons and in such manner as the Senate shall be pleased to direct; and that Mr. Madison do communicate the said message." He did so, and the Senate gave Charles Thomson, veteran secretary of the old Congress, the pleasant duty of serving the summons at Mt. Vernon. Madison had written to Washington earlier in the day that Thomson would bear the message, so there must have been either prescience or planning in the harmony.

# CHAPTER XIX

## IN THE NEW CONGRESS

THE first Congress was heavily loaded with veterans of the old government and framers of the new. In the Senate were Ellsworth and Johnson of Connecticut, Paterson of New Jersey, Robert Morris of Pennsylvania, Butler of South Carolina, Read and Bassett of Delaware, Langdon of New Hampshire—all delegates to the Philadelphia Convention. In New York, following an anti-Clinton legislative sweep, Hamilton picked his father-in-law, General Schuyler, and Rufus King, who, defeated for the Senate in Massachusetts, decided that his marriage to an Alsop heiress made him a New Yorker.

In the House, Madison found himself with Gerry, Sherman, Fitzsimons, Clymer, Carroll, Baldwin, Gilman, all of whom had helped draft the Constitution. Former President Boudinot of the old Congress was on hand. There was an upsurge of new federal men—Fisher Ames and Theodore Sedgwick of Massachusetts, Egbert Benson of New York, the two Muhlenbergs of Pennsylvania—one of them so modest that he believed his friends made him Speaker of the House to prevent James Wilson from becoming Chief Justice. From the deep South came a militant Georgia republican, James Jackson, money-minded William Smith and antifederal Aedanus Burke of South Carolina.

Madison's Virginia colleagues were longer on good intentions than genius. He had prospective allies in John Page, Richard Bland Lee, John Brown of Kentucky, Alexander White, Samuel Griffin and Andrew Moore. Against him, on the original issue of the Constitution, were Isaac Coles, Jonathan Parker and his ancient antagonist Theodorick Bland. He had hopes of two of them.

For clerk of the House, Virginia's vote helped produce a tie and then a victory for John Beckley. Madison thus gained the use of the keenest pair of ears in the country. Both men (also Page,

White and Brown of Virginia) lived in the boardinghouse of Mrs.
Dorothy Elsworth at 19 Maiden Lane.[1]

Madison opened the legislative business on April 8, 1789. His
doing so was typical of an initiative which caused him to take the
floor 124 times in the five-months session, against sixty and fifty-
five times for next-high Gerry and Fitzsimons. He took the liberty, he said, of introducing a subject that required first attention
and united exertions—duties on imports as a means of paying the
national debt.

"No gentleman here can be unacquainted with the numerous
claims upon our justice; nor with the impotency which prevented
the late Congress of the United States from carrying into effect
the dictates of gratitude and policy. The Union, by the establishment of a more effective government, having recovered from the
state of imbecility that heretofore prevented a performance of its
duty, ought, in its first act, to revive those principles of honor and
honesty that have too long lain dormant."

In laying duties, he said, two points would occur—regulation
of commerce and raising a revenue. Believing that commerce
should be as free as possible, but not being ready to deal with so
complicated a subject, he proposed a temporary system based on
the revenue proposals of 1783 (his own), which had been approved by all the states in some form or other; plus a tonnage duty
on vessels. He then offered a resolve for specific duties (the
amounts left blank) on rum, liquors, wine, molasses, sugar, tea,
cocoa and coffee, and a general ad valorem duty on all other imported articles. Tonnage duties were to be at three rising levels—
on American vessels, on those of nations having treaties with the
United States, and on vessels belonging to other powers.

This was too simple for a Congress of complicated interests.
Fitzsimons wanted special levies to "protect our infant industries,"
and proposed them on everything from four-wheeled chariots to
nutmegs. Southern congressmen saw a New England shipping
monopoly in the proposal of graduated tonnage taxes. Madison
advised more study of a permanent plan, but insisted on emergency
action. The prospect of a revenue from spring importations was
daily vanishing. If the South felt unjustly burdened it should

recall that a thinly populated region had extra need of national security. He would approve of protection of new industries which had been fostered by state legislation, but wanted attention paid to the general interests of the Union.

"I own myself the friend to a very free system of commerce, and hold it as a truth that commercial shackles are generally unjust, oppressive and impolitic; it is also a truth that if industry and labor are left to take their own course, they will generally be directed to those objects which are the most productive, and this in a more certain and direct manner than the wisdom of the most enlightened legislature could point out."

The shoemaker, said he, would gain nothing by making his own clothes to save the tailor's bill, nor the tailor by making his own shoes to save the shoemaker's charge. The same was true between arts and agriculture, between city and country, between nation and nation, and between parts of the same nation. The only need was to discover the exceptions to the free-trade rule. Some of these he was ready to list:

American shipping, which would be driven off the sea if discrimination in foreign ports were not met by counterdiscrimination.

Duties to develop domestic production of the raw materials of manufacture.

Sumptuary duties, to discourage luxury spending.

Embargoes in time of war.

Duties to develop the means of national defense—though it would be much easier to obtain future supplies overseas "because our national character is now established and recognized throughout the world."

Finally, duties for revenue.[2]

Since all amounts were blank, he did not object to the Fitzsimons list being added to his own. Spokesmen for rum importers and domestic distillers then broke their deceptive silence. Facing an effort to cut Jamaica rum from fifteen to twelve cents a gallon, Madison said he would tax this article with as high a duty as could be collected, and it was the sense of the people that it should be weighty indeed. A New Yorker answered that if they were to act

as moralists, every member would wish to prevent the use of
ardent spirits altogether. But he thought anything over eight cents
would induce smuggling. The House made it fifteen.

Next came molasses, imported in huge quantities from the West
Indies by New England distillers. Madison suggested an eight-
cent tax—low enough to give American rum an advantage over
the Jamaican product. By taxing this ingredient of manufacture
they would gain the effect of an excise on domestic rum without
having to resort to that unpopular system. New Englanders yelled
with pain. The distillers couldn't pay such a tax. Massachusetts
imported more molasses than all the other states combined. It was
a tax on a necessity of the poor, who used molasses in place of
sugar and drank country rum.

Madison replied that rum consumers in all states would pay the
molasses tax while those who ate molasses would escape the tax
on sugar. He didn't want the cost of rum so low that the continent
would be flooded with inferior liquor. Pennsylvanians came to his
support. They didn't want the price of rum so low that it would
hurt the brewing industry. The tax was fixed at six cents, but
that didn't end the fight. Fisher Ames launched his national
career as a golden-tongued orator with a passionate defense of
Bay State rum against Madison's nefarious assault upon it. He
knew the purpose of government:

"I conceive, sir, that the present Constitution was dictated by
commercial necessity more than other cause. . . . We are not to
consider ourselves, while here, as at church or school, to listen to
the harangues of speculative piety; we are to talk of the political
interests committed to our charge."

Rum manufacture, said Ames, was not only a direct source of
New England wealth but the bulwark of the fishing industry.
Fish exports paid for molasses imports; without this exchange
markets and industries would be ruined. The distillers' spokesman
swung to pathos:

"Mothers will tell their children, when they solicit their daily
and accustomed nutriment, that the new laws forbid them the use

of it, and they will grow up in detestation of the hand which proscribes their innocent food and the occupation of their fathers."

Loss of foreign markets, Madison replied, had not put any distilleries out of business—it had been offset by growth of population. Virginia imported three times as much as Massachusetts, and would pay three times as much to the Treasury. The South imported many things for the poor. Might not Southern children, for want of clothes, be taught to breathe this same vindictive spirit?

"Why these apprehensions for one part of the Union more than the other? Are the northern people made of finer clay? Do they respire a clearer air? Do their breasts burn with a more generous ardor for their rights as men, or for their country's happiness and glory? Are they the chosen few? Are all others to be oppressed with accumulated burdens and they to take their course easy and unrestrained? No . . . the general government . . . was instituted for the protection of all and it is expected it will accomplish the end for which it was established. But this can only be done by acts of justice and impartiality."

Writing to a friend in Boston, the eloquent Ames gave his impression of this first encounter with the nonoratorical Virginian:

"I made two speeches, the latter in reply to Madison, who is a man of sense, reading, address and integrity, as 'tis allowed. Very much Frenchified in his politics. He speaks low, his person is little and ordinary. He speaks decently, as to manner, and no more. His language is very pure, perspicuous and to the point. Pardon me if I add that I think him a little too much of a book politician and too timid in his politics, for prudence and caution are opposites of timidity. He is not a little of a Virginian and thinks that state the land of promise, but is afraid of their state politics and of his popularity there more than I think he should be. . . . He is our first man."

The six cents stood, whereupon Ames argued for an excise on rum rather than a tax on its chief ingredient. That would relieve those who used molasses as a food. Admitting this, Madison replied that the excise would produce greater evils than it cured. He hammered at a theme which Ames persistently evaded—that the fisheries and distilleries already were paying heavier state duties. How could they be hurt by a shift to lighter federal taxes? He had agreed to a duty on salt, which bore heavily on cattle raisers. Congress was laying a protective tariff on steel, so necessary to agriculture that it ought rather to be favored with a bounty. Duties were being imposed for the benefit of Northern manufactures; the burden was falling on the South. He wanted the North prosperous, but enough favors had been granted. By a margin of two votes, the House cut the molasses tax to five cents.[3]

Told that all duties were so high as to encourage smuggling, Madison replied that the real object of the protest was to cut the duty on spirits. He did not agree with Jackson that all the creeks and rivers of Georgia would be filled with smugglers' boats. The smuggling that Americans did under the British government was to combat oppression. Their virtue would be more strongly fortified when it was "understood that the man who wounds the honor of his country by a baseness in defrauding the revenue only exposes his neighbors to further and greater impositions."

The House held to its rates. Another fight developed when Parker of Virginia moved a tax of $10 per head—the constitutional limit—on every slave brought in. The deep South at once protested, with biting remarks on Virginia's superabundant supply of homebred slaves, while Sherman renewed his 1787 protest against labeling human beings as property. Madison, who had sided with Sherman in the convention, now came to Parker's support. The evil was not in enumerating persons as merchandise on paper, but in treating them as such in fact. The tax would reduce that evil, and give expression to the moral purpose for which it was authorized by the Constitution:

"It is to be hoped that by expressing a national disapprobation of this trade we may destroy it, and save ourselves from reproaches, and our posterity the imbecility ever attendant on a country filled with slaves."

The weakening effect of slavery, said Madison, made any increase of it a matter of national concern. However, because of the threatened delay to the tax bill, he would be willing to see the matter made the subject of a separate bill—to which Parker agreed. These two were not trying to protect Virginia's domestic slave trade. They assailed slavery itself, Parker pointing to its conflict with the Declaration of Independence, Madison emphasizing its demoralizing effect upon the community.[4]

When tonnage taxes came up Madison had no difficulty in securing a small levy on American vessels, needed, he said, for the support of lighthouses, hospitals for disabled seamen and other establishments incident to commerce. Most congressmen were willing to tax foreign ships heavily, though South Carolina protested. The hard fight would be against his proposal that nations having commercial treaties with the United States pay a lower tax than those having none. He told how France had relaxed its regulations and of Moustier's efforts to gain further concessions. Ought these advantages to be jeopardized by putting France on a parity with ex-enemy England, who would not even let British ships be repaired (except trivially) in American ports, or American ships in British ports? Every American harbor was open without restriction, but the most valuable British ports—those of the West Indies—were closed to American vessels and they could carry nothing but American produce to the British Isles. Commerce with continental Europe was channeled through England by the inordinate weight of British shipping. Here was substantial reason for making a discrimination, and it would suit the temper of the people. The cost of favoring American vessels might save the country from a greater one.

"If it is expedient for America to have vessels employed in commerce at all, it will be proper that she have enough to answer all the purposes intended; to form a school for seamen, to lay the foundation of a navy, and to be able to support itself against the interference of foreigners. . . . I consider that an acquisition of maritime strength is essential to this country; if ever we are so unfortunate as to be engaged in war, what but this can defend our towns and cities upon the seacoast? Or what but this can enable us to repel an invading enemy?"

Duties of thirty and fifty cents a ton were voted on the two classes of foreign ships compared with nine cents on American vessels. In working for these rates, Madison stood for the general interests of the Union and squarely against those of Virginia and the South. He displayed not a trace of either the timidity or the catering to local popularity which Ames saw in him. He was pleased, he said, that so little contrariety of sentiments had developed: it foretold the perpetuity of the Union. However, to ease the fears of the South he would suggest that the discrimination in favor of American vessels be made lower at first and raised sharply a few years later. The certainty of increase would stimulate shipbuilding until American ships could handle the whole foreign trade. That would prevent the tonnage duties from raising freight rates. This plan was voted down, partly from fear of British reprisals if discrimination were adopted at all. Madison scoffed at this danger. Should a trade war develop, America could sustain her suffering while Britain would be wounded almost mortally.

"If we were to say that no article should be exported from America to the West Indies but what went in our own bottoms, we should soon hear a different language from any that has ever been held out to us on the subject of commercial regulations. . . . Even at this moment we hear the cry of distress from one part of her dominions, which can only be relieved by the resources they have in this country."[5]

A cry certainly went up from British Consul Phineas Bond, who described affairs in this fashion to Lord Carmarthen:

"I am very sorry to observe that Mr. Madison, who is allowed to be a gentleman of the first abilities in America, seems to be very ill-informed as to the present system of commercial intercourse between G. Britain and these states—and loses sight of the great and equitable principle of reciprocity, which should influence the present regulations. He by no means adverts to that important consideration, that so great an indulgence has been granted by G. Britain to the United States as to put their trade upon a footing with the most favored nations in Europe, our best and oldest allies."[6]

Reciprocity was exactly what Madison was striving for. His purpose was to force Great Britain to modify her monopolistic navigation laws—not merely to place the United States on a parity with other victims. This was reflected in his ardent plea for a slight tax reduction on spirits from nations having treaties with the United States. He said he favored this not (as a New York congressman charged) to show gratitude to France, though there was much to be grateful for, but as a lesson to other countries. As long as the United States did not protect itself, there would be no relaxation of Britain's obnoxious policy. Let the world observe a distinction between commercial friends and commercial adversaries.

"Let us show that if a war breaks out in Europe and is extended and carried on in the West Indies, we can treat with friendship and succor the one, while we can shut the other out of our ports. . . . We possess natural advantages which no other nation does; we can, therefore, with justice, stipulate for a reciprocity in commerce. The way to obtain this is by discrimination."

On three successive tests the majority favoring discrimination mounted from nine or ten to nearly forty. The opposition, Madison observed, was chiefly abetted by New York City's Anglicism. But hardly had the tonnage bill gone to the Senate when he heard that his policy was in disfavor, with Lee and Grayson active in the opposition. Their success was reflected in the British consul's advice not to abandon the highly profitable British monopoly of the West Indian carrying trade. There would be no counterregulations from a people overwhelmed by debt, who would be totally ruined if their crops rotted on the land for lack of ships to carry them abroad.[7]

Just as the import bill was approaching passage, Madison offered an amendment limiting its duration, to avoid the reproach of levying a perpetual tax. His less obvious aim, he revealed, was to avoid protection of manufactures beyond the time needed to put them on their feet. The proposal was overwhelmingly approved, everybody who objected to any particular duty jumping to its support.[8]

In these opening weeks, Madison exercised a leadership in which his theoretical desire for free trade was modified both by his own recognition of the obstacles to it and the powerful influence of the small but aggressive manufacturing interests of the country. Defeated by the Senate in his attempt to use commercial discrimination as a defensive weapon, he laid the groundwork for a later political revolt against the disciples of submission, and outlined the future American policy of pressure for the open door and freedom of the seas.

# CHAPTER XX

## Majority Leader

"Yesterday arrived the illustrious George Washington, President of the United States, amidst the joyful acclamations of every party and every description of citizens. . . . Absorbed and agitated by the sentiment which our adored leader and ruler inspired, the printer apprehends that he cannot with perfect precision describe the various scene of splendor."

Luckily somebody connected with the New York *Advertiser* was still able to set type, so it is of record that the President-elect, greeted on April 23 by a committee of Congress, embarked at Elizabeth in a specially built barge and was rowed to New York by thirteen pilots in white uniforms. Behind trailed a long procession of boats and sailing craft, the counterpart of the shouting throngs which converted a quiet ride from Mt. Vernon into a procession of pageantry and acclaim. In New York City itself, the *Gazette of the United States* reported, old people who had not expected to see Washington until they went to heaven were still limited to that prospect when they were pushed out of range by the eagerness of multitudes of children.

Owing to delay in revamping the old City Hall in which Congress was meeting, Washington's formal induction into office was postponed a week. At noon on April 30, a procession escorted him from his home in Cherry Street and Chancellor Livingston administered the oath in the Senate gallery overlooking Broad Street. The President's modest inaugural address, instead of recommending particular measures, praised the talents, rectitude and patriotism of the men who were to devise and adopt them. Inviting constitutional amendments, he was sure that Congress would avoid alterations injurious to an effective government, but would fortify the rights of freemen and promote public harmony. He closed with a perfect blend of Franklin's speech on prayer in

255

the Federal Convention and Madison's concluding remarks to the ratifying delegates in Virginia. A note written by Washington leaves little doubt that Madison wrote the address.[1]

In England, Commons and Lords always replied to addresses from the throne, so House and Senate must respond to the President. Madison did the writing for the House, and helped produce the first spat between the two branches of Congress. At the instigation of Vice President Adams the Senate directed its half of the joint inaugural committee to report titles for President and Vice President. The committee's House branch, of which Madison was a member, had an idea of its own: let the President be called the President. Madison described the situation to Jefferson:

"Adams espoused the cause of titles with great eagerness. His friend R. H. Lee, although elected as a republican enemy to an aristocratic Constitution, was a most zealous second. The projected title was: His Highness the President of the United States and Protector of their Liberties. Had the project succeeded it would have subjected the President to a severe dilemma and given a deep wound to our infant government."

The death blow was engineered by Madison. On May 5, the House approved a joint committee report advising against any style or titles beyond those specified in the Constitution. Without waiting for Senate action, the Virginian addressed the House reply "to George Washington, President of the United States." By casting off degrading appendages in favor of naked dignity, he commented, this House action would show the friends of republicanism "that our new government was not meant to substitute either monarchy or aristocracy, and that the genius of the people is as yet adverse to both."[2]

The enraged Senate rejected the joint committee report and asked for a conference. House hotheads, led by Parker and Page, wanted to refuse. Adams, they thought, was promoting "His Highness" for himself, as Washington's successor. Madison calmed them. Let us, he advised, "proceed with due respect to the Senate, and give dignity and weight to our own opinion, so far as it contradicts theirs, by the deliberate and decent manner in which

we decide." Titles were not dangerous, just foolish and unrepubli-
can—ridiculous if invented by luxuriant fancy, odious and ridiculous if borrowed from the pompous sovereigns of the East or the
inferior potentates of Europe. "The more simple, the more republican we are in our manners, the more rational dignity we shall
acquire." Appointment of a conference committee would not
sacrifice dignity; it would tend to cement that harmony, good will
and urbanity between the two houses which were necessary for
public business.

Madison headed the House conferees; Lee the Senate's. They
disagreed. Lee's group advised the Senate to address the President
as "His Highness," etc., but it decided instead to conform with
the practice adopted by the House. As Madison described it, the
House action was spontaneous, the imitation by the Senate was
extorted.[3]

Three years later, heavily cudgeled in print for his passion for
titles, the Vice President explained to an unidentified correspondent that he merely asked the Senate how he should address the
chief executive, observing that it appeared "better to give him no
title but 'Sir' or 'Mr. President,' " than to put him on a level with
his own ambassadors by calling him "Your Excellency." The
Senate appointed a committee and that was all there was to it.

In this address to posterity Adams sought to create the impression that he favored "Mr. President" when he said it was better
than "Your Excellency." Did he? On May 8 the Senate rejected
both titles and appointed a new committee headed by Adams' alter
ego Lee, which brought in the resounding smacker "His Highness," etc. The next day, according to Senator Maclay, the Vice
President orated for forty minutes, insisting that the President's
title must include and be greater than all the dignities of the
diplomatic corps. Call George Washington merely President and
the common people of foreign lands "will despise him to all
eternity." The pseudo-monarchism thus choked off found vent in
social forms and protocol, pushed on Washington against his will,
which disgusted Madison and alarmed many other republicans.[4]

Madison's reply informed Washington that, having received
many tokens of the people's affection, he now possessed proof "of

their gratitude for your services, of their reverence for your wisdom, and of their confidence in your virtues." In sacrificing his
desire for repose he would be rewarded by the satisfaction of
promoting the happiness of his fellow citizens. The President's
statement that he would refuse any compensation beyond actual
expenses drew praise, so worded as to invite him to abandon that
course, as he soon did. The only reference to public policy was a
promise to consider constitutional amendments.

Receiving the reply in the House audience room, Washington
made a brief answer, saying that he felt overpaid for past services
to his country and feared his future ones might not fulfill antici-
pations, though directed by an honest and ardent zeal. The answer
was prepared for him by Madison, to whom Washington had
written on May 5:

"Notwithstanding the conviction I am under of the labor which
is imposed upon you by public individuals as well as public bodies;
yet, as you have begun, so I could wish you to finish, the good
work in a short reply to the Address of the House of Representatives (which I now enclose) that there may be an accordance in
this business."

It is evident from this note that Madison prepared the inaugural
address, since the prior service mentioned was for a public *individual*. So all three of these state utterances—the President's
address, the reply of the House, and the final response of the
President—came from his mind and pen, and he rounded out the
job by writing Washington's response to the Senate.[5]

With the executive head firmly in place, the House set out to
put a body under it. On May 19 Madison moved that there be a
Department of Foreign Affairs, a Treasury Department, a War
Department, each to be headed by a secretary appointed by the
President, by and with the advice and consent of the Senate; and
removable by the President.

Hot controversy was stirred by the provision for removal. Smith
of South Carolina believed there was no way of removing a man
except by impeachment. Madison protested. That would keep
every officer in place during good behavior. Such a fatal error

would ultimately destroy the system, but he thought the construction illogical and faulty.

"I think it absolutely necessary that the President should have the power of removing from office; it will make him in a peculiar manner responsible for their conduct, and subject him to impeachment himself if he suffers them to perpetrate . . . crimes . . . or neglects to superintend their conduct so as to check their excesses."

Benson, Vining and Boudinot reinforced Madison's position, but many agreed with Bland that the power which appointed must also remove, wherefore the Senate's consent was necessary. Was it really natural, rejoined Madison, that the power which appointed should remove? That violated a principle which pervaded the whole system. If a department head could be removed by the President, the secretary was fully responsible to the chief executive and the latter was responsible to the public. But if the officer could not be displaced without the consent of the Senate, the President no longer was answerable for his conduct. "You here destroy a real responsibility without obtaining even the shadow."

The removal clause was left in the resolution, but White of Virginia moved to strike it out of the bill to create the Department of Foreign Affairs. Smith supported the motion with a telling quotation from No. 77 of *The Federalist,* a work which he understood "to be the production of two gentlemen of great information." It asserted flatly that the Senate's consent "would be necessary to displace as well as appoint." Madison could have said that this came from Hamilton. Instead, pursuing a thought suggested by Clymer, he said that a rereading of the Constitution had convinced him that Congress did not even have power to abate the President's responsibility in this field. Quoting the clauses which placed the legislative power in Congress, the executive power in the President and the judiciary power in the courts, he averred that there could be no deviations from this separation of powers except where the Constitution made exceptions. It had done so in appointments to office. It had not done so in removals. So, as the power of removal was executive, it was beyond the reach of the legislative body.

Madison's argument, Ames remarked, was so conclusive that it was needless to go over the ground again. Sherman, however, contended that the power to create an office implied legislative discretion in determining how it should be vacated. Madison pointed out that this would permit the total exclusion of the President from a share in removals. He emphasized the importance of what they were about to do:

"The decision that is at this time made will become the permanent exposition of the Constitution. . . . It will depend, perhaps, on this decision whether the government shall retain that equilibrium which the Constitution intended, or take a direction towards aristocracy or anarchy among the members of the government."

Safety against abuse of the President's power, he argued, lay both in impeachment and in his need to go before the people every four years. The chief executive could be impeached either for keeping an unworthy man in office or for removing one whose continuance was necessary, "for I contend that the wanton removal of meritorious officers would subject him to impeachment and removal from his own high trust." Following a 20-to-34 failure to strike out the removal clause, Benson and Madison reshaped the proposition so that Congress would not appear to confer a power which was in fact conferred by the Constitution. They inserted a clause containing the words "whenever the said principal officer shall be removed by the President," thus resting the power on inference. The debate was notable for Madison's assertion of the right of Congress to interpret the Constitution.

"I acknowledge, in the ordinary course of government, that the exposition of the laws and Constitution devolves upon the judiciary. But I beg to know, upon what principle it can be contended that any one department draws from the Constitution greater powers than another, in marking out the limits of the powers of the several departments. . . . If the constitutional boundary of either be brought into question, I do not see that any one of those independent departments has more right than another to declare their sentiments on that point."[6]

The War Department was established without a battle, and the Treasury occasioned only minor conflicts. Madison's proposal for a single head encountered some opposition. It faded when he declared that he wanted the comptroller and auditor to exercise checks upon the secretary, which would be impossible if all three were coequal members of a board. To make the comptroller more independent he moved that he serve for a fixed number of years, unless removed earlier by the President, and be eligible to reappointment. The House was unsympathetic. It was 132 years before fixed tenure was given to the comptroller general in the General Accounting Office, and 145 years before the Supreme Court indorsed Madison's accompanying contention that Congress could modify the removal power of the President in the case of officers performing quasi-judicial functions.

In the debate over the Treasury Madison fought hard to retain a section authorizing the secretary to digest and report (changed later to digest and prepare) plans for improving the revenue and supporting public credit. Page, Gerry and others called this a dangerous invasion of the exclusive right of the House to originate revenue bills. Joining Ames, Boudinot and Laurance in its defense, Madison said he was unable to see the danger. These were the exact words used by the old Congress when it set up the Treasury Board. There was a small probability that an officer might derive weight from this circumstance, and have some influence upon Congress, but far more danger and expense would result from the lack of well-formed and digested plans.[7]

That forecast carried no hint of Hamilton's meteoric rise to power. The issues which were to divide him and Madison had not yet arisen, but the latter's moderate disagreement with Fitzsimons and sharp conflicts with Ames pointed plainly to new alignments. Ames continued to mix praise and disparagement of the Virginian in his letters to George Minot:

"Madison [he wrote on May 18] is cool, and has an air of reflection which is not very distant from gravity and self-sufficiency. In speaking he never relaxes into pleasantry, and discovers little of that warmth of heart which gives efficacy to George

Cabot's reasoning, and to Lowell's. His printed speeches are more faithful than any other person's, because he speaks very slow and his discourse is strongly marked. He states a principle and deduces consequences with clearness and simplicity."

At times, Ames continued, Madison would become declamatory and appeal to such things as the pride of the House in remaining consistent to a former vote.

"I think him a good man and an able man, but he has rather too much theory, and wants that discretion which men of business commonly have. He is also very timid and seems evidently to want manly firmness and energy of character."

Minot made a surprising reply. He delicately rebuked his young friend (Ames was thirty-one) for allowing his feelings to carry him into contemptuous expressions toward an adversary. Admitting his proneness to represent things too strongly, Ames answered:

"But did I express any contempt for Madison? Upon my word I do not recollect a word of it, and there is not in my heart a symptom of its having ever been there. Before I came I was cautioned against pinning my faith on any man's sleeve. I was afraid of it, for I think I am not apt to resist the influence of those whom I esteem. But I see in Madison, with his great knowledge and merit, so much error, and some of it so very unaccountable and tending to so much mischief, that my impatience may have tinctured my letter with more gall than I remember."

Ames could not account for Madison's passionate devotion to the discrimination against British shipping. Though approved by Frenchmen it would not benefit France. Was it, then, the illogical product of his bias toward that country? A reappraisal of Madison followed:

"He is probably deficient in that fervor and vigor of character which you will expect in a great man. He is not likely to risk bold measures, like Charles Fox, nor even to persevere in any measures against a firm opposition, like the first Pitt. He derives from nature an excellent understanding, however, but I think he excels in the quality of judgment. He is possessed of a sound judgment, which perceives truth with great clearness and can trace it through the mazes of debate without losing it. He is admirable for this inestimable talent. As a reasoner he is remarkably perspicuous and methodical. He is a studious man, devoted to public business, and a thorough master of almost every public question that can arise, or he will spare no pains to become so if he happens to be in want of information. What a man understands clearly, and has viewed in every different point of light, he will explain to the admiration of others, who have not thought of it at all, or but little, and who will pay in praise for the pains he saves them. His clear perception of an argument makes him impressive, and persuasive sometimes. It is not his *forte,* however. Upon the whole, he is a useful, respectable, worthy man, in a degree so eminent that his character will not sink. He will continue to be a very influential man in our country."[8]

It seemed to Ames that on protection of commerce, Madison paid too much attention to Adam Smith's *Wealth of Nations,* too little to the conditions of American business. Again, "he is afraid, even to timidity, of his state, and has reasoned to my disgust and surprise about the topics I have mentioned so strongly." To a Massachusetts congressman who never deviated a hair's breadth from the desires of the New England shipping, fishing and distilling interests, a timid man was a Virginian who supported Massachusetts against Virginia only half the time. Right at this time a matter was coming forward which would show whether Madison was afraid of his state. That was his handling of constitutional amendments.

# CHAPTER XXI

## The Bill of Rights

On May 4, 1789, Madison gave notice that he intended to bring up the subject of constitutional amendments on the fourth Monday of the month. Why speak of it so far in advance? To get ahead of Bland, who next day presented the application of the Virginia legislature for a general convention. Delayed a fortnight by revenue matters, Madison moved on June 8 that the House go into committee of the whole. He was ready to offer some propositions which he hoped would receive unanimous approval. Hours of debate followed, some opposing any amendments, others objecting to immediate action. Many wanted a select committee. Balked of an immediate decision, Madison moved the appointment of a select committee and laid his propositions before the House.

This reproduced the earlier situation in reverse. Those who wanted no amendments, those who wanted delay and some who wanted prompt action were now against a select committee. The harassed Virginian said that fearing again to be discomfited he would withdraw his second motion and simply move the adoption of his resolutions. That produced results—a quick reference to committee of the whole. The action pointed to a friendly majority, but it was evident that the amendments faced a coalition of those who wanted none and those who wanted everything demanded by the antifederal extremists.

In framing his propositions Madison went over the amendments asked for by the conventions of Massachusetts, South Carolina, New Hampshire, Virginia, New York and North Carolina, and by minorities in Pennsylvania and Maryland. Piled up in these were innumerable duplications. Most states put emphasis on bills of rights, but there was also a pyramiding of amendments reserving undelegated powers to the states, gutting the power of direct taxation, compelling an increase in the size of the House, and eliminating federal control of congressional elections except when states failed to provide for them.

EDMOND CHARLES GENÊT

PHILIP FRENEAU

WILLIAM B. GILES

JAMES MONROE. BY VAN DER LYN

Madison's amendments were drawn almost entirely from the forty Virginia propositions, but he rejected utterly the notion that he was bound by state action. If several states favored a proposition of which he approved, that was an argument for submitting it. If a still greater number favored one to which he was opposed, it stayed out. On personal liberty, he used everything translatable into definite guaranties. From Patrick Henry's twenty substantive amendments five were taken. Not one weakened the government. Had he wished to secure every amendment recommended by Virginia, he wrote later in the session, he would have asked for no more than he did because "two or three contentious additions would even now prostrate the whole project."[1]

The Madison propositions opened with a harmless prefix (a bow to the Virginia convention) setting forth the purposes of government and the right of the people to alter it. The amendments which followed were to be embedded in the Constitution, not added to it.

Five states had asked that House membership be fixed at one representative for each 30,000 persons until the total reached at least 200. Madison provided also for a maximum but left both numbers blank. Next came a proviso that salary increases voted by Congress to itself should not take effect until after the next election.

A ten-clause bill of rights covered freedom of religion, speech, press and assembly; the right to bear arms; immunity from the quartering of soldiers in peacetime; prohibition of unreasonable searches and seizures through general warrants; a ban on excessive bail and fines; forbidding of cruel and unusual punishments; the right to a speedy, public, fair trial; and a guarantee against deprivation of life, liberty or property without due process of law. These were followed by a clause protecting unenumerated rights.

Amendment No. 5 declared that *no state* should violate the equal rights of conscience, freedom of the press or trial by jury in criminal cases. This came from Madison alone. No convention asked for it. Supplementing the bill of rights were some amendments to the judiciary article. Criminal trials must employ juries of the vicinage. Civil appeals involving less than a minimum sum were forbidden. Higher courts must not re-examine facts found by a jury except in accordance with the common law. A new article concluded the list: No branch of government was to exercise powers assigned to another branch. Powers not delegated by the Constitution, nor prohibited by it to the states, were reserved to the states respectively. This last provision, its sponsor said, was put in only to quiet the public mind. It changed nothing.

Protection of civil rights, safeguards in the organization of Congress, assertions of established principles—these were the characteristics of the Madison amendments. They neither impaired the powers of the federal government nor weakened its structure.

Supporting his proposals, the Virginian observed that some champions of republican liberty thought a bill of rights unnecessary, improper or even dangerous. He himself "always conceived that in a certain form and to a certain extent, such a provision was neither improper nor altogether useless." In contrast with a monarchy, there was little need to place restraint on the relatively weak executive department. It must be leveled against the legislative branch, the most powerful, and most likely to abuse its power because it was under the least control.

Arguing for his bill of rights, the sponsor raised and answered objections which he himself, as a maneuver against conditional ratification, had offered in the Virginia convention. It was said that Congress had been delegated no power over civil liberties. True, but it might invade them through its sweeping power to carry its delegated powers into effect. A law authorizing general warrants would be unnecessary and improper in itself, yet Congress might think such warrants a legitimate aid to the collection of revenue. Better forbid them altogether.

It had been argued that civil rights were solemnly protected in state constitutions. That was an uncertain assurance against federal invasion. It was claimed that the enumeration of certain rights would disparage those not enumerated. That was taken care of by the amendment forbidding such an interpretation.

Some contended that declarations of rights were worthless because those of the states had been violated. Let them be incorporated in the Constitution and independent tribunals of justice would become their special guardians. The federal courts would be an impenetrable bulwark against every assumption of power, but should they fail there was another safeguard:

"Besides this security there is a great probability that such a declaration in the federal system would be enforced; because the state legislatures will jealously and closely watch the operation of this government, and be able to resist with more effect every assumption of power than any other power on earth can do."

Here was not only the doctrine of judicial review but the lusty germ of the Virginia and Kentucky Resolutions, through which Madison and Jefferson tried to remedy the Supreme Court's failure to protect the people against the Sedition Act of 1798. It was an outgrowth of their correspondence. Through solemn declaration in a bill of rights, Madison observed to his friend in 1788, political truths gradually acquired the character of fundamental maxims of free government. In cases of violation by the government, they furnished good ground for an appeal to the sense of the community. Even without a written bill, such rights would be protected against federal invasion by "the jealousy of the subordinate governments." Jefferson agreed, but said the declaration must be written, to furnish a text whereby state governments "will try all the acts of the federal government." He then affirmed the power of the courts to check the operation of unconstitutional laws. Thus it was through Jefferson that Madison was brought to the doctrine of judicial review, and it was from Madison that Jefferson derived the idea (but not the details) of the Kentucky Resolutions.[2]

The House saw no urgency in the proposed amendments. Cynical Fisher Ames wrote that they were the fruit of much labor and research by Madison. "He has hunted up all the grievances and complaints of newspapers, all the articles of conventions, and the small talk of their debates. . . . Upon the whole, it may do some good towards quieting men who attend to sounds only, and may get the mover some popularity, which he wishes." Six weeks passed before Madison begged the House to devote a current moment of leisure to the matter. Instead, the whole day was spent deciding that it would be better, after all, to refer it to a committee of one from each state. The balloting made Vining of Delaware chairman, Madison second. All of the amendments, some shortened and clarified, were reported in a week.³

By this time congressmen were intent on something really important—their salaries. Would $6.00 a day provoke a storm at home? Madison thought that sum too much for the House, too little for the Senate. His fear was that with equal pay, the ablest men would prefer the House, letting the Senate degenerate into an unfitness for the great dignity of its institution. This was no sour-grapes verdict. The Senate had just drafted one of the most important laws in American history—the act creating the federal judiciary system—yet because of its rule of secrecy its work was ignored by a public which crowded the House galleries and pored over newspaper accounts of its debates. In the eyes of the people, the House was Congress. In its own eyes it rated not a penny less than a $6.00 Senate, but responded to a call for economy by reducing the doorkeeper's salary.⁴

Trying on August 13 to bring up his amendments, Madison encountered more devices for delay. Was it wise, he asked, to stir up jealousy among people who believed their most essential rights were in danger? A demand followed for two or three weeks to consider substitute proposals. Realizing (as he wrote to Randolph) that this was a scheme to thwart moderate amendments which would satisfy the people, he replied that the offering of new propositions should not prevent a decision on those in the report. With the end of the session drawing near, any kind of delay would be fatal because the Senate must act too.

The response was an all-day debate on Sherman's motion that amendments be added to the Constitution instead of inserted in it. Madison combated the change and it was voted down. The House proceeded to a clause-by-clause debate.

Religious freedom was Madison's first concern, both in drafting his amendments and in the deliberations which now ensued. His original hesitancy about a bill of rights was largely due to the fear, expressed to Jefferson, that "the rights of conscience in particular, if submitted to public definition, would be narrowed much more than they are likely ever to be by an assumed power."

In Virginia he had seen the Declaration of Rights violated in every instance where it had been opposed to a popular current.

"Notwithstanding the explicit provision contained in that instrument for the rights of conscience, it is well known that a religious establishment would have taken place in that state, if the legislative majority had found as they expected a majority of the people in favor of the measure; and I am persuaded that if a majority of the people were now of one sect, the measure would still take place and on narrower ground than was then proposed, notwithstanding the additional obstacle which the law [the Statute of Religious Liberty] has since created."

From this it is clear that Madison regarded the religious assessment bill of 1784 as a move to set up a religious establishment. He saw it also as a violation of the rights of conscience. Public aid to religion, therefore, was unconstitutional if the basic law either forbade a religious establishment or guaranteed full rights of conscience. The danger came not only from New England, where there was a full-fledged and intolerant state church, but even from his own state. In the Virginia ratifying convention, a pretended defense of religious freedom had been made by Patrick Henry, leader of the 1784 campaign for public support of teachers of religion. He presented a federal amendment based on Madison's "rights of conscience" clause in the Virginia Declaration, but weakened it by adding that "no particular religious sect or society ought to be favored or established by law in preference to others."
Madison asked Congress to submit a far broader guarantee:

"The civil rights of none shall be abridged on account of religious belief or worship, nor shall any national religion be established, nor shall the full and equal rights of conscience be in any manner, or on any pretext, abridged."

The committee shortened this to:

"No religion shall be established by law, nor shall the equal rights of conscience be infringed."

Replying to a New York congressman's fear that this might
have a tendency to abolish religion altogether, Madison said he
understood the meaning to be "that Congress should not establish
a religion, and enforce the legal observation of it by law, nor compel men to worship God in any manner contrary to their conscience." A Connecticut member was afraid this would close the
federal courts to suits to collect contributions pledged to church societies, since "a support of ministers or building of places of worship
might be construed into a religious establishment." In reply:

"Mr. Madison thought, if the word 'national' was inserted before
religion, it would satisfy the minds of honorable gentlemen. He
believed that the people feared one sect might obtain a pre-
eminence, or two combine together and establish a religion to
which they would compel others to conform. He thought if the
word 'national' was introduced it would point the amendment
directly to the object it was intended to prevent."

In his desire to soothe the New Englanders, Madison stated *one*
object of the clause as *the* object. But his proposed alteration did
not limit it to that object. Insertion of the word "national" would
make it plain that the clause did not cover local or state matters
affecting religion. He had no thought of narrowing the scope of
the prohibition in the national field. That was made clear in his
"Essay on Monopolies" (discussed below) wherein he treated
the First Amendment as if the word "national" still were in it
and represented it both as a guarantee of equal rights and a barrier to tax support of religion. Now, however, it was pointed out
that the word "national" was anathema to Antifederalists, who
associated it with consolidation of state and federal governments.
Madison thereupon withdrew his motion, and the House voted
fifty-one to twenty for a clause proposed by the New Hampshire
convention and offered by Livermore of that state:

"Congress shall make no laws touching religion, or infringing
the rights of conscience."

That definitely restricted the prohibition to Congress, but was so broad as to be vague. A few days later, on motion of Ames, the House without debate adopted this substitute:

"Congress shall make no law establishing religion, or to prevent the free exercise thereof, or to infringe the rights of conscience."

There can be little doubt that this was written by Madison. It consisted of the original committee version, plus a middle clause drawn from his speech explaining that version—all reshaped to bear directly on Congress. Ames had taken no part in the debate, but in private wrote jeeringly of the religious and other guaranties as "a prodigious great dose" of medicine which would no more stimulate the stomach than hasty pudding. He was willing enough, however, to co-operate in a rephrasing which left the states free to do as they pleased. Working thus, Madison gained unanimous support for his main objective—an amendment barring any sort of federal support of religion.[5]

It was a different story in the Senate, where New England supporters of established churches were leagued with Senator Lee of Virginia, a partisan of the 1784 assessment scheme. In September they sent the article back with its vitals cut out. Congress was to "make no law establishing articles of faith or a mode of worship or prohibiting the free exercise of religion." By limiting the ban on establishment of religion to creed and ritual, and striking out infringement of the rights of conscience, the Senate left the way open to financial support of churches and church schools by the federal government.

Madison was chairman of the three House conferees. There is no positive proof that he wrote the final version which came out of conference, but it was a House victory and neither Sherman nor Vining had displayed any interest in this subject. The guaranty that became part of the Constitution could be ascribed to Madison on the basis of the legislative history, even if its wording did not clearly identify him as the author:

"Congress shall make no law respecting an establishment of religion or prohibiting the free exercise thereof."[6]

Of all the versions of the religious guaranty, this most directly covered the thing he was aiming at—absolute separation of church and state and total exclusion of government aid to religion. The extent of the prohibition was indicated by him a year later in a debate over the census bill. To aid the agricultural, commercial and manufacturing interests he proposed an enumeration by occupations. During the discussion of it Madison was asked why he had not provided for a count of the professional classes. He would do so willingly, he replied, but added:

"As to those who are employed in teaching and inculcating the duties of religion, there may be some indelicacy in singling them out, as the general government is proscribed from interfering, in any manner whatever, in matters respecting religion; and it may be thought to do this, in ascertaining who [are], and who are not ministers of the gospel."[7]

That interpretation was made in the same Congress that drafted the amendment. The meaning of the clause came officially before Madison as President. On February 28, 1811 (after striking down a church incorporation act), he vetoed a grant of land to the Salem, Mississippi, Baptist church on this ground:

"Because the bill in reserving a certain parcel of land of the United States for the use of said Baptist church comprises a principle and precedent for the appropriation of funds of the United States for the use and support of religious societies, contrary to the article of the Constitution which declares that 'Congress shall make no law respecting a religious establishment.' "

In his "Essay on Monopolies," Madison cited this land grant as evidence of the tendency to break down the strongly guarded separation between religion and government. "The Constitution of the U. S.," he wrote, "forbids anything like an establishment of a national religion." Even the appointment of chaplains to Congress violated this principle because "these are to be paid out of the national taxes" and equal rights were violated by the exclusion of small and unpopular sects. Madison was fourth man on the House side of a joint committee appointed in April 1789 to prepare conference rules and consider "the manner of electing chaplains." There being no constitutional barrier at that time, it would have been futile to make a fight against the system, inherited from the old Congress, and thus it became entrenched.[8]

More than a hundred years elapsed after Madison's vetoes before any serious attack was made upon his ruling against tax support of religion. The issue was slow in arising because during most of that interval the guaranties of the First Amendment were binding only on Congress. It was Madison's intention to subject the states to a similar but separate restriction—one which he called the most valuable in his entire list[9]—but the Senate threw it out. Consequently the guaranty of religious freedom did not become binding on the states until after the Fourteenth Amendment forbade them to deprive any person of life, liberty or property without due process of law. Religious liberty, as defined in the First Amendment, was held by the Supreme Court to fall within that protection.

As the House moved from amendment to amendment it became evident that South Carolina, with some Northern aid, was intent on subordinating Congress to the states. Carolinian Tucker wanted an amendment assuring the people's right "to instruct their representatives." From Madison came a warning that if they expected anything at all they should sheer away from such dubious propositions. By guaranteeing freedom of speech, press and assembly, they were assuring the people's right to advise their representatives. To do more was impossible. Suppose they instructed a representative to violate the Constitution. Was he at liberty to obey? It was true, as Gerry had said, that sovereignty was in the people, but was it to be inferred that detached bodies of people could contravene an act established by them all?

"My idea of the sovereignty of the people is that the people can change the Constitution if they please; but while the Constitution exists they must conform themselves to its dictates."

Gerry agreed with this, but chided Madison for being so devoted to his amendments. "It is natural, sir, for us to be fond of our own work. We do not like to see it disfigured by other hands." Gerry demanded consideration of all the amendments proposed by the various states. The South Carolinians joined him.

Once more Madison protested. The amendments laid before the House were those most strenuously called for by opponents of the Constitution. Protection of rights of conscience, freedom of speech and press, trial by jury—these were attainable and he approved them. To be sure of attaining them he would oppose every amendment of a doubtful nature. The House voted forty-one to ten against subjecting Congress to instructions, then beat down a motion to have all proposals of the state conventions referred to committee of the whole.[10]

Tucker moved to insert the word "expressly" in the final proposition, so that "the powers not *expressly* delegated" to Congress would be reserved to the respective states. On issues to which Congress was alert, Madison was often the last to speak. At this effort to cast out implied powers he was the first:

"It was impossible to confine a government to the exercise of express powers; there must necessarily be admitted powers by implication, unless the Constitution descended to recount every minutia. He remembered the word 'expressly' had been moved in the convention of Virginia, by the opponents to the ratification, and, after full and fair discussion, was given up by them, and the system allowed to retain its present form."

Tucker denied that his amendment would totally exclude implied powers, but it was defeated, seventeen to thirty-two.[11] Antifederalist Burke assailed federal control of the times, places and manner of electing representatives. Gerry supported him, but all others who had been in the Federal Convention stood by the existing clause. The attempt to weaken it, said Madison, tended to destroy the principles and efficacy of the Constitution.

Burke orated on loss of liberty through federal invasion of the electoral process. The patriots of Holland had fought for self-government, but lost it when they gave their general government powers like those in this Constitution. Madison jolted him with the rejoinder that it was the seven state governments of the United Provinces, and not the general government, that robbed the people of the right to choose representatives. By a narrow margin, twenty-three to twenty-eight, the power of Congress was upheld.

The antifederal leaders made a final effort to destroy the power of direct taxation, but polled only nine votes. Seeing how tenacious Sherman was of adding amendments to the Constitution instead of inserting them, Madison gave in on that issue and secured the votes needed for final action. The propositions were accordingly reshaped and sent to the Senate, which compressed them into twelve articles that were submitted to the states.[12]

Of the original sheaf of amendments introduced by Madison, not one was substantially altered in meaning. Three were dropped—the ban on state violation of civil liberties, the declaration about separation of powers, and the limitation of appeals in lawsuits. Two amendments, dealing with the size and pay of Congress, failed of ratification. The others have stood since 1791 as the major portion of the Bill of Rights of the American people.

It is one of the anomalies of history that so great a charter of liberties should have come from a man who had no spontaneous urge to provide it. The explanation lies in the reason for his reluctance—that limitations of language and public opinion might render the basic freedom, that of religion, too narrow for security. If it were infringed, prejudice and intolerance would tear down everything else. Charged with the task of drawing a bill of rights, the very apprehensions which made him hesitate spurred him to superlative performance.

# CHAPTER XXII

## Washington's Right-hand Man

Adjournment was in the air all through August of '89. On the twenty-fourth, Madison and Ames secured a House vote for a recess from September 22 (changed later to the twenty-ninth) until the first Monday in December. Their purpose was to stimulate urgent legislation and exclude new subjects, but the partnership was only skin-deep. Both men were aware that Scott of Pennsylvania was about to bring up the question of locating the national capital. Each knew that regional combines were in the making, and each suspected the other of what both were doing.

The House was plunging at that moment into a fight over the Senate judiciary bill. The incipient State-Rights party, led by Burke and Sumter of South Carolina, undertook to eliminate all lower federal courts except admiralty. Madison rounded out the federal arguments of Smith, Ames, Benson and Sherman. What would follow, he asked, if state courts were declared federal courts? All state judges would hold office during good behavior, by virtue of the Constitution. Filling offices through *description,* instead of presidential appointment, would violate the Constitution. Furthermore the courts of many states could not be trusted with the execution of federal laws.

A despairing lament came from Burke. No matter which way he turned, the Constitution stared him in the face. He followed his allies into a thirty-one-to-eleven defeat. During the entire debate, not one member objected to Section 25, later decried as unconstitutional, which authorizes the Supreme Court to issue writs of error to the highest state tribunals. Even State-Righters recognized a federal duty to check the excesses of the states.[1]

Madison was worried by the sudden attempt to locate the capital. Pennsylvania and the Eastern states seemed to have united in a great push for Trenton, but he doubted the solidity of the coalition. It could be broken by accepting a permanent capital on the Susquehanna and leaving the temporary seat in New York, but that would not do for Virginia. Ames saw quite a different cabal. The Pennsylvanians, he wrote, were making a compact with the Southern people to fix the permanent seat on the Potomac, in exchange for a temporary stay in Philadelphia. It could be carried, but "the Pennsylvanians abhor this in their hearts . . . and as the members east of the head of the Chesapeake outnumber the others, they are pretty sure of preventing the future removal to the Potomac."[2]

That is, Pennsylvania would double-cross the South after getting what she wanted. Madison's forecast was fulfilled. A Northeastern pull, concealed in Scott's motion for a capital near the center of *wealth,* population and territory, was made definite by Goodhue's amendment for the Susquehanna and (temporarily) New York. Madison's answer was a motion by Richard Bland Lee that the seat of government be "as nearly central as a convenient water communication with the Atlantic ocean, and an easy access to the western territory will permit." This virtual description of the Potomac produced a hostile outburst. Why, rejoined Madison, should gentlemen object to stating the truths which were to guide them? One had called the resolutions a bandage over his eyes, leading him toward an unseen object. "They appear to me," the Virginian commented, "to contain those luminous truths which ought to guide him through his embarrassment."

In that case, replied Ames, would they not guide Congress without being stated? The House either did or did not think so, for it voted them down by a two-thirds majority. It then defeated Madison's motion to strike out wealth as a consideration in locating the capital. Hartley of Pennsylvania told of the fine bass and pickerel fishing congressmen could enjoy if they chose the Susquehanna. Madison took the floor again.

Mr. Scott, he observed, had been candid enough to admit that agreements had been reached outside the House. More than half the territory of the United States, and nearly half its inhabitants, had been disposed of without their consent or knowledge. He hoped this candor would be extended to principles. If the seat was to be at or near the center of wealth, population and territory, gentlemen should show that their proposed permanent seat was near the permanent center, and the temporary site near the temporary center. His protests brought a reminder that he had praised the House in the debate on the tonnage bill, saying that if such moderation had been foreseen, many objections raised in the Virginia convention would have been obviated. True, he admitted:

"But give me leave now to say that if a prophet had risen in that body and brought the declarations and proceedings of this day into view, that I as firmly believe Virginia might not have been a part of the Union at this moment."

Newspaper accounts of this speech created a sensation, but he meant only that the half-dozen western votes which carried the Constitution might have been lost if dissatisfaction over the seat of government had been added to that over the Mississippi. There was no deep new schism, he wrote to the alarmed Tench Coxe.

Madison emphasized the need for good connections between the capital, the ocean and the Ohio River, and got into a dispute with Ames over the relative mileage by way of the Potomac and the Susquehanna. According to Maclay, Madison observed Governor St. Clair of the Northwest Territory passing mileage figures to Ames from the House gallery. He moved to reduce the governor's salary by $500—an illustration, commented the senator, of the less amiable side of Madison's character.

Reason and logic, however, were his reliance for the Potomac. No government, not even the most despotic, could persistently violate the idea of justice and equal right which prevailed in the mind of the community. Locate the capital in the territorial center and it would always be right on that score, while growth of population would make it nearer and nearer right from that standpoint. Placed north of center, it would always be wrong geographically and the population center would move ever farther away.

The Northern faction was thoroughly nettled by his repeated remarks about a majority disposing of the South. "It is a notorious fact," burst out Wadsworth, "that the New England members . . . refused all bargaining till they were assured there was a bargaining set on foot to carry them to the Potomac. Why, then, are we

reproached with this?" Madison retorted that he wished everything that had passed on the subject were put on paper. It would
be found that the Southern gentlemen had not listened to a proposition until they had found it necessary to prevent a sudden and
improper decision.[3]

Madison did reduce part of the affair to writing. Early in the
session, he reported to Pendleton, secret negotiations were set on
foot among the Northern states, including Pennsylvania, to place
the capital on the Delaware. With this as a threat, New York and
New England offered the South the Susquehanna site, if they
would keep Congress for a time in New York. Pennsylvania, "full
of distrust and animosity" against the northerly states, offered to
support the Potomac site in exchange for a temporary stay in Philadelphia. Flattering progress was made on this ground until the
original parties were reunited "by circumstances which it would
be tedious to explain."

Senator King of New York began to write where Madison left
off. The guileless New England and New York members learned
that a Potomac treaty was on foot between the South and Pennsylvania. So they held a meeting and after debating "whether the
permanent residence ought to be on the Susequehanna or the
Delaware," they agreed to vote for the Susquehanna provided
Pennsylvania would support a temporary residence in New York.
However, the senator's memorandum discloses a bit of trouble:

"Mr. King and Mr. Goodhue met the Pennsylvania delegates
soon after the meeting, and before the subject was mentioned Mr.
Madison came in and after conversing with the delegates of
Pennsylvania by themselves for some time, the delegates informed
Mr. King and Mr. Goodhue that they were so embarrassed with
a connection with the Southern delegates that they could not confer with us concerning the subject of our meeting then."

Senator Morris, according to Maclay, thought Fitzsimons
tricked him by bringing Madison in. Nobody knew whether the
Virginian was introduced or introduced himself.

"There, however, he was, and occupied a room downstairs
while Goodhue and King sat with Mr. Morris upstairs. Messages

were exchanged. The result was that Messrs. Clymer, Fitzsimons, Heister, Scott and the Speaker [Muhlenberg] declared totally against any treaty with the New England men."

Morris, King wrote in his memo, gave a hint that the breakup might not be final. The later course of the Pennsylvanians was described by Ames:

"After a day's deliberation they complied with the proposition for the Susquehanna, and New York in the meantime. How they got clear of their allies is none of my business."[4]

The House approved the seat on the Susquehanna, thirty-one to seventeen. Madison opposed all compromise, but some of the Virginians weakened and the Marylanders gave in. The opponents succeeded, however, in half destroying the bill with an amendment postponing its effectiveness until Pennsylvania and Maryland should clear the navigation of the lower river. Madison doubted whether the Senate would agree. Those who wished to do nothing, added to those who thought the Susquehanna too far north or too far south, were likely to form a majority against it. They might substitute Trenton or Germantown, neither of which could finally be established, but "either of which might get a majority composed of sincere and insidious votes."

Madison was not guessing. Fitzsimons had written to a friend in Philadelphia that he was at heart against the Susquehanna deal. Senator Morris wrote to his wife that the Susquehanna bill never would pass the Senate, and he still hoped for Trenton, on tidewater. The recipients of both letters disclosed their contents to John Dawson of Virginia, who lost no time in getting the information to Madison.

The latter's forecast was verified when the Pennsylvania delegation in the House advised Morris to switch the deal to Germantown. To hold the shaking coalition together, he and six Penn congressmen gave King a signed promise not to consent to the removal of Congress from New York prior to January 1793. Germantown was then inserted as the permanent site and the bill passed, the Vice President breaking a nine-to-nine tie.[5]

THOMAS JEFFERSON. AFTER ST. MEMIN

Memorandum of agreement made and entered into this 23 of December 1789 between William Duer & William Constable both of Newyork ——————

The Parties having full confidence in each other agree to enter into a Speculation in the Funds generally to create a Capital for which Object it is proposed to purchase on time as many Continental Securities as can be obtained. the Money arising therefrom to be immediately invested in the Debts of North & South Carolina to the extent of Sixteen thousand Specie Dollars, the residue in Indents of Interest or such other Paper as may be determined on ——————

It is lastly agreed that the Speculation shall be finally closed in twelve Months or earlier if desired by either of the Parties, and the Profit or Loss mutually shared between or born by them In Witness whereof they have hereunto sett their hands & Seals the day and state above mentioned

Witness
Joseph Ingles

Wm Duer

Wm Constable

DUER-CONSTABLE SPECULATION CONTRACT SIGNED THREE MONTHS AFTER
WILLIAM DUER BECAME ASSISTANT SECRETARY OF THE TREASURY

The session had but three days to run when the revamped measure came back to the House. Short four votes, Madison affected
to surrender. All he wished, on the day before adjournment, was
a little amendment—a proviso that the laws of Pennsylvania continue to operate in the ceded territory until Congress provided
otherwise. Adoption forced the bill back to the Senate, where it
stayed. Was this innocent mischance? Maclay wrote in his journal:

"Just as I was leaving the Hall, Izard took me aside, asked me
to stay; said a trifling amendment will be made in the lower
House, just enough to bring it up here, and we will throw it
out ... you must not tell Morris of this."[6]

On his way home, Madison was held in Philadelphia by a slight
illness. Here he encountered Senator Morris, who said that if the
Senate failed to pass the bill immediately after the recess he would
speak seriously to the Southern states about a renewal of their
Potomac project. "I told him," wrote Madison to Washington,
"they must be spoken to very seriously after what had passed, if
Pennsylvania expected them to listen to her."[7]

Late in the session the President sent a series of appointments to
the Senate. For months, Madison had been his closest adviser
on the filling of offices and was, in turn, deluged with applications.
Acquaintances were usually coy but willing; strangers eager and
full of reasons, ranging from ten children down. Writing to Jefferson on May 27, Madison said that General Knox would be carried
over from the old war office. John Jay would continue to be
foreign secretary if he desired the place. Chancellor Livingston
wanted the Treasury post, but it would be given to Jay or Hamilton. "The latter is perhaps best qualified for that species of business and on that account would be preferred by those who know
him personally."

About Jefferson himself: The President had asked whether any
appointment at home would be agreeable. "Being unacquainted
with your mind I have not ventured on an answer." Given a long-
desired leave of absence, it was Jefferson's intention to bring his
daughters home, attend to plantation business for a few months,
and return to his well-liked diplomatic duties.

Madison was excluded from the cabinet during his current term by the restriction he himself had planted in the Constitution. He was at the moment virtually a presidential cabinet in himself and some of the lawmakers did not relish this. Senator Maclay in July disparaged a current charge that Madison's discrimination policy represented his courtship of the French nation through Jefferson, but felt "much readier to believe him guilty of another charge— *viz.,* his urging the doctrine of taking away the right of removals of officers from the Senate in order to pay his court to the President, whom, I am told, he already affects to govern."

As the executive offices were created, Washington consulted representatives on local appointments, but turned to Madison for counsel as to Virginian, western and national positions. In August the angered Senate gave the President a slap by rejecting the nomination of a seaport officer. They received in reply a stinging defense of the rejected man, and straightway appointed a committee to confer with the President on the mode of receiving communications about appointments and treaties. If they had the nerve, Senators Izard, King and Charles Carroll were also to tell him what was what in the new field of patronage. The committee assured the President that the Senate would adopt the mode of communication most agreeable to him. The deeper realities were recorded by Maclay after a few days' absence:

"Called on Mr. Izard. He gave me a short history of the court party which (as might be expected) is gaining ground. A conference has been held with the President, in which Mr. Izard declares that the President owned he had consulted the members of the House of Representatives as to his nominations, but likewise said he had not acted so with the senators, as they could have an opportunity of giving their advice and consent afterwards. . . . Mr. Izard was clearly of opinion that all the late measures flowed from the President. Mr. Madison, in his opinion, was deep in this business."[8]

Deeper than they knew. The morning after the first meeting with the committee, Madison received a note from the President, who wished to talk with him about oral nominations as an aid to *viva voce* confirmation, and to tell him what John Jay had said about public office. Would it be *perfectly* convenient for him to call that afternoon—Sunday, August 9?

On Monday the Senate committee received from Washington a detailed analysis of the constitutional relations between President and Senate. Every sentence was stamped with Madison's thought and style. The Senate, in its function of advising and consenting, was only a council to the President. Time, place and manner of consultation should therefore rest with the latter. The Senate agreed, on August 21, but when Washington appeared one day later and sought advice about a treaty with Southern Indians, he met so icy a reception that never again did he attempt a personal consultation. This has been called an early demonstration of the futility of oral discussion between President and Senate. It actually signified the blasting of the first presidential honeymoon less than four months after the inauguration—the only honeymoon, it is safe to say, that ever was wrecked by jealousy of James Madison.[9]

The senators would have felt no happier if they had known of the discussion brought on by Foreign Secretary Jay's desire to be chief justice. Washington's first question may be surmised: With the foreign portfolio open, was it safe to appoint Jefferson before he answered Madison's inquiry? Next, what about Edmund Randolph? At Washington's request, Representative Griffin had asked him whether he would accept any federal appointment. The reply was to Madison. What he would really like would be to refuse a federal office, thus showing up those who were saying he could be neither elected nor appointed to the new government. However, his law practice was crippled by his service as governor, his wife was in bad health, old debts had suddenly become vexatious and a federal salary would be very helpful. "I commit myself to you," he concluded. Familiar with his friend's shuttlecock behavior, Madison did not treat this as an acceptance.[10]

Near the end of August, Washington sent Madison a grist of topics to run through his mind "between this and tomorrow afternoon when I shall expect to see you at the appointed time." William Barton having declined a western judgship, would Edward Carrington or Major Turner fit the place? And here was a tougher problem:

"What can I do with A[rthur] L[ee]? He has applied to be nominated one of the associate judges; but I cannot bring my mind to adopt the request."

Having kept Lee out of the foreign secretaryship in 1781 and engaged in a running fight with him in the Continental Congress, Madison knew just about all there was to know about this turbulent doctor of medicine whose preparation for the Supreme Court consisted of several years spent as a law student in London. The advice was probably what Washington did: nothing. What about Carrington? A few weeks after this conference, friends began telling him that he should be United States marshal. He wrote to Madison at once, entrusting the decision to his judgment and friendship, and sent cheering news. Antifederal state judges were taking the oath to support the Constitution. Also:

"A very considerable change has taken place amongst the antis as to yourself. They consider you as the patron of amendments, and it is no uncommon thing to hear confessions that they had been formerly imposed on."[11]

Another Washington inquiry was part of a comedy of miscues. Weeks earlier, both Turner and Barton applied to Madison for aid in getting office. He suggested the western judgship to Turner, who replied that life in the Indian country would interfere with his children's education. Barton was then appointed, and on the day his name went to the Senate, Turner applied to the President for the place he had rejected. Reading of Barton's appointment, he shifted his application to the marshalship. Scarce had he done so when Barton wrote to Madison, refusing the judgship. Turner was then appointed and confirmed as judge, but the thought of his children overwhelmed him and he refused the place again.[12]

Immediately after this conference, near the end of August, Washington revealed the progress of judiciary and cabinet plans in another undated note to Madison:

"My solicitude for drawing the first characters of the Union into the judiciary is such that my cogitations on this subject last night (after I parted with you) have almost determined me (as well for

the reason just mentioned as to silence the clamors, or more properly *soften* the disappointment of smaller characters) to nominate
Mr. Blair and Colonel Pendleton as associate and district judges.
And Mr. E. Randolph for the attorney general trusting to their
acceptance. . . . I am very troublesome, but you must excuse me.
Ascribe it to friendship and confidence and you will do justice to
my motives."

The high standing of Blair and Pendleton was to keep Arthur
Lee silent. No less striking than Madison's current intimacy with
Washington is the absence of a similar relationship between the
President and Hamilton, who was appointed Secretary of the
Treasury on September 11. The difference can be sensed even in
the ending of letters—"Yours sincerely" to Hamilton, "Yours
ever" to Madison. On September 25 Washington asked Hamilton
to look over a filtered list of thirty-five applicants for office and
tell him whether any of them would make a better postmaster
general than Colonel Osgood—who got the job. An old list of
appointments already made, accompanying this request, reveals
the fact that Washington did not choose the Supreme Court from
a general list of eligibles, but assigned the judgships in blank to six
states. To Hamilton the President finally remarked:

"And, that you may have the matter *fully* before you, I shall
add that it is my *present* intention to nominate Mr. Jefferson for
Secretary of State and Mr. Randolph as Attorney General; though
their acceptance is problematical, especially the latter."[13]

Here is definite evidence that Hamilton was not told of the
Jefferson and Randolph selections until the day before their names
were sent to the Senate. That was four months after Washington
and Madison had their first discussion of a place for Jefferson, six
weeks after the probable decision to name him and a full month
after Randolph's selection was disclosed to Madison.

The new government was set in personnel, except for accept-
ances, when Madison departed for Virginia. Arriving there, he
received word of Randolph's acceptance. And would Madison
please secure him a house in New York at a top rental of $166.66

a year? At home he waited eagerly for the Virginia Assembly's action on constitutional amendments. Senators Lee and Grayson sent them off to a bad start with a letter to the legislature, telling of their vain efforts to secure the radical changes Virginia had asked for. Madison heard that Grayson signed the document (written by Lee) with reluctance, but what suprised him was that he signed at all. The reluctance may have been due to a thrust in it at Madison's failure to revere and obey the state assembly.[14]

From Hardin Burnley, Orange County legislator, Madison heard that the first ten amendments went through the House of Delegates with hardly a dissenting vote. The eleventh and twelfth were at first defeated, due to one of Randolph's irrationalities, then approved. And what was the great opponent doing all this time? Mr. Henry, Carrington reported in December, was disposed to do some antifederal business; but, finding that the pulse of the House did not beat in unison with his own, he took his departure about mid-session. He never would have left, Carrington commented, had he foreseen the antifederal heat the debate would generate.

In the state Senate, Burnley wrote, things were worse. That body was inclined to reject all amendments, not from dissatisfaction with them, but being "apprehensive that the adoption of them at this time will be an obstacle to the chief object of their pursuit, the amendment on the subject of direct taxation."[15] The game of the opposition was to attack the most popular amendments on the ground that they were too weak, throw the whole subject back on Congress, and thus open the way to destruction of the taxing power. By a vote of eight to seven, four amendments were stricken out. Both houses adhering to their positions, everything failed.

The eight antifederal senators then published a pretended explanation of their action. The religious guaranty, they said, did not protect the rights of conscience. True, it forbade establishment of a national religion, but Congress might "levy taxes to any amount for the support of religion or its teachers." The purpose of this assertion was to create alarm among Baptists and Presbyterians. At the same time it enabled the opponents of direct taxation to pose as defenders of the religious liberty they were jeopardizing by their maneuver. Of the eight senators who played this game only one (and he a nonentity) had a legislative record in support of religious freedom. Three were notoriously on the other side, two having voted for tax support of religion in 1784, and all three to emasculate the Statute of Religious Liberty. Among the seven who voted for ratification, three were outstanding champions of religious liberty and not one had a record of opposition.

The moment Madison heard of the postponement move, he described it to Washington as a maneuver for promoting the war against the general government. The experiment, he felt sure, would recoil on the authors of it rather than inspire the public to a new attack.

"As far as I can gather, the great bulk of the late opponents are entirely at rest, and more likely to censure a further opposition to the government as now administered than [to censure] the government itself. One of the principal leaders of the Baptists lately sent me word that the amendments had entirely satisfied the disaffected of his sect and that it would appear in their subsequent conduct."

Confident of the people's attitude, Madison saw no reason to change his opinion after the Senate's maneuver succeeded. To Washington he wrote:

"On some accounts this event is no doubt to be regretted. But it will do no injury to the general government. On the contrary it will have the effect with many of turning their distrust toward their own legislature. The miscarriage of the third article [on religion, press, etc.], particularly, will have this effect."[16]

Since Congress was to open its second session on January 4, 1790, it was Madison's intention to set out for New York shortly after the middle of December. The critical illness of his mother held him for eight or ten days, but the delay enabled him to perform another service for the President. On December 23 Thomas Jefferson reached Monticello, one month after he landed at Norfolk. While on his way, gaining an impression that the Secretary of State would have heavy domestic duties, he informed

Washington that he had a strong preference for his diplomatic post but would accept any decision the President might make.

After a brief visit with Jefferson, Madison reported to Washington that he was sorry to find him so little biased in favor of the secretaryship. Luckily his unwillingness diminished when he was assured that the domestic duties were trivial. Madison predicted acceptance and pressed Washington to stick to the appointment:

"After all, if the whole business can be executed by any one man, Mr. Jefferson must be equal to it; if not he will be relieved by a necessary division of it."

This was written from Georgetown on January 4. Arriving there on New Year's Day, Madison was smitten with a prolonged dysenteric attack. Weakened by it and still more by the medicine which cured him, he did not reach New York until the twentieth. The next day Washington wrote to Jefferson that he had postponed his answer until Madison's return. Jefferson could choose, but the office of Secretary of State was *very* important, and he knew of no person who could execute it better. If its duties proved too arduous they could be divided under his superintendence. If he accepted he should come at once. He did accept, but his arrival, thanks to slow mails, business, a detour to Richmond and eighteen inches of snow at Alexandria, occurred two months later.[17]

Even in this final interval, advisory duties were thrust on Madison. How should the President submit communications from the several states to Congress? By personal messenger, Madison replied, not through a letter from the Secretary of State.

Requested to comment on a proposal to seek a treaty of commerce with Great Britain, he asked whether the treaty of peace should not first be fulfilled. That is, should not the western posts be freed of British troops? He denied reports that the policy of discrimination against Great Britain was dead in Congress. A considerable number objected to his measure as defective in energy rather than wrong in principle, and the last move in both houses was to bring in stronger bills. From all this it appears that efforts already were being made to have Washington commit himself to the policy which five years later produced the ignominious Jay

pay and farmers' and contractors' claims for war supplies and services. Other certificates covered wartime loans by citizens and continental currency redeemed after its forty-for-one devaluation in 1780. An unliquidated debt of $2,000,000 was the value Hamilton placed on about $80,000,000 of old currency still outstanding. (Redeemed later at 100 for one.)

Knowing the American dislike of taxes, the Treasury chief delivered a basic lecture on the need to lift national credit by punctual performance of contracts. The soaring prices of public securities testified to a belief that this would be done, and "the most enlightened friends of good government are those whose expectations are the highest." A proper provision for public credit would win their confidence and cement more closely the union of the states. Public securities would then become a virtual part of the money system, promoting national prosperity.

There were other ways of stating these things. Previous to the making of the report, Madison wrote, the avidity of speculators sent prices up from a few shillings to eight or ten in the pound, "and emissaries are still exploring the interior and distant parts of the Union in order to take advantage of the ignorance of holders."[3] Bluntly stated, Hamilton's precept was: Bind the rich to the government by self-interest.

This brought the Secretary to the storm center of his report. More than once he had read that a discrimination ought to be made between original holders of public securities and those who had bought them at a depreciated price. That would be a breach of contract and would ruin public credit. If the losses of the original holders were to be made up, their claim was against the government.

There is nothing to indicate whether Madison ever discussed this subject with Hamilton in their occasional talks and rambles in New York. No hint of it, certainly, is to be found in the recorded recollections of an old dame who, as a girl, saw them "talk together in the summer, and then turn, and laugh, and play with a monkey that was climbing in a neighbor's yard."[4] Nevertheless, the Secretary thought it wise to buttress his case with the address to the states which Madison wrote for the old Congress in 1783.

It would be unnecessary and invidious, said that paper, to discriminate between those who originally made loans to the government and those who showed confidence by receiving transfers.

For the refunding of the domestic debt, creditors were to be given their choice of long-term or lifetime annuities, provided they would agree to a reduction of interest from six to four per cent. In theory the exchange was voluntary, but those who clung to their six-per-cent bonds were to receive no more interest than the others. Hamilton expected by this means to reduce the annual cost of the debt from $4,600,000 to $2,240,000. The "cement to the Union" would stick for at least forty years.

Finally, the Secretary asked that the federal government take over the debts, estimated at $25,000,000, incurred by the states during the Revolution. He said it was wrong to distinguish between local and general defense, but his main object, stated privately, was to tie state creditors to the national government.[5]

Assumption of state debts originated with Madison in 1783, but Congress struck it out of his revenue plan. This background made Hamilton confident of Madison's support, without full reason. The latter wanted assumption in order to win ratification of the federal impost. That issue was dead, and the state securities, like the federal, were passing into the hands of big speculators.

From every quarter came reports about the buying up of federal certificates. Senator Maclay heard that Robert Morris' New York partner, William Constable, had one contract for forty thousand dollars' worth. Boston people were involved. "Indeed, there is no room to doubt but a connection is spread over the whole continent on this villainous business."

Newly arrived Senator Hawkins of North Carolina reported that he passed two expresses with great sums of money on their way south. Wadsworth (Connecticut congressman) had sent off two money-laden vessels. Other members of Congress were reported deep in the business. Nobody doubted that the speculative commotion originated from the Treasury. Most people blamed Assistant Secretary Duer, but Maclay believed it stemmed from Hamilton.[6]

Madison took no part in the early debate on Hamilton's report.

Jackson wanted action postponed so that the speculators would burn their fingers. Gerry, Sedgwick and others called for quick action. Speculation was inevitable, even useful, they argued, and the only way to end it was to bring securities up to their face value. Smith, reported to have sent a money ship south, moved that no discrimination be made between original holders and assignees. Scott and Livermore called for devaluation of the debt. It was inflated paper issued to pay for goods and services at extravagant prices—not even an obligation of the government, but an old claim of one part of the people against the whole of them. Scott's motion was beaten, whereupon Burke moved a discrimination but withdrew his motion before debate, saying he did not favor it. That brought Madison to the floor.

Anxious to profit from the thoughts of others, he had chosen to be a listener, but the turn affairs had taken required him to speak now if at all. The debt, he affirmed, was fully valid. By whom was it contracted? By the United States in a national capacity, by the government as agent of the whole people.

"The change in the government which has taken place has enlarged its national capacity, but it has not varied the national obligation, with respect to the engagements entered into by that transaction. . . . Although the government has been changed the nation remains the same . . . the obligation remains the same."

What then was the amount of the debt? It was the amount the United States received and had promised to pay. No logic, no magic, could diminish it. "The only point on which we can deliberate is, to whom the payment is really due." There were, said Madison, four classes proper to notice:

Original creditors who still held their securities.

Original creditors who had alienated them.

Present holders of alienated securities.

Intermediate holders, who had acquired securities but no longer held them.

The first group was entitled to full payment. The fourth should be dismissed offhand. The second and third groups—the original and present holders of alienated securities—had rival pretensions.

The second group, Madison believed, had a claim in which humanity reinforced justice. The value they delivered to the government had never been repaid to them. The securities they were forced to receive had less real value, even at the time of issuance, than the sums due. The debt was not extinguished. The sufferings of the soldiers could never be forgotten while sympathy was an American virtue—to say nothing of the injustice of requiring those who lost seven eighths of their due to contribute to those who made a sevenfold gain.

Holders by assignment, he continued, had a valid claim upon the public faith. The two sets of claims interfered. That being the case, they must either pay both, reject one, or make a composition between them. To pay both would far exceed the value received by the public. To reject wholly the claims of the assignees would be fatal to public credit. To load the entire loss on the other group was an idea at which human nature recoiled.

"A composition then is the only expedient that remains; let it be a liberal one in favor of the present holders, let them have the highest price which has prevailed in the market; and let the residue belong to the original sufferers."

By this plan, all but a few of the present holders would make a profit. The others would lose nothing and would get a sound six-per-cent investment. It would be said the plan was impracticable. But all it required was a knowledge of the present holders, which was shown by the certificates, and of the original holders, whose names were in office documents. Some might say it would injure public credit. That would be prevented by the honesty and disinterestedness of the policy, which would not save the government a farthing—also by full provision for the foreign debt and punctuality in future domestic payments.

The present case was so extraordinary, it seemed to Madison, that ordinary maxims could not be applied to it. The American situation was like that of England in the South Sea scheme, where a thousand-per-cent change in the value of stock produced government interference. If the condition existing in American national securities were to happen among individuals a court of equity would interpose to give redress.

"If a tribunal existed on earth, by which nations could be compelled to do right, the United States would be compelled to do something not dissimilar in its principles to what I have contended for."[7]

Madison then offered a motion for discrimination and the 1790 fight was on. Nobody denied the injustice suffered by the original holders. With Boudinot leading off and Sedgwick, Ames, Smith and Laurance adding their weight, the opponents argued that nothing could be done about these losses. The instant a claimant assigned his claim, he was through. It was not even possible to discover who were the real first holders, since innumerable certificates were issued in the names of government clerks. To attempt a refund would lay a foundation for frauds and perjuries. "Do not rob on the highway to exercise charity," cried Ames. Madison's measure would destroy the property and faith of foreign investors, violate the sacred rights of property, duplicate the evils of state tender laws, produce confusion, corruption and expense. Ames would not charge Madison with a deliberate intent to produce these mischiefs:

"I think so highly of his probity and patriotism that if he can be made to see that these consequences will follow, or only be apprehended, he will give up his scheme. But if government has this right, what right of private property is safe?"

Arguments based on sympathy for veterans and dislike of speculators did not seem so bad to Jackson of Georgia, Seney of Maryland, White, Page and Lee of Virginia. Soldiers had been forced to receive certificates with a current value, when received, of two shillings sixpence for a twenty-shilling note. It was said now that they should have held onto them. And leave their children to starve on a dunghill?

This drew no tears from Livermore. "Esau had sold his birthright for a mess of pottage, and heaven and earth had confirmed the sale." That remark boded ill for Madison's motion. The New Hampshire man and several others were eager to scale down the domestic debt in order to cut taxes. If it must be paid in full, why worry over who was to get the money?[8]

Taking the floor again on February 18, Madison refused to admit "that America ought to erect the monuments of her gratitude, not to those who saved her liberties, but to those who had enriched themselves in her funds." Claimants entitled to receive gold or silver had been given a piece of paper worth at the moment of delivery one eighth of its face value.

"Was this depreciated paper freely accepted? No. The government offered that or nothing. . . . The same degree of constraint would vitiate a transaction between man and man before any court of equity on the face of the earth."

The speaker said he had been criticized for appealing to the heart as well as the head. He would be bold to repeat that in great and unusual questions of morality the heart was the better judge. Gentlemen should consider "not the form, but the substance—not the letter, but the equity—not the bark, but the pith of the business."

Opposition speakers had reminded Madison repeatedly of his authorship of the address of Congress which rejected a discrimination. At that period, he replied, the certificates to the army and citizens at large had not been issued. Transfers, few in number and entailing little loss, were confined to loan-office certificates.

"At present, the transfers extend to a vast proportion of the whole debt, and the loss to the original holders has been immense. The injustice which has taken place has been enormous and flagrant, and makes redress a great national object."

This change of circumstances, Madison insisted, destroyed the argument from the act of 1783. But if it were to be adhered to implicitly, how could anybody justify the compulsory reduction of interest called for in the Treasury plan? He denied that one set of men was to be robbed to pay another. If there had been robbery, it was committed on the original holders. He wished a part to be withheld from each of two creditors, both of whom could not be paid the whole. The audience was enlarged at this point by an influx on the floor which Maclay tells about:

"The Senate now adjourned and we went into the lower House to hear the debates on Mr. Madison's motion. Madison had been up most of the morning and was said to have spoken most ably indeed. He seemed rather jaded when I came in. He had, early in the business, been called on to show a single instance where anything like the present had been done. He produced an act of Parliament in point in the reign of Queen Anne. But now the gentlemen [Laurance and Ames] quitted this ground and cried out for rigid right on law principles. Madison modestly put them in mind that they had challenged him on this ground and he had met them agreeably to their wishes."

Benson wanted to know whether an original creditor who had assigned his certificate could, in conscience, accept a reimbursement in the manner proposed. In general, Madison answered, assignments were made with reference to market value and the uncertainty of government policies. No scruples could arise out of that. In turn he would ask whether a present holder who got his certificate from a distressed fellow citizen for one tenth of its ultimate value might not feel some remorse in retaining so unconscionable an advantage. The embarrassed Benson could reply only that if a soldier made such an application to him as a matter of right, he would reject it, but if his benevolence were appealed to—what he would do would depend on other principles.

Madison showed that the Treasury plan cut the interest on the liquidated debt and violated the pledge of redemption written on the face of the old currency. If contracts were immutable, all should be enforced. If not, Congress should attend to the correction of injustice. There were difficulties, but the true ownership of securities could be traced. There would be more frauds and perjuries in the collection of duties than were likely in this case. Devote the same ingenuity to removing difficulties that was employed in raising them and they would vanish.

Expecting Madison's motion to be defeated, Senator Maclay sought him out at his lodgings on the day the vote was to be taken. It had occurred to the Pennsylvanian that he could offer a good deal of useful guidance. House Clerk Beckley, he noted in his journal, was very intimate both with Speaker Muhlenberg and with Madison.

"I can, through this channel, communicate what I please to Madison; and I think I know him. But if he is led, it must be without letting him know that he is so; in other words, he must not see the string."

Maclay's suggestion was simple—slash interest to three per cent and pay everything by making debt certificates and nothing else receivable in sales of public lands. The senator had taken his plan to Congressman Scott, who declared that if Madison would join it could be carried. "I wished him to communicate with Madison. He was afraid of Madison's pride." It was at Scott's suggestion that Maclay called on Madison and read the resolutions to him, first telling him with typical delicacy that his own proposition hadn't a chance to succeed.

"It hurt his *Littleness*. I do not think he believed me. I read the resolutions. I do not think he attended to one word of them, so much did he seem absorbed in his own ideas. I put them into his hand. He offered them back without reading them. . . . His pride seems of that kind which repels all communication. . . . The obstinacy of this man has ruined the opposition."

To those who wanted to scale the debt or defeat the funding of it, Madison's attitude might indeed seem obstinate and full of pride. What he desired was a fair distribution of what the government was to pay, not an escape from paying it. The pious land speculator, Manasseh Cutler, was in the gallery when the vote was taken on February 22. For a week, he wrote, the House had been debating a very unexpected motion by Mr. Madison—a motion which would have been smiled at had it come from a member of less consequence, "but his character gave it importance. . . . On taking the question, Mr. M. had the mortification, which he appeared sensibly to feel, to be in a minority—only thirteen for the motion."[9]

The thirteen-to-thirty-six vote was far more one-sided than Madison's advance estimate. Nine Virginians and four other Southerners supported his motion. The causes of this, he wrote to Randolph, could not altogether be explained, and some of them he preferred to discuss orally. Actually he faced a five-way combination: congressional speculators, cementers of the rich, those who feared injury to public credit, those who thought a revision desirable but impracticable, those who preferred Hamilton's plan because it scaled the debt by reducing interest. The political weakness of Madison's position lay in the fact that the justice he called for would hurt the rich, help the poor and save nothing to the taxpayer.[10]

Unshaken, he wrote to his father that his proposition was much better relished in the country at large than in New York. Abigail Adams thought he was "acting a covered and artful part." Youthful John Quincy Adams reported that Madison's reputation had suffered from his conduct, Judge Dana being his only respectable Boston supporter. It was a nonrespectable one who wrote in the *Columbian Centinel*: "Happy there is a Madison who fearless of the blood suckers will step forward and boldly vindicate the rights of the widows and orphans, the original creditors and the war worn soldier." Anger and cynicism stirred other good men to bad poetry, such as these newspaper lines "On the rejection of Mr. Madison's motion":

> "Pay the poor soldier!—He's a sot,"
> Cries our grave ruler B-ud-not.
> "No pity, *now*, from us he claims,"
> In artful accents, echoes Am-s:
> "In *war*, to heroes let's be just,
> In *peace*, we'll write their toils in dust;
> A soldier's pay are rags and fame,
> A wooden leg—a deathless name.
> To Specs, both *in* and *out* of Cong,
> The four and six per cents belong."[11]

Throughout this business, Madison informed a critic, he had carefully refrained from attacking the title of the actual holders of securities because he did not wish to influence popular prejudices. He nevertheless believed that in many instances the purchases had been vitiated by fraud or impaired by lack of a valuable consideration. Finally, he doubted whether the buyer was more

entitled than the seller to the benefits resulting from establishment
of the new government—an event "as much out of the contempla-
tion of both parties as a miraculous shower of gold from heaven."[12]
His own and later generations have agreed on the sincerity of
Madison's motives in proposing a discrimination among security
holders. Three factors, however, have interfered with recognition
of the rightness and wisdom of his proposal:

1. His deliberate understatement of his own case to avoid stirring up an already excited public.

2. Failure to realize that public credit was restored by the
setting up of a strong government with taxing power, rather than
by the specific nature of the plan adopted, which violently impaired contracts by cutting part of the interest to three per cent
and deferring another part until 1800.

3. The vagueness of the charges about wholesale speculation
by government officials and other insiders.

The influence of the first factor is self-evident. A hint of the
second came from Maclay, who complained that Madison's system
did not reduce the burden, but distributed the benefits more
fairly, and was, perhaps, "on that account more dangerous, as it
will be readier submitted to." The third handicap—vagueness of
the speculation charges—can be removed.

The day before Madison delivered his principal speech on discrimination he received an anonymous letter signed "Foreigner."
After giving an account of European purchases the writer forgot
his origin and drew on personal knowledge of Revolutionary
finance to combat Madison's charge of injustice to veterans. The
only person who could have marshaled that particular combination of facts and perversions was William Duer, Hamilton's assistant, who had been secretary of the old Board of Treasury.

Certain agents, his story ran, offered to contract with Hollanders
to furnish a large amount of the domestic debt of the United States.
The careful Dutch wanted assurance against discrimination, so
"the secretary of the Board of Treasury under the seal of his office
gave attestation to confirm the facts." Great amounts were purchased by Dutch bankers at fifteen shillings in the pound. The
bankers then issued "actions"—little notes backed by the American

securities—and sold these at higher prices (at or near par) to thousands of Dutch investors. If Madison's amendment should prevail European faith in America would be shattered.[13]

Who were the "certain agents" who contracted to deliver these securities? For that, read a memorandum dated December 21, 1788, in the papers of Rufus King. "Some days since," King recorded, "Colonel Duer mentioned to me that his situation required that he should pay some attention to his pecuniary concerns." A Geneva banker, M. de Claviere, approaching through Brissot de Warville, wanted him and other Americans to join in buying up the American debt to France. Duer "told me that he had conferred with Wadsworth, General Knox and Mr. Osgood [member of the Treasury Board] on the subject—that he had informed them that Robert and Gouverneur Morris . . . proposed to unite with him (Duer) and that Gouverneur Morris was going to Europe with this among other views."

The design was "that Duer, Robert Morris and Gouverneur Morris should be the principal Americans, that Constable and Duer's friend (Osgood) should be admitted," along with some others who could not be left out, and the three principals should split all profits above those of the limited shareholders. Should this fail, the idea was to accomplish the measure through an American minister in Holland. Duer invited King to enter the speculation and said that Knox and Wadsworth wished to know whether he would accept an appointment to Holland. King gave an ambiguous answer on the first point, but told Duer that he was not indisposed to a foreign appointment. It would be a great satisfaction to promote the interest of his friends if he could do so with propriety, but the opinions of Jay and Hamilton were of consequence. "Previous to any decision on my part I must be ascertained of their opinions."[14]

Gouverneur Morris went to Europe bearing letters from Duer (so said King) to promote the speculation. Madison gave him a letter of introduction to Jefferson with this note added in cipher: "I am a stranger to the errand on which G. Morris goes to Europe. It relates, I presume, to the affairs of R. Morris, which are still much deranged." Nothing came of the French scheme, but Holland produced a flourishing alternative in speculative purchases of American securities. Jefferson, going to Amsterdam to borrow money with which to meet interest on the *foreign* debt, protested to the Board of Treasury that Dutch purchasers of the *domestic* debt made this impossible. What banker would pay ninety-six per cent for one public security when he could buy another of the same nation for fifty-five per cent? The Stanitzky house, he reported, held $1,340,000 of the American domestic debt and was trying to blackmail the United States by refusing to service the foreign debt unless paid a year's interest on its domestic securities. Little did Jefferson suspect that his bitter complaints went straight to the chief American organizer of the European speculations, soon to become Hamilton's principal assistant.[15]

In all that followed there is no hint that Hamilton stood to make a dollar, but King's memorandum leaves no doubt that he knew exactly what Duer was, and what he was doing and likely to do, when he chose him in September 1789 to be assistant secretary of the Treasury. What Duer proceeded to do is recorded over his own signature in a "Memorandum of agreement made and entered into the 23 of December 1789 between William Duer and William Constable both of New York." Signed by both parties before a witness, and preserved in Constable's papers, this contract between Hamilton's chief assistant and New York's leading financier begins as follows:

"The parties having full confidence in each other agree to enter into a speculation in the funds generally to create a capital for which object it is proposed to purchase on time as many continental securities as can be obtained, the money arising therefrom to be immediately invested in the debts of North and South Carolina to the extent of sixteen thousand specie dollars, the residue in indents of interest or such other paper as may be determined on."

This speculation was far more ambitious than the reference to $16,000 indicates. Borrowing on what they bought and pyramiding their loans, they could hope for a tremendous profit through the rise of security prices when the funding plan came into effect.

Success depended on two things—advance knowledge, which
Duer possessed, that assumption of state funds was to be part of
the Hamilton program; and ignorance of that fact by the Carolina
security holders. December 1789 was late, but Duer's agents had
been in the field since July, inquiring after securities and con-
cealing their real object by holding up "the idea of purchasing
rights to lands." There is nothing to show the total operations of
Duer and Constable, but their certificate account with Richard
Platt has a maximum figure of $170,114.65 for activities in which
he shared.[16]

Really big speculations could be financed only in Europe. To
bring in Amsterdam bankers risks must be passed along to Dutch
farmers, mechanics and widows. That called for long-term paper
in small denominations, with interest sustained over the whole
term of the speculation. Constable worked that out and put his
scheme on paper in these words:

"Suppose one million of dollars in the debt of South Carolina
to be purchased at two shillings in the pound. Suppose the 'actions'
to be disposed of at 80 per cent, security to be given for the punctual payment of interest at 5 per cent on these 'actions.'

"After deducting the original cost of the purchase, the balance
remaining to be placed in the British or other equally solid fund,
bearing interest at 4 per cent.

"The deficiency of the interest payable annually on the 'actions'
to be taken from this capital—what would be the result?"

The answer was satisfactory. The million-dollar state debt would
cost $100,000, but could be handled with $20,000 "as certificates
would be transmitted and disposed of to raise funds for discharge
of our drafts." The "actions," payable at the Peter Stanitzky bank-
ing house in Amsterdam, would bring in $800,000. Deduct the
full cost of the collateral, $100,000, and it would leave $700,000 to
be invested in British bonds. For the first year, Constable's group
would owe $50,000 interest in Holland and receive $28,000 interest
in England. They would have to sell $22,000 of the British bonds
to make up the deficit. In the fourteenth year the interest payable
in Holland would still be $50,000, the interest received in England

would be only $13,367, and it would be necessary to sell $36,633 of the shrinking British capital. By that time the state securities were sure to reach par, sale of them would pay off the Amsterdam "actions" and the speculators would still have $297,558 in British bonds—their profit on an original capital of $20,000. The speculators risked little, the bankers nothing. The risk was to be borne by hundreds of Dutch burghers who were to put up $800,000 for state bonds with a market value of $100,000.

Constable's papers do not show whether this precise plan was put into effect. But when he made a list of his foreign obligations on August 16, 1790, at the height of his speculative activities, the Stanitzky house was in for $840,000, Gerrit Nutches and others for $2,156,479.32, Etienne Lespinasse and others $700,000. The grand total was $5,447,042.27.[17]

This was the cold reality behind Hamilton's plea that good faith, honor and public credit forbade a partial restitution of losses to soldiers of the Revolution out of the profits of assignees—or, to state it another way, behind his plan to make the self-interest of the rich a cement to the Union. Speculation in public funds was not merely the automatic pay-off of past transfers, or the result of a spontaneous rush of gamblers. It was the planned work of international syndicates of European bankers and American politicians and financiers, operating in millions of dollars, with the second highest officer of the United States Treasury as organizer and manager of the most brazen part of the speculation.

Rumor, planting itself in Maclay's journal, could put down a comment on "Wadsworth with his boatload of money," or assert that Constable early in 1790 cleared $35,000 on a contract for $70,000.[18] The closed pages of account and memorandum books concealed the record of a multi-million-dollar conspiracy of bankers and politicians to draw huge unearned profits out of the trustfulness of Dutchmen and the ignorance of American soldiers and farmers—with the speculators headed by Hamilton's chief assistant and basing their actions on advance knowledge of the plans to be laid before Congress.

James Madison had no knowledge of the Duer-Constable contract, or of the conspiratorial terms under which American specu-

lators fed securities into the financial houses of Commeline, Lespinasse, Nutches, Stanitzky, Willink and other Dutch and Flemish
participants in the exploitation of the public debt. He *did* know
that clever men were using the Hamilton funding plan to rob
their fellow citizens, and the knowledge drove him into political
revolt against the financial machine that was taking over the
government.

Madison sacrificed his congressional leadership when he undertook the fight for Revolutionary War veterans and other small
creditors against speculators in and out of Congress. By the same
course he split the original Federalists asunder, fused one part of
them with the radical wing of the vanishing Antifederalists and
gave direction to the political cleavage which swiftly divided the
American public into Federalists and Republicans. Had he possessed personal glamour the next political phenomenon in America
would have become known as Madisonian democracy. As it was,
he planted the seed and started the growth of the party which
received the Jeffersonian label. He did this before Jefferson re-
entered the national scene from his diplomatic exile.

# CHAPTER XXIV

## Assumption of State Debts

MADISON listened in silence to the debate over assumption of state debts. On the simple basis of public finance he could be expected to favor it, but to oppose the unadjusted transfer Hamilton was asking for. In 1783, when Madison proposed assumption to gain support for the federal impost,[1] Virginia's $5,000,000 Revolutionary debt was larger than her share of the taxes required to pay all state debts. Now, $2,000,000 of the Virginia debt had been paid and straight assumption would force her to pay part of it twice, in an excessive proportion of national taxes. Also, mistrusting all class appeals, Madison was hostile to a planned shift of the economic allegiance of the wealthy from states to nation.

In Congress as a whole strong support came to Hamilton's policy from two groups. Delegations of states which had lagged in payment of their war debts were eager to get rid of them—notably Massachusetts and South Carolina with $5,000,000 apiece and Connecticut with $2,000,000. The heavy pull came from speculators who were scouring the country for defaulted state securities. Priced at two shillings in twenty at the start, they promised even higher profits than were being reaped in national certificates. Senator Morris, deep in speculation, addressed the Pennsylvania delegation a few hours after the defeat of Madison's discrimination motion opened the way for the question of assuming state debts. "By God, it must be done," he exclaimed. Seldom did Morris make so long a speech.[2]

Stone of Maryland typified the reaction of the State-Rights, agricultural South. If the general government was to pay the debts it would absorb all the revenue, acquire all the power, and throw the burden of debt-paying on the importers of foreign goods. Normally all South Carolinians except Smith would have upheld these contentions until the windows rattled. Instead, Burke forgot his Antifederalism as he pictured his state burdened with the cost of defending Charleston and supporting the armies of Gates and Greene. Smith, reputed sender of a money ship, demanded prompt action. Speculators, he remarked with brazen hypocrisy, were said to have bought up much of the continental debt. "If we postpone this business I fear that the state debts will find their way into the same channel."

Warnings and threats followed. If Massachusetts had to bear its load of debt, the westward flight from direct taxes would keep up and there would be grave danger of new insurrections. Transfer the debts, and all opposition to settlement of federal-state war accounts would vanish. To Madison, this was a refusal to settle without a transfer. He heard something else which did not get into the *Annals*—a threat to vote against any provision for the *national* debt unless state debts were taken over. This brought him into the debate.

It was preposterous and improper, he told the House, to make the passage of this resolution a condition for the payment of an acknowledged debt of prior date and deeper obligation. Assumption would lead to a new concentration of securities and put them in foreign hands. However, justice between state and state required a settlement of accounts, and settlement was possible only if it went hand in hand with the proposed transfer. He moved therefore as an addition to the assumption motion that provision be made at the same time for liquidating and crediting all state war expenditures. A state which paid its share of the war cost would not be taxed to pay for another state's failure to do so.

The amendment was adopted unanimously, but defeat of a strengthening clause made him suspect that the action was a sham. He therefore moved that the amount of debts actually paid by any state to its creditors since the close of the war should be repaid to such state as a part of the assumption plan. Opponents protested that this would add $15,000,000 to the cost. They then voted to refund $12,000,000 interest paid by the states, and cried out that the additional $27,000,000 put too heavy a burden on federal finances. Madison asked Ames to explain the inconsistency between his vote and his argument. He did not get the obvious answer: The $15,000,000 increase would go to states, not to speculators, therefore should be built high enough to defeat the whole amendment. And so it resulted, twenty-two to twenty-eight.[3]

On the morning of March 8, Maclay noted that "the crew of the Hamilton galley" was being piped to quarters for a House decision on assumption. It was put over a day so that Vining, who came in from Delaware, could "be prepared by the Secretary." Senator Butler heard someone say that he would give Vining a thousand guineas for his vote, but this seemed improbable to Maclay since it could be had for a tenth of that sum. The House, he wrote next day, was overrun with "officers of government, clergy, citizens, Cincinnati, and every person under the influence of the Treasury; Bland and Huger carried to the chamber of representatives—the one lame, the other sick." So assumption won in committee of the whole, thirty-one to twenty-six.

The fight, Madison assured a friend, was not over. North Carolina's delegation would come soon and was hostile. In basic merit there was good and bad in the plan, but the injustice to Virginia put the whole delegation against it except Bland.[4] At this point, assumption was crowded aside by a fight over the slave trade. Philadelphia and New York Quakers asked Congress to put an end to its inhuman tyranny. The Pennsylvania abolition society, headed by Franklin, followed with a memorial for the complete ending of human bondage. From South Carolina and Georgia members came threats. If these petitions were sent to committee it would "blow the trumpet of sedition in the southern states."

Madison tried to calm the Southerners while opposing them. If the memorials caused alarm it would be because of the outcries against them. Congress could not abolish the slave trade, yet there were ways by which it could countenance the abolition. Also it could regulate the introduction of slavery into new states. He thought the object well worthy of consideration. The House thought so too and received a mild committee report, denying the power of Congress to end the slave trade before 1808, but asserting its authority to insure humane conditions on ships and cut off foreign participation, as well as to lay the authorized $10 head tax.[5]

The true policy of Southern members, in Madison's opinion, was to make little noise and obtain a statement of the restraints imposed on Congress, along with its powers. Instead they plunged into a "shamefully indecent" debate, describing slaves as inherently inferior beings who would be harmed by freedom. They denied that slavery detracted from the nobility of Southern manhood or the softness and delicacy of its womanhood, and denounced the Quakers as spies, traitors, pacifists and hypocritical moneygrubbers.

Trying to restore peace, Madison clarified the statement of the powers of Congress and moved that both the original and amended reports be placed in the Journal. By publicly declaring the meaning of the Constitution they might allay Southern fears over emancipation. Four Virginians joined Madison in producing the slim majority by which the motion carried. This harrowing experience warned him against agitation of the subject. Asked later by Quaker Robert Pleasants to present the petition of the Virginia Abolition Society against slave-trade cruelties, he declined because of its general strictures on slavery and advised him that a proposed abolition memorial to the Virginia Assembly was likely to result in repeal of the voluntary manumission law. A similar memorial in North Carolina actually produced a law allowing anybody to seize emancipated Negroes and sell them. Heart-rending affidavits of the resulting cruelties were placed before Congress. The best advice Madison could offer was that the victims appeal to the courts to sustain rights which neither the judges nor Congress dared to vindicate.[6]

Franklin's move against slavery was the last act of his long career. A few weeks later, Madison arose and "in a very handsome manner," as a young man in the gallery described it, offered a resolution which was agreed to without dissent:

"The House being informed of the decease of Benjamin Franklin, a citizen whose native genius was not more an ornament to human nature than his various exertions of it have been precious to science, to freedom and to his country, do resolve, as a mark of the veneration due to his memory, that the members wear the customary badge of mourning for one month."[7]

Assumption, it seemed to Madison, lost ground daily during the slave-trade interlude. North Carolina produced the two-vote mar-

gin by which, on April 12, 1790, the scheme was rejected. The
minority, he wrote next day to Henry Lee, were not abandoning
their project. He did not share Lee's fear that the country must
choose between insolent Northern tyranny and a dissolution of
the Union. The novelty and difficulty of Hamilton's task formed
"no small apology for his errors," which might be diminished
and in any event would not prove fatal.

Reports from Virginia were one-sided. The people, David
Stuart wrote to Congressman Lee, were exasperated by assumption, and by vermin from the northward who were riding around
and buying up securities. Mr. Madison, who was "so harshly
spoke of" by self-interested men for his discrimination plan, had
now become extremely popular. Dr. Benjamin Rush of Philadelphia wrote glowingly to Madison, praising his stand, while his
associate Dr. James Hutchinson reported collateral effects to Albert Gallatin, the young Swiss who was rising to agrarian leadership in western Pennsylvania:

"Mr. Madison's influence is much increased. He has brought in
a navigation bill which is of importance and a bill for increasing
the tonnage duty of foreign vessels that are not in alliance. This
has occasioned very warm debates and will probably pass this
session."[8]

Concluding that England was "itching for war" with Spain,
Madison revived his 1789 project of a discrimination against British
shipping and carried it to thirty-two-to-nineteen approval on May
13. Next day he moved to exclude all ships of nontreaty nations
from carrying unmanufactured American produce. Replying to
Sedgwick's charge that this was a measure of passion, he described
it as a cool and proper action, designed to force the repeal of discrimination against American ships and to foster a navy for national defense. The House, he told Randolph, seemed disposed to
make a pretty bold experiment. By the time his bill was called
up, cool heads were less noticeable than cold feet. Commercial
interests anxious for low British freights, Southerners who feared
a New England shipping monopoly and others who thought the
action too bold joined forces and rejected it. Shifting ground,

Madison proposed that disabilities on American ships be matched in kind. The House found this too "interesting and important" for immediate consideration. They would wait for Europe to explode.[9]

After making his own pressure move, Madison encouraged the sending of David Humphreys to Europe for a purpose known only to Washington, Jefferson, Hamilton, John Brown of Kentucky and himself—to explore the possibility of forcing Spain to open the Mississippi and keep Britain from conquering Florida. This decision—an offshoot of the warlike reaction to Spain's capture of British ships in Nootka Sound—followed a conference between Jefferson and Madison, held at the President's request. What should the United States do if Britain attempted to conquer Louisiana and the Floridas? Reporting that Madison concurred on every point, the Secretary of State replied that such a conquest would lead to the loss of all American territory west of the Appalachians, while the remainder of the country would be encircled by land and sea. But war should be thought of only if France joined Spain.

Their recommendation was that Spain and France be sounded out on making Louisiana and the Floridas independent, with the United States guaranteeing their independence. Britain should be told that complete reciprocity was the price of a treaty of commerce, and that in the event of war, the United States would "view with extreme uneasiness any attempts of either power to seize the possessions of the other on our frontier." Before the end of 1790, Spain's surrender of Nootka ended both the danger and the opportunity. One cannot say how much of this outlined policy stemmed from Madison's ten-year campaign to save the Mississippi, but the lines are plainly visible from it to the Louisiana Purchase and the Monroe Doctrine.[10]

Again and again, during the perfecting of the funding plan, efforts were made to bring in state debts. With each failure the advocates became more desperate. Their state of mind was described by Madison to Monroe:

"The eastern members talk a strange language on the subject. They avow, some of them at least, a determination to oppose all provision for the public debt which does not include this, and intimate danger to the Union from a refusal to assume. We shall risk their prophetic menaces if we should continue to have a majority."

In mid-May, Madison sent word to Randolph (held in Virginia by his wife's almost fatal illness) that the zealots for assumption were still trying to alarm the zealots for funding. Before long he shared the apprehension. It was increased by the wave of influenza and pneumonia which swept the country and threatened to render it leaderless. "The President has been at the point of death but is recovered," Madison wrote on the first day of June. He himself had been in bed for some days. His colleague Bland died. (So did Senator Grayson, but earlier and of other causes.) Alarming reports came from Boston of the ravages of the disease.[11]

At this unsettled moment, a new complication hit the funding deadlock. On May 31 the House voted that the next session of Congress be held in Philadelphia. "*We* are sold by the Pennsylvanians, and the assumption with it," exclaimed Ames. The Pennites, he believed, had bargained to vote against assumption in exchange for the temporary capital. If that was true Madison won at both ends. Not only was he against assumption, but he had concluded that the surest way to bring the permanent capital to the Potomac was to take Congress first to Philadelphia. That would block any bargaining between Pennsylvania and the North over the two sites. Unluckily, half a dozen Southern senators wanted to combine the permanent with the temporary question.

By the House vote for Philadelphia, Madison hoped to press the Southern senators into line and settle the matter before the newly elected senators from Rhode Island should come in and bolster New York. To his chagrin the sextet from the deep South refused to co-operate. Johnson of Connecticut, ill with influenza and wearing a nightcap, was carried in a bed from his house to vote against Philadelphia. Rumors that Hamilton was exerting his influence gave weight to the belief that the Senate action was a maneuver to save assumption. Two days later, on June 10, Parker renewed the House motion for Philadelphia. He did so because it was raining. If the measure reached the Senate before the rain stopped it would pass, because Johnson couldn't be taken out in bad weather. The maneuver produced the first filibuster in congressional history, not in the Senate but in the House, where Gerry of Massachusetts and Smith of South Carolina—leaders of the speculator cohorts—held the floor until the sun came out.[12]

Pressing their advantage, the assumptionists moved that Congress go to Baltimore. Three Marylanders rose to this bait and the motion carried thirty-one to twenty-eight—"a very unexpected result," remarked Madison to his father. He doubted whether the Senate would fall in, but saw only a remote chance now that the permanent capital would go to the Potomac. The Pennsylvania-Virginia coalition had nothing to work on.[13]

This turn shifted the initiative to the Senate, and to Secretary Hamilton. The vote for Baltimore was on a Friday. On Monday morning Senator Maclay called on Tench Coxe, who had just taken Duer's place as assistant secretary of the Treasury. Coxe proposed a bargain: Pennsylvania to have the permanent residence on the Susquehanna, and her delegation to vote for assumption. The senator rejected this the more emphatically because of his belief that "Hamilton, the principal in this business, was not sincere." Later in the morning Maclay learned that Coxe and William Jackson (the President's secretary) had made the same proposition to Clymer, Fitzsimons and Senator Morris a few hours after the vote for Baltimore. Said Morris to Maclay:

"I did not choose to trust them but wrote a note to Colonel Hamilton that I would be walking early in the morning on the Battery, and if Colonel Hamilton had anything to propose to him (Morris) he might meet him there, as if by accident. I went in the morning there and found him *on the sod before me.*"

As they strolled along the water front Hamilton put his proposition before the Pennsylvania senator:

"Mr. Hamilton said he wanted one vote in the Senate and five in the House of Representatives [for assumption]; that he was willing and would agree to place the permanent residence of

Congress at Germantown or the Falls of Delaware if he would procure him these votes."

Morris, preferring a bird in the hand, asked that the temporary residence of Congress in Philadelphia be the price. Morris and Fitzsimons then took Read of Delaware for a ride in the country and found him willing to provide the senatorial vote Hamilton needed. The Secretary however sent Morris a note next day saying that his friends objected to negotiating about the temporary capital. This was interpreted to mean that Hamilton had the votes to keep Congress in New York and still carry assumption. In reality it meant that he couldn't deliver. The New Yorkers would not help send Congress to Philadelphia. If the bargaining could be shifted to the permanent site, Ames wrote, "that would make the friends of the assumption the umpires, and enable them to dictate their own terms." Unfortunately the greedy Pennsylvanians thought only of Philadelphia. The virtuous Bay Staters didn't know what to do. Sedgwick was "a perfect slave" in his search for a solution, while "Goodhue frowns all day long, and swears as much as a good Christian can, about the perverseness of Congress."[14]

Hamilton now realized that the deal must produce a margin of safety to cover losses caused by it. Pennsylvania was not enough. He must win Virginia and Maryland. That meant giving them the permanent seat of government. Their votes were needed, not merely to carry assumption, but primarily to offset New York and New England opposition to an interim removal to Philadelphia.

Madison controlled the Virginia delegation. He must be won at least to silent agreement, but how? Four months of bitter conflict made direct negotiation difficult. Hamilton turned to Jefferson, who, between disabling attacks of migraine headache, was just getting squared around in his new office of Secretary of State. As Jefferson recalled the facts in his "Anas," he arrived in New York in the midst of the fight over assumption, knowing nothing of it. Thus he was "most ignorantly and innocently made to hold the candle" for Hamilton's game of plunder. Here is his description of what took place after the initial defeat:

"Hamilton was in despair. As I was going to the President's one day, I met him in the street. He walked me backwards and forwards before the President's door for half an hour. He painted pathetically the temper into which the legislature had been wrought; the disgust of those who were called the creditor states; the danger of the *secession* of their members and the separation of the states."

It was probable, said Hamilton, that an appeal by Jefferson to some of his friends would rescue the proposition. The Secretary of State disclaimed any knowledge of the subject, but invited Hamilton to dine with him next day. A friend or two would be brought in and, all being reasonable, they could hardly fail "by some mutual sacrifices of opinion to form a compromise which was to save the Union." In another reminiscent paper he named Hamilton and Madison as his guests and again emphasized that all he did was encourage them to consider the thing together.

"They did so, it ended in Mr. Madison's acquiescence ... though he would not vote for [assumption], nor entirely withdraw his opposition, yet he should not be strenuous but leave it to its fate."

Passage of the measure, Jefferson said in the "Anas," would be a bitter pill to the Southern states. So, "to sweeten it a little to them," the seat of government should go to Philadelphia for ten years and then permanently to the Potomac. "Two of the Potomac members (White and Lee, but White with a revulsion of stomach almost convulsive) agreed to change their votes [on assumption] and Hamilton undertook to carry the other point." He did so with the aid of Robert Morris, "and so the assumption was passed, and twenty millions of stock divided among favored states and thrown in as a pabulum to the stock-jobbing herd."[15]

This account, which reflects Jefferson's deep hunger for posthumous fame, has the common defect of such apologies—it exaggerates the need for one. Rives performed the same disservice to

Madison, saying that he stood aloof from the bargaining, "and his correspondence affords no clues to its mysteries." In reality, Madison disclosed a reluctant readiness to compromise before Hamilton ever broached the subject to Jefferson. On June 17, about three days before the dinner, Madison wrote to Monroe:

"The assumption still hangs over us. The negative of the measure has benumbed the whole revenue business. I suspect that it will yet be unavoidable to admit the evil in some qualified shape."

The same thought was in his mind when he wrote to Pendleton immediately after the bargain was made:

"The funding and revenue systems are reduced by the discord of opinions into a very critical state. Out of this extremity, however, some effective provision must, I think, still emerge. The affair of the state debts has been the great source of delay and embarrassment, and, from the zeal and perseverance of its patrons, threatens a very unhappy issue to the session, unless some scheme of accommodation should be devised."[16]

The Potomac, he remarked in the first letter, might show up in the vicissitudes of the business. After the dinner: If success came for the Potomac it would be the happy effect of a coincidence of causes which might never be repeated.

Jefferson's thoughts were similar, and more to his credit than his later self-portraits of innocence led astray. On June 13, harking back to Madison's March 2 proposal, he told George Mason that to avoid something worse, the opponents of assumption might be wise to compromise by having the federal government repay to the states what they already had paid to individuals. Writing to Monroe on the twentieth, immediately after the famous dinner, he fully accepted both the new plan and the urgent reasons for it. Without mutual sacrifices on funding and the national capital, no funding bill would pass. National credit, lately risen high in Amsterdam, would "burst and vanish, and the states separate." In the plan worked out there would "be something to displease and something to soothe every part of the Union but New York." If the subject was so foreign to Jefferson, why did he unconsciously echo the "bait" and "pill" language Madison and he had exchanged in the spring of 1783, when Madison told him of the defeat of his original assumption proposal?

The agreement with Hamilton was actually made on Madison's terms, foreshadowed three months earlier and revised to meet new conditions. The "qualified shape" in which he said he would admit the evil was obtained when Hamilton abandoned assumption in gross, thus removing the injustice to Virginia.

If Congressman White's stomach turned over when he agreed to vote for assumption, Richard Bland Lee's was perfectly steady. "We have a plan which is ripe for execution tomorrow," he wrote on June 27. It would decide the fate of the Potomac forever, conciliate the wealthiest portion of the country, produce a harmonious and permanent arrangement of finances, and close with honor a congressional session "which otherwise would break up abruptly in disgust and confusion." The secret was so closely guarded that New Englanders raged against the only part they heard of—a South-Central combination to carry Congress to the chosen locations. Thirteen roll calls were needed to get that part through the Senate. Uninformed House members then tried to upset the Potomac site by substituting Baltimore. Madison warned the Marylanders that this would send the bill back to the Senate, where Baltimore had many times been defeated. "By amending we give up a certainty for an uncertainty." Carroll and Gale of Maryland, who were leagued with White and Lee in the general compromise, produced the votes to defeat the amendment and to carry the capital bill, thirty-two to twenty-nine. These four and Pennsylvania united to carry assumption by the same margin.[17]

Madison voted against assumption, but did not take the floor. "If the measure should be adopted," he wrote to Monroe just before the final action, "I shall wish it to be considered as an unavoidable evil, and *possibly* not the worst side of the dilemma."[18] That statement furnishes the key to Madison's attitude, and to Jefferson's. They were not won by the dangled bait of a southward seat of government, nor was either of them deceived. Madison, who made the first move for the Potomac site seven years before, thought mainly of the national stability that would accrue from a central location accessible to the expanding West. Finding that assumption was the extorted price of national safety he made the Potomac the price of assumption. His letters written before the meeting with Hamilton make it plain that he would have accepted assumption without the capital, had that been necessary. His primary concern was to prevent national credit from being ruined and the Union destroyed by a group of blackmailing financiers in and out of Congress.

Hamilton's men of enlightenment—those who were to bulwark the new government and cement the Union—had served an ultimatum: No assumption, no funding. They would get their profits, or let the nation go to pieces. Madison could have defeated assumption, but he could not ignore the consequences of defeating it. He realized the desperation of Hamilton's uncontrollable followers, but did not know the full reason for it—that big speculators in the public debt of the United States had *reinvested their gains* in state debts, many of them borrowing to the limit of their capacity. If assumption failed, debtors' prison would stare them in the face.

Secretary Hamilton turned to Madison, with Jefferson as go-between, because he was caught in his own toils. Madison was caught in them too. By acting as he did he saved Hamilton's entire fiscal program from being done to death by the men whom the Secretary of the Treasury regarded as the pillars of national government and props of the social order.

# CHAPTER XXV

## PIEDMONT FARMER

OWING to a shift in election time, Madison planned a quick journey to Virginia after Congress adjourned in August 1790. Learning that his candidacy was unopposed, and invited by Jefferson to wait and ride down with him, he convinced himself that he should postpone travel until a break in the terrific heat reduced the danger of bilious attacks. Systematic exercise was. overcoming the effects of close confinement in Congress. Young Thomas Lee Shippen told of a Sunday afternoon horseback trip into the country with Madison and Randolph, and of a stop at a teahouse where they met Jackson and Humphreys of Washington's staff. They proposed drinking tea with the President. "I went accordingly and . . . remained nearly two hours . . . with the good man."[1]

A few minutes sufficed for Madison's re-election campaign—an identical letter to a friend in each of eight counties, to be handed around confidentially. This conveyed his opinion that the revenue measures might have been worse, funding probably would be handled without direct taxes, and it would jeopardize his health to hurry home. On no account should the letter get into print lest it give an impression that the candidate was seeking votes. He suggested that Ambrose and William attend the polls in Louisa and Culpeper counties. Sudden coups must be guarded against.[2]

On August 31 Madison and Jefferson were ready to set out in the latter's phaeton. Madison owed his landlady £58 16s. 10d. for board, at about £2 a week for himself and half as much for a servant, also for "calleco . . . makeing gound . . . shewmaker," etc. Poor Mrs. Elsworth had to convert "186 doulers" into pounds, deduct her bill and refund the difference. She dropped the third column and lost tenpence. After a week in Philadelphia the two travelers did some figuring on their open account. Madison owed Jefferson $73.91, gave him $65, paid a book bill for him, then took care of traveling expenses and was reimbursed in cash after the balance shifted.[3]

To these two, a journey from New York to the Virginia Piedmont was nothing to write about. But to Tom Shippen, who overtook his "two valuable friends" at Rock Hall on the Eastern Shore, the trip from there to Georgetown was delightful on all accounts—the excellent company, the fare, the weather and the roads. To his father, ex-chief of army hospitals, young Thomas wrote:

"We waited all that day for want of a vessel to take us over, and I never knew two men more agreeable than they were. We talked and dined and strolled and rowed ourselves in boats, and feasted upon delicious crabs."

They sailed across the bay in six hours, but the horses in another boat required eighteen. Shippen picked up a friend who undertook to show Annapolis to them inside and out.

"We passed three hours on the top of the State House steeple from which place you descry the finest prospect in the world, if extent, variety, wood and water in all their happiest forms can make one so. My good friend Shaaff was not displeased at my comparing him to the Diable Boiteux, whose office he seemed to fill in opening the roofs of the houses and telling us the history of each family who lived in them."

Fresh from European travels, Shippen described Mann's Inn (Madison's stopping place during the Annapolis Convention) as among the most excellent in the world. "I never saw so fine a turtle or so well dressed a dish as he gave us the second day for dinner." After that feast they proceeded to Queen Anna's, a dirty village thirteen miles west. "Mosquitoes, gnats, flies and bugs contended with each other for preference," and the supper was so poor that to eat was hardly more pleasant than to be eaten. So, after an early good-by to their little companions, they

"Breakfasted next morning at Bladensburgh with an old black woman who keeps the best house in the town and calls herself Mrs. Margaret Adams. She diverted us with an account of the resentment which discovered itself towards her because the President and his family had preferred her house to lodge at as he passed through Bladensburgh."

Of course, the mob dared not destroy a house in which Washington had slept. So, as Shippen modestly described it, they invaded Mrs. Adams' back yard and pulled down her temple of Cloacina. "And there was the demolished building when we arrived, a monument at the same time of the envy of her fellow citizens and her own triumph."

The destruction of this historic bit of Washingtoniana probably occurred on September 10, 1790, the day before Jefferson, Madison and Shippen gazed on its shattered timbers.[4]

At Georgetown, Congressman Carroll headed a group of citizens who invited the travelers to stay overnight and take an early morning ride through the beautiful country in which the nation's capital was to be located. After breakfasting at the attractive home of Motley Young, they traversed the whole country, and, gaining recruits at each estate, "had at last a cavalcade of thirteen." In the afternoon they dined at Colonel Forrest's and went in a boat to the Little Falls of the Potomac, four miles upstream. Romantic scene, Shippen remarked. Boatmen, one half dollar, Jefferson recorded.

Shippen went ashore in Virginia to visit one of his ten Lee uncles, then went on to Mt. Vernon, where he arrived just as his recent companions were leaving. The youth wrote to his father that day: "My having joined those charming men Jefferson and Madison, though it gave me infinite pleasure, cost me money—so that when I arrived here I found that I was by thirty dollars poorer than when I left you." Washington's servants were somewhat richer, receiving fourteen shillings in tips from Jefferson alone, and Shippen didn't do so badly if his father sent him the $50 he asked for.[5]

Madison's journey ended on September 18, but he lent a servant and horses for the run to Monticello. After these were sent back, Jefferson confirmed a proposal to buy one of the animals but refused to let Madison state its value. "I know nobody," said he, "with whom it is so difficult to settle a price and with whom I should be so likely to differ. Witness the money disputes on our journey." To prevent a sale at less than real value, Jefferson demanded that a good judge be called in. Madison delivered the horse, set the price at £25, and all was well until, with dismaying suddenness, the animal lay down and died. Here was a test of Damon and Pythias. Their reaction to that grim stroke could mold the political destiny of the United States.[6]

The dread issue did not arise until January 10, 1791, before which time Madison had lent Jefferson the cost of his return to Philadelphia and had received $50 on account. "Will you be so good," wrote the latter, "as to let me know how much I am in your debt for travelling expenses and the horse? My monstrous bill of freight [from France] rendered the question useless till now."

Madison demurred. The $50, he reported, overpaid the traveling expenses by £4 9s. 6d. If the horse was to be paid for, the balance would be on the other side. However, his scruples against taking the money were increased by his having discovered, from the servant who drove Jefferson to Monticello, that on his return the horse was taken very ill and drenched. Undoubtedly this was a prelude to the fatal malady. To get rid of all embarrassment, let a common friend—Senator Hawkins for instance—serve as umpire. It was not made clear whether the North Carolina senator was to be brought in for his veterinary skill or his notable gift for making peace among the Indians. However, an ultimatum from Jefferson kept those talents idle:

"It being impossible to entertain a doubt that the horse I bought of you was fairly sold and fairly bought, that his disorder was of the instant and might have happened years after as well as when it did . . . I should as soon think of filching the sum from your pocket as of permitting the loss to be yours. I therefore send you a check on the bank for 95.26 dollars including the two balances."

In his eagerness to pay for the dead horse, Jefferson added the balances instead of subtracting them. Madison refunded $23.26.[7]

All this lay in the future when the Montpelier farmer plunged into plantation affairs in September. His share of the family hold-

ings was divided into a lower and an upper farm called Broad
Meadows and Sawney's, the latter tract extending over the Southwest Mountains. One was managed by Mordecai Collins, a white
overseer, the other by the slave Sawney who had driven Madison
to Princeton twenty-two years before. Lewis Collins, Mordecai's
brother, was farm carpenter.

Before going to Philadelphia Madison gave each of his three
managers a set of written instructions. Mordecai, a new man, was
to choose one of the milch cows for his own use, and let the rest
be milked for the Negroes. He must keep the Broad Meadow
Negroes supplied with meal, filling their thirteen-peck barrel
three times in a fortnight. He was "to take particular care of the
horses and stock, to avoid riding the horses without the approbation of my father." He must "treat the Negroes with all the
humanity and kindness consistent with their necessary subordination and work."

Madison is revealed as a practical farmer who could give advice
on the mixing of timothy with oats or flax, the preparation of a
red clover field, the interplanting of corn and potatoes, the forging
and fitting of new and old plows, the building of stables. The
trend toward home manufactures is suggested by the order to
Lewis Collins to make a loom, along with two good wheelbarrows,
three wagons and three carts.

Most notable, however, is the picture of Madison as a pioneer in
erosion control. Mordecai was "to make the meadow dams in the
manner already prescribed to him." (They broke in four years and
were replaced with stone.) In plowing there should be no long
straight furrows for rains to gully. He was instructed:

"To fallow with the large plows all the ground for oats and
corn, laying off the ground in convenient parcels with horizontal
outlines, particularly on the sides where there will be double open
furrows; and plowing all around each parcel, instead of the common way by lands."

The instructions to Sawney reveal not only Madison's direct
oversight of farm operations but the responsibilities placed on an
intelligent and trusted slave. He was directed:

"To have a patent plow, L. Collins to do the wooden work; and to fallow the little field allotted for meadow first; then the field on the old mountain. He is to plow his ground all around in the manner prescribed for M. Collins. . . . To plant about 200 apple trees either before Christmas or very early in the spring in the little field on the top of the mountain. . . . To plant his corn 5½ feet by 5½ and lay off his ground by stakes. To plant all the tobacco ground on the top of the mountain in Irish potatoes; and as much more as he can find that is worth planting."[8]

Sawney went around freely on plantation business. In a three-year account given Madison in 1790 by Fontaine Maury of Fredericksburg "the Negroe Sawney" was named each year as a purchaser of goods. This account included the expense of inspecting and carting about six hogsheads of tobacco shipped annually to Liverpool and sold by James Maury, Fontaine's brother. Madison's 1789 shipment, he was told, was above the average of a generally inferior crop, but some of it was shipped too early and lacked the summer or spring aftergrowth which was important in the European market.[9]

On November 8, 1790, Francis Taylor wrote in his diary: "Heard that Messrs. Jefferson and Madison passed by on their way to Philadelphia." It was Jefferson who waited this time, delaying a talk with Washington on the piracies of Algiers and Morocco, and on the piratical hope of Northern congressmen to carry away the capital.

"Mr. Madison and myself [wrote the Secretary of State] have endeavored to press on some members of the [Virginia] assembly the expediency of their undertaking to build ten good private dwelling houses a year for ten years in the new city, to be rented or sold for the benefit of the state. Should they do this, and Maryland as much, it will be one means of ensuring the removal of government thither."[10]

In Philadelphia the two men took stock of things political. Monroe, elected to fill out the term of Senator Grayson, was invited to join the Virginia group at Mrs. House's. William B. Giles, brilliant and radical successor to Bland, came to Madison with an introduction from John Marshall. Word arrived that the Virginia legislature had denounced assumption of state debts as unconstitutional, but Jefferson believed that this masked the implacable hostility of Patrick Henry to the new order.

"The measures and tone of the government [wrote he] threatens abortion to some of his speculations; most particularly to that of the Yazoo territory. But it is too well nerved to be overawed by individual opposition."

As at the time of the inauguration, the President called on Madison to draft his message to Congress—but with important portions coming from Hamilton. The House as usual gave Madison the job of writing the reply, and Washington once more sent a request "to finish the good offices you have begun for me" by writing the presidential response to House and Senate.[11]

At Hamilton's suggestion, the President expressed satisfaction over the rise of public securities and credit and the productivity of import duties. Madison's hand is recognizable in advice to admit Kentucky into the Union, to render commerce and agriculture less dependent on foreign shipping and to reduce the national debt through sales of public lands.

Drafting the House reply, Madison put in definite commitments for his own favorite propositions. Swift attacks followed. Smith of South Carolina admitted that the style of composition "was such as might be expected from the acknowledged abilities of the gentleman who drafted it," but Madison had failed to be properly ambiguous. He had given it as the opinion of the House that foreign bottoms ought to be excluded from carrying American produce—a course harmful to Southern agriculture.

In rebuttal Madison cited the reply to the President in January 1790, written by Smith himself when Madison was ill and absent. It promised concurrence in several matters. Smith promptly read from that address to prove that the language was so vague that it promised nothing. The House agreed with Madison that if measures were proper, there was no harm in saying so.

For some time the Virginian remained on the fringe of debate.

A bill to organize the militia brought him up with amendments to exempt conscientious objectors, and to eliminate the exemption of members of Congress except when they were attending its sessions. Both motions were received with disfavor, the second creating such a shock that he withdrew it.[12]

In spite of his opposition to assumption of state debts, Madison supported Hamilton's request for $826,000 additional revenue to carry the costs of it. Southern congressmen violently assailed the proposed excise on domestic liquor and higher duties on the imported product. Madison told them that he would prefer direct taxation, but both the people and Congress were opposed to that. An excise on liquor was the least objectionable of all excises, and this particular plan was free of their most obnoxious features. The plan was what he himself suggested to Hamilton a year earlier. It carried two to one.[13]

This minor harmony meant nothing. When Hamilton submitted his plan for a national bank in December of 1790, the third great conflict was on. The government was to subscribe for twenty-five per cent of the stock. Private stockholders could pay one quarter in cash, three quarters in public securities at face value. Hamilton elaborated on its usefulness as an aid to government finances. Madison raised the issue of constitutionality.

# CHAPTER XXVI

## THE NATIONAL BANK

EVENTS at the end of 1790 were verifying a prediction made by Madison. The exposition of the Constitution, he wrote soon after it came into effect, would be a copious source of trouble until its meaning on all great points should be settled by precedents. From Judge Pendleton, faced with the issue of British debts, came questions on treaties as the supreme law. Did the peace treaty of 1783 automatically repeal state laws in conflict with it? Yes, Madison replied. Was the supreme law, as applied to treaties, unchangeable? A treaty, he answered, could be annulled by the parties that made it, or by one party if the other broke it.[1]

Presidential elections brought up a knotty question in January 1791. Under the Constitution each *state* chooses its electors in such manner as *the legislature thereof* may direct, but Congress may determine the time of choosing them. A bill to fix a uniform time was objected to because in some states they were chosen by the legislatures, which might not be in session at the date fixed. From a Maryland congressman who helped frame the Constitution came this remark:

"Mr. Carroll said that it appeared to him necessary, in the first place, to determine who shall choose the electors. For his part, he was fully convinced that this power is exclusively vested in the people by the Constitution."

Giles agreed that the legislatures were not authorized to exercise that power themselves. Also, the power of Congress to say when they should be chosen imposed "a necessity for one mode, and that the mode should be uniform and be by the people." Jackson and Goodhue argued that the matter was discretionary, while Ames wanted to pass the problem along by planting the words of the Constitution in the bill—"in such manner as the legislature thereof may direct." Supporting him:

"Mr. Madison said a question arose here which was whether the power of Congress extends to determining the manner of choosing, by virtue of possessing the power of determining the time of their being chosen. He was, however, disposed to think that the best idea was that suggested by the gentleman from Massachusetts."

To sidestep the issue the proviso for a uniform time was stricken out. The position taken by Carroll and Giles was fully warranted by the proceedings of the convention of 1787, but it was not until 1823 that Rufus King, one of the last surviving framers, went to the Journals to prove it.[2]

The national bank bill came from the Senate, which passed it without a roll call. In the House the bill was shoved ahead of a militia measure and went through committee of the whole with nobody rising in opposition. Jackson asked a recommittal, condemning national banks as instruments of monopoly, useless to farmers. Madison wanted it sent back for discussion of constitutionality, but was told that the present stage of the bill was ideal for that purpose. So he talked on it all next day—speaking, an opponent remarked, with great earnestness and in very animated language.[3]

The Virginian saw more good than harm in banks, if several were distributed over the country, but only harm in a concentration of wealth and influence in a metropolis. But Congress had no authority to charter one. His impression was the stronger because a power to grant charters of incorporation had been rejected in the Federal Convention. From what clause could the claimed authority arise?

Not from the power to lay and collect taxes for the general welfare. The bill did not lay a tax, and the power to devote money to the general welfare was limited to objects set forth in the enumerated powers.

Not from the power to borrow money. It was a dangerous and forced construction to hold that the power to borrow includes a power of creating the ability to do so.

No power to charter a bank could be found in the "necessary and proper" clause. That only enabled Congress to pass laws

"DOLLEY MADISON, ALASS! ALASS!" LETTER TO ELIZA LEE. THE SECOND "ALASS!" HAS BEEN TORN OFF

necessary to the end and incident to the nature of the specified powers. Stretch it as proposed and "the essential characteristic of the government, as composed of limited and enumerated powers, would be destroyed." He pointed to the chain of reasoning by which the bill was supported. To borrow money is the end, to create capital the means. Creation of capital then becomes the end, a bank the means. Finally, the bank is the end, a charter of incorporation is the means.

"If implications, thus remote and thus multiplied, can be linked together, a chain may be formed that will reach every object of legislation, every object within the whole compass of political economy."

The proposed bank, Madison asserted, might be convenient, but it could not be called necessary to the government. All benefits expected from it could be obtained by other means—by taxation, by loans from individuals, by command over other banks. No inference could be drawn from the fact that the old Congress incorporated the Bank of North America in 1781. That bank was the child of necessity.

He turned to the explanations of the Constitution given in state conventions, especially in Pennsylvania, Virginia and North Carolina. The debates, the acts of ratification, the amendments asked for, all pointed to a rule of construction excluding the sweep of power now contended for. If the power was not in the Constitution, the exercise of it was usurpation, and established a precedent "leveling all the barriers which limit the powers of the general government, and protect those of the state governments."

Ames led off in reply. He expanded Madison's admission of the utility of banks into a concession that a public bank was little short of indispensable. After total silence in committee of the whole, objections were offered which never had been suspected, "and had not the acute penetration of that gentleman brought them to light, I am sure that my own understanding would never have suggested them." He cited the reliance of European governments on banks and asked what would happen if a war should break out. Could it be financed at the outset by taxes or loans of citizens? Was the

ruinous issuance of paper money to be resumed? Should we send
across the sea for loans? He did not contend that the power to pass
necessary and proper laws extended to everything, but power to
establish a bank was a necessary incident to the entire powers to
regulate trade and revenue and provide for the public credit and
defense.

Sedgwick, Laurance and Boudinot reinforced Ames. Madison
listened to his own arguments repeated by Giles and Jackson, and
then closed the debate with a detailed rebuttal. The House overrode his objections, thirty-nine to twenty.[4]

Before signing the bill, the President asked his cabinet officers
for opinions on its constitutionality. Randolph and Jefferson took
one side, and their briefs were given to Hamilton for rebuttal. In
general it was a repetition of the Madison-Ames debate, but with
a rushing out into wider extremes. Besides using Madison's arguments, Jefferson declared that the Constitution restrained Congress
"to those means without which the grant of power would be
nugatory"—an interpretation which would keep the government
on the brink of collapse. Hamilton relied on the inherent principle that "every power invested in a government is in its nature
sovereign and includes, by force of the term, a right to employ all
the means requisite and fairly applicable to the attainment of the
end of such power." To erect corporations was an incident of
sovereign power. The necessity of the bank to government financial operations was evidence of the power to establish it.[5]

Washington held the bill almost to the last hour allowed him.
Its constitutionality, Madison stated in a memorandum, was a question on which his mind was greatly perplexed.

"He held several free conversations with me on the subject, in
which he listened favorably, as I thought, to my view of it, but
certainly without committing himself in any manner. Not long
before the expiration of the ten days allowed for his decision, he
desired me to reduce into form the objections to the bill, that he
might be prepared in case he should return it without his signature."

This Madison did, inferring from the request that a veto would
follow. The delay produced intense excitement. In New York, he

reported, Tories and speculators attacked the President with inconceivable licentiousness. "The meanest motives were charged on him and the most insolent menaces held over him." The truth was that Hamilton's defense of the bank bill did not reach Washington until two days after Madison wrote the veto draft. Though not fully convinced, he decided to accept the will of Congress.[6]

In his main speech against the bank bill Madison hinted at a theory he developed later—that the Constitution was to be judged by the opinions expressed in the ratifying conventions. He told what would follow if it became a law—predicting, by way of warning, almost the whole scope of federal expansion during the ensuing 150 years. Yet all the time he was arguing against himself. The doctrine of implied power originated in his report to the old Congress in 1781. He deliberately preserved it when he wrote the Tenth Amendment to the Constitution. Hamilton's basic contention was a paraphrase of Madison's explanation of the "necessary and proper" clause in *The Federalist* No. 44. The latter could escape from his own logic only by denying that a bank served a purpose incidental to the government's money power.

For nearly two years Madison had been advocating an unimportant action which could be justified only under Hamilton's interpretation of the Constitution. Early in 1789 a "rude genius" named John Churchman came to him with a letter from Dr. Samuel Stanhope Smith of Princeton. Churchman desired a copyright on some charts based on Captain Cook's round-the-world record of deviations of the magnetic needle and also wanted the United States to send him to Baffin Bay to determine the cause of the deviations. Aided by Madison, he presented his memorial. A committee advised postponement of the scientific voyage because of deranged finances. Madison protested:

"Well aware as I am that public bodies are liable to be assailed by visionary projectors, I nevertheless wish to ascertain the probability of the magnetic theory. If there is any considerable probability that the projected voyage would be successful or throw any valuable light on the discovery of longitude, it certainly comports with the honor and dignity of government to give it their countenance and support."

Just before the bank bill debate Madison renewed his effort, suggesting that the voyage might furnish aids to navigation. The answer came that a ship captain did not need to know the cause of compass deviations in order to use the charts recording them. The fact was that he wanted to send out a purely scientific expedition, which could be justified only by a sweeping interpretation of the power to spend for the general welfare.[7]

These two questions, one trivial, the other important, involved the same principle of broad or narrow construction of the Constitution. In one of them Madison took the broad way, in the other the narrow, with no apparent feeling of inconsistency. He saw in the bank an instrument of monopoly and feared it would fortify the new money power grasping for control of the nation. He saw the need to impose general checks against a mounting federal imperialism. Facing hostile majorities he turned to the Constitution, whose ends and means presented a panorama of uncertainties. The issue came to him at the one spot—bank incorporation—where he had a record of strict construction, contrasting sharply with his generally broad concept of federal power. By conviction and compulsion he chose the narrow path on this issue, and by that action was driven into lasting adherence to it. In policy he remained an advocate of the use of federal power for the public good, up to the limit of its discernible existence. But the spectacle of chronic abuse of that power propelled him into a lifelong argument against some of the most important principles he had helped to plant in the Constitution.

In the first Congress, which came to an end a few days after the bank bill was signed, Madison rose to national leadership as organizer of the machinery of government and framer of policies designed to strengthen the nation without giving advantage to any section or class. He gave lasting strength and independence to the executive, and planted responsibility in it, by successfully affirming the power of the President to make removals from office. He fixed the basic rights of personal liberty on an enduring basis by sponsoring the first ten amendments to the Constitution, and in doing so smothered the dangerous fire of Antifederalism.

Having done this, he deliberately abandoned his majority leadership when he saw that the price of keeping it was to become a tool of financial oligarchy. In the second phase, Madison just as definitely rose to leadership of the opposition. Championing veterans and other small fry against powerful speculators, he found himself at last defending farmers, mechanics, storekeepers, small manufacturers—the America of wayside life—against organized commercial and financial interests with the government as their instrument. The result was to make him the fusing agent of a new and powerful political movement. Into this, just as it was taking shape, came the challenging figure of his closest friend, Thomas Jefferson.

Kindred in spirit, far superior in magnetic pull on men, Jefferson needed the chastening influence of Madison's analytic mind on his own anarchic intellect, needed also his talent for political strategy and his relentless perseverance. The progressive effect of the developing conflict was to pit Hamilton against Madison, then Hamilton against Madison and Jefferson, and finally, as parties took shape and issues merged with personalities, Hamiltonian federalism against Jeffersonian democracy. Mind coped with mind, will met will, passion encountered passion, tenacity matched tenacity. Rival skills, all offered to the country's service, were driven against one another by clashing concepts of the public good. The power and influence of organized wealth determined immediate results. The pains and hopes of the people shadowed and lightened the horizon.

# CHAPTER XXVII

## Madison and Jefferson

Three days after the bank bill was signed, Jefferson wrote to the poet Philip Freneau, who was editing the *Daily Advertiser* in New York, and invited him to become clerk for foreign languages in the Department of State. The salary was only $250 a year, but the duties were so slight as not to interfere with any other calling the person might choose. They did not interfere with the founding of Freneau's *National Gazette*. When Hamilton, under various pseudonyms, accused Jefferson of using public office to subsidize his own political organ, the latter denied to Washington that he either controlled or wrote for Freneau's paper. But his memory of its genesis was extraordinarily uneven.

While the government was in New York, and again in Philadelphia, the Secretary of State "was applied to on behalf of Freneau" for a place in his department. On this second occasion, or afterward, he was told Freneau had a thought of setting up a newspaper there. That seemed a good arrangement. As clerk, Freneau would furnish translations of European news. As editor of a good Whig newspaper, he would combat monarchical and aristocratic principles such as "Davila" (John Adams) was planting in John Fenno's *Gazette of the United States*. Fenno, an ex-Bostonian of great vituperative gifts, had established a newspaper in New York in 1789 with the help of Treasury and Senate printing and moved it to Philadelphia with Congress.[1]

Jefferson told the President that he might have talked to some people of the editorial line he hoped for, but to Freneau himself "I think I could not because I had still seen him but once, and that was at a public table, at breakfast at Mrs. Elsworth's, as I passed through New York the past year." Had his memory been a little more acute, he would have said that he was applied to by Madison, who with Henry Lee had tried once before to find a place for their old college chum. When the government moved to

334

Philadelphia the translation clerk refused to go along in a half-time, half-pay job. Madison said he was moved to recommend Freneau "by a respect for his talents and by a knowledge of his merit and sufferings in the course of the Revolution." Was it because of the poet's experience on a prison ship that his friend spent most of the year urging him to take a job he did not want?

Replying to Jefferson's offer, Freneau said he had commitments to establish a weekly in his old home town, so must decline the generous unsolicited proposal. When Congress adjourned in April, Madison hastened to New York. Freneau, he informed Jefferson, had mistakenly supposed that he was expected to translate from English into French.

"Being now set right as to this particular, and being made sensible of the advantages of Philadelphia over New Jersey for his private undertaking, his mind is taking another turn. . . . The more I learn of his character, talents and principles, the more I should regret his burying himself in the obscurity he had chosen in New Jersey. It is certain that there is not to be found in the whole catalog of American printers a single name that can approach towards a rivalship."[2]

Later in May, Jefferson joined Madison at the Elsworth boarding house. They looked across the table (according to the report to Washington) and there was Freneau. Strangers being present, they couldn't talk. However, Jefferson seemed to know what Madison was referring to when he wrote in midsummer, during a later visit to New York, that Freneau was abandoning his Philadelphia project. Jefferson replied that he was sincerely sorry.

"I should have given him the perusal of all my letters of foreign intelligence and all foreign newspapers; the publication of all proclamations and other public notices within my department and the printing of the laws, which, added to his salary, would have been a considerable aid. Besides this, Fenno's being the only weekly or half weekly paper and under general condemnation for its toryism and its incessant efforts to overturn the government, Freneau would have found that ground as good as unoccupied."[3]

Armed with this promise, Madison used all his persuasive powers. Freneau's New York publisher promised capital and a partnership. One week later, Madison was writting letters of introduction
for Publisher Childs to influential republicans of Alexandria and
Fredericksburg, praising Freneau as a man of genius, experience
and great integrity. The first issue of the *National Gazette* came
off the press on October 31, with Madison, Lee and Jefferson all
turning in lists of subscribers. Except for the offering of the public
job, Madison was far more responsible than Jefferson for launching
this highly controversial and controverted newspaper.[4]

Through the *National Gazette,* the sharp wit and acid pen of
Freneau were set against the heavy invectives of Fenno. Hamilton
and Adams felt the menace and sting of satiric laughter, and
Washington suffered when the biting jibes no longer spared him.
The impact of this paper on a part of the people was due to their
eagerness to be led. The qualities of leadership they sought were
set forth in the *Maryland Journal:*

"Keep always before your eyes the steps by which a Jefferson
and Madison have gradually ascended to their present pre-eminence of fame. Like them you must devote your whole leisure
to the most useful reading. Like them you must dive into the
depths of philosophy and government . . . keeping and holding
fast, as to the rock of your political salvation, their unshaken integrity and scorn of party."

This was printed on March 22, 1791, at almost the last moment
that philosophical preparation could be emphasized above political action. The coupling of the two names reflected the rise of
Jefferson to political primacy, owing to personality and cabinet
position, at a time when Madison was still the main formulator
of republican policy.

When Jefferson joined Madison in New York late in May, it
was to set out on a long drive through the Northern states. David
Rittenhouse (who had been debating the anatomy of the opossum
with Madison) planned to go with them but could not find a
good horse. Though it had political overtones, the trip reflected
common interests and a common desire for travel. "Health,

recreation and curiosity being my objects, I can never be out of my way," Madison remarked when an itinerary was submitted.[5]

The journey was an enlargement of local diversions. "What say you to taking a wade into the country at noon?" queried Jefferson after a heavy spring rain. "It will be pleasant above head at least, and the party will finish by dining here." "Here" was the house a few blocks up Market Street to which the Secretary of State moved in January. Hearing that the British diplomatic agent, Colonel Beckwith, was taking quarters with Mrs. House, he invited Madison to escape that disagreeable association by taking a bed and plate with him.

"It will be a relief from a solitude of which I have too much; and . . . it will not increase my expenses an atom. When I get my library open you will often find a convenience in being close at hand to it. . . . Let me, I beseech you, have a favorable answer."[6]

Instead, the presence of Colonel Beckwith proved convenient. Jefferson could not deal with him officially because he was a private agent of the governor of Canada. So Madison told Beckwith that the President had information that Indians in American territory were receiving war supplies from places held by the British. Beckwith assured him that his government was opposed to Indian hostilities. Might not the supplies have been the usual amount furnished for hunting? "As the Indians at war traded with British subjects only, their being able to carry on hostilities was of itself sufficient evidence in the case," answered Madison. When Beckwith learned that this was the nearest he could come to official word from the President, he expressed hope that a "more authentic character" would take his place. The meeting was a virtual prelude to the coming of Minister George Hammond half a year later.[7]

On March 17, four days after that wade in the country, bluebirds were warbling on the fence posts. Weeping willows were in leaf next day, lilacs and gooseberries on the twenty-fifth. Spring was moving north and Madison and Jefferson followed. Meeting in New York and going by boat from there to Poughkeepsie, they took to the road on May 23 and drove to Albany in three days.

The equipment was Jefferson's, with Madison's saddle horse as a spare. Each had a servant (Matthew and James). On the twenty-ninth, leaving their phaeton behind, they sailed up Lake George— "the most beautiful water I ever saw," commented Jefferson, its mountainous shores covered with fir and pine, aspen and birch; its waters filled with speckled trout, salmon trout and bass, whose abundance "added to our other amusements the sport of taking them." Lake Champlain was a pond of a different color, muddy and turbulent. After penetrating twenty-five miles they were obliged "by a head wind and high sea, to return, having spent a day and a half in sailing on it."

From eight miles above Crown Point they sailed sixty-two miles back to Fort George in two days (spending a night at Ticonderoga) and headed their horses toward Bennington, Vermont. Held there by the law against Sunday travel, Jefferson sent an account of the trip to Martha's husband of a year, Thomas Mann Randolph. More pleasing than the historic forts were botanical objects unknown or rare in Virginia. A small red squirrel was so plentiful that twenty-odd were killed within ten yards of their lodging-house opposite Crown Point, the morning they arrived.

The night of June 11 was spent on Long Island Sound, crossing from Guilford to the eastern tip. On the level island they really traveled—128 miles in four days—but found time to visit the Unquachog Indians and look at William Prince's famous fruit nursery at Flushing. Madison stopped in New York, but Jefferson went on. His horses closed the journey on June 18 with a sixty-mile run from South Amboy.

Madison's account of the tour, written to his brother Ambrose, has been lost. Jefferson said of his companion a few weeks later that "his journey with me to the lakes placed him in better health than I have seen him; but the late heats have brought on some bilious dispositions."[8]

From Philadelphia, Jefferson sent Madison $35 to balance their account, also $200 which he collected at Madison's request from Thomas Leiper, their new tobacco buyer and Jefferson's landlord. Madison gathered up some new clothing for Jefferson and paid the tailor. Commissioned to buy maple sugar to allure Piedmont farmers into tree planting, he found the quality too far below the product of his imagination. Maple seed from the North had not arrived, but birch bark for Jefferson was ready to be forwarded by sea. Nearly all of eighty maple trees which Madison sent to Monticello from the Prince nursery died in transplantation. A year later seeds from Bennington were divided by Jefferson with Washington and Madison. The sender of them, Colonel Joseph Fay, disclosed that "after you and Mr. Madison left this, I obtained Mr. Payne on the Rights of Man," and he would now retract all he had said in favor of the British constitution.[9]

Madison had planned a supplementary excursion to Portsmouth with House Clerk John Beckley, but the illness of his horse (in bad shape after 900 miles on the road) made it impossible to start when Beckley came through. The stage traveled too fast for way-side stops and he didn't want to go alone. Hearing of this, Henry Lee rode in from Philadelphia to join him, but by that time Madison's bilious attacks forbade the journey.[10]

New-type Federalists saw deep meaning in these 1791 travels. "There was every appearance of a passionate courtship between the Chancellor, Burr, Jefferson and Madison, when the two latter were in town," wrote Robert Troup to his Treasury boss on June 15. John C. Hamilton enlarged this into an assertion that "after frequent interviews with Chancellor Livingston and Burr, they made a visit to Clinton under the pretext of a botanical excursion to Albany, thence extended their journey to Vermont; and having sown a few tares in Connecticut, returned to the seat of government." Later writers have expanded this into creation of the Clinton-Burr-Livingston axis, with an agreement among the whole quintet to support Clinton for Vice President against Adams.

That is too pat. Clinton had already helped ex-enemy Burr take away Schuyler's seat in the Senate, but it was October 1792 before Burr subordinated his vice-presidential ambitions. Spending several months in New York, Madison no doubt worked to unite Burr and Livingston, who was still brooding over Hamilton's rejection of him for the Senate seat given to King. Jefferson's two-day stop in that city allowed little time for politics. If their northward trip was a pretext to cover a conference with Clinton,

it was strange indeed that they drove twenty-six miles on the day
they reached Albany and twenty-two miles on the morrow.[11]

One motive—political inquiry—was self-evident in Madison's
plan for a second journey with Beckley, the country's champion
inquirer, but quite different was Jefferson's request that he "continue the inquiries relative to the Hessian fly." Madison had been
worrying for three years over the spread of that destructive insect
since it appeared on Long Island, and Jefferson headed a committee
of the American Philosophical Society to study its life habits.[12]

Madison relayed Beckley's reports to Jefferson. The heresies of
Adams—that is, the hints that French experience proved the need
of an aristocratic branch of government—were patronized by
virtually nobody. Then came a revelation—the true identity of
"Publicola," the mystery man of current journalism.

In the previous April Beckley received from England a copy of
Thomas Paine's *Rights of Man,* defending the French Revolution
against Burke's attacks. After arranging for its republication, he
lent it to Madison, who passed it along to Jefferson. At Beckley's
request, Jefferson forwarded it to the printer, and sent with it a
covering note saying that he was glad something was to be published against the heresies which had sprung up. When the
pamphlet came off the press in May, Jefferson's note appeared as
a foreword hitting straight at Adams. This, he promptly told
Madison and others, was without his consent.[13]

Madison was inclined to relish the situation. Adams, he remarked, had no right to complain. In 1787 under a mock defense
of American institutions he had attacked them with all his might.
As Vice President he had continued that course. "Surely if it be
innocent and decent in one servant of the public thus to write
attacks against its government, it cannot be very criminal or indecent in another to patronize a written defense of the principles
on which that government is founded."

That was not the way it looked to the Adamsites. While Madi-
son and Jefferson were on their trip, the *Columbian Centinel* of
Boston began (on June 8) to publish a series of articles signed
Publicola, attacking Paine and Jefferson. Assaults and counter-
assaults spread over the country, with everybody convinced that
John Adams was Publicola. Jefferson thought so too, but termed

the attacks on the Vice President very indecent. They didn't seem to bother Madison, who wrote late in June:

"Mr. Adams seems to be getting faster and faster into difficulties. His attack on Paine, which I have not seen, will draw the public attention to his obnoxious principles, more than anything he has published."[14]

In Boston, Beckley was told that Publicola was really twenty-four-year-old John Quincy Adams. Madison agreed, on reading the articles, that the actual writing was not done by the elder Adams. There was too much method, too little clumsiness in it. Receiving this information, Jefferson aimed an olive branch at the Vice President. He explained the accidental nature of his connection with Paine's pamphlet, condemned those who criminally charged that Adams was Publicola (thus in effect condemning the Adams teamwork while appearing to have no suspicion of it) and denied that he himself was Agricola, Brutus or any other of the anonymous gentry who were taking pot shots at the statesman from Quincy. Adams quickly replied that he had nothing whatever to do with Publicola, with never a hint that his son did.[15]

Jefferson-Adams relations were improved, but the controversy brought the French Revolution squarely into American politics. Randolph described the ups and downs to Madison: "Since the standard of republicanism has been erected . . . the crest of aristocracy has fallen." The other side began to blame Jefferson for the general cleavage, and to make him the butt of slanderous attack. Madison was not exempt. Countering the whisper of a supposed connection with Patrick Henry's Southwestern speculation, he wrote to his father in July:

"The report in Georgia relating to me is as absolute a falsehood as ever was propagated. So far am I from being concerned in the Yazoo transaction that from the nature of it, as it has been understood by me, I have invariably considered it as one of the most disgraceful events that have appeared in our public councils."[16]

Madison was in New York when the bank shares were offered to the public. He witnessed a frenzied scene of speculation as they were struggled for, issued and jobbed within a day. The plan of the bank, he remarked to Jefferson, gave a moral certainty of gain to the subscribers with scarce a physical possibility of loss. Not only were they paid for with public securities at face value, though purchased for a fraction of it, but they could be transferred instantly at forty to fifty per cent above the full price.

"The subscriptions are consequently a mere scramble for so much public plunder which will be engrossed by those already loaded with the spoils of individuals."

Of all the shameful circumstances, he finally remarked, it was among the greatest "to see the members of the legislature who were most active in pushing this job openly grasping its emoluments." Day after day the ferment kept up, with quotations rising and speculators borrowing at one per cent a week. "Stock-jobbing drowns every other subject. The Coffee-House is in an eternal buzz with the gamblers." In August he observed a phenomenal rise in the deferred debt, on which interest was not to be paid until 1800. Hamilton was said to have hinted at earlier payment. Madison was unwilling to believe this without proof, but——

"It is said that packet boats and expresses are again sent from this place to the southern states, to buy up the paper of all sorts which has risen in the market here. These and other abuses make it a problem whether the system of the old paper under a bad government, or of the new under a good one, be chargeable with the greater substantial injustice. The true difference seems to be that by the former the few were the victims to the many; by the latter the many to the few."

Should this new job be piled on top of the funding and bank speculations, with Congress adhering to its course—then, said he:

"My imagination will not attempt to set bounds to the daring depravity of the times. The stockholders will become the pretorian band of the government, at once its tool and its tyrant; bribed by its largesses and overawing it by clamors and combinations."[17]

Coming from Madison, language like that meant a transition from the philosopher in politics to the fighting politician. Once more he was the goad to Jefferson, preceding him in hostility to the plunderers, yet willing to take second place in their political alliance.

Madison's long stay in New York did not please his friends. "All your acquaintances," Jefferson wrote on August 18, "are perpetually asking if you are arrived. It has been the first question from the President every time I have seen him for this fortnight. ... Come on then and make us all happy." He had been in New York since April, with time out for the northern trip, and no evidence of pressing duties. In his "idle situation," he even tried to perfect one of Jefferson's inventions—a cruet stand designed to overhang a dining table and be carried to any part of it by a movable arm.

Perhaps he had interests of which he left no record. In 1802 Dr. Samuel Latham Mitchill wrote after a visit with Madison: "While Congress sat in New York it was reported that he was fascinated by the celebrated Mrs. Colden, of our city, she who was so noted for her masculine understanding and activity, as well as for feminine graces and accomplishments." Madison was not very likely to want a rival in masculine understanding around the house, and Mrs. Colden was on the Tory side. Nevertheless, if theirs was merely an intellectual friendship, it was conspicuous enough to be recalled a dozen years later with implications of romance. He certainly didn't spend four months in New York wooing Freneau, Burr and Livingston.[18]

Madison reached Philadelphia on the twenty-fourth, ready to set out with Jefferson for Virginia. First, however, at Washington's request, the two looked over L'Enfant's new plan for the national capital. Soon afterward the impetuous Frenchman tore down a new house which Daniel Carroll of Duddington (not the commissioner of the same name) was building for himself where L'Enfant wanted a street. Jefferson and Madison, in conference, prepared so strong a rebuke for the President's signature that it helped produce the impasse which led to L'Enfant's discharge.[19]

The start of the Madison-Jefferson homeward journey was governed by another large boil at the upper end of President Washington's thigh. While it was coming to a head, Jefferson hunted for a partner for his carriage horse Romulus. Its old teammate was near death from the same sort of illness that had stricken Madison's mount. Luckily the latter animal recovered enough to become a temporary Remus. From Georgetown on September 9 (the eighth day out), they took the westerly hill-and-swamp road through Fauquier and Culpeper counties. Jefferson's new odometer, bought for ten dollars in Philadelphia and repaired for fifty cents en route, went out completely. Apparently it couldn't stand the road or the country, described by the Monticello farmer as "hilly, stumpy, stony ... frogeaten, stony ... frogeaten, clayey."[20]

On the return of the two men to Philadelphia, beautiful Maria Jefferson went with them. Madison's frog-eaten horse was replaced by a half-broken animal which thought that the downhill push of a carriage was something to run away from. After two days of hairbreadth escapes the horse behaved better but came through "preserving the fierceness of his spirit to the last." Recognizing current distinctions among slaves, Jefferson handed $2.00 to his temporary valet at Mt. Vernon, 45c at Montpelier. At Georgetown he paid Madison $15.33 for expenses, then borrowed 25c from him for a third-class valet.

They needed that equine liveliness now, for Washington had just learned that Congress was to meet on October 24—seven days off—instead of a week later. The President went with them to Georgetown, to attend the opening sales of lots in the new capital. The price thrilled them—about $2,400 an acre for land which cost the government £25—insuring easy payment for all public buildings. At Martha Washington's invitation, Maria rode in the presidential carriage, which recently had had its center of gravity lowered and no longer turned over when a wheel hit a stump. Five days through a slashing southeast storm brought the travelers to Philadelphia.[21]

Now there were supplies to ship to Virginia by water—400 pounds of sugar, 150 of coffee, clothing for Mother Madison, chinaware for Ambrose, but no shoes. None could be got "owing to a variance between the shoemakers and their journeymen on

ALEXANDER HAMILTON, ALIAS CATULLUS. FROM A BUST BY CERACCHI

HAMILTON'S PRESIDENTIAL YEARNING. MANUSCRIPT OF AN UNPUBLISHED ATTACK ON JEFFERSON

the point of wages." A chip hat for Miss Boynton was shipped before word came that she wanted a fur hat instead.[22]

Washington's message to Congress on October 25 betrayed the hand of Hamilton in its jubilation over the revival of confidence and the rapid subscription of bank stock. The House reply, written by Madison, was mildly congratulatory, but he remarked to Henry Lee that if his palate alone had been consulted, "the cooking would not have been precisely what it was."[23] Reapportionment of the House to conform to the census produced a sectional fight. If each state had one member for each 30,000 population—the constitutional limit—larger fractions would be left unrepresented in the Northern than in the Southern states. The bill that passed gave extra members to eight states with big fractions. Madison attacked it as unconstitutional. Jefferson and Randolph urged a veto, Hamilton advised signing. The President finally told the pair that if Madison shared their view he would reject the bill. The result was the first veto in history.

The Northern states achieved their aim by raising the base to 33,000, which gave them the fractional districts without violating the limit, but Madison saw more gain than loss in the outcome. The President, he observed to Henry Lee, had exerted his power of checking the unconstitutional career of Congress. Furthermore, the judges had pronounced a pension law (which put nonjudicial duties on them) unconstitutional and void. They might be wrong in the execution of their power, but "such an evidence of its existence gives inquietude to those who do not wish Congress to be controlled or doubted whilst its proceedings correspond with their views."[24]

Raising the House membership from 65 to 105 enlarged Virginia's delegation to nineteen and forced a drastic cut in Madison's district. "Your *friend* French Strother," a different kind of friend wrote, "has planned a district for himself and to get rid of you." Madison had noted the continued personal animosity of Cabell and Strother. The game now was to take away Culpeper and Spotsylvania. Instead, the legislature gave him the friendly counties of Orange, Spotsylvania, Louisa and the portion of Culpeper just set apart as Madison County. His two enemies were outside.[25]

During the winter of 1791-1792, Madison was a newspaper columnist, writing unsigned essays for Freneau's *National Gazette*. First came a treatise on "Population and Emigration." Man, like other animals, had a reproductive capacity far beyond what was needed to preserve the species. Unlike them, he had no enemies in nature to get rid of the surplus. What was to become of it?

"It is either, 1st. destroyed by infanticide, as among the Chinese and Lacedemonians; or, 2d. it is stifled or starved, as among other nations whose population is commensurate to its food; or, 3d. it is consumed by war and endemic diseases; or, 4th. it overflows, by emigration, to places where a surplus of food is attainable."

The general interests of humanity, Madison concluded, called for freedom of emigration, but the existence of a means of escape was likely to insure the continuous breeding of a surplus. Presumably Thomas R. Malthus had not read this when he published his famous essay on population in 1798, nor had he seen Madison's 1786 letter to Jefferson on the inescapable misery attending over-population.[26]

In the second article, an argument against consolidation of the states led to the conclusion that defenders of them should do more than guard against federal encroachment. They should work with their opponents "to erect over the whole, one paramount empire of reason, benevolence and brotherly affection." Subsequent articles display the democratic drift of Madison's thinking:

January 2, 1792—Republican government requires that the people be a sentinel over their rights, also over the authority of the federal government and the authority and rights of the intermediate governments.

January 19—Charters of government are to be used by republicans to defend liberty against power and power against licentiousness.

January 23—Political parties are inescapable. Their evils are to be avoided by political equality and by the silent operation of laws tending to equalize wealth.

January 30—The equilibrium of the British government has been maintained less by the distribution of powers than by the force of public opinion, which has sustained it through centuries of enormous change.

February 2—The hope of universal and perpetual peace is visionary, but the folly and wickedness of war demand that everything be tried to eliminate it. In a republic, war should be declared only by the authority of the people, and every generation should bear the cost of its own wars.

February 6—Division of government in the United States between general and state governments and into legislative, executive and judiciary departments may prove "the best legacy ever left by lawgivers to their country, and the best lesson ever given to the world by its benefactors."

February 20—The springs which operate government are either permanent military force, corruption, or the reasoned will of the society. In the last class "are the republican governments which it is the glory of America to have invented, and her unrivaled happiness to possess."

March 5—Citizens who provide their own food and raiment are "the most truly independent and happy . . . the best basis of public liberty, and the strongest bulwark of public safety."

March 22—The Prince of Wales, by choosing between buckles and shoestrings, decides whether 20,000 persons are to get or go without their bread. What a contrast to the independent, manly American whose work insures subsistence and inspires a dignified sense of social rights.

March 29—A man has property in land, merchandise, money, opinions and their communication, religion, the safety and liberty of his person, the free use of his faculties. The United States should equally respect the rights of property, and the property in rights.

April 2—The real friends to the Union are those who are friends to the authority of the people, to liberty, to the limited and republican system of government; those who resist tyranny, who consider a public debt injurious, and regard usurpation and monarchy as the dissolvers of union.

With this article—the first that struck closely at Hamilton's policies—Madison cut off his writing for some months. He resumed in September with "A Candid State of Parties." On one side were those who had debauched themselves into a persuasion that mankind were incapable of governing themselves. The other division was offended at every measure that did not conform to republican principles. The Anti-Republican party, weak in numbers, would cater to moneyed men and take advantage of all prejudices to divide and weaken their opponents. "The Republican party, as it may be termed," would seek to banish every difference except that which divided the mass of the people from the enemies of republican government.

Up to this time, the phrase "republican party" was the expression of a state of mind. Madison gave it a political christening. His concluding article, "Who are the best Keepers of the People's Liberties?" was a dialogue between Republican and Anti-Republican. One found the keeper in the people themselves; the other condemned them as stupid, suspicious and licentious. The rising temperature of American politics can be felt in the final exchange:

"*Anti-Republican.* . . . I denounce you to the government as an accomplice of atheism and anarchy.

"*Republican.* And I forbear to denounce you to the people, though a blasphemer of their rights and an idolator of tyranny.— Liberty disdains to persecute."[27]

Specific events were heightening this tension. One of them was Hamilton's "Report on Manufactures." With the general purpose Madison had no quarrel—for years he had been urging the national advantage of industrial development. One word aroused him—bounties—and the argument used to sustain them. The national legislature, Hamilton said, had express authority to lay taxes in order to provide for the general welfare. The objects to which money could be devoted were not narrower than the general welfare itself, and Congress could say what those objects might be.

Madison saw all bars let down. The greatest champions for latitude, he commented to Henry Lee, had hitherto limited the federal government to the specified powers. "If not only the *means,* but the *objects* are unlimited, the parchment had better be thrown into the fire at once." The issue came up in debate on bounties to cod fishermen—not real bounties, supporters said,

ᴼᴼᴼᴼᴼᴼᴼᴼᴼᴼᴼ

but merely a means of making sure that fishermen and not merchants would receive the drawback in the duty on salt. Madison indorsed the proposal but drew a distinction between such a bounty, granted under the power to regulate trade, and one granted under the supposition that Congress could do anything it thought conducive to the general welfare. The words "common defense and general welfare" were drawn from the Articles of Confederation, where they were considered as limited to the enumerated powers. "I ask the gentlemen themselves whether it ever was supposed or suspected that the old Congress could give away the moneys of the states in bounties, to encourage agriculture, or for any other purpose they pleased?"[28]

The proper answer to that was Yes, though nobody gave it. What power, except that of spending for the general welfare, was exercised by the old Congress when it paid the tuition of Indian children at Princeton and Dartmouth? Madison's argument was a deduction drawn from another deduction based on a premise, and the premise was erroneous. His changing attitude was evident in his choice of words. Never, before the combat with Hamilton, would he have referred to the old Congress giving away "the moneys of the states." Always he had emphasized the sovereign power of Congress to tax the states. In the codfish debate he secured an amendment changing the word "bounty" to "allowance" and voted for the bill.[29]

The rift with Hamilton was becoming personal. In the summer of 1791, Hamilton falsely charged Jefferson and Madison with intriguing to make Tench Coxe comptroller.[30] In the following March, he took offense at a normal legislative procedure. Following the passage of Madison's bill for better protection of the western frontiers, it was moved that the Secretary of the Treasury report a mode of raising supplies for the expedition. To maintain its own independence, Madison protested, the House should first call on the Treasury head for facts, then form its own opinions and submit them to the Secretary for him to systematize. The motion carried by four votes. Pouring out his resentment by letter, Hamilton said Madison "well knew that if he had prevailed a certain consequence was my resignation; that I would not be fool enough to make pecuniary sacrifices and endure a life of extreme drudgery, without opportunity either to do material good or to acquire reputation." He continued:

"To accomplish this point an effectual train, as was supposed, was laid. Besides those who ordinarily acted under Mr. Madison's banners, several who had generally acted with me—from various motives, vanity, self-importance, etc., etc.,—were enlisted.

"My overthrow was anticipated as certain. And Mr. Madison, laying aside his wonted caution, boldly led his troops, as he imagined, to a certain victory. He was disappointed. Though late, I became apprised of the danger. Measures of counteraction were adopted; and when the question was called, Mr. Madison was confounded to find characters voting against him whom he had counted upon as certain."[31]

Hamilton wrote this, and far more, to one of Madison's warmest friends, Edward Carrington. Appointed United States marshal for Virginia at Madison's suggestion, Carrington was drawn close to Hamilton by natural conservatism and by his work in collecting the excise. The 6,000-word letter which Hamilton wrote to him in the late spring of 1792 was a declaration of war on Madison and Jefferson. The design was to organize a federal machine against them in their own state.

# CHAPTER XXVIII

## War with Hamilton

"When I accepted the office I now hold," wrote Hamilton to Carrington, "it was under a full persuasion that from similarity of thinking, conspiring with personal good-will, I should have the firm support of Mr. Madison in the general course of my administration. Aware of the intrinsic difficulties of the situation, and of the powers of Mr. Madison, I do not believe I should have accepted under a different supposition."

A letter from Madison as late as 1789, on finances, contained "not a lisp of his new system," but in conversation he had cited the extensive alienation of the debt as a reason for his change of views. Hamilton had heard rumors of unfriendliness based on rivalry, but it was not till the last session that he became convinced "that Mr. Madison, cooperating with Mr. Jefferson, is at the head of a faction decidedly hostile to me and my administration; and actuated by views in my judgment subversive of the principles of good government and dangerous to the union, peace and happiness of the country."

The Secretary cited Madison's share in bringing Freneau to Philadelphia, and continued:

"The opinion I once entertained of the candor and simplicity and fairness of Mr. Madison's character has, I acknowledge, given way to a decided opinion that it is one of a peculiarly artificial and complicated kind. For a considerable part of the last session Mr. Madison lay in a great measure perdu. But it was evident from his votes and a variety of little movements and appearances that he was the prompter of Mr. Giles and others who were the open instruments of the opposition."

The Secretary accused him of insidious insinuations that the Treasury had purchased public securities at an artificial price for the benefit of speculators. He would concede that there was

351

reason to show hostility because "I had some short time before . . . declared openly . . . my determination to consider and treat him as a political enemy."

In public, said the Secretary, Madison had disavowed any intention to undo the funding of the public debt, but a Maryland senator reported that he said Congress had no right to fund it because it "had no right to bind posterity"—Jefferson's doctrine. On almost all questions Jefferson and Madison sought to narrow the federal authority, the latter "sounding the alarm with great affected solemnity," and holding up the bugbear of a faction unfriendly to liberty.

"This kind of conduct has appeared to me the more extraordinary on the part of Mr. Madison, as I know for a certainty it was a primary article in his creed that the real danger in our system was the subversion of the national authority by the preponderancy of the state governments."

Madison always held an exalted opinion of Mr. Jefferson and the sentiment was probably reciprocal. Whether Jefferson's peculiar ideas concerning debts affected Madison he could not say.

"Certain it is that a very material change took place and that the two gentlemen were united in the new ideas. Mr. Jefferson was indiscreetly open in his approbation of Mr. Madison's principles, upon his first coming to the seat of government. I say indiscreetly because a gentleman in the administration in one department ought not to have taken sides against another in another department. The course of this business and a variety of circumstances which took place left Mr. Madison a very discontented and chagrined man, and begot some degree of ill-humor in Mr. Jefferson."

The result, said Hamilton, was a systematic effort to get rid of him. To achieve this they would render the government itself odious, forgetting that it was easier to raise the devil than to lay him. Concluding, he declared himself affectionately attached to the republican theory. A few people on his side might be less republican than Jefferson or Madison, but these two had associates who would ride in the whirlwind and direct the storm. He did not believe this was true of Madison and was inclined to disbelieve it of Jefferson, "but I read him upon the whole thus: A man of profound ambition and violent passions."[1]

In this letter Hamilton displayed utter inability to recognize that a man once friendly could be detached from him on principle. He was incapable of judging the effect on others of his alliance with corrupt and grasping speculators. Disliking Jefferson's traits and opinions, he wished to believe that Madison had been led astray by them. But he was forced to admit that it was Jefferson who was approving the anti-Hamiltonian policies of Madison, formulated before Jefferson arrived at the seat of government.

The only definite accusation of subserviency was senatorial gossip that Madison accepted Jefferson's doctrine that a living generation could not bind posterity. That was contradicted by Madison's public record and disproved by his correspondence with Jefferson. The latter, just before he left Paris, wrote that no government charter or public debt could properly be valid for more than nineteen years—the median life of a generation. Madison replied: "Debts may be incurred with a direct view to the interest of the unborn as well as of the living." He pointed to injustices and anarchic tendencies in the nineteen-year rule and affirmed that all men born into society gave tacit assent to established government and laws.[2]

The complaint to Carrington made Hamilton the inactive victim of Madison's jealousy and Jefferson's ambition. Actually the Treasury machine had been working against them for months. Here are the beginning and end of a conversation, recorded in the previous year by Hamilton's political scout N. Hazard, with a young republican at Petersburg, Virginia:

Hazard: "Sir, you profess yourself my friend. . . . You will find me at least your political enemy if you oppose the system adopted for this country, which I think all ought to support."

Young Republican: "I shall not renounce my acquaintance with M[adiso]n and J[efferso]n as men of science."[3]

It was more than coincidence that the Treasury head burst out against his two opponents at a moment of severe financial panic stemming from the speculative orgy. On March 25, 1792, Madison wrote to Pendleton:

"The gambling system which has been pushed to such an excess is beginning to exhibit its explosions. Duer of New York, the prince of the tribe of speculators, has just become a victim to his enterprises, and involves an unknown number to an unknown amount in his fate. It is said by some that his operations have extended to several millions of dollars; that they have been carried on by usurious loans from three to six per cent per month; and that every description and gradation of persons, from the church to the stews, are among the dupes of his dexterity and the partners of his distress."

Money-mad Duer extended his operations as profits grew narrower and costs increased. In August of 1790 one of his North Carolina buyers found the Hillsboro region thronged with speculators who "bid upon each other with such a spirit of mischief" that he could do nothing. Three months later Duer's Philadelphia agent was begging for $1,200 to cover a draft he had accepted. "Do for goodness sake relieve me instantly or I shall be ruined." A plunge into bank speculation followed. European agents of his Scioto Land Company robbed him. The Treasury sinking fund in August 1791 eased his plight by redeeming $52,685 of his deferred securities, taking them off his hands a few days after Madison reported a "phenomenal rise" in their value on rumors of general redemption before 1800. On March 8, 1792, Duer wrote out a list of his obligations: notes and indorsements not paid, $456,183.37, and a thousand of them overdue. A final appeal to Hamilton brought advice and sympathy: "Do not plunge deeper. Have the courage to make a full stop. . . . I have experienced all the bitterness of soul on your account which a warm attachment can inspire." Duer went to debtors' prison and died there seven years later.[4]

Two weeks after the collapse Madison wrote that New York continued to be a scene of bankruptcies. "Every day exhibits new victims and opens new scenes of usury, knavery and folly." Hamilton saw folly in the downward slide of prices. "Does Duer's failure affect the solidity of the government?" he exclaimed to

William Seton of the Bank of New York, and sent him $50,000 for purchases of government securities at par. Seton sent back word that Alexander Macomb had failed—Duer's partner in bank speculation. "This misfortune," Hamilton replied, "has, I fear, a long tail to it," and forwarded an additional $100,000 to support the funds and "relieve the distressed." Wrote Seton:

"At noon I went into the market but the applications were so numerous and . . . every one . . . so eager that I could only take down names upon a declaration that I would average the whole. . . . The great and universal distress . . . is such that it would be impossible to make purchases equal to the relief."

These purchases at par for the benefit of speculators produced the protest in Congress by Madison which led Hamilton to accuse him of making false insinuations of that very thing. There were others who needed relief too. Duer's Ohio land contracts were taken over by the Reverend Manasseh Cutler (author of the religion and morality clause of the Ordinance of 1787) and his associates, subject to a promise never to call on the settlers for their share of certain expenditures. "Their wanting now to take away the lands of these poor people," wrote an observer, "is a scandalous piece of injustice and should be prevented if possible."[5]

Under such conditions the country approached the 1792 elections. Madison thought the truth would soon force itself upon people misled by fallacious prosperity and newspaper declamations. The issues were so explosive that the country's safety might depend on what Washington did about a second term.

On May 5—three days before Congress adjourned—Madison called on the President at his request. Washington observed (Madison wrote in a memorandum) "that having some time ago communicated to me his intention of retiring from public life on the expiration of his four years, he wished to advise with me on the *mode* and *time* most proper for making known that intention." He had spoken to no others of his purpose except Hamilton and Knox, who opposed it strongly; Jefferson, also opposed, and lately Randolph.

In the past, Madison told the President, he had said nothing against what seemed to be a fixed determination. Under present conditions retirement might have effects that ought not to be hazarded. Washington replied that he found himself deficient in many essential qualifications, declining in health, tired and vexed. He would rather work for his bread with a spade. Party spirit was dividing the secretaries of State and Treasury, public discontents were increasing, and he was being attacked indirectly. Madison told him that his judgment, aided by official opinion, was as good as anybody else's, and in many cases better. The new spirit of party was an argument for his remaining. If he retired, who would succeed him? Jefferson disliked public life and was opposed by the North. Adams had obnoxious monarchic principles and Jay was believed to share them.

Washington changed the subject but at parting repeated his request. A few days later, still protesting, Madison advised a direct address to the public. He thought the matter was dropped, for the President's only response was to ask him to submit ideas for his next message to Congress. However, at Georgetown on May 25, Madison met Washington returning from Mt. Vernon and was given a letter asking him to draft a statement to the people. He did so, producing a preliminary version of the Farewell Address delivered four years later.

Having gratified Washington's wishes, Madison remarked, he would gratify his own by pleading for "one more sacrifice, severe as it may be, to the desires and interests of your country." This appeal reached the President in the wake of a similar one, long and strong, from Jefferson, who told Washington that his being at the helm was the only safeguard against monarchical policies driving the people into violence and secession. That was written three days before Hamilton told Carrington that efforts were being made to destroy him because "Jefferson aims with ardent desire at the presidential chair." Washington retained the wish to retire in 1792, but gave up the intention.[6]

Going home, Madison rode into a country suffering from six weeks without rain. Flax and oats were destroyed, corn dying, no tobacco planted, wheat injured in weak lands but benefited in strong. But when he wrote to Jefferson on June 12, there had been constant rain for days. The only danger now was of too much wet for the wheat, "which I am happy to find has effectually supplanted tobacco in the conversation and anxieties of our crop-mongers, and is rapidly doing so in their fields."

On his arrival Madison received a first-hand report on Kentucky land purchases made by his brother for both of them. First writing his will, Ambrose rode over the mountains in the winter and bought five tracts totaling 7,000 acres. There were 2,000 on Panther Creek, 1,000 on Elk Creek, 1,000 opposite Rough Creek—all tributaries of the Green River—and an original entry on 3,000 poor and hilly acres on Sandy River. Ambrose gave his lawyer-cousin Hubbard Taylor (who moved to Kentucky in 1790) power of attorney over the whole business.[7]

The Panther Creek lands were almost opposite 10,000 acres which the elder Madison owned. And that gave them something to talk about, for the title to this land was being jeopardized by some of the fiercest litigation in American history, though much of the story has never been told. In the spring of 1780 Land Scout Hancock Lee went into the wilderness and picked out 8,400 and 8,300 acres for George Mason, 10,000 for William Moore and 10,000 for James Madison, Sr., all in a solid block. The claims were duly entered, the 8,400-acre tract by description, the others by reference to it. In October it was discovered that the key tract was described as four miles above the junction of the forks of Panther Creek instead of above the junction with Green River. This was corrected in a special entry. The whole 36,700 acres were surveyed in 1783 on the basis of the corrected entry, the surveys recorded and the land paid for—approximately $47,000 to the State of Virginia.

A few months after this, one George Wilson entered 30,000 acres including this entire area except the corrected entry of 8,400 acres, which he used to describe the remainder. He then entered caveats against Mason, Moore and Madison, asking the Kentucky Supreme Court (a part of the Virginia judiciary) to validate his claim. At the trial of the Mason caveat it was brought out that Wilson was in partnership with Assistant County Surveyor Handley. An employee of the office testified that the Wilson entry was made by means of a study of the Mason survey "in a late hour of the night and that he held the candle to give them light."

Mason's death in 1792 interrupted the litigation, but it was renewed against his infant grandson in federal district court in 1797. In 1800 District Judge Harry Innes ruled Wilson's claim fraudulent, since he had full notice, by reason of his partnership with the assistant surveyor, that he was infringing a recorded claim older than his own.

Wilson's appeal to the United States Supreme Court was argued by Joseph H. Daveiss, a protégé of George Nicholas both in law and land piracy, and later famous as the prosecutor of Aaron Burr for treason. To Chief Justice Marshall the case was simple. Mason's revised entry was a removal, not an explanation, therefore did not carry the other entries with it. The land belonged to Wilson under the rule laid down by Lord Kaims that in order to protect himself against loss a man is free to take advantage of another man's error. He did not quote the next sentence by Kaims, that if this is done to gain an advantage over the other man it is a fraud.

Daveiss celebrated his victory by marrying Chief Justice Marshall's sister, and then proceeded to collect. A month before the case was to come up in Supreme Court, he had written to Madison (whose father had died within the year) informing him that he was the real claimant to the entire 30,000 acres under the Wilson entry and suggesting an agreement. Let each of them promise to be bound by the coming decision and drop the Madison-Wilson suits pending in the state courts. Madison ignored this trap. Later Daveiss presented a transcript of Marshall's opinion and persuaded the Register of Lands to give him a patent on Madison's 10,000 acres without a trial of the case. The story of Mason, Madison, Wilson, Daveiss and Marshall is not told in any life of Marshall.[8]

In 1792 another conflict was in Madison's mind. From Jefferson he received reports of the negotiations with Minister Hammond on enforcement of the peace treaty of 1783. For nine years everything had been going in a circle. Great Britain would not give up Detroit until British merchants were allowed to collect their prewar debts. Southern states would not permit collection until their planters were compensated for slaves carried off in violation of the treaty. Madison no longer believed the 1787 statement of Foreign Minister Jay that American violations were of earlier date than the British. He read and corrected Jefferson's letter to Hammond, which then was submitted to Hamilton. Jefferson sent him the latter's criticisms.

"Your answer to Hammond," he responded, "has on the whole got triumphantly through the [cabinet] ordeal." What really surprised Madison was the position Hamilton took on state sovereignty. Jefferson had argued that the state governments and people, as subjects of the nation, were not bound by the treaty until they were notified by Congress of its ratification. Hamilton objected. As members of the federal league were not the states themselves the contending parties, therefore bound from the moment the treaty was ratified? No, answered Jefferson: "As to matters of treaty, the state governments were mere subjects." He was consistent, for he had said in 1784 that in all international matters the United States were a consolidated nation. Hamilton was reversing his views in order to force the United States into a conciliatory attitude toward Great Britain, with repercussions against the French Revolution. The doctrine that would make the states the contracting parties, Madison commented, was as irreconcilable with Hamilton's general views as with the Confederation.[9]

Late in June word came that Chief Justice Jay had beaten Clinton for governor of New York on the face of the returns, but Clinton went ahead when the Otsego County vote was thrown out on the ground that an ex-sheriff delivered the returns. Jefferson wished he would decline the place and thus avert a party schism, but Madison was not so ready to write the governor off. If a majority of *legal* honest votes was cast against him, he ought not to force himself on the people, but on a contrary supposition there was no such obligation. It was curious to see Schuyler who was "supposed to have made millions by jobbing in paper under his own measures," accusing and abusing Clinton for doing the same in land.

Hamilton, Jefferson reported, eagerly desired to have John Marshall in Congress. "I think nothing better could be done than to make him a judge." Smith of South Carolina might be driven out of the congressional field "by the story of the modern Colchis." (That is, by his shipload of money sent for the Golden Fleece of speculation.) John Adams had shipped his furniture home, leading to rumors of his retirement, but it probably meant only that Abigail would not be with him in the ensuing term.[10]

Jefferson came through on July 22 for a three months' stay at Monticello. With Washington, Madison and Monroe also in Virginia, the way was open for something Hamilton had in mind—a newspaper war on his leading opponents. He could neither be stopped by the President nor countered quickly by the others. His first plan, revealed by four unpublished manuscripts, was to launch an attack on Madison and Jefferson without naming them. Who but Madison was in his mind when (echoing the phrases of his letter to Carrington) he denounced those whom "personal rivalship and competitions" threw against the funding measures, who chose opposition "as the supposed road to popularity and preferment," who tortured the Constitution into objections to measures they deemed inexpedient? Of whom but Jefferson was he thinking when he railed against "a kind of POPES in government . . . men of sublimated imaginations and weak judgments; pretenders to profound knowledge yet ignorant of the most useful of all sciences—the science of human nature"? These men, wrote Hamilton, were throwing suspicions of prostitution and corruption in office, of improper connection with brokers and speculators, upon men (*i.e.* upon one man) "who it is notorious have sacrificed and are sacrificing the interests of their families to their public zeal."[11]

Choosing another plan, he put these articles away. On July 25, in Fenno's *Gazette* a writer signing himself "T.L." asked whether Philip Freneau's public salary was paid for translations or for articles vilifying the government that fed him. Freneau made a brief reply, upon which "T.L." changed to "An American" and launched a full-scale assault on Jefferson. How could he remain in the cabinet while sponsoring the vilification of measures adopted by Congress and sanctioned by the Chief Magistrate of the Union? He accused Jefferson of opposing the Constitution before its adoption and of desiring to head a party whose aim was to depress national authority. It might be true, as Freneau asserted on oath, that his coming to Philadelphia was not urged, advised or influenced by the Secretary of State, but was not this done "by a *particular friend* of that officer"? "An American" baldly proclaimed that his real aim was to expose a public officer "who has been the prompter, open or secret, of unwarrantable aspersions on men who"—well, to state it fully, on T. L., An American, Amicus, Metellus and A Plain Honest Man. That is to say, on Hamilton, whose identity, under all these aliases, was recognized by the public long before the original drafts of the vituperative articles were found among his papers.[12]

It was Hamilton's intention to attack Madison by name also in one of his later articles. He wrote to Elias Boudinot who had told him of the Freneau negotiations, and asked for "the particulars of all the steps taken by Mr. Madison—the when and where"—supported by affidavit if possible. Boudinot's informant vaguely remembered that he heard it from Freneau himself, who accused Jefferson of wanting to infringe on his independence. That was not what the inquirer wanted to hear.[13]

Hamilton's methods may be judged by his handling of Freneau's initial reply. In his second "T.L." article the Secretary of the Treasury quoted and denounced Freneau's explanation of his dual employment. "He intimates that he 'receives a small stipend for services rendered as French Translator to the Department of State, and, *as editor of a free newspaper.'*" What Freneau wrote was that he received a small stipend as translator "and, as editor of a free newspaper, admits into his publication impartial strictures on the proceedings of government." Jefferson's public record was misrepresented with the same obvious purpose—to cause a split with the President that would drive Jefferson from the cabinet.[14]

Hamilton's deepest motive was his own hidden ambition to be President. He laid it bare in a partially crossed-out portion of one article which he did not send to the press:

"Mr. Jefferson fears in Mr. Hamilton a formidable rival in the competition for the presidential chair at a future period and there-

fore the sooner he can ruin him in the public estimation the better
for his purpose. . . . After he [Jefferson] entered on the duties of
his station, the President was afflicted with a malady which while
it created dismay and alarm in the heart of every patriot only
excited the ambitious ardor of the secretary to remove out of his
way every dangerous opponent. That melancholy circumstance
suggested to him the probability of an approaching vacancy in
the presidential chair and that he would attract the public attention as the successor to it were the more popular Secretary of the
Treasury out of the way."[15]

As soon as he saw Hamilton's "extraordinary maneuver of
calumny," Madison rode to Albemarle County to consult Jefferson and Monroe. His first thought was to publish a signed statement about the charges concerning himself, but since he was not
named that seemed inappropriate. The conclusion was that Madison and Monroe should unite in a defense of Jefferson, to be published serially in the *American Daily Advertiser* of Philadelphia.

The opening article was to consist of extracts from Jefferson's
Paris letters to Madison, proving that he supported the Constitution from the start. The second article, also by Monroe, would
drive home what these letters made self-evident. After that, Madison was to deal with the Freneau affair. There followed a great
scurrying back and forth, Madison's servants taking materials to
Monroe, the latter stopping at Montpelier, Jefferson carrying the
second article north. Madison fell into a panic when it appeared
that it might have been dropped along the road. "The possibility
of its falling into base hands at the present crisis cannot be too
carefully guarded against," he warned. Jefferson delivered the article to the printer. He then wrote to Washington that on arrival he
"found that many of my letters had been already put into the papers,
by the gentleman possessed of the originals, as I presume, for not a
word of it had ever been communicated to me, and the copies I had
retained were under a lock of which I had the key."[16]

While they were at work, a defense of Jefferson signed "Aris-
tides" appeared in Fenno's *Gazette* of September 8, 1792. Commonly ascribed to Madison, it was not in his style and used

evidence inferior to what he possessed. This article caused Hamilton to convert himself into "Catullus" and lay himself wide open to the devastating effect of the Jefferson-to-Madison quotations. When they appeared, all he could do was resort to insinuations:

"How far they are genuine letters or mere fabrications; how far they may have been altered or mutilated, is liable, from the manner of their appearance, to question and doubt."

This was said just after Hamilton himself had mutilated one of Jefferson's official letters to make it appear that he wished to swindle Dutch investors in a transfer of the American public debt from France to Holland.[17] By his vulnerable attacks on Jefferson's public policies Hamilton weakened his valid criticism of Freneau's connection with the State Department. Replying on that subject, Madison pointed out that the clerk's paltry salary forced him to do other work. Was it dishonorable to make the rest of his living out of a newspaper? Or was that complained of only because he was a Whig and a Republican? The two jobs were unrelated, each proper, and each well done. When he came to the founding of the newspaper, Madison handed the pen to Monroe for an implied disclaimer which only denied bad motives:

"A gentleman for whose public and private virtues . . . the good people of these states have long entertained the most exalted esteem, has been represented as the negotiator; and for the purpose of subverting the government which he contributed so essentially to establish. Can the public mind, when these slanderous imputations are passed in review, withhold from their author the contempt and abhorrence which are deservedly his due?"[18]

When Hamilton changed his aliases he didn't change his style. His adversaries pursued and identified him through his chameleon course, while the people laughed, cheered or raged. Demanding a sight of the Jefferson letters, and retreating when offered them on terms that would pierce his anonymity, he finally claimed victory and fled the field.

If the *hoi polloi* enjoyed this, Washington did not. Discovering what everybody else knew, that the differences between Jefferson and Hamilton were personal as well as ideological, he asked for mutual forbearance. Hamilton promised, and kept right on with his anonymous assaults. Jefferson called attention to the charges which a principal minister was indecently making behind a screen of anonymity. He intended to retire as soon as he could do so without seeming to be driven out by slanders, and would reserve his own newspaper writing until he had become a private citizen. Not one syllable of dissension in the press had come from him.[19]

Monroe left Montpelier on October 7, with arrangements for Madison to join him at Fredericksburg for the trip to Philadelphia. On the eleventh a messenger came to Orange bearing a letter addressed jointly to Madison and Monroe, from Melancton Smith and M. Willett of New York, and one from John Nicholson of Philadelphia to Madison. Both carried the same proposal, to substitute Aaron Burr for Governor Clinton as the Republican candidate for Vice President. Monroe had read the joint letter and sent word that he would sign anything Madison might write, being sure from past talks that they were opposed to the move. He suggested that Burr be given the most soothing assurances of esteem and confidence, resting the advice solely on his youth and late arrival on the national stage. Madison postponed the formal reply until he joined his friend on the seventeenth, but the emissary was told what it would be. Their joint answer, in Monroe's writing, said nothing about Burr and contained language previously used by Madison about Clinton. By adhering to him, they would have a candidate more known and "warmly supported by sundry influential characters."[20]

The question was settled before this written advice was received. Smith, representing all New York Republicans, met on October 16 with "the principal movers of the same interest" in Philadelphia— that is, with Jefferson, Beckley, Butler of South Carolina, Pennsylvanians and others. The result, wrote Beckley to Madison, was a unanimous decision to exert every endeavor for Clinton. Madison should write to Virginia leaders, urging concerted activity. Beckley relayed Revenue Collector Heth's statement that "Mr. Hamilton unequivocally declares that you are his *personal* and *political* enemy."[21]

Madison reached Philadelphia on November 1. His party, he found, had carried Pennsylvania against odds created by western defiance of the President's warning against resistance to the excise. He brought word that Virginia probably would be solid against Adams for Vice President. Over the country, he noted, Adams was being pictured in all his monarchical trappings, while Clinton was presented in the antifederal colors he wore in 1788. Adams probably would win (and so he did, 77 to 50), but since the opposition was leveled entirely against his political principles and under great disadvantages (from Clinton's clouded re-election as governor) the vote should satisfy him that the people were not ready for his aristocratic system. He added to Pendleton:

"I throw in for your amusement an anonymous pamphlet which makes pretty free with the characters of several of your friends. In what respects myself everything happens to be pretty notoriously false which I would wish not to be true."

The pamphlet contained a general assault on Madison's policies in Congress from 1789 onward. In the outline of an unpublished reply left among his papers, he called it "a continuation of the attack on Republican principles commenced by the American etc." He would have been even surer that Hamilton wrote it had he known of similarities to marked-out passages in the latter's other anonymous writings. The attack on himself, Madison wrote, rested on two absurd and impossible suppositions—that Jefferson, while in Paris, foresaw a rival in Hamilton, and that Madison sacrificed his principles "to the ambitions and malicious views of his friend." The lengthy defense which followed was more or less a résumé of his congressional career. The incident points to Hamilton as author of the long-lived fiction that Madison broke with him and stultified himself to advance the political fortunes of Jefferson.[22]

Hamilton himself faced more serious false charges. It was just after Madison's return that Messrs. Reynolds and Clingman, arrested for fraudulent misuse of Treasury records, secretly accused the Secretary of using the former as his agent in speculation. This caused Hamilton to disclose to Speaker Muhlenberg, Senator

Monroe and Representative Venable that the money for which
Reynolds held receipts was blackmail occasioned by adulterous
relations with the latter's wife. Jefferson's December 17 "Ana" contains a note about the meeting, all scratched out except the
names of those present and the comment: "Known to J M[adi-
son], E R[andolph], Beckley and Webb." The matter was
dropped, but rose unpleasantly five years later.[23]

Madison was impatiently awaiting a new ally, his boyhood
school friend John Taylor of Caroline, elected to succeed R. H.
Lee, who escaped defeat by resigning. The new senator made
a better impression on others than his job did on him. He had
been at work only two months when Madison wrote to Taylor's
uncle and foster father, Judge Pendleton:

"I seized the opportunity . . . to tell you how much we have
been charmed with the successor to Col. R. H. L. and to entreat
your cooperation with a number of his other friends in overcoming his repugnance to his present station. His talents during
the fraction of time he has been on the federal theater have been
of such infinite service to the republican cause and such a terror
to its adversaries, that his sudden retirement, on which he is
strongly bent, ought to be regarded as a public calamity and
counterworked by all the means his friends can use."[24]

Washington's message to Congress, delivered on November 6,
1792, was written chiefly by Hamilton. It told of the continuing
hostilities of Indians after the humiliating defeat of General St.
Clair. Public revenues were in a prosperous state except for the
impediments to collection of the excise on distilled spirits. Madison was made chairman, as usual, of the House committee to
prepare a reply, but dictating its contents were Federalists Benson
and William Vans Murray. Madison didn't like what they wrote
about the excise. To say first that a free government should listen
to and redress grievances, and then adversely prejudge the petitions, did not seem very consistent. Added to that was an insinuation that opponents were selfishly trying to avoid their share of the
tax burden, "an insinuation not generally true and more likely to
inflame than heal the wound." He was beginning to discover that
whisky was the western farmer's substitute for money.[25]

Congress was thoroughly aroused over the Indian war and started to take up a committee report, made six months earlier, on St. Clair's defeat. To bolster Hamilton and Knox, administration leaders sought to invite them to appear in Congress. Madison objected on constitutional grounds. Let the officers report in writing. The House agreed, and thereby cut off the possible rise of cabinet government in the United States. Madison obtained a reference to a new committee, whose moderate report was written by Giles. It cut down some of the findings which most distressed Hamilton and Knox. The powder furnished the troops was not really worthless: it was ruined by being stored in worthless tents. The pack saddles were not defective: they were so big that few could be used. Guns were not out of order when received: inexperienced soldiers ruined them. The contractors failed miserably in furnishing supplies, but part of the failure occurred before the secret transfer of the contract to William Duer. The army had bad luck too. Sixty Kentucky militiamen deserted just before the battle began and 300 soldiers had to be detached to keep them from robbing a supply train. The Indians, not being gentlemen, attacked by surprise just as the army finished parading. The non-deserting militia ran away through the regulars, unsettling their aim and morale. Hamilton's friends in Congress prevented debate or action on the report.[26]

The fight was now on over Treasury domination of Congress. Madison opposed a motion asking Hamilton to report a plan for reducing the public debt. Revenue measures must originate in the House, yet a tax plan from the Treasury, being supported by one-sided argument, would actually have more force than one from the Senate. He took the twenty-five-to-thirty-two defeat as a matter of course, but was disgusted when Hamilton came back with a high-sounding sinking fund system for debt retirement, supported by dividends on Treasury-owned bank stock and a graduated tax on carriage horses—$1.00 per horse in a one-horse family, $2.50 per horse on four and up. Wasn't that a direct tax, therefore unconstitutional in the form proposed? How much more would be paid by the equestrian South than the pedestrian East? Wasn't it mockery to start a sinking fund with a tax that would raise only forty-odd thousand a year?[27]

Debating a motion to borrow $2,000,000 to repay a loan from the national bank, Madison remarked that only $200,000 a year would be due. Why borrow ten times that sum? Adequate funds were lying dormant in the Treasury. Were they appropriated by the executive or were they not? If they were, if this dormant money was borrowed in Europe to pay a debt of justice and gratitude, he would like to see it sent on the wings of wind. He would listen to any reason for diversion except the one he heard *out of Congress*—that the debt to France, if paid now, might have to be paid over again, following restoration of the king.

Madison was trying to force Congress to express an opinion on Hamilton's unwillingness to make debt payments to revolutionary France. Some people, he remarked, might vainly presume that this new government had not reached maturity, but the rational part of mankind could see that it was solidly established. By a two-to-one vote, the House refused to strike out the bank-repayment loan, but the Speaker had to create a tie to prevent it from being cut to $200,000.[28]

The President was asked to furnish an account of all foreign loans and balances—a move which disclosed several transfers to America of money borrowed to pay France. Calling this perplexing, Giles offered a set of resolutions asking for copies of the authorities under which the loans were negotiated, a detailed account of payments on debts to France, Spain and Holland, and the state of the various balances. Hamilton burned midnight candles.[29]

The Treasury forces recognized Madison as author and manager of all the moves against them. Wrote Ames in January 1793:

"Virginia moves in a solid column, and the discipline of the party is as severe as the Prussian. Deserters are not spared. Madison is become a desperate party leader, and I am not sure of his stopping at any ordinary point of extremity. We are fighting for the assumption of the balances, which shall be declared due the creditor states. He opposes, *vi et armis*."[30]

This additional assumption carried when the Speaker broke a tie. Hamilton's reports, coming in a stream through February, were scanned eagerly. Madison gave Pendleton his opinion of them:

"You will have discovered from the newspapers that a pretty interesting scrutiny has been started into the administration of the Treasury Department. The documents furnished show that there has been at least a very blameable irregularity and secrecy in some particulars of it, and many appearances which at least require explanation. With some, suspicions are carried very far; others resolve the whole that is wrong into favoritism to the bank, etc., whilst the partisans of the Fisc. either see nothing amiss or are willing to ascribe everything that is so to venial, if not laudable motives."[31]

Hamilton informed the House that he had been instructed by the President to borrow up to $14,000,000 under two laws. The first law authorized the borrowing of $12,000,000 exclusively for payment of public loans in Europe; the second, $2,000,000 for buying up the domestic debt. Hamilton borrowed under the two laws *combined,* and divided the loan *equally* between their purposes. Altogether, he devoted $5,150,000 of foreign loans to the foreign debt and brought home $2,305,000. His action, he asserted, was useful and not unlawful.

With the adjournment of Congress only a few days off, something had to be done to prevent Hamilton's printed reports from being the last word to the public. So Giles offered resolutions of censure, accusing him of violating the law. To keep these resolutions from being the last word, Hamilton's friends joined in calling them up for two days of debate with evening sessions. What the Secretary did under both laws together, they said, was lawful under one of them. He must have acted with the President's approval because there was no sign of dissatisfaction. Even if all the charges were true the government had not lost a penny.

Madison undertook to prove that both the law and the President's instructions had been violated. He showed by Hamilton's written orders that on the very day the Secretary received them back in 1790, he acted contrary to them. Could it be true, as Hamilton claimed, that he transferred these European funds to the United States for the convenience of Congress? In that case why was Congress not told that the money was so drawn? Instead, to repay the bank's loan before it was due, he tried to induce Congress to break the public faith by repealing the existing appropriation for discharge of a debt of justice and gratitude to the French nation—then engaged in desperate combat with Prussia and Austria. Madison took satisfaction in one fact: no more was heard of that $2,000,000 loan. "The bill had dropped from the hand of its patron with the first light that broke in upon the House."

The Giles resolutions were overwhelmingly defeated, only fifteen votes being cast for them on the most favorable roll call. Jefferson called this the natural action of a majority consisting of bank directors, stockholders, stockjobbers, blind devotees, mental loafers and ignoramuses. The first four groups certainly formed the core of the majority, but it was swollen by two persuasive arguments. Condemnation of Hamilton would hit his venerated chief. His irregularities had cost the Treasury nothing. The net effect was to increase the personal bitterness of the conflict and to give notice of an intense new issue—the French Revolution—in American politics.[32]

# CHAPTER XXIX

## The French Revolution

To VIRTUALLY all Americans the French Revolution appeared at the outset to be a peaceable extension of their own. The storming of the Bastille added the kind of violence they could sympathize with. When Lafayette's National Guard and a mob carried the royal family within reach of the National Assembly, when free elections were proclaimed and Jacobin clubs were formed to preach democracy, most Americans rejoiced. A minority trembled. To Madison, in the spring of 1790, the old continent looked like this:

"France seems likely to carry through the great work in which she has been laboring. The Austrian Netherlands have caught the flame and with arms in their hands have renounced the government of the Emperor forever. Even the lethargy of Spain begins to awake at the voice of liberty which is summoning her neighbors to its standard. All Europe must by degrees be aroused to the recollection and assertion of the rights of human nature."

The pleasure this gave to Americans, Madison continued, must be "enhanced by the reflection that the light which is chasing darkness and despotism from the Old World is but an emanation from that which has procured and succeeded the establishment of liberty in the new." But to his neighbor Robert Beverley it was a frightful moment indeed. "In this revolutionary, anarchical, democratical, tyrannical, patriotic age," men of prudence and property should be sent to the United States Senate to offset the follies and ignorance of those who disgraced the lower House. Every man who wished well to humanity must join in curbing "this spirit of *reform* . . . taken from the infamous sans-culottes of the terrible republic."[1] Madison chafed at the slowness of French progress toward liberty, but events in the fall of 1791 elated him.

371

"The French Revolution seems to have succeeded beyond the most sanguine hopes. The king, by freely accepting the constitution, has baffled the external machinations against it, and the peaceable election of a legislative assembly of the same complexion with their predecessors, and the regular commencement of their functions, have equally suppressed the danger of internal confusions."[2]

This new government was conservative, but events flowed by in a radical stream. The royal family fled toward Austria and was brought back. The king's troops committed wholesale murder in the Champs de Mars. Then came the threats of Prussian and Austrian monarchs, France's declaration of war in April 1792, the swift upsurge of mob authority when foreign armies and titled *émigrés* threatened the Revolution. By midsummer the Commune ruled Paris, the Tuileries were stormed, the king arrested. Thousands of royalists were massacred in the streets. Danton rose to power, the monarchy was abolished and a republic proclaimed.

By the time the last news crossed the ocean American opinion on the French Revolution was split almost on the division line between Republicans and Federalists. Madison looked beyond the ill-advised declarations of war to the aggressive purposes of the Germanic monarchs: the combination against the revolution was extremely formidable, and there was "still greater danger within from the follies and barbarities which prevail in Paris." On the other hand, the nation was united against royalty and ready to sustain the government in national defense.

News of the guillotining of the French king reached him just before he left for Orange in March 1793. A Philadelphia dinner group, Jefferson wrote shortly afterward, discussed the beheading with partialities ranging from "the warmest Jacobinism . . . to the most heartfelt aristocracy." The monocrats were cautious, but the society ladies were "open-mouthed against the murderers of a sovereign, and they generally speak those sentiments which the more cautious husband smothers." In his neighborhood, Madison replied, sympathy with the fate of Louis was general, but this was derived from spurious newspaper accounts of the king's innocence and the bloodthirstiness of his enemies. All agreed, when the facts were put before them, that if the king was a traitor he should be punished the same as any other man.[3]

On the heels of this came a letter from the French Minister of the Interior notifying Madison that he had been made a citizen of the new French Republic. The National Assembly voted this honor on August 24, 1792, just two weeks after the storming of the Tuileries. The subject was brought up by a private citizen, Marie Joseph de Chénier, who, the debates record, "singled out Paine, Madison, Dr. Priestley, Wilberforce and several others" who by their luminous writings and constant courage had proclaimed the rights of man and prepared for the reign of universal liberty. Citizen Bazire warned that this aristocracy of demi-talents was likely to include some enemies of liberty, but Citizen Chabot overwhelmed him with the cry: "The Declaration of Rights is the Constitution of the world." Citizenship was conferred on eighteen men, one of whom, the Dutch-Prussian Anacharsis Cloots, became a member of the National Assembly and was guillotined for following the atheistic branch of communism.

Three Americans were in the list—Washington, Madison and Hamilton. Madison was "Adisson" in the debate, which was as recognizable as "Jean Hamilton" or "Georges Masingthon." Apparently Hamilton got in by being in bad company. Madison, thanks to the *Encyclopédie Méthodique,* was looked on as the outstanding American disciple of liberty. A 1792 edition of *Le Federaliste* named "MM. Hamilton, Madisson et Gay" as its authors. Men whose writings and courage had paved the way to emancipation should not be regarded as foreigners by a nation which had been made free by their enlightenment. So said the decree, and continued:

"If it cannot be hoped that men will some day form but a single family, single society, before the law, as they do in nature, the friends of liberty and universal brotherhood ought not to be cherished less by a nation which has proclaimed its renunciation of all conquests and its desire to fraternize with all peoples."[4]

The preliminary phase of the Reign of Terror was known to Madison when this award reached him. He could reject it (as the German poet Klopstock did), testify to his continued faith by accepting it, or say nothing. He wrote a cordial acceptance, with emphasis on international fellowship. It was with peculiar satisfaction, Madison added, that he accepted this honorable adoption, because the United States had done so much to banish prejudice and reclaim the lost rights of mankind, and was so intimately bound to France by the affinities of their mutual liberty. He ended with anxious wishes for the glory of the French nation and the final triumph of liberty by a victory over the minds of all its adversaries.[5]

News that Great Britain had entered the war caused Madison to hold back this letter until affairs should clear up. On April 22, President Washington issued his neutrality proclamation, announcing, for the government "a conduct friendly and impartial towards the belligerent powers" and calling on the people to avoid all acts and proceedings tending to contravene that disposition. Fully aware that acceptance of French citizenship would violate the proclamation, Madison asked Jefferson to forward his letter or return it for revision. It should not be sent if developments in France (following General Dumouriez' desertion to the Austrians) made it "totally malapropos *there.*" If it was proper there, and consequently proper in itself, "I shall not trouble myself about any comments which the publication attending all such things may produce here."

This was so shocking to Editor Gaillard Hunt that he expurgated the paragraph from Madison's *Writings.* Jefferson read the letter and "found every syllable of it strictly proper." However, Monsieur Roland was out of office, so he was sending it merely to the Minister of the Interior. Roland, a year later, committed suicide after his wife was beheaded. It was she who exclaimed, when led to the guillotine: "O Liberty! What crimes are committed in thy name!"[6]

Washington's proclamation shocked Madison. The United States was bound by treaty to defend France's American possessions against attack. Hamilton's unsuccessful attempt in cabinet to "shuffle off" the treaty seemed to him "equally contemptible for the meanness and folly of it." If a change of government absolved a country from public engagements, was that not equally true of domestic affairs?

"In fact, the doctrine would perpetuate every existing despotism, by involving in a reform of the government a destruction of the social pact, an annihilation of property, and a complete establishment of the state of nature."

The longer he thought about it, the less he liked the "Anglified complexion" of executive policies. Peace was no doubt to be preserved at any price that honor and good faith would permit, but the least departure from these was likely to bring war or other evils. To Jefferson he wrote on June 19:

"The proclamation was in truth a most unfortunate error. It wounds the national honor, by seeming to disregard the stipulated duties to France. It wounds the popular feelings by a seeming indifference to the cause of liberty. And it seems to violate the forms and spirit of the Constitution by making the Executive Magistrate the organ of the disposition, the duty and the interest of the nation in relation to war and peace—subjects appropriated to other departments of the government. . . . If France triumphs, the ill-fated proclamation will be a millstone which would sink any other character and will force a struggle even on his."[7]

Madison hoped that France would be given one seasonable plum to match the bitter pills—such a reception of the incoming French minister, Genêt, as would testify the real affections of the people. On the day he expressed that hope, British Minister Hammond protested the first actions of Genêt in South Carolina, following his April landing. French privateers, fitted out under his orders, were capturing British ships, which then were condemned by French consuls, commissioned by Genêt to conduct prize courts on American soil. Genêt himself was on his way north, applauded by multitudes or greeted with cold reserve. "I hear," Madison wrote, "that the fiscal party in Alexandria was an overmatch for those who wished to testify the American sentiment. Georgetown it is said repaired the omission." The minister would be misled if he took either the fashionable cant of the cities or the cold caution of the government for the sense of the public.

Anxious to know the state of mind in Virginia, Washington sent Randolph to inquire into it. The Attorney General, as usual, messed things up. Drawing his first information from "tainted sources," Madison reported, he could not be set right, though his brothers-in-law W. C. and John Nicholas did their best. As to the state in general:

"The great danger of misconstruing the sentiment of Virginia with regard to liberty and France is from the heretical tone of conversation in the towns on the post road. The voice of the country is universally and warmly right."[8]

War between France and Great Britain was reviving the old loyalties and hatreds of the American Revolution. England was once more the enemy, France the ally. But men who had acquired wealth through speculation or expanding business felt a fear of the French Revolution which united them with the old Tories.

The effect of this became quickly evident in the conduct of Genêt, whose initial statements were so modest and peaceful that Madison wished to distribute them by pamphlet. In the adulation of people and press, the minister saw evidence of devotion to France running counter to official policies—a current strong enough, if rightly led, to overrule them. Why not lead it? Trouble started when Jefferson tried to explain that although France could send warships and prizes into and out of American ports, she had no right to use those ports as outfitting points or bases of operation. The Secretary of State restrained himself until July, then exploded to Madison:

"Never, in my opinion, was so calamitous an appointment made as that of the present minister of France here. Hotheaded, all imagination, no judgment, passionate, disrespectful and even indecent towards the President in his written as well as verbal communications, talking of appeal from him to Congress, from them to the people, urging the most unreasonable and groundless propositions, and in the most dictatorial style. . . . He renders my position immensely difficult. . . . I am on a footing to advise him freely, and he respects it, but he breaks out again on the first occasion."

Astonished and dismayed, Madison answered:

"Your account of G[enêt] is dreadful. He must be brought right if possible. His folly will otherwise do mischief which no wisdom can repair. Is there no one through whom he can be *effectually* counselled?"

To darken the picture still more, Jefferson sent copies of Hamilton's letters of "Pacificus," upholding the neutrality proclamation and seeking to destroy the binding force of the treaty with France. When the first of these came out in Fenno's paper (June 29, 1793) Jefferson lamented that none but bunglers and brawlers were available to answer it. The second and third produced this anguished appeal to Madison:

"For God's sake, my dear sir, take up your pen, select the most striking heresies and cut him to pieces in the face of the public. There is nobody else who can and will enter the lists with him."

Isolated from news and counsel, Madison was reluctant to undertake the task but did so and reported it the most grating one he ever experienced. He did the work "in scraps of time, with a distaste to the subject, and a distressing lassitude from the excessive and continued heat." The result was that Hamilton's eight letters of "Pacificus," running through July 1792, were followed by Madison's five letters of "Helvidius," beginning August 24. The public recognized the authors.[9]

Jefferson had managed to keep the word "neutrality" out of the proclamation (written by Randolph), thus minimizing the repudiation of the French treaty. Hamilton as "Pacificus" thrust in all that the President omitted. The territorial guarantee, he alleged, ran counter to the sense of the proclamation, which therefore was "virtually a manifestation of the sense of government that the United States are, *under the circumstances of the case, not bound* to execute the clause of guaranty." It was the President's duty, Hamilton argued, to preserve peace until Congress declared war. In fulfilling this duty he "must necessarily possess a right of judging what is the nature of the obligations which the treaties of the country impose on the government." His power in this field was broad, that of Congress narrow, because the powers of war and peace were by nature executive.

There was nothing mild about the opening words of "Helvidius" in reply:

"Several pieces with the signature of PACIFICUS were lately published, which have been read with singular pleasure and applause by the foreigners and degenerate citizens among us, who hate our republican government and the French Revolution."

Madison's five articles all assailed Hamilton's first. The others were to be dealt with after he learned more about events in Europe and at home. Not knowing whether the President really intended to disparage the treaty, he denied that the proclamation required such a construction and struck at the foundation of the case. The executive had no lawful power to do what Hamilton said he had done. Under the guise of vindicating a loved chief executive principles were advanced which struck at the honor and true interest of the country and at the vitals of its Constitution. The basis of them was "the extraordinary doctrine that the powers of making war and treaties are in their nature executive." This was a fallacy growing out of the fact that these are high acts of sovereignty, and European writers have discussed them with their eyes on monarchical governments, where sovereignty is in the prince. A declaration of war repeals the laws of peace. Decisions of war and peace, if not purely legislative, partake so much more of that quality that no other department can assert a rival claim. To nail this down he quoted similar words from *The Federalist* No. 75, and identified Hamilton as the author by dissenting from a minor part of the passage quoted.

Madison agreed that it was the President's duty to preserve peace until Congress declared war. He denied that this allowed him to decide what obligations were imposed on the country by its treaties—in other words, whether peace ought to be preserved. Hamilton had admitted that the power to judge the need of war was part of the power to declare it, but claimed that the lesser power was concurrent in Congress and the President. If it was, Madison replied, the power of which it was a part must be concurrent too but the Constitution gave that exclusively to Congress. Where did "Pacificus" get his doctrine, vicious in theory and dangerous in practice? From but one possible source: treaty and war powers "are *royal prerogatives* in the *British government,* and are accordingly treated as *executive prerogatives* by *British commentators."*

He challenged Hamilton's contention that abolition of an old government threw treaties into abeyance until the new one was recognized. The right of the people to change their rulers "is not only recorded in every public archive, written in every American heart, and sealed with the blood of a host of American martyrs; but it is the only lawful tenure by which the United States hold their existence as a nation."

Hamilton's loose and slashing letters were easier to read than Madison's close-knit, analytical replies. One reason for the latter's reluctance to enter the field was his knowledge of Hamilton's "prolixity and pertinacity," which made it unlikely that the business would be terminated by a single shot. But it was. Hamilton, with his main position riddled, said no more, and changing conditions as well as inclination kept Madison from completing his attack.

Among the handicaps was the weather. An exceedingly wet early season produced a remarkable stand of wheat. Inspecting several fields on June 16, Madison concluded that the luxuriant growth would offset the damage from rust and rot. The harvest, favored at first by a few dry days, stretched out through a cloudy, rainy, hot and humid month, as bad as could be. Corn throve till hit by an August drouth that baked the saturated fields to brick. Seven weeks went by without rain.

No wagons went to Fredericksburg during the wheat harvest, so no letters arrived, and no news. Later came an important letter from Jefferson, partly in cipher, and Madison's key had been left in Philadelphia. He stared at this enlightening passage: "We have decided unanimously to 130 . . . interest if they do not 510 . . . to the 636. Its consequences you will readily seize but 145 . . . though the 15 . . . to it." He knew that this related to Genêt and the President, but what was it?[10]

More satisfactory was the receipt of two plows made for him by Dr. Logan of Philadelphia. One, after a special pattern, realized Jefferson's theory of a proper moldboard, in which the iron wing took the friction instead of being buried uselessly under wood. He planned a change in it: the detached colter would not stand the shocks of rough and rooty land and rougher plowmen. He attached it directly to the point of the share and it worked well.

When Jefferson paid for these plows for Madison, he handed the $34.70 to William Gardner. And who was Mr. Gardner? He was the ex-slave Billey who ran away from Madison in 1782, was recaptured, and was given his freedom subject to a seven years' indenture, because his master could not punish him for taking the Declaration of Independence seriously. Employed as a free man by Mrs. House, he was relied on by Madison for the shipment of goods to Virginia, and may have acted as his paid valet during the sessions of Congress. In 1795 Madison wrote to his father: "Let old Anthony and Betty know that their son Billey is no more." He shipped as a seaman to New Orleans, fainted from seasickness in a storm and was swept overboard.[11]

On June 2, 1793, Jefferson wrote that old Mrs. House was dead. She went out like a candle. Mrs. Trist, who had suffered great losses in keeping her mother's place open, intended to dispose of it at once. So passed the famous congressional boardinghouse, Madison's home in all Philadelphia sojourns since 1780, and the center of Virginian activities.

Just as he was getting well into the Helvidius writings Madison received the second of two bulky packages from Senator Taylor—drafts of his famous pamphlets attacking the Hamilton funding policy and the national bank. Consign them, Taylor requested, to the printer or the flames. Needing to consult Monroe about publication of these hard-hitting papers, Madison completed his own five articles and set out for Charlottesville.[12] There, Philadelphia papers brought him up to date. Jay and King had published a certificate testifying to Genêt's threat to appeal to the people. It was plain, he wrote to Jefferson, that the minister's indiscretions and the popularity of the President were to be used to turn the country against France. To repel local attempts, he and Monroe were planning "expressions of the public mind in important counties" by respectable people.

As Madison was about to return to Orange, at the end of August, young Davie Randolph came in from Philadelphia with a letter whose contents, Jefferson said, must be sacredly guarded from everybody but Monroe. The special secrecy was upon a paper (later published in the "Ana" of August 6, 1793) describing a talk with the President about Jefferson's resignation. In spite of strong protests by Madison[13] this had been submitted on July 31, to take effect two months later. Calling on the Secretary at his country home, Washington told him that Hamilton planned to retire late in the coming session of Congress, and begged him to postpone his own departure so that both places could be filled at once. They talked of political parties, Jefferson saying that the Republicans would desert Genêt when the truth about him became known, while Washington termed the monarchists (if there were any) insane. Then——

"He returned to the difficulty of naming my successor. He said Mr. Madison would be his first choice, but he had always expressed to him such a decision against public office that he could not expect he would undertake it."

A number of men were regretfully dismissed by Washington as speculators and the meeting closed with a plea to Jefferson to stay in the cabinet at least till the end of the year. Knowing this, Jefferson commented, Madison could shape his plans. If the Senate were not unsound, "it would be the moment for dividing the Treasury between two equal chiefs of the customs and internal taxes." (A sure method of forcing Hamilton out.) The House, by declaring the true sense of the Constitution, could divorce the national bank from the government. Hamilton's reports to Congress should be censured, etc. Turning to Franco-American affairs, the Secretary confirmed all that Madison deduced from the newspapers. Genêt's conduct was inspiring universal indignation. The towns were proclaiming their loyalty to the President. If the popular leaders had not sense enough to go with the people, the people would desert them. It would be true wisdom to approve neutrality and abandon Genêt entirely, with expressions of strong friendship and adherence to his nation. "In this way we shall keep the people on our side by keeping ourselves in the right."

Jefferson had adhered to Genêt as long as there was a hope of getting him right, but "finding at length that the man was absolutely incorrigible, I saw the necessity of quitting a wreck which could not but sink all who should cling to it." Then came the information which was buried in the cipher of the earlier letter. It had been determined *to insist on Genêt's recall*. In spite of that, Hamilton and Knox were pressing an appeal to the people with an eagerness never before seen in them. Hamilton had made three forty-five-minute speeches to the President attacking the new democratic societies as agencies of sedition set in motion by Genêt, which would draw the people into their vortex and overset the government.

"The President was strongly impressed by this picture. . . . I opposed it totally, told the President plainly in their presence that the intention was to dismount him from being the head of the nation and make him the head of a party: that this would be the effect of making him, in an appeal to the people, declare war on the Republican party."

Randolph was guided by Washington's indecision and secured a postponement. Madison's absence was felt. "The President," wrote Jefferson, "is extremely anxious to know your sentiments on the proclamation. He has asked me several times. I tell him you are so absorbed in farming that you write to me always about ploughs, rotations, etc."[14]

Madison reported the situation in Virginia. Friends of France were turning away in disgust, their feelings intensified by habitual veneration for Washington. The Anglican party was making the worst of everything:

"The only antidote for their poison is to distinguish between the nation and its agent, between principles and events; and to impress the well meaning with the fact that the enemies of France and of liberty are at work to lead them from their honorable connection with these into the arms and ultimately into the government of Great Britain. If the genuine sense of the people could be collected . . . the calamity would be greatly alleviated if not absolutely controlled."

In abandoning Genêt, Madison observed, he concurred with Monroe that silence was better than open denunciation. The errors of the American government should not be forgotten—its refusal to favor French over British commerce, the unfortunate appointment of Gouverneur Morris as minister to France, the language of the proclamation, the attempt of Hamilton to explain away and dissolve the treaty of alliance. He sent resolutions to keymen over the state, designed to guide the country people against the insidious inflammation of the towns. These praised the illustrious George Washington and his efforts for peace, approved the glorious contest of France for liberty, and declared that disbelievers in the American Revolution were propagating prejudices against the French Revolution in order to mold the American government to the form and principles of British monarchy.

To an increasing extent, Madison felt, national-bank influence was strengthening the opposition. W. C. Nicholas talked like a sincere friend to the French cause, but confidence in him was impaired by his constant borrowing at Richmond and his connection with John Marshall. The latter's great purchase from Fairfax had been aided by the bank or people connected with it, and Madison was sure "he must have felt, in the moment of the purchase, an absolute dependence on the moneyed interest," which would explain his anti-Gallic activities. A few weeks earlier, Madison had suggested "young Marshall" as the only person in the state who could safely be used by Jefferson as a secret American observer of Spanish policy in New Orleans, but said there were objections of several sorts to him.[15]

Reading the Washington-Jefferson notes, both Madison and Monroe felt that the President showed a real anxiety to keep the Secretary of State in office. Jefferson should stay where he was, but Madison was glad that his own determination to stay out was understood. It seemed doubtful now whether he should go on with the Helvidius writing. At any rate he would postpone it—a decision reinforced by the fact that on his return from Albemarle he found "a house full of particular friends who will stay some weeks."[16]

While Madison was advising silence about Genêt, that worthy was blowing himself to bits. He published his correspondence with Jefferson, putting the entire record of his own misbehavior before the nation. "His conduct has been that of a madman," Madison wrote to Monroe. "He is abandoned even by his votaries in Philadelphia. Hutchison [who died of yellow fever while his letter was en route] declares that he has ruined the Republican interest in that place." Luckily, his course was so flagrant that people were likely to blame him rather than his government. Also——

"I find that the Anglicans and monocrats from Boston to Philadelphia are betrayed by the occasion into the most palpable discovery of their real views. They already lose sight of the agent; and direct their hostilities *immediately against France.* This will do good if proper use be made of it."

To cap all, Great Britain had declared war on American commerce by seizing noncontraband goods bound to unblockaded ports. This, Madison asserted, would bring on a crisis unless the order was revoked on American demand, of which he saw not the slightest probability.[17]

The "Anglicans and monocrats" made no attempt to hide their jubilation. "You will be delighted," wrote John Adams' Boston son-in-law to Hamilton, "with the anti-Gallican spirit which has lately burst forth in this state." But there was little joy in Philadelphia. "All the inhabitants who can, flying from it in every direction," was Madison's picture—flying from the malignant fever which struck down thousands and killed three fourths of those attacked. The account came to him from Jefferson, who could not refrain from putting in a thrust at Hamilton, who believed he had yellow fever and called in two physicians. Said his cabinet colleague:

"A man as timid as he is on the water, as timid on horseback, as timid in sickness, would be a phenomenon if the courage of which he has the reputation in military affairs were genuine."[18]

Jefferson himself was caught between his retirement and his pride. Having announced that he would go home on October 1 for six weeks, he didn't like "to exhibit the appearance of panic" by going earlier. A week later (September 15) he joined the exodus and stopped with Madison on the twenty-fifth. The latter went to Monticello in October for a three-way conference with Jefferson and Monroe—their business probably some final editing of Taylor's attack on Hamilton.[19]

Starting north just after Madison's visit, Jefferson stopped as usual at Montpelier. He was so pleased with a new brand of sweet corn, "three weeks forwarder" than others, that he took a seed ear with him rather than risk the miscarriage of some sent to Albemarle for him and Monroe. Madison undertook to grow pecans and coffee berry trees from Kentucky. His incessant experiments did not always come off so well—as when he planted sulla seed and cork oak acorns sent him from France by Jefferson, or a few grains of upland rice from Timor given him by Captain Bligh of the *Bounty*. Turned out by a mutinous crew for forty days in a longboat, the captain saved only a little rice out of a fine collection, but the detailed directions he gave Madison did not make it a Virginia staple.[20]

Madison received an inquiry from Washington. With yellow fever raging in Philadelphia, had the President power to summon Congress to another place? Madison said No (as had Jefferson, earlier), but indorsed Washington's alternative plan to suggest a meeting elsewhere, and drew up a requested proclamation.[21] No epidemic was needed to bring death to the Madison household. On October 3, 1793, Ambrose died, leaving a tuberculous widow and twelve-year-old daughter. He had the substantial qualities of his father, and was closer to James than the other brothers were. This event increased the worry with which the family saw Madison set off late in November toward the plague center. At Fredericksburg, where Senator Monroe arrived one day ahead of

him, letters were picked up from Jefferson and Beckley saying that
the fever was gone—washed away apparently, in a series of heavy
rains. ("The frost came—the distemper disappeared," wrote
Fisher Ames, but nobody suspected mosquitoes.)

With northerly stages uncertain, and Jefferson warning that he
had been robbed of $70-odd in horse hire, the two travelers cast
their eyes on an ancient vehicle. "We set off in five minutes,"
Madison wrote, "in a machine we have procured here and which
we shall keep on with till it fails us or we can do better." His
saddle horse Damon didn't fit the new arrangement, so he bought
a carriage horse at Dumfries and sent his father's servant Sam
home with the gaited animal. Living quarters awaited them at
Germantown, where the President was staying—no mere shake-
down in a hotel hallway, such as Jefferson was forced to accept
for a few days, but (the latter reported) a pleasant private room
with two beds and a fireplace which he had found for them. However, the people of Philadelphia were by this time streaming back
to their silent metropolis, and Congress and the cabinet followed
them in.[22]

Washington's address to Congress on December 5, 1793, left
no doubt of the effect of Madison's reply to "Pacificus." Jefferson,
who wrote the passages on foreign affairs, was able to describe the
neutrality proclamation merely as a declaration of the legal state
of things, designed to prevent Americans from engaging in hostile
acts. This was the same as saying that Hamilton ("Pacificus")
had no warrant for calling it a denial of future obligations under
the treaty with France. Writing the reply of the House, Madison
no longer hesitated to approve the President's vigilance for peace,
but he took care to repeat the narrow definition of the proclamation.[23]

Madison's affection for Washington was evident in the opening
paragraph congratulating him on his unanimous re-election.
Nevertheless, the bond between the two was broken. The President had been drawn deeply into Federalist policy. The disclosure
of Madison's connection with "that rascal Freneau," as Washington called him, had a chilling influence, even though the *National*

*Gazette* ceased publication as receipts fell off in the furor over Genêt. Personal relations were friendly, but there were no more confidential requests for Madison's aid in important matters. Little lingering fevers, wrote Jefferson, were affecting Washington's looks, and he was extremely affected by the newspaper attacks on him. It was a tragic trend, which Madison had foreseen from the start, as revealed by Jefferson's comment:

"I think he feels those things more than any person I ever yet met with. I am sincerely sorry to see them. I remember an observation of yours made when I first went to New York, that the satellites and sycophants which surrounded him had wound up the ceremonials of the government to a pitch of stateliness which nothing but his personal character could have supported and which no character after him could ever maintain. . . . Naked he would have been sanctimoniously reverenced, but enveloped in the rags of royalty, they can hardly be torn off without laceration."

It was about time for Martha Washington to make her classic remark (if she ever did so) that a greasy spot on her wallpaper, above the sofa, indicated the presence of "a filthy Democrat." A Federalist wrote to Rufus King: "I am to sup with a set of Jacobins . . . and I would almost as leave be whipped as go."[24]

The new Congress produced (it was thought) a solid Republican delegation from Virginia. John Nicholas, brother of Wilson and George, was among the newcomers. White was out, defeated five to one, according to Madison, because of his vote for a second assumption of state debts. "When Colonel Bland was the only good member of that delegation, he died; and now we have lost White!" the Adams son-in-law lamented to Hamilton.[25] But White began a cordial correspondence with Madison, referring to himself always in loyal Republican terms. The Senate was enriched for a few months with the fiscal and political talents of Albert Gallatin, but he was thrown out by a partisan vote of 14 to 12 on the convenient theory that his citizenship did not start until six years after he came to America, fourteen years before. The bitter animus against him resulted from his suggestion that the

Secretary of the Treasury make regular reports to Congress. In the tumult over Gallatin, the Senate threw open its doors, blinked at the dazzling light and kept them open.

On the last day of 1793 Jefferson retired. The vacillating Randolph was put in his place. Hamilton, riding high, decided not to resign. His power was not diminished by the choice of a new Attorney General. William Bradford had been Madison's closest friend in college, but neither his law career nor marriage into the Boudinot family tended to perpetuate their common outlook. It was not in the executive branch, however, that the next crisis was to arise. By a bold plunge into international affairs, Madison became the storm center of American politics and policy.

# CHAPTER XXX

## MR. MADISON'S RESOLUTIONS

BEGINNING on the third day of 1794, a wave of discussion swept over the United States. The subject was "Mr. Madison's Resolutions," three years in the making. In February 1791 the President informed Congress that Britain showed no disposition to enter into a commercial agreement. This gave such impetus to Madison's campaign for tonnage discrimination that, to head it off, the Secretary of State was directed to make a report on foreign commercial restrictions and suggest remedies.

While Jefferson gathered material from overseas, Tench Coxe and Madison made domestic tonnage and trade studies. The report, completed before Congress adjourned in 1792, was held back because of changing world conditions and the desire for effective timing. Jefferson sent it to the House on December 16, 1793.[1]

It arrived at a moment of angry tension. Britain had issued a general order for seizure of American food ships, France following with a similar decree in reverse. Then came Jefferson's report showing that prior to these actions American commerce was being well treated by France, Spain and Portugal, but was subject to severe British restrictions. The remedies he suggested were those which Madison had been urging for years—a strict system of reciprocal favors and retaliations.

Supporting the report, Madison described the transition from interstate chaos to unity under the new government and the common effort to conciliate all friendly countries. Four years' experience had proved the need for a moderate, firm and decisive attitude toward those who would not meet us on terms of reciprocity. He then offered his resolutions, calling for higher tonnage taxes on vessels of nations having no commercial treaty with the United States. Port restrictions were to be met in kind. Finally, if unable to obtain reparations, Congress was to reimburse citizens who sustained losses from foreign regulations which contravened the law of nations.

The United States, Madison pointed out, produced necessities and imported luxuries. It could stand a curtailment of trade better than the countries it traded with. American exports were bulky, imports compact. If each country carried its own goods the chief benefit would be to American ships. To avoid needless irritation and a loss of revenue, he would not go every length at first. But by doing no more than most nations and less than some, "our country may make her enemies feel the extent of her power."

Ames, leader of the anticounterdiscriminationists, was able to secure a week's postponement. During the interval a minor issue bore curiously on Madison's final resolve. Three thousand fugitives from war-torn Santo Domingo landed in Maryland. The legislature begged for a federal appropriation to supplement its dwindling relief fund. A committee advised a grant but met opposition. Madison wished to relieve the sufferers but was afraid of establishing a dangerous precedent which might thereafter be perverted to the countenance of purposes very different from those of charity. He could not "lay his finger on that article in the Federal Constitution which granted a right to Congress of expending, on objects of benevolence, the money of their constituents."

Clark advised him to be consistent. He had asked Congress to indemnify all citizens who suffered losses by the British pirates. Was there any more authority for that in the Constitution? Madison replied that the two cases were different. American vessels "were under our protection, by the Law of Nations, which the French sufferers unquestionably were not."

Elias Boudinot was astonished at Madison's statement that nothing like this had been done before. Did not the Indians frequently come to the capital on embassies, and did not the executive pay their lodgings for whole months together, merely because they were unable to pay for themselves? By the eighth section of Article I, "Congress were warranted to provide for exigencies regarding *the general welfare,* and he was sure this case came under that description."

Madison's scruples were finally satisfied by a clause charging the cost to France if that country would pay it. In spite of the amendment it was expenditure for the general welfare. More extraordinary was what Madison said to justify his own proposal to reimburse the victims of piratical warfare. It would be constitutional because it was to remedy a violation of international law. To avoid reliance on the welfare clause, he set up a welfare spending power based on the power to *define and punish* offenses against the law of nations![2]

It was the hand of William Smith that gestured, but the words of Hamilton that were heard, when the South Carolinian took the floor for an all-day attack on Madison's commercial resolutions. Jefferson said instantly, when Madison sent him the thirty-four-column speech, that every tittle of it was Hamilton's except the introduction. The first draft of it lies among Hamilton's papers in his handwriting.

The strategy was to undermine the resolutions by discrediting Jefferson's report. Through Smith, Hamilton charged the Secretary of State with understating the commercial hostility of France and exaggerating that of Great Britain. A commercial conflict with the latter country would end in defeat and disgrace for the United States, with war probable. France was pictured as selfish, hostile and impotent.

Madison held the floor all next day. He was a believer, he said, in free trade. But that required what did not exist—freedom everywhere. British ships carried eleven twelfths of the country's commerce because the Navigation Act gave a preference which was not offset by the laws of rival nations. American ships were totally excluded from the West Indies, and could do no indirect carrying to the British Isles. But the United States allowed Britain to bring in anything she might please, from her own or from other ports, and in her own or in other vessels.

Britain, he stated, sold to the United States more than twice as much as the American products she bought. France bought seven times as much as she sold in return. Nine tenths of all imported manufactures came from Britain, but that country "refuses not only our manufactures but the articles we wish most to send her— our wheat and flour, our fish, and our salted provisions." The balance of trade with France was $2,630,000 in favor of the United

States; with Britain, $5,922,000 against the United States, and re-exports would nearly double that. To correct this condition by retaliation was in accord with the usage of nations, and the House had voted twice to do so. Of all the objections he had heard, the most extravagant was the idea of war. On what imaginable pretext could an independent nation be attacked by another for following its example in commercial regulations? If war resulted it would prove a fixed predetermination to make it.

The proposed regulations, their sponsor said, would immediately benefit the Northern states and put a temporary burden on the Southern—stimulating manufacturing and navigation in the former, cutting exports in the latter. His own state would suffer the most, yet he believed that Virginia would cheerfully concur in a temporary sacrifice. The long-range effect in the South would be favorable, furnishing a home market for produce and creating a shipbuilding industry. British policy was bottomed on the belief that the United States would be ruled by conflicting sectional interests and local prejudices. To reject the propositions "must convey the most unfavorable impressions of our national character and rivet the fetters on our commerce," as well as prolong other causes of injury.[3]

The debate raged into February. Newcomer John Nicholas made his oratorical debut in Madison's support, but Parker, impressed by the injury to Virginia trade, went over to the opposition. Richard Bland Lee paid a long "tribute of gratitude and thanks" to Madison's part in founding the present happy government. Then he too joined the opposition, apparently on the ground that farmers were more virtuous than manufacturers and French privateers were depressing the price of Virginia tobacco. Griffin deserted also, but Giles came strongly to Madison's aid. So did Findley and Clark, while Ames, Boudinot and Fitzsimons offered heavy opposition.[4]

Speaking for nearly two full days in final rebuttal, Madison defended Jefferson against unwarranted charges of misrepresentation, accused Britain of fomenting Indian war and Algerian piracy, and built up his own case. His resolutions, if adopted, would produce these results:

1. Inform the British nation that we can, by fair and pacific means, make it her interest to be just.

2. Increase the American marine, thereby reducing costs and providing for the national security.

3. Encourage domestic manufactures.

4. Break up the British monopoly of manufactured imports.

5. Win the nations in treaty, notably France, into arrangements still more favorable to American commerce.[5]

In spite of the hostility of New England leaders, the resolutions had support among Northern members influenced by British spoliations on their commerce. The outcome was a tossup. On February 3, opponents observed that Madison was absent and moved to strike out his first resolution. Nicholas and Giles pleaded for a delay of ten or fifteen minutes. Dayton, Smith and Wadsworth began to insinuate that Madison had "fled the question." Smilie of Pennsylvania rebuked them. Never in all his life had he witnessed such an attempt to take advantage of a man's absence. "Money Ship" Wadsworth made the blundering retort that characters in all ages and all countries had fled the question and a majority of the Pennsylvania Assembly once did so.

Pennsylvania could take insults, but not from Connecticut, which tried to swindle her out of the Wyoming Valley. By the time Congressman Findley finished his defense of the assembly, Madison was in the doorway. His first resolution carried 51 to 46. Following this action, as he explained to Jefferson, several friendly New Englanders insisted on a postponement until March, so that they could gain home backing. Both sides then plunged into a pamphleteering campaign. Madison worked day and night writing out his speeches for nationwide distribution, with time off to read the newspaper slanders upon himself. He described developments to Jefferson on March 2:

"The interval has produced vast exertions by the British party to mislead the people of the eastern states. No means have been spared. The most artful and wicked calumnies have been propagated with all the zeal which malice and interest could invent. The blackest of these calumnies, as you may imagine, have fallen to the lot of the mover of the resolutions. The last Boston paper contains a string of charges framed for the purpose of making the eastern people believe that he has been the counsellor and abettor of Genêt in all his extravagances, and a corrupt tool of France ever since the embassy of Gerard."

In spite of "all these diabolical maneuvers," public meetings in Boston and New York showed leanings the other way. The new French minister, Joseph Fauchet, was reversing Genêt's errors. Washington had received him with "affectionate solicitude for the success of the republic." Fauchet, writing to his government, paid Madison the highest tribute in his power: "Madison, le Robespierre des Etats Unis."

Washington's friendly words did not cancel unfriendly policies. Madison was shocked when he heard that American vessels were being chartered to carry provisions to the British armaments in the West Indies:

"This is really horrible. Whilst we allow the British to stop our supplies to the French dominions, we allow our citizens to carry supplies to hers, for the known purpose of aiding her in taking from France the islands we have guaranteed to her, and transferring these valuable markets from friendly to unfriendly hands. What can be done?"

His inclination was to cut off supplies to the British as long as supplies to France were obstructed, but he doubted whether such a measure could stand the clamor of seaboard merchants, farmers and shipowners. It was a different clamor that he reported to Jefferson on March 12:

"The merchants, particularly of New England, have had a terrible slam in the West Indies. About a hundred vessels have been seized by the British for condemnation, on the pretext of enforcing the laws of the monarchy with regard to the colony trade. . . . This new symptom of insolence and enmity in Britain shows either that she meditates a formal war as soon as she shall have crippled our marine resources, or that she calculates on the pusillanimity of this country and the influence of her party in a degree that will lead her into aggressions which our love of peace can no longer bear."

The partisans of England, Madison reported, were now trying to curry favor with the people by taking the lead in defensive preparations. It was proposed to build six frigates against the Algerines. Better hire the Portuguese navy, or continue to imitate the British tribute system, he advised, than rely on too few ships which could hardly be started within a year for lack of cedar and live oak. (An understatement.) Following approval of the ship program, Sedgwick called for 15,000 auxiliary troops. Induced to enlist by the gift of a $12 suit of clothes, and given two days of training per month, they and the 5,000 regulars could conquer Canada, and their higher discipline would prevent them from looting the property of their neighbors as the militia did.[6]

To Madison, this proposal by a pro-British Hamiltonian didn't ring true. "His immediate prompter," he remarked to Jefferson, "will be seen both in his speech and in his propositions." One purpose, possibly, was to embarrass Madison's resolutions, but that was not all. "You understand the game behind the curtain too well not to perceive the old trick of turning every contingency into a resource for accumulating force in the government." He found one satisfaction. The foolish military reason offered for the move (retaliatory invasion of British dominions) made it impossible to continue the charge that his own resolutions tended to provoke war by alarming and irritating Great Britain. A committee converted the proposal into a call for organization of 80,000 militiamen, who couldn't be ordered out of the country.[7]

The chief objection now to Madison's resolutions was that they did not go far enough. He admitted that more might be needed, but contended that they would be useful—in peace, as a means of peaceful pressure; in the event of war, as a vantage point in subsequent negotiations. The South was keen for a thirty-day embargo. Northern congressmen defeated it, 46 to 48, then heard such an uproar over West Indian ship seizures that they put it through by a huge majority. The Senate concurred next day.[8]

Praise for Madison was ringing out everywhere now, though not among all classes. "The manly manner in which you came forward, at a time when the legislature were designedly thrown into a state of torpor, does you honor," wrote Senator Butler. And

General Horatio Gates: "Go on, my friend, persevere in the glorious cause you have uniformly supported, and there will not be a true Republican in the U. S. that will not with heart and voice be ready to support and exalt you."

New England merchants, clinging to their trade with Britain, were glumly silent. But the American ship captains held prisoner in the West Indies felt a different stirring. Joshua Barney and twenty-one others, in a joint letter to Madison, told how their hearts bounded with joy when they read his speech and resolutions. The Republican Society of Charleston, South Carolina, sent congratulations to "Citizen Representative" James Madison. "They with pleasure behold in you, Citizen, the firm patriot and true Republican." A few nights later these same people beheld, or caused others to behold, the hanging and burning in effigy of their own Congressman Smith, along with Ames, Benedict Arnold, Dumouriez and the Devil, "en groupe," as Madison described it.[9]

Meanwhile, on a motion by Giles, a committee was probing into Treasury bookkeeping and the loans made in Holland under the two acts of 1790. The inquiry brought this from Madison:

"I understand that it begins to pinch where we most expected— the authority for drawing the money from Europe into the bank. H[amilton] endeavored to parry the difficulty by contesting the right of the committee to call for the authority. This failing, he talks of constructive written authority from the President, but relies on parol authority, which I think it impossible the President can support him in."

Apparently Madison did not know what lay behind Hamilton's reluctance. In 1791 while Washington was touring the South, the Treasury head obtained from him a letter approving what he *already had done* in Holland and assenting to further steps proposed. The approval was based on "the opinions offered in your letter," and indicated only a vague knowledge of the matter. The sequel was related by Edmund Randolph to Madison many years afterward. Following the defeat of the Giles-Madison resolutions in 1793, Hamilton by an "indirect conduit" reminded Washington that he had sanctioned the transfer of funds from Europe. "The

President," Randolph wrote, "mentioned the circumstance to me with surprise and passion, declaring, in the most excluding terms, that he never did write or cause to be written letters to that purport." Some days later Hamilton delivered the 1791 correspondence to the President, who, discomfited, gave it to Randolph with an instruction that he write to Hamilton and avow it.

Now, in the 1794 inquiry, after other defenses failed, Hamilton turned Washington's letter over to the House committee. The committee promptly asked him to submit it to the President, along with his written instructions, and obtain a declaration touching "the point of authority." The distressed Secretary did so, and was told that the letters spoke for themselves. As for oral communications, Washington did not doubt that he had approved what was proposed, "upon the condition that what was to be done by you should be agreeable to the laws."

Madison displayed no grief as he told Jefferson of the reaction. The President's letter was inexpressibly mortifying to Hamilton's friends. However, the effect was to hamstring the committee. Criticism of the Secretary for violating the law would hit his chief, so the report merely set forth the facts and (at Hamilton's request) absolved him of any suspicion of misusing funds.

In mid-April, with the embargo in effect but to be dropped because both France and Britain disliked it, three other proposals were before the House: to sequester British debts, establish a lien on arriving British imports and suspend importations from that country until spoliations were paid for and the peace treaty was executed. With such drastic measures pending, Madison thought it imprudent to force his commercial resolutions to a vote.[10]

At this point a greater obstacle appeared. The President was to send a special envoy to Great Britain to negotiate a treaty, instead of taking the risks involved in coercive legislation. Hamilton would be named, Madison suspected, unless overruled by fear of "the disgust to republicanism and to France." Personal protests to Washington by Monroe and Nicholas emphasized the feeling. A fortnight later to Hamilton's "great mortification," he was set aside and Chief Justice Jay was named. Hamilton, King and others pressed him strongly to accept—their anxiety increased by discovery that Randolph had proposed the envoyship to Madison, who wanted Jefferson named.[11]

Recalling Jay's unpopular course as foreign minister—his support of British contentions regarding violations of the treaty of 1783, his failure to press the American claim to the Mississippi—Madison saw no hope of national advantage in the appointment. But it might produce partisan gain.

"If animadversions are undertaken by skillful hands there is no measure of the executive administration perhaps that will be found more severely vulnerable."

The Democratic Societies, he wrote on May 11, were beginning to open their batteries upon the appointment, but it was paralyzing all measures for extorting redress from Great Britain. A North Carolina congressman incautiously pushed one of Madison's discrimination resolves to a vote and "placed us in a very feeble minority." Diverse motives were in this reaction—the desire for peace, reliance on England as a bulwark against Jacobinism, the feeling of merchants that bad relations with a good customer were better than none. Nobody, it seemed to Madison, had real confidence in the success of the mission, while the distrust of Jay made his appointment the most powerful blow ever suffered by the popularity of the President.[12]

Hamilton's control of Congress was shown in the tax measures made necessary by national defense. Excises were laid on carriages ($2.00 on a chaise, $10 on a coach), snuff, sugar and auction sales (with auctioneers licensed). As Ames told of it: "Madison spouted against excise, and in favor of land tax, hoping to prevent anything, or to get only that voted which would raise enemies to the government." As Madison described it: "The aversion to direct taxes, which appeared by a vote of 70-odd for rejecting them, will saddle us with all these pernicious innovations without ultimately avoiding direct taxes in addition to them." (He was right.)

The snuff and carriage taxes were aimed at the South. Madison assailed the first because it hit the poor, the second because it hit the rich. Furthermore, a tax on carriages was a direct tax and unconstitutional unless apportioned according to population. (The

Supreme Court disagreed.) If constitutional barriers were broken down to permit the taxation of luxury, *as such,* the wealthy might soon discover that, as Paine said, the greatest of all luxuries is a great estate.

Madison's desire for laws to equalize wealth was not fulfilled by luxury taxes piled by congressional speculators on honest Southern planters. The answer was an amendment to Hamilton's pending stamp act, putting a tax on transfers of public securities and bank stock. Horrified Fisher Ames cried out that the Massachusetts members did not draw income enough from funded stock "to buy the oats for the southern members' coachhorses." Unluckily, Dexter swung to the left and the sinister ingredient was implanted in the bill. There, Madison reported, it served as an effective poison. The "sentinels of stock" turned around and helped him defeat the whole measure. "This distresses Hamilton exceedingly," wrote Ames.[13]

Not confining himself to poison, Madison reported that the Senate's plan to give the President power to raise an army of 10,000 men "was strangled more easily in the House of Representatives than I had expected." This was the third or fourth attempt "to get a powerful military establishment, under the pretext of public danger, and under the auspices of the President's popularity." A bill forbidding American enlistments in foreign armies (designed, Madison intimated, to curry favor for Jay in England) went through the House, but the Virginian killed the only important section of it—one stopping the sale of French prizes in the United States. The President, he pointed out, had authorized such sales. If Congress declared that course unneutral, Britain could collect damages for all the sales already made. That was an argument New England could understand.[14]

At the height of the conflict, Senators King and Ellsworth argued privately to Senator Taylor for a dissolution of the Union. King said that Madison, whose conduct he had narrowly watched, "had some deep and mischievous design." Taylor reported this seriously to Madison, who jotted the comment "probably in terrorem" on the synopsis of the talk. He was spurred, however, to put out a 10,000-word pamphlet of *Political Observations,* justifying his resolutions,

upholding moderate defense measures, opposing war and defending friendship with revolutionary France. The opposition, Madison
remarked, was "ever ready to invoke the name of Washington" to
garnish their heretical doctrines with his virtues, arousing "a fair
suspicion that they who draw most largely on that fund are hastening fastest to bankruptcy of their own."[15]

Congress adjourned on June 9. Surveying the scene, Madison
took comfort only in the future. Executive influence on events,
coupled with public confidence in the President, overmatched all
the efforts of republicanism. "The party of that sentiment in the
Senate is completely wrecked," he affirmed to Jefferson, "and in
the House of Representatives in a much worse condition than at
any earlier period of the session."

Madison and Monroe left Philadelphia together, the latter to
take ship for France at Baltimore. It could have been the other
way around. When, in retaliation for the Genêt ouster, France
demanded removal of unfriendly Gouverneur Morris, Madison
headed a committee which asked the President to appoint Aaron
Burr. Instead, he offered the place to Madison himself, then to
Livingston, finally to Monroe, who was advised by Madison to
accept. Fearful that ocean travel would bring back the dreaded
convulsions of his youth, Madison would have declined the place
in any event. But there was another personal reason why neither
ships nor wild horses could have dragged him out of the United
States at that particular time.[15]

# CHAPTER XXXI

## DOLLEY MADISON

AMONG the casualties of the yellow-fever epidemic which swept Philadelphia in 1793 was a young Quaker lawyer named John Todd. Escaping by a narrow margin was the attractive young woman he had married three years earlier, Dolley Payne Todd. A year later she became Mrs. James Madison, destined to acquire more fame in her own right than many a President of the United States.

Dolley Payne, like Madison, was descended from substantial Virginia farm families. Her grandfather Josias Payne of Goochland County married Scottish Anna Fleming. Grandfather William Coles came from Wexford County, Ireland, and took to wife Lucy Winston, whose sister Sarah became the mother of Patrick Henry. John Payne was twenty, Mary Coles sixteen, when they married in 1761 and went to live on a 200-acre farm on Little Bird Creek, in Goochland County, given them by the former's father and uncle, Josias and John Payne. In 1765, following young John's conversion to his wife's religious faith, they set off with their two-year-old son for the New Garden Quaker settlement in North Carolina. There, near the present Guilford College, they bought 2,500 acres of land. On their return to Virginia four years later, they brought with them two sons and Dolley.[1]

That name—the only one she ever owned, knew or used during eighty-one years—was too plain to suit early biographers. So, just as Eleanor Rose was invented for Madison's mother Nelly, Dolley had to be Dorothea or Dorothy. The "e" was then knocked out and the triumph of convention was complete. It is said in the 1886 *Letters and Memoirs* of her grandniece Lucia B. Cutts:

"Dorothy Payne first opened her eyes on this world, which she was destined so thoroughly to enjoy, on the 20th May, 1768, in North Carolina, where her parents were visiting; and was named Dorothy for her mother's aunt, Mrs. Patrick Henry."

Dorothea Spotswood Dandridge, who became the second Mrs. Patrick Henry, was eight years old at this time. If the infant was named after her, the pet name of one became the real name of the other. A church official, registering births, does not write "Dolley their daughter" if the parents have told him "Dorothea." Dolley herself disclaimed both of the embellished versions, as well as the spelling "Dolly." In 1826 the sculptor John H. I. Browere wrote to the Madisons that his wife had determined to name their new daughter after the "amiable spouse" of the ex-President.

"Uncertain of the real signature of Mrs. Madison [who usually signed her letters D. P. Madison] we have awaited her name in full—some here saying it was Dorothea, Dorothy, Dolly, Dolli, etc. . . . . You will much oblige me by transmitting it in full."

He wrote again next month: "Our young daughter has been named Dolley Madison Browere."[2]

Dolley's name could be what she chose, but it was a more dubious proposition when she undertook to control her age. Late in life she wrote to Margaret Bayard Smith that she believed she was eleven or twelve (though actually fifteen) when her parents moved to Philadelphia. Finally she decided she was ten, as revealed by an 1839 letter to another friend: "Being anxious to disavow the affectation of curtailing some precious years I will give you a true copy of the notice of me in our family Bible. Dolley Payne, born May 20, 1773." The date recorded on her tombstone, May 20, 1768, is the same that was written down in the North Carolina church record.[3]

Some years after the return to Little Bird Creek, John Payne bought Patrick Henry's former home in Hanover County, ten miles west of Ashland. The big old hip-roofed, clapboard house, a hundred feet long, was called "Scotchtown" in memory of a bygone settlement. Here Dolley spent her childhood, retaining memories which, in her old age, gave prominence to black marble mantelpieces, bright fires and spacious rooms. With her brothers Walter and William Temple she went to the Cedar Creek Quaker school, and at home beheld the coming of more children—Isaac, Lucy, Anna, Mary and John.

John and Mary Payne might have spent their lives as slave-own-ing Virginians had not the former taken his new religion so deeply to heart. It was opposed to slavery and so was he, but until 1782 Virginia law forbade the freeing of slaves. In the following year John Payne manumitted all his Negroes, well knowing that without them he must sell his plantation. Son Walter had gone to Philadelphia in 1779, when he was seventeen. His mother visited him there in 1781 and took counsel with the Quakers Henry and Elizabeth Drinker, whose people, like her own, had come from Wexford. Mrs. Drinker, who recorded the visit in her journal, wrote again on July 9, 1783: "John Payne's family came to reside in Philadelphia." While the senior Payne made and sold starch, Dolley acquired as much schooling as was considered fitting for a girl, and learned that young men liked her. She had been in the city just a year when Mrs. Drinker wrote:

"1784 July 10. Sally Drinker and Walter Payne, Billy Sansom and Polly Wells, Jacob Downing and Dolly Payne, went to our place at Frankford. Sally and Josey Sansom and Nancy Drinker (from Par la Ville) met them there. A squabble. Nancy returned home in the evening with her sister, etc."

Sixteen-year-old Dolley (not eleven, certainly!) was younger than most of these. Sally, Nancy, Walter, Billy and Jacob were in their early twenties and Polly married in a year. The squabble remains unexplained. However, Jacob Downing was then court-ing Nancy Drinker, who unluckily had gone out to the Schuylkill three days earlier. Whatever happened, it happened after Nancy found herself the odd girl in a gathering to which her young man had taken a black-haired, blue-eyed, pink-cheeked maiden just arrived at the most dangerous age known to eighteenth-century man. Dolley was never named in another Drinker chroni-cle. Jacob soon afterward drove to New York with Nancy, in a chaise-for-two portion of a family excursion. He married Sally.[4]

In spirit Dolley Payne was no Quaker, though she followed the discipline imposed by her parentage. On March 27, 1789, Quaker records reveal, Sarah Bertier (late Bartram) was disowned by the church for marrying out of unity, and Elizabeth Miller (late

Wistar) was condemned for marrying contrary to discipline. Very different was Dolley's gleeful welcome of these unions. To a friend who had been her guest a year earlier she wrote:

"A charming little girl of my acquaintance, and a Quaker too, ran off and was married to a Roman Catholic the other evening—thee may have seen her, Sally Bartram was her name. Betsy Wistar and Kitty Morris, two plain [garbed] girls have left to effect a union with the choice of their hearts, so thee sees Love is no respecter of persons."[5]

Those lighthearted words gave no hint of the blow about to strike her family. Through the hard days of the late eighties, John Payne's meager capital dwindled. Money was scarce and living costs ruinous. In 1789 the starch business failed. Among Philadelphia Quakers financial solvency was part of godliness, and the Pine Street Monthly Meeting greeted Payne's misfortune by expelling him for failure to pay his debts. The two blows crushed him. He went to his bedroom and stayed there until he died, while his wife converted the home into a boardinghouse.

The failure tested the worth of a suitor and brought his wooing to a crisis. Dolley, one of her girl friends wrote, was likely to marry a young man named John Todd who had been her constant lover for many years and was never more faithful than during and after her father's trouble. There might be no radiant joy in such a union, but it gave assurance of quiet happiness and security.

Dolley and John, aged twenty-one and twenty-six, passed meeting for the first time on "fourth day" (Wednesday), November 25, 1789. That is, they stood up at the Pine Street Monthly Meeting and declared their intention of marrying. Another couple were married at that meeting, and the two events brought so big and gay a crowd of young people that somebody said it was like a playhouse. They crowded after Dolley, into a private room, disregarding the protests of the mighty Nicholas Waln, who at second meeting (December 23) was named along with James Bringhorst to supervise the wedding.

Eighty persons, representing leading Quaker families, signed the register as witnesses when the marriage took place on January

7, 1790. Among them were Eliza Collins and Anthony Morris, who found themselves face to face again at Dolley's funeral in 1849. It was said that they had been bridesmaid and groomsman at this wedding. At any rate, Eliza was Dolley's closest friend always.[6]

Toward the end of 1791, the Todds moved from a rented house to one of their own in Fourth Street between Chestnut and Walnut. Dolley gave birth to a son on the twenty-ninth of February. During the spring John Payne died, easing the family burdens. In the summer of 1793, fifteen-year-old Lucy Payne eloped with George Steptoe Washington, the President's nineteen-year-old nephew and ward, then a college student in Philadelphia. They went to live at Harewood, the young man's inherited estate in the Shenandoah Valley. The marriage caused grief to Mrs. Payne, who had warned Lucy of the church expulsion which swiftly came, but it was a fine thing for both of the George Washingtons. "In God's name," Uncle George had written when he first learned that he must support three orphans, "how did my brother Samuel contrive to get himself so enormously in debt?" After George S. went home as Lucy's husband, he put an end to the mismanagement of his father's estate, and won George Washington's confidence so completely that his $2,500 school debt was canceled and he was named as an executor of his uncle's will.[7]

On July 2, 1793, John Todd made his will, leaving all "to the dear wife of my bosom and first and only woman upon whom my all and only affections were placed . . . trusting that as she has proved an amiable and affectionate wife to her John, she may prove an affectionate mother to my little Payne and the sweet babe with which she is now enceinte."[8] That babe was born in August, and Dolley was not yet on her feet when yellow fever began its devastation. John Todd took his family to Gray's Ferry, where Mrs. Payne and her three young children also found refuge, then returned to the city. For two months he remained in the plague center, burying the dead, succoring the sick, writing wills for the dying, making brief trips to the Schuylkill to relieve his and his wife's anxiety.

Men, women and children died—hundreds in a single day—in

the hospitals, in their homes, in the gutters. "They have burnt tar in the streets, and taken many other precautions," Elizabeth Drinker reported. On October 2 John Todd's father died. On the twelfth he buried his mother. On the twenty-first Mrs. Drinker wrote: "A delightful, cool, frosty morning. 'Tis generally agreed that the fever is very much abated." Todd's work was finished. He would go back to his wife and children. He went, on the twenty-fourth, but the fever was in his veins. "I must see her once more," he cried to Mrs. Payne. And so he did, but before the afternoon ended he was dead.[9]

Soon Dolley was near death, and her infant son died. The natural supposition is that this was yellow fever too, but direct contagion was impossible and there was a striking absence of infection outside the city itself, where the mosquito carriers bred in water barrels behind every house. On her recovery Dolley went back to her empty home—a widow of twenty-five with a son less than two years old. Lucy and George Steptoe invited Mrs. Payne to live at Harewood. Apparently the mother left Philadelphia before the end of the year, taking Mary and John with her, but Anna probably remained with her older sister.[10]

Mrs. Todd was not barred long, either by widowhood or sorrow, from the pleasures of social life. Having an estate to settle, she made William W. Wilkins her attorney. He promptly fell in love with her, and in return was given the status of a brother. Senator Burr became her trusted friend and adviser. One spring day in 1794 Eliza Collins received this excited note from Dolley:

"Thou must come to me. Aaron Burr says that the great little Madison has asked to be brought to see me this evening."

From the tone of the message it is plain that this was no casual event. Madison was at the height of his fame. The affairs of the nation, with political storms to match, were revolving around him because of his retaliatory measures against Britain. He was "the great little Madison" to the whole country. And he was unmarried. There must be chaperonage, so she called in her closest friend, the fiancée of Congressman Richard Bland Lee.

Because of Aaron Burr's later reputation as a lady killer and the trust Dolley placed in him, their friendship has led to many harmless sentimental conjectures. On May 13, 1794, Dolley signed a will naming her mother and brother-in-law as executors, and Burr as sole guardian of little John Payne Todd. In the light of history, shining on the profligate pages of Burr's journal of his life in Paris, such a choice seems incredible. But he was then of better repute, and a constant visitor in Quaker homes. His wife, in New York, was fatally ill of cancer, though her death on May 18 of that year was unexpected. Not long before, advising ten-year-old Theodosia to record her scholastic progress in a daily journal, Burr sent her an imagined entry ending with: "Ma better—dined with us at table, and is still sitting up and free from pain." Dolley's estate, had her will become effective, would have provided for her son's care and education. The trait that made Burr seem a fitting guardian was that which caused a biographer to write that "he had a veritable passion for adopting and rearing children."[11]

It should not be assumed that Madison was totally unacquainted with Dolley Todd when he asked for this meeting. For several years they had been living less than three blocks apart—Madison one block north of the State House, Dolley two blocks east of it in Chestnut, later one block east of it in Fourth. She was a cousin of Congressman Isaac Coles of Virginia (whose wife witnessed her will), one of Madison's firm supporters. Both of the Todds were known in official circles. Abigail Adams turned to John when she wanted to find a position in England for an educated Negro. Former Congressman White referred to his acquaintance with Dolley when he congratulated Madison on his marriage. Certainly, if they had not met, they must have seen each other many times. He was either thoroughly in love with her before this overture or was ready to fall in love with extraordinary rapidity.[12]

At forty-three, Madison was not a "confirmed bachelor." He was an unwilling one, who had outgrown some of his youthful handicaps. No drawing-room favorite, he now had assurance and social graces—witness the impression he made on the unconventional Madame de Brèhan, the intellectual companionship (if nothing more) with Mrs. Colden. There was no timidity, no hurt memory of the 1783 jilting by Kitty Floyd, in his approach through an intermediary. He chose a method of introduction which virtually notified Dolley in advance that he was going to ask her to marry him. Burr was a natural emissary, the recent political break between Madison and Congressman Lee ruling the latter out.

That Madison worked fast is evident from what followed. A dubious story has come down in the Madison family, recorded by Lucia Cutts, that Mrs. Washington requested Dolley to come to see her and asked if it was true that she was engaged to James Madison. No, she thought not. Upon which Martha advised her that James would make her a good husband, all the better for being so much older. Whether or not this incident ever took place, the hesitating denial credited to Dolley fits the facts. When Madison set off in mid-June he was just short of a positive acceptance. His departure did not break the wooing. Dolley was to visit relatives near her old home in Hanover County, then go to her sister's place near Winchester, where it appears he was to meet her. But things went wrong. In Hanover she was stricken with severe illness, probably malaria. At Orange a young Frenchman named Antoine, Madison's guest, became deathly sick. To leave him might be disastrous, since he was utterly ignorant of English and nobody in the family except Madison understood a word of French. Beset with anxiety and frustration, the suitor was at last lifted to the heights by a letter from Dolley which settled their future. His reply, partly missing and almost worn out from much folding and handling, begins as follows:

"Orange Aug. 18, 1794. I received some days ago your precious favor from Fredericksburg. I cannot express, but hope you will conceive the joy it gave me. The delay in hearing of your leaving Hanover, which I regarded as the only satisfactory proof of your recovery, had filled me with extreme [illegible] inquietude, and the confirmation of that welcome event was endeared to me by the style in which it was conveyed. I hope you will never have another deliberation on that subject. If the sentiments of my heart can guarantee those of yours, they assure me there can never be a cause for it."

He explained the dilemma created by the plight of his French friend, which had upset the efforts and sacrifices he had made to meet her earlier than planned when they parted. "In the meantime allow me to hope that this unavoidable delay will not extend its influence to the epoch most"—the rest is gone.[13]

Dolley wrote another letter at Fredericksburg, to one who wished to be in Madison's place—William Wilkins. She wanted to know what property settlement to make on her son. And did she have his approval in this match? He met the test nobly:

"Mr. M——n is a man whom I admire. I knew his attachment to you and did not therefore content myself with taking his character from the breath of popular applause—but consulted those who knew him intimately in private life. His private character therefore I have every reason to believe is good and amiable. He unites to the great talents which have secured him public approbation those engaging qualities that contribute so highly to domestic felicity. To such a man therefore I do most freely consent that my beloved sister be united and happy."

The sentence did not end there. Somebody—presumably Dolley— scratched out the rest, but fading ink has made it decipherable: "and am satisfied that an honorable asylum is offered to my gentle friend who has been so undeservedly and vindictively persecuted and over whose safety I have long anxiously watched."

Wilkins then told his dear Julia (he called her that repeatedly though addressing the letter to "Mrs. Dolley P. Todd") something of his own feelings:

"Heaven is my witness that nothing is less selfish than my attachment to you. That I have not been insensible to your charms ought not I think to be regarded as a fault—few persons in similar situations would not have felt their irresistible influence; but none I will venture to say could have mingled in their emotions more true respect and more fraternal affection than I have."

As to a settlement—Mr. Madison was a man of genteel though not of large property who would not expect all of hers. Her house and stables in Fourth Street might be placed in trust for the sup-

port and education of her son, and conveyed to him when he
reached twenty-one. This, said the lawyer, would take care of a
critical situation. "The eyes of the world are upon you and your
enemies have already opened their mouths to censure and condemn you"—presumably for taking Todd property out of unity.[14]

To Eliza Collins Lee, who left in June on a honeymoon trip to
England, Dolley wrote on her wedding day that a settlement of
all her real property, with a considerable addition of money, had
been made on Payne "with Mr. M——'s full approbation. . . . You
also are acquainted with the unmerited censure of my enemies on
the subject."

James Madison and Dolley Todd were married at Harewood on
September 15, 1794. The Reverend Alexander Balmain of Winchester, whose wife (Lucy Taylor) was Madison's cousin, performed the ceremony before a small family group. Wrote Dolley
to Mrs. Lee:

"And as a proof, my dearest Eliza, of that confidence and friendship which has never been interrupted between us I have stolen
from the family to commune with you—to tell you in short that
in the course of this day I give my hand to the man of all others
I most admire. You will not be at a loss to know who this is as I
have been long ago gratified in having your approbation. In this
union I have everything that is soothing and grateful in prospect—
and my little Payne will have a generous and tender protector. . . .
Tell your dear Lee that he must not supplant D. P. T. in your
affections but suffer her whilst she deserves it to share with him
your ever valuable esteem. Adieu! Adieu! It is yet uncertain
whether we shall see you before the meeting in Philadelphia.
Mama, Madison, Lucy, George, Anna and Harriot join in best
love to you and yours.

                                        DOLLEY PAYNE TODD
Evening—Dolley Madison! Alass! Alass!"[15]

It was nearly three weeks before Madison notified his own
parents that the marriage had taken place. He could send a letter
only when his father's servant went home, and, said he apologetically, he couldn't spare Sam any earlier. His own course, prior to

the wedding, seems to have been governed by his theory that procrastination is the thief of bliss. He was able, during Antoine's convalescence, to make a flying trip to Monticello, where he alarmed Jefferson by saying that he wanted to drop out of Congress. Then to Harewood. "On my arrival here," he wrote to the senior Madison on October 5, "I was able to urge so many conveniences in hastening the event which I solicited that it took place on the 15th ult."

Four days after the wedding they set out with Anna Payne and Harriot Washington, spent a night in Winchester with the Balmains, and continued up the valley to Long Meadows Farm, near Strasburg, the home of Madison's sister, Nelly Hite. There Dolley came down with malaria, but "a decisive administration of the bark" expelled the complaint. Back to Harewood and then——

"In eight or ten days we expect to set out for Philadelphia. Your daughter-in-law begs you and my mother to accept her best and most respectful affections, which she means to express herself by an early opportunity. She wishes Fanny also to be sensible of the pleasure with which a correspondence with her would be carried on."[16]

Madison, Dolley, Anna and little Payne drove to Philadelphia over the route Madison had followed on horseback eight years before, through Harper's Ferry and over rugged mountain roads. The autumn foliage was at the height of brilliance, but there were drawbacks. Madison's carriage, "a very neat and costly one, was so infamously executed and suffered so much . . . that it is a perfect wreck," he informed his father. No coachmaker would give $100 for it though it cost almost four times that much. Writing to the Monroes of the new acquaintance who would be presented on their return from Paris, he added: "We are at present inhabitants of the house you occupied last winter, and shall continue in it during the session." Rent was half as much again.

The cost of living really hit Madison now. He had encouraged his father to buy a millsite, but how was he to help pay for the mill? He had some money coming in, he reported, to supplement a salary too small to live on. This would be enough for all pur-

poses were it not for the enormous expense of living and the need
to buy costly equipment. "Prices of all kinds are 50 per cent
higher than the last year, when they were thought to have reached
their ultimate point of extravagance." As a last resort, he could
sell his land in the Mohawk Valley, but the advice from there was
to hold it. At his suggestion his father sold his public securities,
then above par. Thus the elder Madison's work as wagon repairer
for the Continental Army supplied the deficit caused by the son's
need of a new carriage. Other deficits were taken care of too.
Unable to buy hams and bacon for Madison in Fredericksburg,
Joseph Jones sent half of his own supply; he also forwarded
chinaware shipped from Montpelier. Wanting something finer,
Madison induced Monroe and his wife to shop in Paris for second-
hand bed and window curtains, parlor curtains, two carpets, tea
and china sets, and such debris of the Revolution, but in the spring
of 1796 he was still looking for them "by every vessel that escapes
the British depredations."[17]

Dolley's house in Philadelphia had been rented for Payne's
benefit, and the little boy was to be brought up as a Friend. That
did not prevent the monthly meeting from expelling Dolley on
December 26, 1794, for marrying outside of unity—three months
after Eliza Collins Lee fared likewise. Dolley thus became the
sixth member of her family to be disowned in five years. Her
brother Walter, who headed the list, returned in 1787 from two
years in England. He was disowned in 1789 and disappeared from
family annals. Isaac was expelled for immorality on the day
Dolley and John Todd passed second meeting. William Temple
was put out two years later for entering the army. The father
and Lucy completed the list. On January 5, 1795, Elizabeth
Drinker entered in her diary:

"I heard this evening of the death of two of Molly Payne's sons,
Temple and Isaac—the latter offended a man in Virginia, who
sometime afterward shot him with a pistol."[18]

For the Madisons, marriage brought a new social life and a
stream of congratulations. "I hear with real joy," wrote Henry
Lee, "that you have joined the happy circle and that too in the

happiest manner. To your lady present my most respectful congratulations. She will soften I hope some of your political asperi-
ties." The last remark reflected Lee's own asperity as he hardened
into a Federalist.

Philip Freneau, living tranquilly in his boyhood home, promised
the Madisons "if not a costly welcome, yet a kind," should they
visit Monmouth. Horatio Gates offered to add the hospitality of
Rose Hill to other earthly felicities. Jefferson, emerging from a
two months' rheumatic disability, ended a short note with: "Adieu.
A thousand respects to Mrs. Madison and joys perpetual to both."
From John Francis Mercer came congratulations that Dolley had
induced Madison to become a Free Mason.[19]

The felicitations which came last harked farthest back. Charles
Pinckney, writing in 1800, recalled that he and Madison used
often (in 1787) to talk about matrimony. Said the Carolinian:

"I have much curiosity to see your lady. I have heard everything
I could wish of her, for certainly if ever a man deserved a good
wife you did. Had you unfortunately got, as Dr. Johnson says,
into a state of gennococracy (is it right spelt) or petticoat government, I know no man I should have pitied more nor none I could
have more sincerely wept over."

There was no petticoat rule in the Madison household, and no
male sway, but mutual deference and zestful outlook. The deep
love Madison felt was met first by admiration and liking, soon by
a love that matched his own. Jefferson saw from the first that
Dolley would be a major influence in Madison's life. Domestic
happiness might enforce the wish to retire from public office. To
counteract it, Jefferson dangled the Presidency before them both.
The political ship, he wrote in December, was nearing the end of
its leeward swing and would soon fetch up.

"Hold on then, my dear friend, that we may not shipwreck in
the meanwhile. I do not see in the minds of those with whom I
converse a greater affliction than the fear of your retirement; but
this must not be, unless to a more splendid and a more efficacious
post. There I should rejoice to see you; I hope I may say, I shall

rejoice to see you. . . . Present me respectfully to Mrs. Madison, and pray her to keep you where you are for her own satisfaction and the public good, and accept the cordial affections of us all."[20]

If the thought of retiring was still in Madison's mind, it vanished when rumors of such an intent were circulated through his district. "Perhaps I ought on many considerations to do so," he remarked to his father, "but I have said nothing from which the report could spring, and find myself constrained again to sacrifice both my inclination and interest."[21] That decision kept him at the center of a political struggle which was advancing from crisis to crisis. He was too much the unseen manager of party strategy, too little the popular symbol of democratic principles, and too devoted to Jefferson, to win or even seek top place in the fast-growing party of the common people. But now, in addition to a major national position and intimate personal and political alliances, he had fulfillment, harmony and happiness in his domestic life. Dolley Madison not only brought these to him, but made their home a radiating center of good will and gracious hospitality.

# CHAPTER XXXII

## Freedom in Jeopardy

Pennsylvania's Whisky Insurrection was at its dangerous anti-climax when James and Dolley Madison reached Philadelphia in October 1794. Violence was at an end, and public hysteria and military power were being channeled against democracy. The acute trouble started in July, when long resistance to the excise progressed from tar and feathers into shooting and house burning. The western militia swarmed to arms to aid the tax resisters. President Washington, deeply alarmed and spurred by Hamilton, called 15,000 men from four states into federal service, but Randolph persuaded him to delay the march and appoint commissioners to seek peaceful submission.

Moderate leaders induced the angry farmers to drop their guns and promise to refrain from violence. The government's demand for written pledges of submission was accepted in public meetings, but few individuals would confess guilt. So the army came on, led first by Washington as the symbol of national authority, then by General Henry Lee (governor of Virginia), with Secretary Hamilton going along as unofficial manager. They marched into a land showing no disorder or hostility. The leaders of violence had fled, but Hamilton had no intention of returning empty-handed.

Acting on the principle, as he explained to Washington, that "every man may of right apprehend a traitor," the Secretary induced army officers to ignore judicial processes and summarily "take hold of all who are worth the trouble." He would have liked but did not dare to fasten treason charges on Gallatin, H. H. Brackenridge (Madison's classmate at Princeton) and Congressmen Findley and Smilie, the quartet who had suppressed the insurrection by persuasion before the army arrived. Brackenridge, wrote Hamilton, was the worst of all scoundrels. Back to Philadelphia he sent bedraggled prisoners. Guarded by spick-and-span cavalry from the best families, they were paraded through the streets with the placard "Insurgent" stuck on their hats. Out of

150 arrested, two obscure farmers were convicted, and sentenced to death, but Washington pardoned them.[1]

Madison had no sympathy with the insurrection, though he remarked that many explanatory circumstances were imperfectly known. What he saw clearly was that resistance to law advanced "the business of despotism" through the use made of it by Hamilton. "You will perceive his coloring to all the documents which have been published during his mentorship to the Commander-in-Chief," he wrote to Jefferson. For the suppression of the affair Madison gave credit to the people in general, who, with a spirit truly republican, obeyed the call to vindicate the authority of the laws. To Monroe:

"If the insurrection had not been crushed in the manner it was I have no doubt that a formidable attempt would have been made to establish the principle that a standing army was necessary for *enforcing the laws*. When I first came to this city about the middle of October, this was the fashionable language."

Hamilton went infinitely farther, wishing by "a peace process of outlawry" to override the constitutional guarantees of civil liberty. To Rufus King he wrote from his military headquarters:

"The best objects of punishment will fly, and they ought to be compelled by outlawry to abandon their property, homes, and the United States. This business must not be skinned over. The political putrefaction of Pennsylvania is greater than I had any idea of. Without rigor everywhere our tranquillity is likely to be of very short duration, and the next storm will be infinitely worse than the present one."[2]

The President's annual message, read in Congress on November 19, left Madison in no doubt as to Hamilton's real aim. First came a denunciation of prejudice, passion and violence in the western counties, then these significant words:

"The arts of delusion were no longer confined to the efforts of designing individuals ... certain self-created societies assumed the tone of condemnation."

The tremendous weight of Washington's prestige was being thrown against the Democratic Societies. The damning epithet "self-created" indorsed the current notion that ordinary people had no right to come together for political purposes. These societies in general had no connection with the insurrection. Imitative of the Jacobin clubs of France, they were the scattered seeds of a national party. All were Republican, all pro-French, but in local matters they had the diversity of local interests and sentiment. Societies in western Pennsylvania supported the insurrection; those in other parts sent their members to help put it down. Madison gave Monroe his opinion of the official denunciation:

"The introduction of it by the President was perhaps the greatest error of his political life ... The game was, to connect the Democratic Societies with the odium of the insurrection—to connect the Republicans in Congress with those societies—to put the President ostensibly at the head of the other party, in opposition to both, and by these means prolong the illusions in the North and try a new experiment on the South."

"Porcupine" Cobbett left no doubt that this was the intent, and made Madison a principal target, when he republished the toasts drunk by French and American citizens in a Southern city in the previous February. They began:

"1. The Democratic Societies throughout the world—may they ever be the watchful guardians of Liberty.
"2. Citizen *Maddison* and the *Republican party* in Congress."

Madison had to choose between Washington's friendship and his own principles. Again he headed the House committee to draft a reply to the President, but Sedgwick and Scott were put on to control him. Hoping to keep out any reference to the societies, he made his draft as strong as possible on other points. It condemned the insurrection as a flagrant outrage and praised the President's efforts to restore order without bloodshed. Happily, the crisis had demonstrated that the great body of the people were as ready to crush licentiousness as to defeat usurpation:

"In a word, that they are capable of carrying into execution that noble plan of self-government which they have chosen, as the guarantee of their own happiness, and the asylum for that of all, from every clime, who may wish to unite their destiny with ours."

This, Madison explained to Monroe, was meant as an antidote to the poisonous move for military rule. In committee, he convinced Scott that silence as to the societies was best for the President's sake and for general harmony. When the draft was reported it ran into trouble. The Senate speeded a reply which drew from the President a further criticism of the societies. All this was rushed to the newspapers, said Madison, to influence the House.[3]

Promptly on Monday, Fitzsimons moved to insert a reprobation of the self-created societies. By a two-vote margin, the House struck out the word "self-created" and ruined the resolution. Concluding that total silence was now impossible because of the implied rebuke to Washington, Madison pushed a revision censuring "certain combinations of men" who had taken active part in the uprising. He assailed the original proposition. Congress ought not to interpose where it had no jurisdiction—within the reserved rights of the people. As quoted in the *Annals:*

"He conceived it to be a sound principle that an action innocent in the eyes of the law could not be the object of censure to a legislative body. . . . Opinions are not the objects of legislation."

It was proper, said Madison, that Congress should investigate persons in the public service; the Democratic Societies were not in it. Start criticizing people for abuse of their reserved rights and the censure might extend to liberty of speech and press. And what of the people who are thus condemned by Congress?

"It is in vain to say that this indiscriminate censure is no punishment. . . . Is not this proposition, if voted, a bill of attainder?"

He then laid down this fundamental rule:

"If we advert to the nature of republican government we shall find that the censorial power is in the people over the government, and not in the government over the people."

No harm could come from following that rule, for everything published in a free press would stand or fall by public opinion. An attempted reply came from Dexter, who warned against the prostitution of the press to "the base purposes of party and falsehood." Wild extremes of liberty would lead to anarchy and usurpation. Let slander run unchecked and "we shall need a master." For a moment, the enemies of free speech won. Forty-seven to forty-five, they put "self-created societies" into the new resolution. The Republicans, with the Speaker breaking a tie, then limited the application to four Pennsylvania counties. At that the Federalists gave up. The amended resolution received only nineteen votes and a harmless substitute was adopted.[4]

This result, Madison reported, was looked on by the Federalists as a Republican victory. But when the President, in a rejoinder to the House, called on the people to check the artful approaches to insurrection, no doubt was left in his mind that Washington was being used in a dangerous game.

"If the people of America are so far degenerated already as not to see, or to see with indifference, that the citadel of their liberties is menaced by the precedent before their eyes, they require abler advocates than they now have to save them from the consequences."[5]

If Madison felt pessimistic, Ames was despairing and angry. Speaker Muhlenberg, he charged, was a member of the Democratic Club and broke that tie to clear himself. "Madison and Parker are honorary members. Oh shame! Where is thy sting!" Time, Ames feared, was running against his side. State factions were spreading. Jacobinism and Gallomania were stronger in Congress than anywhere else. The best men were weary, and in danger of being driven out. If the government was not to prove utterly impracticable the people must save it "by excluding mobocrats from legislation." Let New England, then, move in a phalanx, while waiting for the South to reform.[6]

Though they did not know it, Madison and Ames were firing the opening guns in the great combat over the Alien and Sedition laws of 1798. Madison was well satisfied with the first political repercussions. To Jefferson at Monticello he wrote that this attack "on the essential and constitutional right of the citizen" was not having the effect intended. Edward Livingston was elected to Congress through the exertions of the Democratic Society of New York. The state delegation would be half Republican. New Jersey was ejecting its old congressmen. As to that Eastern phalanx:

"In Massachusetts . . . the two Republican members have stood their ground. . . . Ames is said to owe his success to the votes of Negroes and British sailors, smuggled under a very lax mode of conducting the election there. Sedgwick and Goodhue have *bare* majorities. Dexter is to run another heat but will succeed." (He ran four heats, and lost by eleven votes.)

In Pennsylvania the Republicans won nine out of thirteen seats, with Fitzsimons' defeat by Swanwick "a stunning change for the aristocracy." Virginia's two representatives who deserted republicanism (Griffin and R. B. Lee) were ousted. Two good Republicans, Henry Tazewell and Stevens T. Mason, were to succeed Senators Taylor and Monroe, resigned, but the Senate would remain overwhelmingly Federalist. Henry Lee came back from his Pennsylvania military campaign an ultraconservative. He toasted Madison at a dinner as a prelude to charging him with making "frequent remarks reflecting upon his reputation as an individual." Giles assured him that there had been no criticism except of his official acts and wrote to Madison that "his feelings are hurt beyond description from the late political occurrences."[7]

Robert Goodloe Harper, elected as a Republican, came up from South Carolina with a letter to Madison from Senator Butler, who, after Harper turned out to be a Federalist, wrote an abject apology for having introduced the miserable fellow. But when retiring Federalist Samuel Dexter sent Madison a note asking to be told in confidence why a man of Madison's talents and integrity should have changed his political position, he was promptly invited to Sunday dinner, as a prelude to being persuaded that there had been no change of principles.[8]

In Congress antialienism flared up when Madison submitted a naturalization bill requiring three years' notice of intention and five years' residence. The applicant must take an oath of allegiance and renounce his former ties. To Sedgwick these easy terms invited a duplication of the cruelties and assassinations inflicted upon England by the Saxon, Danish and Norman invasions. The big fight was over a Giles amendment requiring renunciation of titles of nobility. Dexter asked why they didn't extend that to the Pope and exclaimed that priestcraft had done more mischief than aristocracy. This brought Madison bouncing out of his chair.

"He did not approve the ridicule attempted to be thrown out on the Roman Catholics. In their religion there was nothing inconsistent with the purest republicanism. . . . They had, many of them, proved good citizens during the Revolution. As to hereditary titles, they were proscribed by the Constitution. He would not wish to have a citizen who refused such an oath."

The debate went on for days, the opponents trying to clog the amendment with an antislavery test. They were fearful of alien radicals and alarmed at the abolition of titles in France. Madison defended that action as essential to a republican revolution and offered a home comparison:

"The sons of the Cincinnati could not have inherited their honors, and yet the minds of the Americans were universally disgusted with the institution."

Unable to escape a roll call, the Federalists saw their ranks wither. Renunciation of titles was made compulsory, 59 to 32. This safeguard and the requirement of attachment to the Constitution, according to Madison, had reference both to aristocracy and licentiousness. "It seems not amiss that we should be on our guard against both extremes."⁹

Hamilton was resigning from the Treasury and in "an arrogant valedictory report," as Madison termed it, reported a plan for reducing the public debt which would require thirty years to produce results. Coupled with this was a frontier defense measure which did away with the prohibition against using regular troops for law enforcement. On January 16, 1795, Madison struck at both of these. Permanent taxes, he proposed, should be used for permanent purposes, including debt reduction, and the temporary taxes be applied to the Indian campaign. If the public was really to be freed of the evil of debt, there must either be excises or a general tax on property. He thought the prejudice against the latter could be overcome by a choice of different objects in different states—a land tax in some, other articles elsewhere. A million or two a year could be raised by this means.

Horror and exultation competed in Ames. Madison's proposal was the trick of a man out of power, "clamoring against excises and for the land tax, meaning really to do nothing." But he advised New Englanders to read the speech and see the purpose avowed, even though, "having heard that it will ruin them among our Yankees, they try to wrap up the land tax in the hypocrisy of a tax on *property*." That charge was forgotten by the time Ames got to a P. S. denouncing Boston Republicans:

"Unluckily too for them, Madison's speech, recommending land tax, comes out here on the day that the *Chronicle* asserts that the Madisonians are opposed to it."[10]

That term "the Madisonians" marked Madison's position in the party struggle of that day, as seen by his opponents. Jefferson was universally thought of as the presidential prospect, but for six years Madison had been the chief formulator and executor of Republican policies in Congress. The only rivalry between the two men at this time was in pushing each other toward the presidency. Jefferson began it with his appeal to Dolley to keep Madison in line for promotion. The most insuperable and obvious reasons, the latter replied, "shut my mind against the admission of any idea such as you seem to glance at." There was a great deal with respect to Jefferson which he would reserve for a free conversation. "You ought to be preparing yourself, however, to hear truths which no inflexibility will be able to withstand."

That brought from Jefferson a reassertion of his wish to see Madison become President. "I expressed it with entire sincerity," he wrote, "because there is not another person in the U. S. who, being placed at the helm of our affairs, my mind would be so completely at rest for the fortunes of our political bark." There were now, Jefferson continued, stronger reasons than ever why he was determined to reject all office high or low. His health was entirely broken down (from rheumatism), his age required him to put his affairs in a clear state, and above all else were the delights of his family life and his eagerness for agricultural pursuits. In the past only his enemies had discussed his supposed ambitions for the presidency. This was the first opening to say that he had none. "The question is forever closed with me." Instead of taking this as an avenue to his own promotion Madison saw it as an obstacle to be overcome.[11]

Pleurisy, which hit Dolley and Anna, and bad roads after that delayed the journey to Virginia after Congress expired in March. April was well advanced before the party set out. Madison's parents, aged seventy-two and sixty-three, now had their first glimpse of their new daughter-in-law, whom they knew through friendly letters to Mother Madison and sister-in-law Fanny. James and Dolley visited in Hanover County, where both had relatives, before the malaria season set in, and stopped at Monticello on the way. The senior Madisons spent a good part of the summer at Healing Springs. Wealthy Isaac Zane of Winchester, with less than three months to live, made his will on June 17 and bequeathed ten guineas apiece to Jefferson and Madison, with which they were "to purchase a memorial of our long and mutual friendship." When the complicated estate was settled, eight years later, Jefferson took a set of Zane's pistols in lieu of money.

In August Hubbard Taylor came in from Kentucky. He needed money for taxes on Madison land, but had learned nothing definite about the "mind"—some said a lead mind, others a silver mind—which was reported to be on or near the Sandy River tract. (A year later the man who knew about it came to see Taylor but refused to talk.) There was other business too. The late John Payne had left his widow Kentucky land warrants for 2,000 acres and Taylor was trying to locate the tracts. One appeared to be near the Upper Blue Licks and might be valuable. Things grew no simpler when it was discovered shortly after this that John Payne's uncle of the same name had likewise left his heirs 2,000 unsurveyed acres, and his son had mistakenly surveyed the property of his cousin's widow.

A friendly lawsuit, Taylor advised, would be necessary to divide

the lands jointly owned by Madison and the widow of his brother
Ambrose. Oral contracts made by Ambrose might bring difficulties. And one tough fight was looming. A man named John
Mays had made a survey badly overlapping the Madisons' 2,000
acres on Panther Creek. George Nicholas, the dear friend on
whom Madison bestowed the Kentucky district attorneyship,
bought Mays's claim and intended to sue for it. No more would
his sparrow-claw handwriting find its way into Madison's files,
marked "interesting" to prove that the letters could be read.[12]

Jay's treaty was now the great public issue. Signed in November 1794, it did not arrive until after Congress adjourned in March.
The President kept it rigidly secret, pending a special session of the
Senate called for June 8, but rumors of its contents had been rife
for two months. In February Madison wrote:

"I suspect that Jay has been betrayed by his anxiety to couple
us with England, and to avoid returning with his finger in his
mouth. . . . Those most likely to be in the secret of the affair do
not assume an air of triumph."

The curiosity and disappointment of the public at the secrecy, he
remarked later, could easily be guessed. Combining his own conjectures with information scraped up by Robert Livingston, he
sent Monroe a disquieting outline of the new treaty:

1. The western posts to be surrendered after June 1796, but to
remain open to British trade with the Indians.

2. Other 1783 treaty provisions to be executed, with American
and British losses from violations to be referred to commissioners.

3. Compensation for unlawful seizures at sea to be dealt with
judicially and diplomatically.

4. American and British ships to go on the same footing in
direct trade between Great Britain and the United States—wiping
out a ten-per-cent tax advantage to American vessels.

5. American craft under 100 tons, or possibly only under
seventy-five, to be admitted to the West Indies; this clause to
continue only four years.

From some circumstances, Madison said, he would not doubt
the limitation on West Indian trade if it were not so strikingly

revolting. It was late June before he was sure what was in the treaty. The Senate continued the secrecy—otherwise, wrote Butler, it could not be ratified. Convinced that this secret was "much safer with you than in the hands of many to whom it is confided," the Carolinian sent the sheets of the treaty to Madison as fast as they could be copied.

The compact appalled him. Aside from the agreement to transfer the frontier posts (already required by a previous treaty), its one valuable feature was the creation of bi-national commissions to settle boundary disputes and fix compensation for various kinds of losses, including British debts and unlawful seizure of American ships. Not a word about compensation for slaves. Nothing about impressment of seamen. The doctrine that free ships make free cargoes was given up. Tax preferences to American ships were wiped out. Contraband lists were extended. The West Indian trade was opened to American vessels under seventy tons, until two years after the current fighting should cease—a palpable device to use such vessels as a military aid against France. The United States agreed not to export sugar, molasses, coffee, cocoa or cotton. Sale of French prize goods in America was forbidden.

Worst of all, it seemed to Madison, was a clause granting favored-nation status to Great Britain with nothing whatever in return. What nation, he asked Livingston, would grant a trade favor to the United States, knowing that it must be passed along to Great Britain without being paid for? It would surprise nobody that so insidious an article should occur to Lord Grenville. But why did the American envoy concur?

"It seems impossible to screen him from the most illiberal suspicions, without referring his conduct to the blindest partiality to the British nation and government and the most vindictive sensations towards the French Republic."

Such a treaty, Madison declared, would have been scorned by the United States at the time of its greatest embarrassments. From one end to the other, it proved that the Federalists were "a British party, systematically aiming at an exclusive connection with the British government, and ready to sacrifice to that object, as well the dearest interests of our commerce, as the most sacred dictates of national honor."[13]

Washington withheld his signature. He disliked the treaty, but would sign if the Senate approved. By an exact two thirds that body ratified the treaty on June 24. In doing so it excepted Article XII and thus got rid of the vicious provision on West Indian trade and the ban on exports. A week later Senator Mason defiantly gave the treaty to the Philadelphia press, whence, wrote Madison, "it flew with an electric velocity to every part of the Union."

Urged by Livingston to write to Washington against the treaty, Madison replied that he had good reason for doubting the propriety or utility of uninvited communications from himself. However, the President must be aware of the universal feeling in Virginia, where even strong Federalists joined in the indignation. The national reaction he described in retrospect to Monroe:

"The first impression was universally and simultaneously against it. Even the mercantile body, with the exception of foreigners and demi-Americans, joined in the general condemnation. Addresses to the President against his ratification swarmed from all quarters, and without a possibility of pre-concert or party influence. In short it appeared for a while that the latent party in favor of the treaty were struck dumb by the voice of the nation."

Philadelphia and Boston chambers of commerce warned that rejection would result in war, but the President, Madison said, was shaken by the general reaction. Then came news of British orders, due to near-famine in France, for renewed seizure of American food ships. Washington agreed with Randolph that to sign the treaty now might confess the validity of the seizure order, and left for Mt. Vernon. Soon after came a startling and decisive incident.[14]

Informed by Randolph of the President's position, British Minister Hammond handed Secretary Wolcott an intercepted dispatch (received only six days previously) written in the fall of 1794 by French Minister Fauchet. Secretary Pickering translated it. After referring to certain "precieuses confessions" of Randolph concerning the Whisky Insurrection, it said that two or three days before the President issued his proclamation (of August 7, 1794), the Secretary of State came to him with an anxious countenance

". . . and made the overtures of which I have given you a detail in my No. 6. Thus with some thousands of dollars the Republic would have decided for a civil war, or in favor of peace. Thus the consciences of pretended patriots in America have already a price."

Wolcott, Pickering and Bradford called Washington back to Philadelphia. The President promptly signed the treaty, then put the letter before Randolph at a cabinet meeting. The Secretary protested his innocence, found himself disbelieved and resigned. From Fauchet, recalled to France and on the point of sailing, he received a sweeping exoneration. Randolph had told the minister that British agents were seeking to turn the Pennsylvania uprising into a civil war, and suggested that Fauchet counteract them through the talents of three or four of the men from whom he was buying flour for the French army. These men were likely to be in debt to British merchants and might be saved from harassment by early payments on their contracts. He had no suspicion that Randolph was seeking money for himself. The "pretended patriots" were those who would not aid their government unless given protection. Randolph published a long *Vindication,* including a passage from No. 6 which quoted him as saying that "four men" could avert a civil war, but might owe British debts. "Could you lend them instantaneously funds sufficient to shelter them from English persecution?"

This defense saved Randolph neither from the scurrilous epithets of "Peter Porcupine," the violent condemnation of Federalists, nor lasting suspicion. "Randolph's *Vindication,*" Madison observed in the wake of the Cobbett assault, "has just undergone the lash of the author of the 'Bone to Gnaw' "—an attack handled with satirical scurrility and enough plausibility to aid the plan of running him down. Madison's own conclusions about Randolph were definite:

"His greatest enemies will not easily persuade themselves that he was under a corrupt influence of France, and his best friend can't save him from the self-condemnation of his political career, as explained by himself."

Randolph was done to death, in reputation, by the malice of Pickering and Wolcott, the snap judgment of Washington and blunders in translation which have gone uncorrected to this day. Chief Clerk George Taylor of the State Department, translating No. 6 for Randolph, thought "momentanement" meant "instantaneously." The suspicion-breeding sentence should have read: "Can you lend them funds for the time being?"—a request perfectly fitting the suggestion of a prepayment of flour purchases. Pickering transliterated "precieuses confessions" into the evil-sounding "precious confessions." It means "valuable disclosures" and referred merely to indiscreet remarks about cabinet alignments. These things sharpened the reference to "four men," though these were plainly synonymous with the indefinite "three or four" of Fauchet's certificate, written from memory. To the Federalists, no more was needed: names could be supplied. Two days after Randolph resigned, Senator Butler wrote to Madison:

"There is a vile underhand game playing with a view of injuring unspotted characters. In this an attempt is making to implicate you. If I was to mention by whom, you would be surprised. 'Man is to man the surest sorest foe.' "

Randolph did not pen a line to Madison until the *Vindication* was on the press, to keep him clear of a defense which charged Washington with trying to destroy the Republican party. "But every nerve has been strained to combine your name in a business to which you were the most absolute stranger. I mean the insurrection, and a general revolution of government." Livingston told Madison of more specific slanders based on Fauchet's letters:

"The name of every man they wish to hunt down is inserted with the specific sum given to purchase him. I suppose I need not tell you that neither you nor Mr. Jefferson have escaped."[16]

Fauchet, it seems, was a good witness only when it suited Federalist purposes. He had said in his intercepted letter that Hamilton's financial system turned the whole nation into a stockjobbing, speculating, selfish people, that Minister Monroe was a patriot, "his friend Madison is also an honest man," and Jefferson was the presidential hope of their party.

Madison picked up some of this information at Fredericksburg (November 6, 1795) as he drove to Philadelphia with Dolley, Anna and Payne. It was a quiet trip except that, having borrowed an unmanageable horse from his brother William, he had to buy a substitute en route. Knowing the high price of feed in the national capital, he also bought twenty barrels of old corn at Fredericksburg and shipped them by water, along with two wagonloads of goods from Montpelier. In Philadelphia they moved into a three-story brick house (two rooms and a kitchen on each floor), in Spruce Street between Fourth and Fifth. Congressman Swanwick had secured it for them at £200 a year, and saw to it that the winter's supply of wood, ordered in advance by Dolley, was in the cellar. Still economizing, they sent three of their horses to board in the country at $4.00 a month.[17]

Not until now was the issue of Jay's treaty effectually before Madison. In August he had written an extensive analysis of it for several correspondents, but only second-rate writers publicly attacked the treaty. Meanwhile Hamilton went all out in its defense. Working jointly with King, he poured out a flood of articles signed Camillus. Even Jefferson burst into unwilling praise as he appealed to Madison in September:

"Hamilton is really a colossus to the anti-republican party. Without numbers, he is an host within himself . . . there is nobody but yourself who can meet him . . . For God's sake take up your pen and give a fundamental reply to Curtius and Camillus."[18]

Hamilton's technique was to defend the inoffensive treaty clauses, ignore the indefensible ones, and picture its opponents as a Jacobin rabble trying to foment a war with Britain. The result of rejection would be disastrous defeat, or, if not war, a total and disgraceful failure to stop the violation of American rights.

Madison saw no logic in Washington's decision to sign. How did Randolph's conduct, whatever it was, affect the merits of the treaty? However, he discovered a change in public opinion. As soon as the signing became known, he wrote to Monroe, "the British party were reinforced by those who bowed to the name of constituted authority, and those who are implicitly devoted to the President." Bank directors and British capitalists were coercing merchants to sign addresses of approbation. Exaggerated pictures of prosperity and the bugbear of war affected many, yet he felt that the real sense of the nation was still opposed to the treaty.[19]

His own plan of action was now taking shape. Jay's treaty would need legislation to put it into effect. Enlarging an idea he had expressed in the Virginia convention, he would assert the right of the House to pass independent judgment on that legislation, and thereby decide the fate of the treaty.

# CHAPTER XXXIII

## FIGHTING JAY'S TREATY

SURVEYING the political scene in December 1795, Madison felt uncertain whether the Republican gains would alter control of the House. He soon saw the Federalists, by a slim margin, oust Speaker Muhlenberg in favor of Jonathan Dayton. The other branch was so hopelessly Federalist that Senator Jackson did not hesitate to resign in order to clean up the bribe-taking Georgia legislature and rescind its scandalous sale of 50,000,000 Yazoo acres. The endangered speculators, he wrote, would try to sell their claims to Congress, but "I feel confident that neither the voice nor vote of a Madison will be engaged on the side of avarice and aristocracy." He didn't count on the Supreme Court, which denied the legislature's power to repeal an act of sale put through by bribery. Such action would impair a contract.[1]

Madison knew nothing about cabinet appointments. He would not have believed the report that Patrick Henry was invited to head the State Department, had not Congressman Coles been shown the letter from the President. Henry's Yazoo company had lost out to its corrupt competitors, but he made a fortune out of Georgia securities bought up as an intended payment. No longer antifederal, he was attached to the Union by the best Hamiltonian cement. Four others refused the State portfolio, so the President transferred Pickering to it, appointed James McHenry to the War Department, and named Charles Lee to fill the vacancy caused by the death of Attorney General Bradford. Jay had been elected governor of New York while still in England and Ellsworth became Chief Justice. Washington was completely surrounded by second-rate followers of the absent but active Hamilton. "Through what official interstice," exclaimed Madison, "can a ray of republican truths now penetrate to the President?"

As usual, the Virginian headed the committee to frame a reply

431

to the President's message. The report was delayed five days while he tried to cajole his two hostile associates, who were afraid to favor the treaty directly. Federalist policy was "to blazon the public prosperity, to confound the treaty with the President, and to mouth over the stale topics of war and confusion."

Sedgwick and Sitgreaves forced a passage into the reply which Madison believed would never be swallowed. It affirmed the confidence of the President's fellow citizens to be undiminished, "which will be denied by many who sincerely wish it to be the case." Enough did deny it to cause a recommittal. Madison accepted a general indorsement of treaties "compatible with our national rights and honor," on condition that they add, "with our Constitution and great commercial interests." This established the basis for his coming attack on the treaty itself.[2]

Ames, ill at Dedham, heard that Madison would have a majority, and cried out: "What are we to hope from a body so deeply infected with the spirit of folly or Jacobinism?" Jefferson at Monticello expected every post to "bring us the first movements of your campaign."

But Madison held off. His party had been put in a bad spot, he felt, by the conciliatory tone of the President's address (written by Hamilton) and the clever device of telling the House about the treaty without asking for necessary laws and appropriations. To bring the subject up on their own initiative, he told his friends, would antagonize treaty opponents who were particularly devoted to the President or to formalities. When the opportunity came they should strike hard and quickly. A clear majority disapproved of the treaty, he told Monroe, but it would dwindle "under the influence of causes well known to you."[3]

In the meantime the House was in a turmoil over a proposal blandly made by two agents of Canadian and American speculators. They wanted Congress to turn the Michigan peninsula over to a land company which would deliver two thirds of its stock to the members of Congress who voted for the bill. The House, with its big speculators most agitated of all, ordered the men arrested, refusing to pause for a single day to debate its jurisdiction. Madison was more alarmed over the punishment than the crime. A

part of the charge, he wrote to Jefferson, was based on the slanderous assertion that nearly a majority of the House had embarked
in the job. This was false, but was the House to punish slander
as a matter of constitutional privilege?

"What an engine may such a privilege become, in the hands of
a body once corrupted, for protecting its corruptions against public animadversion, under the pretext of maintaining its dignity
and preserving the necessary confidence of the public! . . . Apply
the principle to other transactions and the strictures which the
press has made on them, and the extent of its mischief will be seen
at once."

The case, actually tried by the House, evaporated for lack of
tangible proof that the stock was not to be paid for. But the
arbitrary effort at self-protection marked this as one more step
toward the Sedition Act, now only two years off.[4]
It was becoming evident, Madison wrote to Monroe in February, that the President would not serve beyond his second term.
"The British party had Jay first in view," but shifted to Adams
during the reaction against the treaty. His running mate would
be somebody to split the Southern vote.

"The Republicans, knowing that Jefferson alone can be started
with hope of success, mean to push him. I fear much that he will
mar the project and insure the adverse election by a peremptory
and public protest. The candidate for the Vice President is not
yet designated."

Here is evidence of informal party organization centering in
Congress, with Jefferson not the planner but the beneficiary of
the planning. Ties ran from individual senators and representatives to local leaders. Madison, Burr, Gallatin, Blount, Butler,
Baldwin, Dearborn, the Livingstons and some others could decide
on a presidential slate. The Federalist party was ruled by Hamilton and a coterie of conservative senators, bulwarked by eastern
merchants and the New England clergy, with its pulpit thunder
against atheists and Jacobins.
Reports came to Madison of order in France and victories under

a new general named Bonaparte. England, short of bread, was placing a bounty on foreign wheat and flour. The latter article had soared to $14 a barrel in Philadelphia and a shortage was feared. Said Madison:

"In this attitude of things, what a noble stroke would be an embargo! It would probably do as much good as harm at home, and would force peace on the rest of the world, and perhaps liberty along with it. But you know . . . the clamors that would be raised among the merchants, the millers and farmers, to say nothing of the Tories, etc., who would make more noise than any of them."[5]

Late in February the President laid two treaties before the Senate. To Madison that with the Algerines was "stamped with folly" because the tribute promised to the piratical monarch was to be paid in naval stores, outrageously undervalued. Thomas Pinckney's Spanish treaty, opening the Mississippi and settling boundaries, gave general joy. In everything bearing on the law of nations "it presents an honorable contrast to Jay's stipulations."[6]

In this moment of satisfaction the President sent Jay's treaty to the House, but still did not ask for legislation. Livingston lighted the fireworks by moving that the President be requested to lay Jay's instructions and correspondence before the House. That was Madison's plan, but prematurely offered and too abrupt. By his advice Livingston toned it down by omitting such papers as ought not to be disclosed. There was a cry that the House had no business with any treaty papers unless the purpose was to impeach the President or the envoy. Madison sought to hold the debate to the basic issue: Must the House pass any bills needed to implement a treaty, without consulting its own judgment? Smith of South Carolina epitomized the protreaty case: "Can the House repeal the treaty? No; then they must obey it."

Gallatin raised the constitutional issue, but full development of it awaited Madison's entry on the fourth day. Taken literally and without limit, said the Virginian, the legislative and treaty powers clashed. The powers to regulate commerce, declare war, raise armies and borrow money were specifically vested in Congress, but came within the scope of treaties. There were five ways of construing this relationship.

1. The two powers could be considered not to touch the same objects—but that would narrow the treaty power too much.

2. They could be considered concurrent and equal over the same objects—but that called for too much prudence and moderation in their exercise.

3. Each could be supreme over the other, when last exercised—but this involved the absurdity of an *imperium in imperio*.

4. The treaty power could be viewed as unlimited in its objects and completely paramount—the view of the Jay treaty supporters.

5. The congressional power could be viewed as co-operative with the treaty power, *on the legislative subjects submitted to Congress by the Constitution.*

If the treaty power was unlimited, President and Senate could put the United States into a war. The true construction left the power of making treaties with them, but required the sanction of the whole Congress in all cases which involved powers specifically given to that body. The House, in such matters, must exercise its reason. Otherwise it would be the mere instrument of the will of another department. An omnipotent treaty power was utterly inadmissible in a Constitution marked with checks and balances.

Ames, not yet strong enough to debate, thought Madison strangely wary in giving his opinion: "Conscience made him a coward. He flinched from an explicit and bold creed of anarchy." Sedgwick, trying to prove a reversal of Madison's views, read his strong affirmation in the Virginia convention that treaties were part of the law of the land. Actually, in the broad terms there used, he was claiming the supremacy of treaties over state law.[7]

Madison felt sure that the House would affirm its right to refuse to pass laws for executing a treaty which overlapped the legislative powers. Whether it actually would refuse in this instance was more doubtful. Sixty-two to thirty-seven, that body called for the treaty papers, and six days later received an aggressive rejection. The assent of the House being unnecessary, the President could not see that an inspection of the papers was relevant to any constitutional purpose except impeachment. Reading this unexpected, improper and indelicate refusal, Madison had little doubt "that the message came from New York"—that is, Hamilton wrote it. In reality it was drawn up before Hamilton's 4,000-word draft arrived.[8]

The Republicans caucused on April 2 and decided that Blount should offer a set of resolutions drawn by Madison. The House did not claim an agency in making treaties, but when a treaty dealt with subjects committed to Congress, it was the right and duty of the House to deliberate on the expediency of carrying such a treaty into effect. Also, when information was requested of the executive, relating to the constitutional functions of the House, it was not necessary to set forth the purpose for which the information was sought.

Expecting a climactic fight, Madison led off in debate. The President, he conceded, might withhold executive documents on grounds of safety, but the House alone could decide whether they were relevant to legislative objects. He agreed that the treaty power was exclusively vested in President and Senate. But the power of making laws was exclusively vested in Congress. No doubt it was true, as Washington had said, that the Federal Convention defeated a motion that no treaty should be binding unless ratified by a law. That had no bearing on a treaty which was not made effective by ratification. He challenged the propriety of an appeal to the convention, nine years dim in memory. Then he laid down the rule which for the rest of his life enabled him to escape from his 1787 nationalism:

"But after all whatever veneration might be entertained for the body of men who formed our Constitution, the sense of that body could never be regarded as the oracular guide in expounding the Constitution. As the instrument came from them it was nothing more than the draft of a plan, nothing but a dead letter, until life and validity were breathed into it by the voice of the people, speaking through the several state conventions. If we were to look, therefore, for the meaning of the instrument beyond the face of the instrument, we must look for it, not in the general convention, which proposed, but in the state conventions, which accepted and ratified the Constitution."

In 1821, when publication of the Yates notes revealed his nationalism as a framer, Madison admitted that in their anxiety over besetting dangers, he and others might have been inclined to give the Constitution too much energy. Regardless of that, it was the duty of all "to support it in its true meaning as understood *by the nation* at the time of its ratification."[9] If this argument was accepted, he could not lose. In the Virginia convention, he had allowed destructive amendments to be indorsed as a harmless sop to Antifederalists. Now, the desires of the State Righters were to be linked with the mollifying words and silences of the Federalists to produce something utterly alien to what was said and done at Philadelphia. His apotheosis of the state conventions was pure afterthought, to sustain his altered attitude toward federal power.

By a vote of 57 to 35 the House slapped the President and upheld its right to reject the Jay treaty. The Madisonians then moved to the concrete test—a motion to reject. The debate went on all through April 1796. Madison set the pattern and drew unceasing fire. He pointed out the lack of reciprocity—Americans to pay damages but receive none for mutual violations of the peace treaty. The terms for surrender of the posts would perpetuate British influence over Indians. He assailed the contraband lists, the relinquishment of freedom of the seas, the grant of equal rights to Britain in the Mississippi River, the one-sided commercial clauses.

To induce Great Britain to receive our raw materials (which she must have) and to sell us her manufactures (which she wanted to do) the United States was to give up the preferences which had built the American merchant marine. On West Indian trade, it abandoned the main objective for which the treaty was sought. Finally, if the United States on the basis of reciprocity extended favors to any other country, it must likewise extend them to Great Britain without getting a thing in return.

Having thus riddled the treaty, he attacked the continuing impressments and ship seizures. If, as the executive once declared, such practices jeopardized our neutrality and peace, what must be thought of giving effect to this treaty while they were going on? On the other hand, what would happen if they refused to carry the treaty into effect? The executive would seek a modification of the offensive passages. The idea of war was visionary and incredible. Was it conceivable that Britain, amid all her embarrassments, would wantonly attack her best customer, and cut off supplies essential to her dominions?[10]

Madison estimated on April 18 that he had a twenty-vote majority. But vast exertions were on foot. Merchants hoping for compensation for past losses, or fearful for their "floating speculations" (ships at sea), were circularizing the nation in support of the treaty. At the same time "the banks, the British merchants, the insurance companies were at work in influencing individuals, beating down the prices of produce [by refusing to insure ships] and sounding the tocsin of foreign war and domestic convulsions." A flood of petitions rolled in upon Congress, partly inspired by terror, partly by pressure. The banks, said Madison, were powerfully felt.

"Scarce a merchant or trader but what depend on discounts, and at this moment there is a general pinch for money. Under such circumstances, a bank director, soliciting subscriptions, is like a highwayman with a pistol, demanding the purse."[11]

The fear-of-war cry was echoed in Congress, and the debate was stretched out on Hamilton's advice to give effect to outside pressure. Ames's speech of April 28, the most eloquent of his career, has sometimes been called the decisive factor. With its frightening picture of war and destruction—Indians fattening the western cornfields with blood, midnight aglitter with burning homes, the desolating storm descending from Europe, and Jay's treaty a rainbow of peace at its edge—it was superlative demagogy. But it probably did not change a vote—the issue already was decided by the fever and delirium (the terms are Madison's) of which this speech was an oratorical climax.

As he saw his weak supporters succumb to the mercantile lobby, Madison tried to use what was left of his majority. They should drop the effort to reject the treaty, but, in accepting it, ram a condemnation down the throats of its supporters. Half a dozen anti-treaty extremists, led by Parker, would not yield an inch. In a race against time, Madison argued and pleaded. He must win at one end before losing more at the other. It was no use. "Before some were ripe for the arrangement," he wrote to Monroe, "others were rotten."

In committee of the whole, the House voted 50 to 49 to accept the treaty. In the House itself, Dearborn offered a preamble describing the treaty as objectionable and injurious but reciting reasons for acceptance. The ensuing fury confirmed Madison's belief that the treaty forces would regard this as a bitter defeat. "A few wrong-heads, however, thought fit to separate, whereby the motion was lost by one vote." The treaty was then accepted 51 to 48. Disgusted, Madison wrote to Jefferson:

"The progress of this business throughout has to me been the most worrying and vexatious that I ever encountered; and the more so as the causes lay in the unsteadiness, the follies, the perverseness and the defections among our friends, more than in the strength or dexterity or malice of our opponents."

He was ready enough to concede their strength and dexterity in the country at large:

"The people have been everywhere made to believe that the object of the House of Representatives in resisting the treaty was war, and have thence listened to the summons 'to follow where Washington leads.'"

Most damaging of all were the political results outlined to Jefferson:

"The New England states have been ready to rise in mass against the House of Representatives. Such have been the exertions and influence of Aristocracy, Anglicism and Mercantilism, in that quarter, that Republicanism is perfectly overbalanced, even in the town of Boston. I hope it will prove but a transitory calamity and that the discovery of the delusion will ultimately work a salutary effect."[12]

Before May was past, elections in New York, Massachusetts and other states had taken a wrong turn. A crisis, said Madison, which ought to have strengthened the Republican cause had crippled it.

France was expected to take hostile steps in consequence of the treaty, and every artifice would be used to blame the Republicans for that.

It seemed that Adams would be Jefferson's opponent. Madison did not know that Hamilton, fearing inability to control Adams and wishing to split the South, was working through King, Marshall and Henry Lee to induce Patrick Henry to run for President. On May 24 Marshall replied that Henry was "unwilling to embark in the business" because of the difficulties the holder of high office would face. Hamilton thereupon proclaimed Adams and Pickering to be his ticket, but wrote to King advising that they work to put Thomas Pinckney (popular because of his Spanish treaty) in place of Adams.

Neither party had fully settled on a vice-presidential candidate when Madison left for Virginia early in June, but Beckley wrote in a fortnight that Burr had the support of Gallatin, Rittenhouse and Chancellor Livingston, which assured him Pennsylvania and New York. Brown, Blount and Cocke were to line up Kentucky and the new state of Tennessee. "North Carolina and Georgia you know to be fixed," remarked Beckley—a statement which implied that Virginia was too.[13]

Madison learned also that Washington was to publish a Farewell Address. Hamilton had disclosed this, leading to the instant assumption that the American Catiline, as Beckley called him, would make it a campaign document. Madison no doubt thought of the retirement address he prepared for the President four years earlier. He would have been surprised indeed had he known that the draft which Washington gave to Hamilton for revision included the entire 1,200 words of the 1792 letter, within quotation marks. The President's own text began as follows:

"Friends and Fellow Citizens: The quotation which you will find in the following address was composed and intended to have been published in the year 1792 . . . but the solicitude of a few friends who were apprised of my intention and on whose judgment I did very much rely (particularly in one who was privy to the draught)* [footnote *Mr. Madison], that I would suspend my determination, added to the peculiar situation of our foreign affairs at that epoch, induced me first to hesitate, and then to postpone the promulgation; lest among other reasons my retirement might be ascribed to political cowardice."[14]

Hamilton, at a personal meeting, advised against naming Madison or using his draft as a quotation. Washington struck out the footnote and the clause to which it referred, but retained the Madison text. "I am attached to the quotation," he remarked as he sent the material to Hamilton for revision. Use of it would demonstrate that he had no intention of overextending the executive department, and thus reduce the pretensions of those who tried to build themselves up by a show of patriotic zeal and watchfulness.[15]

Recasting the address, Hamilton used nearly all of Madison's draft, most of it paraphrased, rewrote many of Washington's additions to it and inserted extensive passages of his own. The first ten paragraphs of the Farewell Address—about one fifth of the whole—are Madison's, but the germ of nearly all he wrote can be found in his notes of a talk with Washington on May 5, 1792, or in the latter's written request of May 20. Hamilton was given even more guidance. A comparison of the Washington, Madison and Hamilton contributions leaves no doubt that practically every important idea came from the President.

Not so the wording. Madison forged the link between Washington and the people, and gave the address its inspirational tone. Hamilton added force and amplitude—also partisan politics—to the advice about public affairs. The concluding personal passages are almost as Washington wrote them. Hamilton saved it from the appearance of a defensive maneuver against Republican critics of the administration, but made it an offensive weapon against them. It was partly owing to the change of form he gave it that the address (published, not spoken) became a great message to posterity.[16]

To Madison the address was all politics. The President had asked him in 1792 to condemn the spirit of parties. He wrote nothing on that head, while Hamilton inflated it to such proportions that Washington cut out much of what he wrote and still failed to exclude a partisan flavor. The advice against foreign entanglements stemmed from Madison's 1783 resolutions in the Continental Congress, but his 1792 draft was silent on that point. Washington dealt with it mildly and Hamilton sharpened the remarks. By the vehemence of his half-concealed attack on pro-French Americans he produced an isolationist doctrine more extreme than either he or Washington believed in.

Madison's opinion of the Farewell Address is contained in a ciphered passage written to Monroe on September 29, 1796. The letter which reached him was a duplicate in Dolley's hand, which came to light in a sale in 1934. Erroneously decoded and obscured by a scrawled interlining, its contents attracted no attention. The President's valedictory, Madison wrote, showed him completely in the snares of the British faction, laboring with all his might to prevent any improvement in commercial relations with France:

"It has been known that every channel has been latterly opened that could convey to his mind a rancor against that country and suspicion of all who are thought to sympathize with its revolution and who support the policy of extending our commerce and in general of standing well with it. But it was not easy to suppose his mind wrought up to the tone that could dictate or rather adopt some parts of the performance."

Monroe decoded "snares" as "sn duce s" and "dictate" as "nis c ta te,"[17] but he probably got the idea. One happening to which Madison thought it furnished a key was something he could hardly credit—the recall of Monroe from France. Actually that was inevitable after French policy turned as sour as Pickering's. In June of 1796 an American vessel conditionally sold to an Englishman and loaded with British-owned goods was followed to sea by a French privateer and seized. Bache's *Aurora* hailed this as the beginning of a new French policy brought on by Jay. How did the editor know this unless he had secret news from France? Monroe *must* be recalled, wrote Wolcott to Hamilton. "We must stop the channels by which foreign poison is introduced into the country or suffer the government to be overturned."

Remote Controller Hamilton suggested C. C. Pinckney to succeed Monroe, though "Sometimes I think of sending [Thomas]
Pinckney who is in England." C. C. was appointed (though France
refused to receive him) and a report was spread throughout the
United States that Monroe had faked a robbery of the American
legation to cover the misuse of government funds in huge speculations.[18]

When Madison first warned Monroe of these tales, the robbery
complaint was merely that he showed lack of caution. Thieves
broke into a locked storeroom in the house of Consul General
Fulwar Skipwith and carried off three silver ingots worth $4,371,
part of a $120,000 shipment to service the American debt in Hol-
land. Skipwith sent Madison the affidavits of consular officials
describing the robbery and attesting that the consul general, to
avoid a default on the debt, had replaced the loss out of his own
pocket. But when Skipwith drew on the Treasury for reimbursement, Wolcott dishonored the draft. If the government paid it
what would become of the story that Monroe had been using the
$120,000 in speculation, and the robbery was a fiction to explain
his delay in sending it to Amsterdam? It was not until Madison
became Secretary of State that Skipwith got his money back.[19]

In the fall of 1796 Secretary Pickering's suspicious nature found
something to play on—a letter in Italian which came to his office,
addressed by Philip Mazzei in Pisa to Secretary Randolph, inclos-
ing an unsealed letter to Madison which in turn covered one to
Jefferson. From a translation he concluded that Mazzei was trying to collect a large debt from Randolph, for support in his old
age, and had made the awful blunder of entrusting the debtor with
appeals to friends for aid in the collection. So he sent all the
letters to Madison, "that there may be a certainty that you and
Mr. Jefferson may receive your own." In reality Mazzei was
begging Randolph for a settlement of his accounts as European
agent for Virginia during the Revolutionary War, while the in-
closures dealt with Madison's ten-year effort to recover $2,700 for
Mazzei on a bad draft given him by Arthur Dohrman when
United States consul at Lisbon. Madison had induced Dohrman
to give a mortgage on a township of western land received in

settlement of his consular claims, and made every effort to avoid foreclosing when it became overdue. Just two weeks after Mazzei penned his last appeal Madison wrote that the ex-consul had closed the business "in a just and honorable manner." Dohrman's closing comment to the collector was: "I shall ever remember your humanity."[20]

Such was the political temper of America as the presidential election came on—Adams and Thomas Pinckney against Jefferson and Burr. It has generally been assumed that Jefferson, after telling Madison he would not run, was prevailed on to agree with real or feigned reluctance. He was not even asked. Madison had been home more than three months, and the election was only six weeks off, when he made this statement to Monroe in his long-buried letter of September 29:

"I have not seen Jefferson and have thought it best to present him no opportunity of protesting to his friends against being embarked in the contest. Whether he will get a majority of votes is uncertain. I am by no means sanguine. His enemies are as indefatigable as they are malignant."

In spite of politics, Madison plunged into farm work. His father had been disabled by sciatica since early spring, barely able to stand or walk. James, Jr., dinned at him to enrich the soil by planting clover. Rotation was an absolute necessity—grain, rest and red clover, with all the help that manures could supply. In a few years, he was persuaded, people would be as careful to sow clover as to sow wheat or rye, and make equal sacrifices to procure the seed. Having none, he ordered his overseers to plant timothy seed and even the sweepings of the hayloft on the exhausted land, to convert it into pasture.

Madison supervised the building of the new flour mill on the Rapidan while his parents spent many weeks at Healing Springs. He was still unable to help finance it. His Mohawk lands had been sold, but the $5,250 received for them was earmarked for use in Philadelphia and to remodel the family home.[21]

This last step reflected a major decision. Madison was about to retire from Congress. He was tired of being an opposition leader, he was intensely interested in experimental farming, and he wanted to be at home with Dolley. Offered a unanimous election as governor of Virginia, he rejected the overture.

An easy ride over the best roads Madison had ever known brought the family to Philadelphia on November 21. They rode into a housing problem, not eased by the fact that twenty-two-year-old Fanny Madison came along for the winter. The house in Spruce Street had been given up. The one Dolley owned was rented to General Stephen Moylan. John Beckley had scoured the city, but every new house was taken before it was finished. The enlarged family finally crowded into cramped quarters and struggled to stow away the furniture, including a sea-soaked shipment sent by Monroe from Paris.[22]

By this time the threat of war with France had further damaged the Republican cause, already tagged with the British menace. In October Minister Adet served notice that his country would treat American ships as the United States allowed them to be treated by Great Britain. Imitating Genêt, he gave his letter to Bache's paper and exhorted Americans to stand with France. Madison described the results to Jefferson:

"Adet's note, which you have seen, is working all the evil with which it is pregnant. Those who rejoice at its indiscretions and are taking advantage of them have the impudence to pretend that it is an electioneering maneuver, and that the French government have been led into it by the opponents of the British treaty."

Madison seemed more concerned with the international conflict itself. Unless healing measures were taken in both countries, enemies of France and America would bring about their perpetual alienation. As he wrote this, in early December, the election was still in doubt. The North was going for Adams, Pennsylvania and the South for Jefferson, with Maryland and Delaware cutting over to produce a Federalist majority. But Madison saw a distinct possibility that Hamilton's intrigues would give the presidency to Pinckney, under the system by which each elector voted for two candidates for President, the second highest becoming Vice President. South Carolina, solid for Pinckney, was expected to give its second votes mostly to Jefferson. To be sure of beating him, Hamilton urged, New England must vote solidly for Adams and Pinckney—advice which could not fail to put Pinckney on top. The Adamsites responded by throwing away twenty-one Pinckney votes, making Jefferson an easy winner for Vice President. Adams seventy-one, Jefferson sixty-nine, Pinckney fifty-nine, Burr thirty— that was the result of a faulty electoral system made worse by plots and counterplots.

As he saw this approaching, Madison directed a strong appeal to Jefferson. He *must* reconcile himself to second place, as well as first, and take either if the country called him. Hamilton feared that Adams was too headstrong to be a fit puppet. The intrigues for Pinckney had turned Adams against the British faction. He was said to be talking of Jefferson in friendly fashion, due to fair treatment during the campaign. For these reasons, Jefferson's nearness to Adams might have a valuable effect on his councils. "It must be confessed," he added in a prophetic understatement, "that all these calculations are qualified by his political principles and prejudices."[23]

The reaction was more than Madison bargained for. He received from Jefferson the draft of a letter addressed to Adams, expressing unfeigned pleasure at the latter's victory. After noting that Adams might yet be cheated "by a trick worthy the subtlety of your arch-friend of New York," he said he would "leave to others the sublime delights of riding in the storm, better pleased with sound sleep and a warm berth below, with the society of neighbors, friends and fellow-laborers of the earth, than of spies and sycophants."

This was sent open for Madison's perusal, to be forwarded or returned as he thought best. The alarmed recipient replied with his usual care for Jefferson's feelings. Owing to want of confidence in himself, he was suspending delivery of the letter until Jefferson should pass on certain reasons for not sending it. Relations with Adams being good, was not the idea of bettering them outweighed by the possibility of making them worse? There was a certain air in the letter which betrayed Jefferson's difficulty in writing it. Might not the remark about riding in the storm be misconstrued to reflect on anybody who took the helm? "You know the temper of Mr. A. better than I do, but I have always conceived it to be rather a ticklish one." What would be the reaction of men who had risked the President-elect's enmity by their zeal for Jefferson, if they were told their candidate was glad to be defeated? Some of them were already sore on this head. And if Adams went wrong it might be very embarrassing to have a written testimonial of compliment and confidence in his possession. The letter was not sent.[24]

This time Madison did not head the committee on the President's message. He and Baldwin formed the Republican minority. The message informed Congress of extensive injuries to American shipping by French cruisers, but said it was the President's ardent desire to maintain cordial harmony with France. It was Madison's desire to nurse this moderation by avoiding altercation in the House. Peaceful words in the reply brought a rejoinder in kind from Washington and gave him hope of healing policies in the critical remaining weeks of the administration. "Yet I cannot look around at the men who counsel him," he wrote to Jefferson, "or look back at the snares into which he has hitherto been drawn, without great apprehensions on this subject."[25]

In these last weeks Madison made a futile attempt to realize the dream of a National University in the new capital. Washington, Commissioner White told him, was offering his Potomac Canal stock as an endowment. Congress would refuse a grant of money, so all they wanted was an act setting up a body to receive donations. For one flickering moment old times came back, as Washington asked Congress for action and handed the commissioners' memorial to Madison. To outwit the economy bloc, his report on it specified only that they "enroll proper persons to receive in trust" donations for "a University within the District of Columbia." Just a public body to sponsor a private seminary. What! exclaimed Nicholas, would this be done for any ten-mile area? The gifts were "to the use of the United States—to the support of a National University." Begin it, and the dignity of government would require that it be finished with public funds.

That was of course the truth. Madison might as well have quoted the words in which White presented the project to him:

"The utility of a National University seems generally admitted, and that it ought to be established at the seat of the general government will hardly be contested." The motion to foster the institution was postponed, 37 to 36. Nobody pointed out to Madison that the visible part of his project contravened his contention that Congress had no power to set up corporations, and that the invisible part of it was out of harmony with his strict interpretation of the "general welfare" clause.[26]

There was sardonic pleasure in Madison's reaction when the crisis with France resulted in higher naval appropriations and these produced a demand for direct taxes. His party was willing to have the three (cut from six) long-delayed frigates completed, but didn't want them equipped and sent to sea to start a war they couldn't finish. The decision was to complete them. The Federalists, he commented, first made direct taxes odious, then made them necessary, and were so nauseated by their own project that it would probably miscarry. He was ready to support a direct tax on land, provided a tax on slaves accompanied it to equalize the load in the South. His party, aided by half a dozen mild Federalists, carried the proposition 49 to 39, while he watched the New England hardshells "sneaking out of the difficulty" by a negative vote which they thought would give them the tax but let them enjoy the popularity of having opposed it. They finally squirmed out altogether by raising customs duties.[27]

The anxiety with which Madison awaited Washington's special message on France was made doubly acute by Secretary Pickering's publication of his own belligerent reply to Adet. Madison described the result:

"The British party, since this overt patronage of their cause, no longer wear the mask. A war with France, and an alliance with Great Britain, enter both into print and conversation; and no doubt can be entertained that a push will be made to screw up the President to that point before he quits the office."

The new British minister, Robert Liston, rejoiced to his chief that "the men of fortune, of weight and of character begin so generally to look forward to a close connection with Great Britain as the only wise system of American politics." He described Pickering as "one of the most violent anti-Gallicans I have ever met with."

Washington's brief message of January 19 had the familiar tone of conciliation. It was the 30,000-word letter accompanying it, addressed by Pickering to Minister Pinckney in Paris, that filled Madison with alarm. Here was no healing lotion but the fester of an incurable gangrene. Adding it to the provocative language and actions of the French, it seemed that the only hope for peace lay in the President-elect, but he knew little of his mind and derived little consolation from what he knew.

What should be done by the House about Pickering's "corrosive letter"? Silence might look like approbation, but a motion to disapprove could not be safely risked. There was still time for remedial steps by Washington. What were they? A January letter to Jefferson pointed to a method but not an expectation:

"It has got into the newspapers that an envoy extraordinary was to go to France, and that I was to be the person. I have no reason to suppose a shadow of truth in the former part of the story, and the latter is pure fiction."[28]

The fiction was half-prophetic. On February 26, Hamilton wrote to Sedgwick (now a senator) that if he were Mr. Adams his first step would be to name Madison, Pinckney and Cabot as an extraordinary mission to the French republic. The mission would need "a man as influential with the French as Mr. Madison, yet I would not trust him alone, lest his Gallicism should work amiss." Fisher Ames carried the Cabot suggestion to Adams. On March 2, Jefferson arrived to be sworn in. His prompt call on Adams was returned the next morning "at Mr. Madison's, where I lodged." Explaining the danger of a rupture with France, Adams said he had concluded to send a mission. Would Jefferson go? No. Assuming that to be the case, Adams "had determined to join Gerry and Madison to Pinckney, and he wished me to consult Mr. Madison for him." Jefferson promised to do so, but held out no hope, as Madison had refused the place when Jefferson retired, though Washington held it open a twelvemonth for him.

Adams had just held his first cabinet meeting when Jefferson informed him of Madison's refusal. It was welcome news, for the new President said with embarrassment that objections had been raised which he had not contemplated. Those objections were described by him in 1809 in a belated reply to Hamilton's pamphlet attacking his administration. Having long wished to avail himself and the public "of the fine talents and amiable qualities and manners of Mr. Madison," he planned to send him and Hamilton to France. After the talk with Jefferson, he broached the subject to the Secretary of the Treasury:

Wolcott: Is it determined to send Mr. Madison?

Adams: No; but it deserves consideration.

W: Sending Mr. Madison will make dire work among the passions of our parties in Congress, and out of doors, through the states.

A: Are we forever going to be overawed and directed by party passions?

W: Mr. President, we are willing to resign.

"I had said nothing that could possibly displease," Adams lamented, "except pronouncing the name of Madison." Had he let them resign, he would have saved himself an infinite amount of trouble, and would have had a good chance to avert the undeclared war with France, insure his own re-election and postpone the "second revolution" until Jacksonian democracy began marching. But he succumbed, as Jefferson's biographer Randall remarked, and his political fate was sealed.[29]

On March 4 Madison became a private citizen, but the rumor of his diplomatic appointment spread. The *Nouvelles Politiques* of Paris announced on April 3 that he had arrived in that city the day before. Thomas Paine read this at Le Havre just after a Boston ship captain who had sailed March 10 told him the appointment was expected. In a letter which Madison never received, Paine sent his congratulations and condolences.

"Individually as Mr. Madison you will be welcome; but as the French government now know that Mr. Monroe was sent with a lie in his mouth they will suspect that this is a second trick of the same kind. . . . If [your instructions] are the least petulant and you act on them, my opinion is they will send you away."

Had Jefferson been elected President such an appointment would have been consistent. But with Adams put in to support the British treaty the French would conclude (said Paine) that Madison was sent to play a contrary game to the treachery and insolence of the clownish Timothy Pickering—"for of all the clowns that ever were entrusted to write public dispatches he is the worst."[30]

Meanwhile Madison warned his father that if Jefferson stopped in Orange and made any effort to put him into the state legislature, it should have not the slightest effect. He was waiting then for March winds to dry the rain-soaked roads. Ahead, by water, he sent five bushels of precious clover seed. After him, by the same route, went eighteen chairs, sixteen boxes and trunks and twenty bundles of nail rods. Overseer Collins came to Philadelphia with extra horses to take part of the load.

Madison and his personal party—Dolley and her sister Anna, Fanny Madison and five-year-old Payne Todd—took the westward route through Harper's Ferry. They would visit Mrs. Payne and Madison's relatives. The roundabout way and leisurely pace of this return journey were symptomatic of the coming years. Freed of the relentless pressure of public affairs, James and Dolley were ready to settle into the quiet occupations of rural Virginia.[31]

# CHAPTER XXXIV

## THE VIRGINIA RESOLUTIONS

DEEP green forests were broken by the brightness of pastures and young wheat fields when James and Dolley Madison drove into their home acres in May of 1797. The meager national news was more ominous than surprising. John Dawson, the new congressman, was "sorry to find all your apprehensions verified" by the warlike address of President Adams to a special session of Congress. Jefferson filled out the story.

C. C. Pinckney's dispatches told of studied affronts by the French Directory before he was expelled from the country, and drastic new orders for the confiscation of American ships. By the time the special session opened the war fever had been sharply cooled by the failure of the Bank of England. Adams called passionately for the arming of merchant vessels and extensive military and naval preparations, but said he intended to send a new mission to seek a peaceful understanding.

Before the end of May C. C. Pinckney, Marshall and Francis Dana were named. A Virginia congressman, asked by Attorney General Lee whether Marshall would be acceptable, replied that Madison was preferable. "Nobody of Mr. Madison's way of thinking will be appointed" was the answer. On that, the holdover cabinet still ruled. When Hamilton tried late in March to have Madison included, this was Secretary Wolcott's answer:

"I have no confidence in Mr. Madison; he has been a frequenter of Adet's political parties. I have been just informed that Adet has suggested the idea of sending this gentleman. . . . If the government suffers France to dictate what description of men shall be appointed to foreign courts, our country is undone. . . . Mr. Madison would insist upon a submission to France, or would obstruct a settlement and throw the disgrace of failure on the friends of government."

Hamilton stuck to his position. The victories of Bonaparte might lead to a general peace. Where would that place the United States in the event of a rupture with France? A mission to that country must include one man in whom both France and the American opposition had full reliance. What risk could there be in sending Madison, if coupled with others? His intrigues could not operate, and anyway it was "possible that too much may be taken for granted with regard to Mr. Madison."

Jefferson saw things from a different angle. The brilliant successes "of that wonderful man Bonaparte," he remarked to Madison, were likely to restore peace to Europe and thereby preserve it for the United States, which otherwise would be pushed into war in six months by the anti-Gallic rage. With Austria knocked out of the coalition, Congress defeated its main military bills and adjourned, wondering why it had been called.[1]

A July 11 entry in Jefferson's account book, "Mr. Madison's valet .25," dates a long talk on foreign and domestic affairs. Three Virginia congressmen had gone over to the Federalists, taking the balance of power with them. Congress was more pacific than the executive, Adams more so than his cabinet. It was cheering that the President had disregarded his counselors and appointed Gerry—a friend of France—to the special mission when Dana declined. They talked of so many things (so Jefferson wrote on August 3) that he did not bring up the letter to Philip Mazzei imputed to him in the newspapers—a letter which in substance was his, though changed considerably in translations from Italian to French to English. A monarchical Anglican party including the executive, judiciary and most of Congress, wrote Jefferson to Mazzei, had supplanted the American love of liberty with the forms of the British government and wished to add the substance.

"It would give you a fever were I to name to you the apostates who have gone over to these heresies, men who were Samsons in the field and Solomons in the council, but who have had their heads shorn by the harlot England."

The published version, with its errors, could neither be avowed nor disavowed. Should Jefferson explain it or say nothing? His reference to the "forms" of the British government, which meant, he said, its birthdays, levees and inaugural pomposities, had been changed in print to "form," making him seem hostile to the Constitution. It would be impossible to explain this publicly "without bringing on a personal difference between General Washington and myself."

Monroe, in a letter now sent for Madison to read, urged Jefferson to avow and defend the missive. Answers to partisan challenges, Madison replied, were likely to bring on unforeseen dilemmas. Washington was silent for years about forged letters imputed to him. "Mr. Adams has followed the example with respect to Callender's charge, probably well founded, of advising the extermination of the Tories." (Those spoon-feeders of posterity, Madison's editors, expurgated "probably well founded" from his published *Letters* and omitted the whole letter from his *Writings*.) If Jefferson said anything, the popularity of Washington was likely to make more converts against him than the explanation would make for him.

The silence lasted until 1824, when Jefferson denied to Martin Van Buren that the reference to Samsons and Solomons was aimed at Washington: he had in mind the Cincinnati generally. Historian Hildreth called this a subterfuge, since Jefferson had written to Madison that the letter could not be avowed without bringing on a personal difference with Washington. In reality, Jefferson wrote that he could not explain the word "form" without bringing on this personal difference—convincing evidence that he did not think of Washington in connection with the harlot-shorn Samsons.[2]

In December the President renewed his call for military preparations. Even his tone was evidence to Madison of further apostasy from Revolutionary principles, but he had hope that the tide of evil was near flood and would soon ebb back. He was at Richmond (having joined Dolley in a visit near by) when first reports came via Norfolk about the envoys in France. War seemed near, and many feared that it would enable Britain's partisans to warp the public mind toward monarchy. At least, Madison commented, that was a useful argument for peace.

At home in February 1798, Madison received better news from

Jefferson. Talleyrand, back from exile, was now foreign minister of a country moving from revolution into imperialism. He disliked the American claims but was reported to have said there would be no declaration of war by France. Madison still saw two great obstacles—the lack of a cordial spirit on either side, and the difficulties produced by the British-American treaty. It was admitted by the House of Representatives that American policy should put France and England on an equality.

"How can this now be done? In one of two ways only: either by dissolving the British treaty, or by stipulating with France that she may plunder us, as we have stipulated that Britain may plunder us."

The first course was obviously unwise. France could not agree to the second without formally giving up the principle that free ships make free goods. She would be better off, Madison concluded, to equalize conditions by retaliation. Should that course be followed the United States either (1) would have to go directly to war, or (2) go to war indirectly by arming and convoying merchant ships, or (3) attempt some defense through commerce regulation. The people would not tolerate the first. The third probably would hurt Britain and America more than France. "The second expedient I conclude therefore will be persisted in."

Here was not only a forecast of the undeclared war on France, but analytical proof that Jay, Hamilton, Pickering, Wolcott and Adams had put the United States into a hole from which (Adams being what he was) there was no other escape. Madison followed with a scathing comparison of the first and second Presidents— "the one, cool, considerate and cautious; the other, headlong, and kindled into flame by every spark that lights on his passions"; Washington a hero in the field, Adams a perfect Quixote as a statesman. The contrast, he remarked, might be pursued much further, the one shunning European connections, the other offering America as a makeweight in the balances of power—

"the avowed exultation of W[ashington] in the progress of liberty everywhere, and his eulogy on the Revolution and people of France posterior even to the bloody reign and fate of Robespierre—the open denunciations by Adams of the smallest disturbance of the ancient discipline, order and tranquillity of despotism."[3]

In April came word of the attempt by Talleyrand's agents (dramatically unidentified as X, Y and Z) to collect a $250,000 bribe from the American envoys. Madison found this almost incredible—not so much for its heinous depravity as its stupidity. How could a man of sagacity, who lived in America throughout the violence at home, fail to realize that such a proposal would be used to widen the breach between the two countries? He would applaud the delivery of the diplomatic dispatches to Congress, he told Jefferson, if it were not evident that the purpose was to inflame the public mind. Their publication a few weeks later by order of the President and Senate seemed to blast every chance of an accommodation with France.

"After this stroke in the politics of those two branches of our government, no one who has not surrendered his reason can believe them sincere in wishing to avoid extremities with the French Republic; to say nothing of the internal views to which they mean also to turn this extraordinary maneuver."[4]

Madison was disturbed at the ease with which the war party used the dispatches to put their military measures through Congress, and still more so at the way Adams was cracking the constitutional barriers against executive war power. By withdrawing his order against the arming of merchantmen, he indirectly authorized that course—something Congress alone had power to do.

Now came alarming information from Jefferson. A bill giving power to send away suspected aliens was being offered in the Senate. One of the war party had disclosed "in a fit of unguarded passion" that there would likewise be a sedition bill, designed to suppress the Whig press, especially Bache's *Aurora,* which had been violently assailing Adams. Freedom of the press, Madison replied, was the only remaining check to desperate projects. The sanguinary faction had better not "adopt the spirit of Robespierre without recollecting the shortness of his triumphs and the perpetuity of his infamy."

A week later, Fenno's pro-Adams *Gazette* was the only paper to come by post. "I hope the bridle is not yet put on the press" was Madison's comment. Another week and the Senate's alien bill arrived—"a monster that must forever disgrace its parents." Yet perhaps these excesses were for the best. The enemies of the people might do more to open their eyes than all the arguments of their friends. As for the President, his language to the young men at Philadelphia was the most abominable and degrading that ever fell from the lips of a Revolutionary patriot. Madison could see now what Adams meant by a remark to him "that there was not a single principle the same in the American and French Revolutions"—to which he had added, when reminded that Washington expressed a contrary sentiment, "that it was false, let who would express it." Abolition of royalty, Madison concluded, was not one of Adams' Revolutionary principles.[5]

He surveyed the President's measures. His law for capture of French privateers meant that war actually was on. The bill suspending commerce with the French dominions was a notice of intent to starve France, while Britain would be fed at the expense of American farmers through the downward plunge of flour prices. A land tax was being imposed at the very moment that ability to pay it was being annihilated. And the answers of Adams to an address of protest formed the most grotesque scene in the whole tragicomedy.

"They present not only the grossest contradictions to the maxims, measures and language of his predecessor, and the real principles and interests of his constituents, but to himself. He is verifying completely the last feature in the character drawn of him by Dr. F[ranklin], however his title may stand to the two first, 'Always an honest man, often a wise one, but sometimes wholly out of his senses.'"

Madison made this comment one month before Adams' vanity and passion, and the general Federalist fury, culminated in the signing of the Sedition Act. Though counting on a political revolt against this, Madison took a grave view of the immediate zeal for persecution. The Federalist Harper, on the floor of Congress, had charged that Monroe was bribed by France, but every demand by the latter for disclosure of the reason for his recall was rejected by Pickering and Adams. Asked for his advice, Madison told Monroe that he should give no opening for his enemies to wreak party revenge on him through the forms of the Constitution. Though out of office, he might still be impeached.[6]

Under the Sedition Act, it was a penal offense to publish any false, scandalous and malicious writings against the government, President or Congress, with intent to bring them into disrepute or stir hatred against them. The first man sent to prison under this act was Congressman Matthew Lyon of Vermont, whose sedition consisted of the publication, after the act passed, of a letter written earlier, in which he charged President Adams with a grasp for power, thirst for adulation and selfish avarice. The trial gave full notice of what Madison already knew, that the Sedition Act, limited in duration to March 3, 1801, was intended to destroy the Republican party by terrorizing its press and leaders during the 1798 and 1800 elections. With Madison out of office and Jefferson holding place without power, they found themselves facing an unparalleled threat to personal liberty and constitutional government. What should they do?

Madison thought about this while engaged in a very different enterprise. Early in 1798 he began the remodeling of his and his parents' home. Orders for nails went to Jefferson's factory in December 1797—50,000 sixes, as many fours for lathing, 12,000 flooring brads, etc. In April he asked Jefferson to buy 190 window-panes for him in Philadelphia (for French windows), also brass hinges for eight doors. In this same month death came to Mrs. Ambrose Madison. The funeral service at the house, attended by "a considerable large number of genteel people," was followed next day by the Reverend Mr. Waddele's funeral sermon at Orange Courthouse.

The elder Madisons made their summer visit to the springs and were informed that "the family have continued nearly as you left it"—Simon complaining, Ralph recovering from dysentery, Joseph worse. "The family" were the slaves. In November a skilled man shifted from Jefferson's employ "for plastering and for adjusting stone to the fireplaces." On December 11 Madison wrote to Monroe that he was just back from Hanover and "in the vortex of housebuilding in its most hurried stage." A week or two later they moved into quarters completed enough for winter use, but purchase of a glasscutting diamond told of work yet to be done.[7]

The remodeling of the Madison house was a long-term job, one-story wings being added in 1809 under the advice of Architect William Thornton, who visited the place in 1802 and 1806. Mrs. Thornton's diary tells how impressed they were by Madison's architectural skill and by the evidence of "a taste for the arts which is rarely to be found in such remote and retired situations." So was British Minister Augustus J. Foster (a student of columnar structures) when he visited Madison in 1804. The house, he noted, commanded a fine view of the Blue Ridge and of a wooded plain from which the rise was so gradual that the building hardly seemed to be upon an elevation.

"There is a portico to it of the plainest and most massive order of architecture, but which Palladio gives as a specimen of the Tuscan. Mr. Madison himself superintended the building, which he had executed by the hands of common workmen to whom he prescribed the proportions to be observed. It is of brick which requires and is intended to be plastered. . . . I mention it as being a specimen of very plain, and except that I object to plinths, of good and massive Doric, which was executed by a proprietor without the assistance of an architect and of very ordinary materials; but he had cases made for the shape of the pillars, of wood, and filled them up with the mortars and bricks according to measure."[8]

Probably Jefferson's knowledge was drawn on, for in 1794, when the Hites were planning their great new home, Madison sent their builder to Monticello to talk especially about the portico. Apparently Madison and Jefferson exchanged not a single letter between June 21 and October 26, 1798. There are records of only two meetings during that interval—Jefferson at Orange on July 2 and 3, Madison at Monticello in October. Yet, before the second meeting, they had undertaken the writing of two papers whose similarity has linked them in history as the Virginia and Kentucky Resolutions.[9]

It is quite possible that these were drawn with no more joint planning than the July visit afforded. The basic doctrine of state opposition to unconstitutional laws had been suggested by Madison to Jefferson in 1788, enthusiastically indorsed by the latter, and restated by Madison in Congress in 1789. At that time, Jefferson had put heavy reliance on the federal judiciary. Now the judges were in the forefront of the assault on civic rights. Justice Chase in 1796 thought Editor Bache should be indicted for publishing Adet's letter. "A licentious press," he wrote, "is the bane of freedom." A year later Justice Iredell, sitting in circuit court at Richmond, induced the federal grand jury to denounce Congressman Cabell for a letter to his constituents. Jefferson wrote a petition to the state legislature against this attempt to "put the legislative department under the feet of the judiciary." Revised somewhat by Madison (to soften criticism of alien grand jurors) it was presented under other sponsorship and approved.[10]

With judicial partisanship driving them to state action, the two Virginians could as easily plan their strategy in July as in September. Certain it is that on October 4, Wilson C. Nicholas acknowledged a set of resolutions sent to him by Jefferson for use in another state. Nicholas said he had taken the liberty of handing them to John Breckenridge, whose visit at his home (en route from Sweet Springs to Buckingham and back to Kentucky) furnished a happy opportunity. To help keep the authorship secret Breckenridge would by-pass Monticello. Jefferson replied that he had thought the resolutions should originate in North Carolina, but Kentucky was probably better. He added:

"I understand you intend soon to go as far as Mr. Madison's. You know of course I have no secrets from him. I wish him therefore to be consulted as to these resolutions."

Severe illness kept Nicholas at his home in Warren, but it is obvious that Madison had been consulted already. Jefferson would not have told Nicholas that he wished the business to commence in outside state without knowing that Virginia was cared for.

Neither he nor Madison would have acted independently in so vital a matter. The latter read the Kentucky Resolutions when he visited Monticello in October, but a copy of them was not sent to him (owing to delay of a messenger) until November 17, one week after Breckenridge put them through his legislature.[11]

Madison turned his own resolutions over to Nicholas, who had already arranged to have John Taylor of Caroline sponsor them in the Virginia Assembly. Indorsed in a Republican caucus, offered on December 10 and warmly supported by Taylor and others, they were adopted on the twenty-first, 100 to 63.[12] The Virginia Resolutions opened with a pledge to defend the Constitution and maintain the Union, then declared that the powers of the federal government were limited by the compact out of which they arose.

"In case of a deliberate, palpable and dangerous exercise of other powers not granted by the said compact, the states, who are parties thereto, have the right and are in duty bound to interpose for arresting the progress of the evil, and for maintaining within their respective limits the authorities, rights and liberties appertaining to them."

The resolution condemned the sweeping construction placed on certain general phrases in the Constitution, with a design to consolidate the states, and protested against the alarming infractions of the Constitution in the Alien and Sedition Acts. Both laws subverted the charter by exercising powers not delegated and contrary to the principles of free government, while the second exercised a power expressly forbidden. Virginia having sought the amendment guarding liberty of the press, it would be criminal degeneracy to ignore so palpable a violation of it.

Proclaiming true anxiety to perpetuate the Union and scrupulous fidelity to the Constitution, the General Assembly called on other states to "concur with this Commonwealth in declaring, as it does hereby declare, that the acts aforesaid are unconstitutional; and that the necessary and proper measures will be taken by each for cooperating with this state, in maintaining unimpaired the authorities, rights and liberties reserved to the states respectively, or to the people."

Jefferson's Kentucky Resolutions covered the same ground, but in a more emotional tone and with a more extreme assertion of state power. Both instruments tended to fling the states apart. Realizing this, Madison restrained his arguments and wound unifying bands around them. Jefferson let his fly.

In the Virginia Resolutions, the *legislature* declared the offending laws unconstitutional and asserted the power of the *states* (not its own power or the power of one state) to take necessary and proper measures of correction. In the Kentucky Resolutions, *each* state was declared to have a right to judge for itself of infractions of the federal compact and the mode of redress. The state *legislature* then declared the Alien and Sedition Acts to be "altogether void and of no effect," and invited the states to concur in declaring them void. Breckenridge added a weakening request for their repeal and struck out an assertion that when undelegated powers are assumed, each state has a natural right "to nullify of their own authority."

Even with this in it, Jefferson thought his resolutions mild. Sending them to Madison, he said that Virginia should distinctly affirm all the important principles they contained, thus taking ground for the future yet avoiding any commitment to push farther than events rendered prudent. What seemed mild to him struck Madison as fallacious and dangerous. So, though declaring the two laws to be unconstitutional, Madison's resolutions said nothing about their being void. Nevertheless when Taylor introduced the protest in the House, it described the Alien and Sedition Acts as "unconstitutional, null, void and of no effect." For this, Jefferson was responsible. Disappointed when Nicholas showed him Madison's draft, he wrote:

"The more I have reflected on the phrase in the paper you showed me, the more strongly I think it should be altered. Suppose you were . . . to make it an invitation 'to concur with this commonwealth in declaring, as it does hereby declare, that the said acts are, and were *ab initio,* null, void and of no force or effect.' "[13]

Just before the final vote, Taylor caused the added words to be struck out. For the key to this action one need but note that

Madison spent the early part of December in Hanover County, only a few miles from Richmond. Undoubtedly he insisted on the elimination. One other change was made. Madison had written that the states, which were parties to the compact, *alone* had power to interpose. Giles (who resigned from Congress to enter the assembly) caused "alone" to be struck out because he thought it excluded the idea of intervention by the people as makers of the social compact. The change, Madison said long afterward, eliminated his doctrine that only the states, not the legislatures, had power to interpose. That applied with far greater force to the Kentucky Resolutions, and to the attempted declaration of nullity in his own. He raised the issue in a veiled criticism which he sent to Jefferson late in December 1798:

"I have not seen the result of the discussions at Richmond on the alien and sedition laws. It is to be feared their zeal may forget some considerations which ought to temper their proceedings. Have you ever considered thoroughly the distinction between the power of the *state* and that of the *legislature,* on questions relating to the federal pact? On the supposition that the former is clearly the ultimate judge of infractions, it does not follow that the latter is the legitimate organ especially as a convention was the organ by which the compact was made. This was a reason of great weight for using general expressions that would leave to other states a choice of all the modes possible of concurring in the substance, and would shield the General Assembly against the charge of usurpation in the very act of protesting against the usurpations of Congress."[14]

It is clear that whatever remedies Madison had in mind, they did not include the power of individual states, or the legislatures of all the states, to nullify federal laws. But in his desire to build up pressure against the Alien and Sedition Acts, he had used language whose gravity suggested such a power, while the implied denial of it was eliminated without being recognized as such. That obscured the legal difference between his position and Jefferson's, and caused the Virginia and Kentucky Resolutions to be lumped together as an assertion of the power to nullify, both in 1799 and in the great controversy which began in 1828.

The resolutions were intended for propaganda. For that, the Kentucky resolves were by far the more powerful. Madison put his emotions into a supplemental paper, an address to the people of Virginia adopted by the assembly in January 1799. Under the sophistry of a distinction between freedom of the press and licentiousness, the bulwark of liberty was being broken down. Where did the Constitution allow Congress to create crimes and inflict punishment?

"This doctrine, united with the assertion that sedition is a common law offense and therefore within the correcting power of Congress, opens at once the hideous volumes of penal law, and turns loose upon us the utmost invention of insatiable malice and ambition, which in all ages have debauched morals, depressed liberty, shackled religion, supported despotism and deluged the scaffold with blood."[15]

Supporters of the Virginia Resolutions felt a sense of personal danger. "I know not which mortifies me most," Jefferson wrote to Taylor, "that I should fear to write what I think, or my country bear such a state of things." In the debate at Richmond affirmative speakers were threatened with imprisonment. The assembly answered by requiring state judges to issue writs of habeas corpus, if legislators were arrested, and by strengthening the militia. Hamilton read the "hostile declarations" of Virginia and called for action. He wanted a federal justice of the peace in every county of the United States, a permanent army on a war footing, and a new law making any criticism of a federal official seditious, if libelous under the common law. A thousand kings could do no wrong.[16]

With the X Y Z delirium at its height, the Federalists made heavy gains in the 1798 election, but by February it seemed to Jefferson that the people wished "to hear reason instead of disgusting blackguardism." He entreated Madison to write one article a week for the press—an incalculable service. Six Virginia congressmen begged him to enter the state legislature, where wise and firm measures were needed. The conduct of the executive party, they said, rendered the inaction of Republican talents deplorable. Taylor of Caroline, renewing an appeal made a year earlier, added a potent argument. Patrick Henry, a supporter of the Alien and Sedition Acts, was a candidate for the assembly with Washington's blessing. "Fathom Mr. Henry's motives and consider your personal situation," urged Taylor. Henry was conspiring to destroy Jefferson and Madison. Nobody but Madison could cope with him.

"Consider that Virginia is the hope of Republicans throughout the Union, and that if Mr. Henry prevails in removing her resistance to monarchical measures the whole body will be dispirited and fall a sudden and easy prey to the enemies of liberty. If you will not save yourself or your friend—yet save your country."[17]

Madison yielded. Henry too was elected, but died in June. Madison spent the summer completing his house, and ran so short of money that he even tried to collect what John Francis Mercer had borrowed of him when they were in Congress together. Monroe was housebuilding too, on a site chosen for him by Jefferson and Madison, and he asked the latter to come to Albemarle where his skill in architecture and farming would be of great use. The Vice President wrote cautiously from Philadelphia, believing that his mail was tampered with, and Madison had no doubt that there was foul play in his own failure to receive newspapers.

Jefferson indorsed the suggestion of a society "between whom and yourself is great mutual esteem and respect" (probably the American Philosophical Society) that Madison publish his notes of debates in the Federal Convention. They would help produce a revulsion of public sentiment against current tax and military measures. Madison demurred. In the current trend toward despotism, some parts of them might be susceptible of a very different use. That was in truth the main reason for fifty years of secrecy—to avoid swelling the concept of federal power.[18]

Sooner or later, of course, news came through. Gerry had stayed in France at Talleyrand's request, after his two associates were spurned, and worked informally to prevent a rupture. His letters, held back for five months, were published after the election along with a report on them by Secretary Pickering. No man of candor, Madison remarked, could fail to see that the letters disclosed an anxious desire by France for a friendly settlement, whereas Pickering displayed "a narrow understanding and a most malignant heart." The result, he noted, was an address by the President to Congress giving France an option for peace, while the Secretary of State endeavored to insult and exasperate her into a refusal of it.[19]

The Republican leaders did not yet know that the Adams administration was being torn to shreds by internal dissension. Hamilton, slated for fourth place in the emergency army, had intrigued with the cabinet to be lifted above Generals Knox and Pinckney, immediately under General Washington. To the public, it was a disgusting quarrel over seniority, but the President discovered that the cabinet was not his own. Hamilton got his command, and talked of conquering Louisiana, Florida, even South America. But Adams refused him his war. Assured by Minister William Vans Murray in Holland that Talleyrand really wanted peace, the President overrode his cabinet and named Murray minister to France and member of a new peace mission. Sending the news to Madison, Jefferson called it a grudging and tardy action, but rejoiced over the dismay of the Northern Federalists, whose reaction showed that war had been their object.[20]

Adams now demonstrated the pin-point accuracy of Franklin's two-way statement about him. The wise and honest Adams, defying Hamilton, Wolcott, Pickering, McHenry and the Senate, refused to allow his undeclared naval war to turn into full-fledged hostilities with France. The Adams "absolutely out of his senses" united with a mad political faction and an insane judiciary in jailing Republican editors and repressing political freedom throughout the nation. Matthew Lyon, re-elected to Congress while in prison, was held there after his sentence expired until Senator Mason raised money for his $1,000 fine. Released, he drove to Philadelphia in a triumphal procession that recalled the Washington inaugural. The people were giving their answer to tyranny.

Late in August, W. C. Nicholas was called to Kentucky by the death of his brother George. Jefferson urged that he come first to

Monticello for a strategy meeting with Madison. Dolley, then in Charlottesville, promised that her husband would be there and carried home a letter in which Jefferson outlined his own ideas: answer the arguments of other states against the resolutions of 1798, reaffirm the position already taken, express warm attachment to the sisterhood of states but declare a determination "to sever ourselves from that union we so much value rather than give up the rights of self-government."

Madison came; Nicholas was unable to do so. That mattered little, judging from Jefferson's comment to the absentee: "I proposed to Mr. M. to write to you, but he observed that you knew his sentiments so perfectly from a former conference that it was unnecessary." Madison's chief concern was to wean Jefferson from his dangerous position on secession. In this he succeeded. Outlining his original idea in rather veiled terms, Jefferson told Nicholas that Madison did not concur in it and added:

"From this I recede readily, not only in deference to his judgment but because as we should never think of separation but for repeated and enormous violations, so these, when they occur, will be cause enough of themselves."[21]

Jefferson intended to call on Madison in November, on his way to Philadelphia, but Monroe prevented this by a last-minute warning. If the two met just before Madison launched his program at Richmond, it would be blazoned all over the continent. The hazard, Jefferson explained, was "the espionage of the little wretch in Charlottesville" (presumably the post-office snooper who tried to connect Jefferson with the "John Langhorne" letter to Washington). He had been the more anxious for this final interview because he intended to trust nothing confidential to the mails during the next twelve months.[22]

At Richmond Madison headed a committee to vindicate the previous resolutions against the replies of other states. The task was made no easier by a week in bed with dysentery and a continuation of debility from it. The five New England states, New York and Delaware had rejected Virginia's invitation, most of them affirming their support of the Alien and Sedition Acts.

Madison's report defended the Virginia Resolutions clause by clause. There could be no tribunal superior to the creators of the federal compact, hence the states must be the rightful judges in the last resort of whether it had been violated. This power should be exercised only when vital principles were in plain and palpable danger. The judicial authority could not be relied on as sole expositor, because usurped power might not be within range of judicial control. Indeed the judiciary itself might exercise or sanction unconstitutional powers. The issue depended on the candid judgment of the people, whose authority over constitutions, as well as the authority of constitutions over governments, ought ever to be kept in mind.

Next Madison took up the resolve against forced construction of general phrases. This he said must refer to the power to spend for the general welfare, which he declared once more to be limited to objects found in the other enumerated powers. In 1791, he recalled, Hamilton had reported to Congress that "whatever concerns the general interests of learning, of agriculture, of manufactures and of commerce are within the sphere of the national councils, *as far as regards an application of money.*" In 1797 a committee of Congress had assumed the same latitude in relation to agriculture—all this without the slightest mark of disapproval from Congress itself.

At this point, unwilling memory told Madison that "this extraordinary doctrine" barely missed being his own. Resolve No. 6 of the 1787 Virginia Plan flashed into his mind, and he wrote what he alone knew was an argument against Madison the nationalist. It would not do to refer the "general welfare" power to cases beyond the reach of individual states, "for, as the authority of the individual states must in all cases be incompetent to general regulations operating through the whole, the authority of the United States would be extended to every object relating to the general welfare which might by any possibility be provided for by the general authority." Why did he rebut an argument which nobody had made? Because he himself had proposed in 1787 that Congress be given power "to legislate in all cases to which the separate states are incompetent," and the convention had used that resolve as a guide to the extent of the enumerated powers. Luckily for him the Virginia Plan was still secret in 1800.

Proceeding to the Alien and Sedition Acts, Madison blasted their constitutionality. The President was given arbitrary power to punish friendly aliens by banishment, without any of the legal safeguards their presence in the country entitled them to. He riddled the two arguments offered for the Sedition Act—that Congress had power to punish crimes under the common law of England and that the amendment forbidding Congress to impair freedom of the press created a power to punish its licentiousness. Was the federal government then destitute of every authority for shielding its officers against libelous attack? It was, except under the same laws that protected all citizens, and any deviation from that rule would bring an end to the power of the people to control their rulers. Said Madison:

"To the press alone, chequered as it is with abuses, the world is indebted for all the triumphs which have been gained by reason and humanity over error and oppression."

Virginia had protested against a law which would stifle free discussion during two congressional elections and the choice of a President—a law which if made permanent would either destroy our free system of government or lead to a fatal convulsion. Where was the impropriety of the protest? The resolutions declaring these acts unconstitutional were not judicial expositions, to be carried into immediate effect by force. They were "expressions of opinion, unaccompanied with any other effect than what they may produce on opinion by exciting reflection." Virginia had suggested no special remedy, but many were available. Had the other states concurred they might have asked Congress to repeal the offensive acts, or requested an explanatory amendment, or required the calling of a constitutional convention.

The report ended in a brief resolution adhering to the resolves of 1798 and renewing the protest against the Alien and Sedition Acts as infractions of the Constitution. Completely baffled, the opposition complained that the report was more moderate than the debate of the previous year, argued that the legislature had no authority to protest, and went down to a two-to-one defeat. "You have really swept the Augean stable," commented Madison's cousin the Bishop.[23]

Widely distributed, Madison's report made little stir in the wild presidential campaign then opening. However, it established a legal foundation for the great popular protest against the Alien and Sedition Acts and spiked the guns which would have been fired at Jefferson had there been no explanation of his state's position. It was the last major constitutional utterance by the man who was to be called the father of the Constitution.

Both in the Virginia Resolutions of 1798 and the 1800 report on them, Madison put political objectives ahead of abstract thought. He was trying to knock out the Alien and Sedition Acts by public opinion expressed through state governments, and to build a constitutional barrier against the expansion of federal power in general. He had no desire to exalt state sovereignty, but used it as a weapon, and sharpened it for that purpose as much, perhaps, as he would have sharpened national sovereignty if all the political conditions had been reversed.

Wherever Madison's argument coincided with his original opinions it was impervious and overwhelming. He exposed the Alien and Sedition Acts as blatant violations of rights guaranteed by the Constitution. He destroyed for all time the notion that Congress could base criminal statutes on the common law. But when he searched for safeguards against a tyrannous Congress, an arbitrary executive and a persecuting judiciary, anxiety led him farther than reason would let him remain. So came an incongruity—the proposal of joint state action, solemnized as a desperate resort to the ultimate sovereignty of the makers of the federal compact, and then explained as a mere attempt to secure an expression of opinion, or to amend the Constitution in accordance with its provisions.

What this meant was that Madison's nationalism, though buried, was as much alive as it ever was. Then as always he put the Union above all other things political. In Congress he was quick to sustain Virginia against Massachusetts, the South against New England, but he stood for national against state and sectional interests, even when that hurt Virginia and the South. He turned against Hamilton's fiscal policies, and toward a strict construction of the Constitution, to promote justice for the whole people and to protect their rights and liberties against tyranny that rises out of exploitation.

The Constitution which Madison took the lead in framing was always in his mind a supreme Constitution of the nation and the people, neither the instrument nor the destroyer of any section or any class. The guarantees of freedom which he placed in it by amendment protected the people against dangers greater than any he foresaw. The powers which he helped to confer, but renounced when they were perverted to base uses, survived both the perversion and the renunciation and became in time the bulwark of the rights and welfare of all.

When James Madison left the Virginia legislature in 1800 he ended a state and federal service spanning twenty-four years. Constitution building was behind him. The life of a farmer lay ahead. But before that goal was reached there would be sixteen years in the highest executive offices of the nation.

# NOTES AND INDEX

# NOTES

MANUSCRIPTS used in this volume include the papers of James Madison, George Washington, Thomas Jefferson, Alexander Hamilton, James Monroe, Patrick Henry, Dolley Madison, W. C. Rives, Richard Bland Lee, Nathan Dane and the Shippen and Breckenridge families, in the Library of Congress; the Constable-Pierrepont Papers, Jefferson Account Book (1791-1803) and collections of letters individually catalogued in the New York Public Library; the papers of Rufus King, William Duer and Albert Gallatin in the New York Historical Society; the Coolidge-Jefferson Papers and Jefferson Account Book (1783-1790) in the Massachusetts Historical Society, and manuscripts in the Historical Society of Pennsylvania, Huntington Library, Virginia State Library (Francis Taylor Diary), Haverford College and the Friends' Center in Arch Street, Philadelphia.

Letters cited by date alone are to be found in the published works of the writers of them, or in Farrand or Burnett. Abbreviations to indicate sources are used in the notes as follows:

A.H.A.: *Annual Report of the American Historical Association.*

Ames: *Works of Fisher Ames,* edited by Seth Ames.

Annals: *Annals of the Congress of the United States.* All references are to the House of Representatives unless the Senate is specified.

Bancroft: *History of the Formation of the Constitution,* by George Bancroft.

Burnett: *Letters of the Members of the Continental Congress,* edited by Edward C. Burnett.

Cutler: *Life . . . of Rev. Manasseh Cutler,* by W. P. Cutler.

Domestic Life: *The Domestic Life of Thomas Jefferson,* by Sarah N. Randolph.

Elliot: *The Debates in the Several State Conventions, on the Adoption of the Federal Constitution,* edited by Jonathan Elliot (1836).

Farrand: *The Records of the Federal Convention of 1787,* edited by Max Farrand.

Grigsby: *The History of the Virginia Federal Convention of 1788,* by Hugh Blair Grigsby.

Hening: *Statutes of Virginia,* edited by W. W. Hening.

Hunt, Madison: *Life of James Madison,* by Gaillard Hunt.

Hunt-Scott: *Debates in the Federal Convention of 1787,* reported by James Madison, edited by Gaillard Hunt and James B. Scott.

JCC: *Journals of the Continental Congress.*

King: See first Madison entry below.

King, *Rufus King: Life and Correspondence of Rufus King,* by Charles R. King.

Lansing: Notes of constitutional debates by John Lansing, Jr., published in *The Delegate from New York,* edited by Joseph R. Strayer.

LC: Library of Congress.

McHenry: See first Madison entry below.

Maclay: *The Journal of William Maclay,* edited by Edgar S. Maclay.

Madison: Name followed by date, without year, indicates Madison's Notes of Debates in the Federal Convention of 1787, published in Farrand, Hunt-Scott, Madison *Writings,* Madison *Papers* (1840), and *Formation of the Union,* edited by Charles C. Tansill. The names of Yates, McHenry and King, similarly used, refer to their notes published by Farrand and Tansill. The notes of Paterson and Pierce, in *Formation of the Union,* are cited by page.

Madison, *Letters: Letters and Other Writings of James Madison* (1865).

Madison MSS: Papers of James Madison, Library of Congress.

Madison, *Writings: Writings of James Madison,* edited by Gaillard Hunt.

MHS: Massachusetts Historical Society.

NYHS: New York Historical Society.

NYPL: New York Public Library.

Paterson: See first Madison entry above.

Pierce: See first Madison entry above.

Rives: *Life and Times of James Madison,* by William C. Rives.

VSL: Virginia State Library.

Warren: *The Making of the Constitution,* by Charles Warren.

Yates: See first Madison entry above.

*Op. cit.* abbreviations refer to full titles in the same chapter.

## CHAPTER I

### (Pages 11 to 22)

[1] Edmund Randolph to Madison, March 27, 1787. Madison to Randolph, April 8, 1787. Madison to Washington, April 16, 1787.

[2] Madison to Randolph and Washington, *op. cit.* Madison to Jefferson, March 19 (mistakenly corrected to 18 in *Writings*), 1787.

[3] Grigsby, I, 95.

[4] Thomas Paine, *Public Good* (concluding words). Alexander Hamilton to James Duane, September 3, 1780.

[5] Madison, "Preface to Debates in the Federal Convention," *Writings,* II, 402. Madison credited Barton's anonymous pamphlet to Pelatiah Webster and said nothing about the latter's 1783 pamphlet. This was due to failing memory and the disappearance of the 1783 pamphlet from Madison's collection some time before 1820. See Madison to Noah Webster, January 1820; Madison to Tench Coxe, November 10, 1820; *Writings,* VI, 21, 21n. Bancroft, I, 24. Hannis Taylor, insisting that Madison made no error, credited both pamphlets to Pelatiah Webster and grossly exaggerated the importance of the one he really wrote. Taylor, *Origin and Growth of the American Constitution.*

[6] Madison, "Notes of Debates in Congress," April 1, 1783.

[7] Madison to Washington, February 21, April 16, 1787. Madison to Edmund Pendleton, April 22, 1787.

[8] Eliza Trist to Jefferson, June 6, 1787, Coolidge-Jefferson Papers (MHS). Madison to James Madison, Sr., April 1, May 27, 1787.

[9] Madison to James Madison, Sr., July 28, 1787, Madison MSS.

[10] Robert Hunter, *Quebec to Carolina in 1785-1786*, 173. Madison to J. K. Paulding, April 1831.

[11] Madison to Jefferson, May 15, 1787. New York *Daily Advertiser*, May 18, 1787. The Cincinnati re-elected Washington president and adjourned on May 19. See Brant, *Madison*, II, 395-396.

[12] Eliza Trist to Jefferson, June 6, 1787, Coolidge-Jefferson Papers (MHS). Randolph to Madison, April 11, 1787, Madison MSS. Madison, "Debates in the Federal Convention" (MS in LC), July 17 (for McClurg).

[13] Franklin to Thomas Jordan, May 16, 1787. *Diaries of George Washington*, May 16, 1787.

[14] *Ibid*, May 17, 20, 23, 24, 27, 1787. George Read to John Dickinson, May 21, 1787. Madison to Madison, Sr., May 27, 1787. George Mason to George Mason, Jr., May 20, 1787. This portion not in Farrand but quoted (p. 128) in Charles Warren, *Making of the Constitution*—excellent for its sidelights on the convention. Charles Pinckney was born October 26, 1757. "I am now forty," he wrote to Madison on March 16, 1801 (NYPL).

[15] Madison, May 25.

[16] Herbert B. Adams, *Life and Writings of Jared Sparks*, I, 560-564, II, 31-36.

[17] Madison, "Preface," *Writings*, II, 410-411.

[18] The notes of Yates, McHenry, King, Pierce, Paterson, Hamilton are published in Farrand and *Formation of the Union*, Lansing's in *The Delegate from New York* (1939).

[19] Madison to Randolph, March 11, 1787, Madison MSS. Lansing, May 25. Yates's manuscript has been lost, and his notes as published in 1821 name Madison in the opening May 25 entry. However, Lansing, who was absent until June 2, copied Yates's prior entries into his own record, and wrote "Mr. Matthewson" in the May 25 list of Virginia delegates present. Lansing copied these entries so literally that he wrote "New York—by Col. Hamilton and myself," "myself" meaning Yates. The June 1 entry ends with: "Thus far Judge Yates—I having been prevented from attending the convention at an earlier day." On June 4, in the notes written by Lansing himself, Madison becomes "Mr. Maddison."

[20] Madison to Joseph Gales, August 26, 1821; to Thomas Ritchie, September 15, 1821; to John G. Jackson, December 27, 1821; to Thomas Cooper, December 26, 1826; to Nicholas P. Trist, December 1831; to W. A. Duer, June 5, 1835. Also draft of unsent letter, Madison to John Tyler, 1833, *Writings*, IX, 502.

[21] Madison to Samuel H. Smith, February 2, 1827. Madison to Jefferson, February 8, 1799.

[22] See, in Chapter VI, account of proceedings of June 29.

## CHAPTER II

(Pages 23 to 31)

[1] Bancroft, II, 6. George Mason to Mason, Jr., May 20, June 1, 1787. Madison to Jefferson, April 23, 1787.

[2] G. W. Otto to the Count de Montmarin, June 10, 1787, Farrand, III, 39-45. Madison to Jefferson, October 24, 1787. Henry Knox to Rufus King, July 15, 1787.

[3] Madison, McHenry, Yates, May 29.

[4] Randolph to the Speaker of the House of Delegates, October 10, 1787. Madison to Thomas S. Grimke, January 6, 1834.

[5] Yates, May 29. C. Pinckney to J. Q. Adams, December 12, 30, 1818. These letters and the spurious Pinckney plan are in Farrand, III, and Hunt-Scott.

[6] Jared Sparks, *Journal*, April 19, 1830; Sparks to Madison, May 5, 1830, May 24, November 14, 1831, January 17, 1832. (All in Farrand.) Madison to Sparks, November 25, 1831. Madison, "Note on the Pinckney Plan," and "Observations on Mr. Pinckney's Plan," Farrand, III, 504, 506-513. C. Pinckney, "Observations," etc., and Pinckney to M. Cary, August 10, 1788, Farrand, III, 106-123; IV, 80. J. F. Jameson, "Studies," A.H.A., 1902, I, 128, 132. A. C. McLaughlin, "Sketch," etc., *American Historical Review*, IX, 735, 741-747. Pinckney plan restoration, Farrand, III, Appendix D. Taylor, *Origin and Growth of the American Constitution.* Charles C. Nott, *The Mystery of the Pinckney Draught.*

[7] C. Pinckney, 1786 speech in the New Jersey legislature, Burnett, VIII, 321-330.

[8] Madison to Sparks, November 25, 1831.

[9] Madison, Yates, McHenry, May 30.

[10] Madison to T. Cooper, December 26, 1826. Madison to N. P. Trist, December 1831. Madison to J. Tyler, 1833 (marked-out portion in *Documentary History of the Constitution*, V, 387-388).

[11] See note 3. Benjamin Rush to Richard Price, June 2, 1787.

## CHAPTER III

(Pages 32 to 45)

[1] Madison, May 29, 30. Madison to Washington, April 16, 1787.

[2] Madison, May 31. Jeremiah Wadsworth to Rufus King, June 3, 1787.

[3] Madison, May 31, June 19. Madison to Washington, April 16, 1787.

[4] Madison, May 31 (see original manuscript). Madison to J. Tyler, 1833, *Writings*, IX, 502.

[5] Madison, May 31.

[6] Madison, June 7. Egbert Benson to Rufus King, February 19, 1799 (NYPL).

[7] Madison, June 6, 7, 8. Yates, June 8.

[8] Madison, June 1, 2, 4. Pierce, in *Formation of the Union*, 91.

[9] *Ibid*, 93 (on King), 94 (on Bedford). Madison, June 6, 13.

[10] Madison, June 5, 13.

[11] Madison, June 4, 5. Yates, Lansing, June 5. The *Journal* of June 4 (from which Madison copied his similar entry) records the change in the court clause as a motion "to add these words." Professor Jameson jumped to the conclusion from this that the Virginia Plan did not originally provide for inferior courts and that Madison put them in by interpolation after June 4. Jameson's inference is completely disproved by a text of the plan which Lansing copied from Yates on June 1, 1787. It contains the exact wording about supreme and inferior tribunals found in Madison's manuscript. For variant texts of the Virginia Plan, see *Formation of the Union*, 953, 963, and Lansing, 113-118, with footnote on 116 by Editor Joseph R. Strayer.

[12] Madison, June 5, 12.

[13] Madison, June 6.

## CHAPTER IV

(Pages 46 to 54)

[1] Madison, June 6, 7.

[2] Madison, June 12.

[3] Paterson, in *Formation of the Union*, 879. Madison, June 9.

[4] Madison to Randolph, August 20, 1782. Madison to Jefferson, October 24, 1787.

[5] Otto to Montmarin, July 25, 1780, Farrand, III, 62 (French text).

[6] Madison, June 11, 12, 13, 14.

[7] Madison, June 15. For variant texts of the New Jersey Plan see *Formation of the Union*, 971-988.

[8] "Luther Martin's Reply to the Landholder," March 19, 1788, Farrand, III, 286. Jameson, "Studies," A.H.A., 1902, I, 140-150. Paterson and Sherman papers, Farrand, III, Appendix E. (Lansing's preliminary draft of the New Jersey Plan is in Paterson's handwriting, but is identifiable by the words "See Mr. Lansing" in Paterson's own draft—an instruction to pick up a clause from the other paper.)

## CHAPTER V

(Pages 55 to 70)

[1] Abraham Baldwin in *Annals*, January 11, 1799. The youngest delegates were Dayton 26, Mercer 28, Spaight 29 plus two months, C. Pinckney 29 plus seven months, Hamilton 30, Davie 30, Gilman 31, King 32, Baldwin 32, Lansing 32, McHenry 33, Randolph 33, G. Morris 34, Broom 35, Madison 36. The oldest: Franklin 81, Sherman 66, Jenifer 63 or 64, Livingston 63, Mason 61 or 62, Wythe 60 or 61, Carroll 56, Washington 55, Blair 54 or 55, Dickinson 54, Read 53, R. Morris 53, Williamson 51, Yates 49.

[2] William Pierce, sketches of members, *American Historical Review*, III, 317-334, republished in Farrand and *Formation of the Union*.

[3] J. Q. Adams, *Memoirs,* Journal of November 19, 1818 (Farrand, III, 426). William Blount to J. G. Blount, July 19, 1787, Burnett, VIII, 623.

[4] "Économie Politique et Diplomatique," *Encyclopédie Méthodique,* II, 401 (1786). (It also contains a large part of Madison's 1783 address on funds, 389-391.) William Short to Madison, May 7, 1787, Madison MSS. Jefferson to Madison, July 31, 1788. Jefferson to M. van Hogendorp, August 25, 1786.

[5] Madison, "Detached Memoranda," *William and Mary Quarterly,* October 1946.

[6] Madison, "Preface," *Writings,* II, 411.

[7] Madison, *The Federalist,* No. 10.

[8] Walton Hamilton and Douglass Adair, *The Power to Govern,* 202.

[9] Virginia, extending to the Mississippi, contained 107,395 square miles in 1787, North Carolina 94,448, Georgia 158,128. The seven states of New Hampshire, Rhode Island, Connecticut, New Jersey, Delaware, Maryland and South Carolina (the last estimated) totaled 70,404 square miles. Massachusetts then included Maine, causing it to be classed as a large state. Outside the state boundaries of that day were Vermont's 9,564 square miles and the 265,878 of the Northwest Territory.

[10] Mason in Elliot's *Debates* (1836), III, 528-529.

[11] George Read to John Dickinson, January 17, 1787, in William T. Read, *George Read,* 438-439.

[12] Madison, "Preface," *Writings,* II, 395, 405.

[13] Madison to J. Tyler, 1833, *Writings,* IX, 510.

[14] Madison to T. Cooper, December 26, 1826.

[15] O. G. Libby, *Geographical Distribution of Vote on the Constitution,* 65.

[16] Archives des Affaires Étrangères, M. et D., États-Unis, 253-287.

[17] Madison, August 30.

[18] *Formation of the Union,* 886.

[19] Madison, June 29 (Hamilton), 30 (Bedford). Yates, June 30.

## CHAPTER VI

### (Pages 71 to 91)

[1] Madison, June 16.

[2] Madison, June 18. Five variant texts of Hamilton's plan are in *Formation of the Union,* 979-988. See also Hunt-Scott, 608-618 for Hamilton's complete draft of a constitution, which he handed to Madison near the close of the convention. John Church Hamilton's charge that Madison reported this speech improperly is rebutted in N. P. Trist: Memoranda, September 27, 1834, Farrand, III, 533-534.

[3] Madison and *Journal,* June 18, 19. Professor Jameson, perplexed by Dickinson's offer of a substitute for the first article instead of an amendment to it, concluded that a totally different article (found in one of the drafts) headed the New Jersey Plan when it was placed before the convention, and that a garbled version of the substitute was accidentally put in

the copies made by Madison and others. (A.H.A., 1902, I, 137-138.) That is impossible, because the *earliest preliminary* draft of the New Jersey Plan contains the exact wording found in Madison's standard version. See Farrand, III, Appendix E, and *Formation of the Union,* 884.

[4] Madison, Lansing, June 19.

[5] Madison, Yates, June 19.

[6] Madison, June 20. Madison to T. Cooper, December 26, 1826. Madison to Andrew Stevenson, March 25, 1826.

[7] Madison, June 20, 21.

[8] Madison, June 21, 22, 23, 24.

[9] Madison, Yates, June 25.

[10] Madison, June 25, 26. Yates, June 25 (quoting Madison).

[11] Madison, June 26.

[12] Madison, Yates, June 27, 28. "The Landholder" No. 10, Farrand, III, 272.

[13] Madison, June 28. Four decades later, Jonathan Dayton told a remarkable tale, published in the *National Intelligencer* of August 26, 1826, of a convention overcome with silent admiration, assent and approbation of Franklin's speech, and of the immediate adoption of his motion for daily prayers—Farrand, III, 471. Madison corrected the erroneous story, but it still appears from time to time, as true. Madison to T. S. Grimke, January 4, 1834.

[14] Manasseh Cutler, "Journal," July 13, 1787, Farrand, III, 58. Robert P. Reeder, in Farrand, IV, 69.

[15] Madison, Yates, June 29. Paterson, June 29, *Formation of the Union,* 906.

[16] Madison to Joseph Gales, August 26, 1821. Madison to J. G. Jackson, December 21, 1821. Madison to J. C. Cabell, February 2, 1829. Madison to N. P. Trist, December 1831. Madison to W. C. Rives, October 21, 1833.

[17] Madison, June 29.

[18] Madison, June 29, 30. Yates, June 30. King, June 29.

[19] Washington to David Stuart, July 1, 1787.

[20] Madison, Lansing, July 2. L. Martin, "True Information" (paragraph 26), Farrand, III, 190.

[21] *Pennsylvania Herald,* July 5, 1787. James Campbell, *An Oration,* etc. (1787), quoted in Warren, 268-269.

## CHAPTER VII

### (Pages 92 to 100)

[1] Madison, July 5, 6. Lansing, July 5. N. Dane to N. Gorham, June 22, 1787.

[2] Yates, July 5. Yates and Lansing to Governor Clinton, Farrand, III, 245.

[3] Madison, July 7. Washington to Hamilton, July 10, 1787.

[4] Madison, July 5, 6, 7, 9.

[5] Madison, July 10, 11.

[6] Madison, July 12, 13, 14.

[7] Manasseh Cutler, whose journal contains many errors, listed Madison as a resident of the Indian Queen. There is not the usual direct evidence that he lived at Mrs. House's, but the indirect evidence is conclusive. George Read gave up his room there to accommodate Edmund Randolph, who could have had no motive except to be with the Virginia group. Read's own colleague Bassett, he said, was "at the Indian Queen, where Mr. Mason of Virginia stays, the last of their seven deputies who came in."—Farrand, III, 25, 58.

[8] Madison, July 14, 15, 16; also (on Pinckney's Senate proposals) June 8, July 2. Yates, June 25.

[9] Madison, July 16, postscript.

## CHAPTER VIII

### (Pages 101 to 112)

[1] Madison, July 17.

[2] Proposals by Roger Sherman, Farrand, III, 615.

[3] Madison to Martin Van Buren, May 13, 1828. Bancroft, II, 88.

[4] Madison, July 17.

[5] *Ibid.* King, June 1. Timothy Pickering to Hamilton, April 5, 1803; Hamilton to Pickering, September 16, 1803; Farrand, III, 397. The manuscript of Madison's notes shows that he first wrote the names of those who favored an executive during good behavior, then scratched them out. Hamilton's name is decipherable.

[6] Madison, July 19, 20.

[7] Madison, July 21.

[8] Madison, July 18, 21.

[9] Madison, July 24, 25, 26.

[10] Madison, July 26.

[11] Madison, July 23.

[12] Madison, July 23, 24.

## CHAPTER IX

### (Pages 113 to 131)

[1] Hamilton to Washington, July 3, 1787. E. Carrington to Madison, June 13, 1787, Madison MSS.

[2] Cutler, "Journal," Farrand, III, 59. *Pennsylvania Packet*, July 19, 1787. Otto to Montmarin, July 25, 1787, Farrand, III, 61.

[3] Madison, *Writings*, IV, 90n, 171.

[4] Henry Knox to Washington, August 14, 1787. Philadelphia *Independent Gazetteer*, August 6, 22, 1787.

[5] John Adams to Richard Cranch, January 15, 1787 (NYPL). Madison to Jefferson, June 6, 1787, May 12, 1791.

[6] Cutler, I, 258, 272-279. William Irvine to Madison, October 19, 1789, Rives Papers.

[7] *Independent Gazetteer*, August 14, 1787. *Pennsylvania Gazette*, August 15, 1787. David Humphreys to Hamilton, September 16, 1787. John Dawson to Madison, June 12, 1787, Madison MSS. Madison to Jefferson, September 6, 1787. Madison to J. G. Jackson, December 27, 1821.

[8] Madison, August 6, 7, 8. McHenry, August 6, 7. McHenry to Maryland House of Delegates, November 29, 1787, Farrand, III, 144.

[9] Madison (footnote), *Documentary History*, V, 439-449; Hunt-Scott, 619-623.

[10] Madison, August 9. Madison in Virginia convention, June 14, 1788, *Writings*, V, 185.

[11] Madison, August 10.

[12] Madison, August 8, 9, 13.

[13] Madison, August 8.

[14] Madison, August 8, 9, 11, 13.

[15] Madison, August 13, 15, July 19 (Randolph's views on executive), 26. James McClurg to Madison, August 5, 1787, Madison, *Writings*, IV, 91. Joseph Jones to Madison, September 13, 1787, Farrand, III, 80.

[16] Madison, August 14, 24, 25. The method of electing the President was postponed "until tomorrow" but was not taken up then.

[17] Madison, August 17.

[18] Madison, August 16, 21, 24, 25.

[19] Madison, August 25.

[20] Luther Martin, "Reply to the Landholder," Farrand, III, 282.

[21] Madison, August 18, 23.

[22] Madison, August 20.

[23] Madison, August 28, 29, September 14.

[24] Madison, "Remarks on Mr. Jefferson's Draught of a Constitution [for Virginia]," *Writings*, V, 294. *Annals*, I, 501; V, 773.

[25] Madison, August 28, September 12.

[26] Madison, August 23, 28.

[27] Madison, August 29, 30. L. Martin left on September 4.


## CHAPTER X

### (Pages 132 to 139)


[1] Warren, 510-512.

[2] Madison, August 18, 20, 22. See also *Journal* and MS of Madison debates, August 18.

[3] Madison, August 22. The sixteenth power was inserted by the convention on August 18: "To make rules for the government and regulation of the land and naval forces." It became No. 16 through the striking out of powers to name a treasurer and subdue rebellions.

[4] Madison, August 18 (Rutledge motion on state debts), 21, 22, 23, 25, 31.

[5] Madison, August 9, 22 (taxation and general power).

⁶ Madison, August 23, 25.
⁷ The clause on commerce with the Indians was in a committee report not acted on. Madison, August 22.
⁸ Madison, September 1, 4, 5.
⁹ Madison, September 4, 5, 6.
¹⁰ Madison to Pendleton, January 21, 1792. Madison, "Report on the Virginia Resolutions of 1798," *Writings*, VI, 354-357. Madison to Andrew Stevenson, November 27, 1830.

## CHAPTER XI
### (Pages 140 to 153)

¹ Madison, August 30. Farrand, III, 85.
² Madison, August 15, 16, 17, 18, 20, 21, 22, 25.
³ Letter of unknown to unknown, Philadelphia, October 11, 1787, copied by Jefferson, Farrand, III, 104. The words *"handed* to you" exclude Jefferson as the addressee, since he was in Paris.
⁴ Madison, June 29, July 5, 23, August 31, September 10. "The Landholder, VIII," Farrand, III, 171.
⁵ Madison, August 16 (Gerry's vote on taxation), 18, 21, 22, 23, 25.
⁶ Madison, September 4, 5, 6. T. Pickering to Hamilton, April 5, 1803; Hamilton to Pickering, September 16, 1803; Sparks, Journal, April 25, 1830; Farrand, III, 395-398, 480. J. C. Hamilton, *History of the Republic*, III, 284, 341-345. Hamilton, manuscript draft of constitution (NYPL). Almost every word of Hamilton's preamble, in the paper to which his son gave a June date, was taken from the preamble reported by the Committee of Style on September 12.
⁷ Madison, September 7, 8, 14.
⁸ Madison, August 29, 30, September 8. Madison to Sparks, April 8, 1831.
⁹ J. McClurg to Madison, September 5, 1787, Madison MSS.
¹⁰ Madison, September 10, 15.
¹¹ Madison, September 12, 13, 14.
¹² Madison, September 15.
¹³ James Wilson, "Considerations on the Bank of North America," *Works*, III, 397-427.
¹⁴ Madison to Jefferson, October 24, 1787.

## CHAPTER XIII
### (Pages 161 to 171)

¹ *JCC*, September 20, 27, 28, 1787. Madison to Washington, September 30, 1787.
² R. H. Lee to G. Mason, October 1, 1787. Madison to Washington, October 18, 1787. Washington to Patrick Henry, September 24, 1787. Replies in Washington, *Writings* (Fitzpatrick), XXIX, 278n.

[3] Madison to James Madison, Sr., September 30, 1787. Madison to Randolph, October 7, 1787. Madison to Jefferson, October 24, 1787.

[4] Washington to Madison, October 10, 22, November 5, 1787. Madison to Jefferson, October 24, 1787. Madison to A. Stuart, October 30, 1787. October letters of Stuart, Jones, Randolph to Madison, in *Writings*, V, 40*n*, 42*n*, 47*n*. Hening, XII, 412.

[5] *JCC*, September 29, October 11, 1787. Virginia delegates to Lieutenant Governor, July 22, 1787.

[6] Virginia delegates to Governor, November 3, 1787. Madison to Jefferson, October 24, December 20, 1787.

[7] Madison to Pendleton, October 28, 1787. Madison to Randolph, October 21, 1787. T. Coxe to Madison, September 28, 1787, J. Jones to Madison, October 29, 1787, Madison MSS.

[8] Madison to Washington, October 18, December 20, 26, 1787. L. Martin, "Genuine Information," Farrand, III, 172-232.

[9] *Observations . . . from the Federal Farmer*, 8, Madison Papers LXXVII, 25 (LC Rare Book Room). R. H. Lee to Madison, August 11, 1785.

[10] Madison to Washington, December 20, 1787. Madison to Jefferson, December 9, 20, 1787. A. Stuart to Madison, November 9, December 2, 1787; Randolph to Madison, April 11, October 23, 1787, Madison MSS. Phineas Bond to Lord Grenville, October 12, 1792 (on western posts), British Foreign Office 4, 16-4 (LC transcript).

[11] Madison to Washington, December 14, 1787. Madison to Jefferson, December 9, 1787.

[12] Madison to Randolph, January 10, 1788. Randolph to the Speaker of the House of Delegates, October 10, 1787, Farrand, III, 123. Meriwether Smith *et al.* to Randolph, in *Virginia Independent Chronicle*, January 2, 1788.

[13] Madison to Jefferson, December 9, 1787.

[14] Washington to Madison, October 10, 1787. William Short to Madison, August 1, 1787; A. Stuart to Madison, November 2, 1787, Madison MSS. Madison to A. Madison, November 8, 1787.

[15] Madison to Washington, November 18, 1787. Madison to Jefferson, August 10, 1788.

## CHAPTER XIV

### (Pages 172 to 184)

[1] Daniel De Leon, *James Madison and Karl Marx, a Contrast and a Similarity*.

[2] Madison, *Writings*, VI, 86. Jefferson to Madison, October 28, 1785. Madison to Jefferson, June 19, 1786.

[3] Madison to Jefferson, December 9, 1787.

[4] *The Federalist*, No. 39.

[5] *Ibid.*, No. 40.

[6] *Ibid.*, No. 44.

[7] *Ibid.*, Nos. 45, 46.

[8] Madison, *Debates,* June 21, 28, 29, 1787.
[9] *The Federalist,* Nos. 47, 48, 51.
[10] *Ibid.,* No. 52.
[11] *Ibid.,* No. 57.
[12] D. Adair, "The Disputed Authorship of the Federalist Papers," *William and Mary Quarterly,* April, July 1944.

## CHAPTER XV

### (Pages 185 to 194)

[1] Madison, bond and receipt, Madison MSS, XII, 13.
[2] Madison to Washington, January 20, February 3, 8, 11, 15, 1788. Rufus King to Madison, January 27, 1788, *Writings,* V, 95n. Jameson, *Constitutional History,* 75. Samuel Adams to R. H. Lee, December 3, 1787.
[3] Madison to Washington, February 8, 20, 1788. Randolph to Madison, January 3, 1788 (NYPL). James Madison, Sr., to Madison, January 30, 1788, Pendleton to Madison, January 29, 1788. Madison, *Writings,* V, 98, 105n, 89n, 107n. Washington to Madison, February 5, 1788.
[4] A. Stuart to Madison, January 14, 1788, Madison MSS. Carrington to Madison, January 18, 1788, *Writings,* V, 89n. Madison to Pendleton, February 21, 1788. Madison to Washington, March 3, 1788.
[5] Madison carried a letter, written in Philadelphia on March 11, to Washington.
[6] Madison to Washington, December 20, 1787 (Washington Papers), February 20, 1788. Washington to Charles Carter, December 14, 1787. Washington to Madison, February 5, 1788. Washington to James Wilson, April 4, 1788.
[7] Carrington to Madison, April 8, 1788. Cyrus Griffin to Madison, April 7, 1788. J. Spencer to Madison, February 28, 1788, Madison MSS. Diary of Francis Taylor, March 24, 1788 (Virginia State Library).
[8] Madison to Jefferson, April 22, 1788. Washington to J. F. Mercer, January 11, 1788. Washington to Charles Lee, April 4, 27, 1788. Washington to Thomas Lewis, May 19, 1788. *Pennsylvania Gazette,* April 2, 1788 (quoting *Maryland Journal,* February 29, 1788).
[9] George Nicholas to Madison, April 5, 1788, *Writings,* V, 114n. *Virginia Independent Chronicle,* May 28, June 4, 1788.
[10] Daniel Carroll to Madison, May 28, 1788, Madison MSS. Broadside, signed J. T. Chase, J. F. Mercer, Madison Papers, LXXVI, 18 (LC Rare Book Room).
[11] Washington to Thomas Johnson, April 20, 1788. Washington to James McHenry, April 27, 1788. Extract from Dr. Brooke to David Stuart, July 10, 1788, Washington Papers, 40, 241. Washington to Madison, May 2, 1788.
[12] *Maryland Gazette,* May 15, 1788. A. C. Hanson to Madison, June 2, 1788. Hanson, "Address to the People of Maryland," Madison MSS, IX, 51, 52, 53.
[13] Madison to Jefferson, April 22, 1788. Madison to Randolph, April

10, 1788. Randolph to Madison, February 29, April 17, 1788, Madison MSS.

[14] Madison to G. Nicholas, April 8, May 17, 1788, Madison MSS.

[15] Madison to Jefferson, April 22, 1788.

[16] C. Griffin to Madison, April 14, 1788, Madison MSS.

[17] P. Henry to unidentified Georgian, November 12, 1790, Henry Papers (LC). Rives, II, 612n (on Marshall).

## CHAPTER XVI

### (Pages 195 to 211)

[1] Grigsby, I, 67.

[2] Elliot, June 3, 1788.

[3] Madison to Washington, June 4, 1788. William Grayson to N. Dane, June 4, 1788, Dane Papers (LC).

[4] Elliot, June 5, 1788. Grigsby, I, 118-119.

[5] *Ibid.*, 96.

[6] The Pennsylvania government failed to protect Congress from military mutineers in June 1783.

[7] Grigsby, I, 79n.

[8] Washington, *Writings* (Sparks), IX, 378n.

[9] Brant, *Madison*, II, 362-363.

[10] Elliot, June 7, 9, 1788. Madison to T. Coxe, June 11, 1788, Madison MSS.

[11] Madison, *Writings*, V, 148n.

[12] Elliot, June 11, 1788.

[13] Elliot, June 7, 9, 12, 1788 (149, 164, 291, 300, 312-313), Jefferson to A. Donald, February 7, 1788 (quoted by Pendleton).

[14] Elliot, June 13, 1788.

## CHAPTER XVII

### (Pages 212 to 228)

[1] Madison to Washington, June 13, 1788. Theodorick Bland to Arthur Lee, June 13, 1788, in R. H. Lee, *Life of Arthur Lee*, II, 337.

[2] Elliot, June 14, 1788.

[3] Madison, *Debates*, August 18, 1787.

[4] Elliot, June 14, 1788.

[5] Elliot, June 17, 1788.

[6] Grigsby, I, 157n.

[7] Elliot, June 17, 18, 19, 1788.

[8] W. Grayson to N. Dane, June 18, 1788, Dane Papers. Madison to Washington, June 18, 1788. Madison to R. King, June 18, 1788, King Papers.

[9] Brant, *Madison*, II, 99.

[10] Elliot, June 20, 1788. 7 Cranch 602. 1 Wheaton 304.

[11] Madison to Washington, June 23, 1788.
[12] Grigsby, I, 325.
[13] Jefferson to W. Short, September 20, 1788.

## CHAPTER XVIII

### (Pages 229 to 244)

[1] *JCC*, July 14, 1788. Madison to Randolph, July 16, 1788. Madison to James Madison, Sr., July 1, 27, 1788, Madison MSS.

[2] Madison to Washington, June 27, 1788.

[3] Hamilton to Madison, May 19, June 8, 21, 27, 1788.

[4] Hamilton to Madison, July 19, 1788, Madison MSS. Madison to Hamilton, July 20, 1788, Hamilton Papers. Both published without date and with textual errors, in Hamilton, *Works*. Madison to Washington, July 21, 1788.

[5] John Randolph to his stepfather, St. George Tucker, July 30, 1788 (NYPL). For newspaper accounts see Burnett, VIII, 765*n*.

[6] John Witherspoon to Madison, August 11, 1788 (NYPL).

[7] Madison to Washington, July 21, 1788.

[8] *JCC*, July 28, 30, August 4, 5, 6, 13, 26, September 2, 3, 4, 12, 13, 1788. Madison to Jefferson, August 10, 23, September 21, 1788. Madison to Randolph, August 11, 1788. Madison to Washington, August 15, 24, September 14, 1788.

[9] Madison to Washington, August 15, 1788. Madison to Pendleton, August 22, 1788. Madison to Jefferson, August 23, 1788.

[10] J. P. Brissot de Warville, *New Travels in the United States of America*, 163-164 (with some changes in translation).

[11] Jefferson to Madison, October 8, 1787. Madison to Jefferson, February 19, 1788.

[12] C. Griffin to Madison, March 17, 24, April 28, May (probably 12), 26, 1788, Madison MSS.

[13] Madison, "Answers to Questions from the Count de Moustier," October 30, 1788, *Writings*, V, 281-284.

[14] Madison to Jefferson, December 8, 1788, May 23, 27, 1789.

[15] Madison to Jefferson, October 17, December 8, 1788.

[16] G. L. Turberville to Madison, October 27, November 13, 1788 (NYPL). Madison to Randolph, October 17, 1788.

[17] Carrington to Madison, October 19, 1788, Madison MSS. Richard Bland Lee to Madison, October 29, 1788, R. B. Lee Papers (LC). Washington to Madison, November 17, 1788.

[18] Madison to Washington, June 13, 1788. G. Turberville to Madison, October 27, November 10, 1788 (NYPL).

[19] Henry Lee to Madison, November 19, 1788, Madison MSS. P. Henry to R. H. Lee, November 15, 1788, Henry Papers. Madison to Randolph, November 2, 1788.

[20] "Decius" in *Virginia Independent Chronicle*, April 8, 1789. R. B. Lee to Madison, November 17, 25, December 12, 1788, R. B. Lee Papers.

[21] Madison to Randolph, November 23, 1788. Madison to James Madison, Sr., December 18, 1788.

[22] *Ibid.* G. Turberville to Madison, December 14, 1788 (NYPL).

[23] Madison to George Eve, January 2, 1789. Madison to Washington, January 14, 1789. H. Williamson to William Blount, February 22, 1789. Tobias Lear to John Langdon, January 31, 1789 (NYPL). Benjamin Johnson to Madison, January 19, 1789, Madison MSS.

[24] Madison to Randolph, March 1, 29, 1789. Madison to Jefferson, March 29, 1789. F. Taylor diary, January 26, 1789. N. Trist memorandum, quoted in Hunt, *Madison*, 165.

[25] F. Taylor diary, February 2, 3, 5, 6, 9, 1789.

[26] Washington to Madison, January 2, February 16, 1789, Washington, *Writings* (Fitzpatrick), XXX, 176n.

[27] Madison to James Madison, Sr., February 24, 1789. Washington to Edward Conway, March 4, 6, 1789. Washington to John Marshall, March 17, April 11, 1789. Washington to James Mercer, March 18, 1789.

[28] Madison to Washington, March 8, 19, 26, 1789. Madison to Jefferson, March 29, 1789. Madison to Randolph, March 1, 1789.

## CHAPTER XIX

### (Pages 245 to 254)

[1] Madison to Washington, April 6, 1789.

[2] *Annals*, April 8, 9, 1789.

[3] *Annals*, April 14, 28, May 11, 12, 1789. Fisher Ames to G. R. Minot, May 3, 1789.

[4] *Annals*, April 15, 24, May 13, 1789.

[5] *Annals*, April 21, May 4, 5, 6, 1789.

[6] P. Bond to Lord Carmarthen, April 29, 1789, A.H.A. *Report*, 1896, I, 595.

[7] P. Bond to the Duke of Leeds, *ibid.*, I, 610. *Annals*, April 25, 1789. Madison to Pendleton, May 17, 1789. Madison to Jefferson, May 9, 1789.

[8] *Annals*, May 15, 16, 1789.

## CHAPTER XX

### (Pages 255 to 263)

[1] *Annals* (Senate), April 30, 1789. Madison, *Debates*, June 28, 1787. Elliot, *Debates*, June 24, 1788. Washington to Madison, May 5, 1789. (See text to which note 5 pertains.)

[2] Madison to Jefferson, May 9, 23, 1789.

[3] *Ibid. Annals*, April 24, May 11 (Senate), April 23, 24, 25, May 7, 8, 9, 12, 14, 1789.

[4] J. Adams to "A Recluse Man," January 19, 1792. William Maclay, *Journal*, May 4, 5, 8, 9, 1789.

[5] *Annals*, May 5, 8, 1789. Washington to Madison, May 5, 1789.

[6] *Annals*, May 19, June 16, 17, 18, 19, 22, 1789.
[7] *Annals*, May 20, June 25, 1789.
[8] F. Ames to G. Minot, May 18, 27, 29, 1789.

# CHAPTER XXI

## (Pages 264 to 275)

[1] *Annals*, May 4, 5, June 8, 1789. Madison to Randolph, August 21, 1789.
[2] *Annals*, June 8, 1789. Madison to Jefferson, October 17, 1788. Jefferson to Madison, March 15, 1789.
[3] F. Ames to Thomas Dwight, June 11, 1789. *Annals*, June 8, July 21, 28, 1789. R. Sherman, draft of report, Madison MSS, XI, 120.
[4] *Annals*, August 4, 6, 7, 1789. Madison to A. Stuart, August 12, 1789.
[5] *Annals*, August 13, 15, 20, 1789. F. Ames to G. Minot, June 12, 1789.
[6] *Annals*, September 21, 24, 1789. Senate Records, September 9, 1789, U. S. National Archives.
[7] *Annals*, January 25, February 2, 1790. Madison to Jefferson, February 14, 1790.
[8] Madison, "Essay on Monopolies," *William and Mary Quarterly*, October 1946. *Annals*, April 9, 17; (Senate) April 7, 15 (report), 1789.
[9] *Annals*, August 17, 1789.
[10] *Annals*, August 15, 18, 1789.
[11] *Annals*, August 18, 21, 1789.
[12] *Annals*, August 19, 21, 22, 1789. Madison to Alexander White, August 24, 1789.

# CHAPTER XXII

## (Pages 276 to 289)

[1] *Annals*, August 3, 24, 29, 31, 1789. Madison to Pendleton, September 14, 1789.
[2] *Annals*, August 27, 1789. Madison to A. White, August 24, 1789. F. Ames to G. Minot, September 3, 1789.
[3] *Annals*, September 3, 4, 5, 1789. T. Coxe to Madison, September 9, 1789, Madison MSS. Maclay, September 8, 1789.
[4] Madison to Pendleton, September 14, 1789. R. King, Memorandum, King Papers, Box 3 (NYHS). F. Ames to G. Minot, September 6, 1789. Maclay, September 2, 1789.
[5] *Annals*, September 7, 17, 22, 1789; (Senate) September 24, 25, 26, 1789. Madison to Pendleton, September 23, 1789. J. Dawson to Madison, undated except Wednesday morning (probably September 14, 1789), Madison MSS, XII, 62. Pennsylvania-New York Agreement, *Rufus King*, I, 374n.

6 *Annals,* September 26, 28, 1789. Maclay, September 28, 1789.

7 Madison to Washington, November 20, 1789.

8 *Annals* (Senate), August 7, 1789. Washington to Madison, August 5, 9, 1789. Washington, on appointments and treaties, August 6, 7, 8, 1789, *Writings,* XXX, 370-374. Maclay, July 1, August 16, 1789.

9 Washington to Madison, August 9, 1789. Washington to Senate Committee, August 11, 1789. Maclay, August 22, 24, 1789. *Annals* (Senate), August 21, 22, 24, 1789.

10 Randolph to Madison, July 19, 1789, Madison MSS.

11 Madison to Washington, undated, but written shortly after August 26, 1789. Washington, Writings, XXX, 393. (See note 13, below.) Carrington to Madison, September 9, 1789 (two letters), Madison MSS.

12 George Turner to Madison, July 19, August 2, 5, 1789; William Barton to Madison, August 26, 1789, Madison MSS. Turner to Washington, August 18, 24, 1789, Washington Papers, applications, XXVI.

13 William Barton to Madison, August 26, 1789, Madison MSS. Washington to Madison, undated, but written shortly after Barton's. Washington to Hamilton, September 25, 1789. T. Lear and Washington, list of appointments, Hamilton Papers, VIII, 1014. Washington's note was given the conjectural date of August 10 by Sparks, which is impossible because it followed Barton's refusal of the judgeship on the 26th. Fitzpatrick guessed September 25, the day on which Washington informed Hamilton of his intention to nominate Randolph. That date is impossible because the note to Madison preceded the nomination of Blair and Pendleton, whose names went to the Senate on September 24.

14 R. H. Lee and W. Grayson to the Virginia Assembly, September 28, 1789, Madison, *Letters,* I, 499. Madison to Washington, December 5, 1789.

15 Hardin Burnley to Madison, November 28, December 5 (misdated November), 1789, Carrington to Madison, December 20, 1789, Madison MSS.

16 *Virginia Senate Journal,* December 8, 11, 12, 1789. Madison to Washington, November 20, 1789, January 4, 1790. Senators John S. Wills, Matthew Anderson and Joseph Jones (of Dinwiddie), who said they voted to postpone the religious guarantee because it was too weak, had past records of 100-per-cent hostility to freedom of religion. Senators John P. Duval, Nicholas Cabell and John Kearnes, who voted not to postpone, supported religious freedom on every previous test. Virginia *Journals;* (House) December 12, 24; (Senate) 23, 1785.

17 Madison to Washington, January 4, 1790, Madison MSS. Washington to Jefferson, October 13, 1789, January 21, 1790. Jefferson to Washington, December 15, 1789, February 14, 1790. Jefferson to T. M. Randolph, March 28, 1790.

18 Jefferson to Washington, April 1, 1790. Madison, Memorandum, undated. (Dated December 1789 in *Writings.*) The reference to Jefferson indicates March 1790 as the time of writing.

19 Madison to Jefferson, May 27, 1789.

## CHAPTER XXIII

(Pages 290 to 305)

[1] Hamilton to Madison, October 12, 1789. Madison to Hamilton, November 19, 1789. Hamilton, *History of the Republic*, IV, 60-64. (Published there with added italics.) Hamilton Papers, VIII, 999 (LC).

[2] *Annals*, II, 1991-2021. Hamilton, *Works* (Lodge), II, 227-289.

[3] Madison to Jefferson, January 24, 1790.

[4] Hamilton, *History of the Republic*, IV, 29*n*.

[5] Hamilton to Carrington, May 26, 1792.

[6] Maclay, January 15, 18, 1790.

[7] *Annals*, January 28, February 8, 9, 10, 11, 1790.

[8] *Annals*, February 11, 15, 16, 17, 18, 19, 1790.

[9] *Annals*, February 18, 19, 22, 1790. Maclay, January 17, February 18, 21, 22, 1790. M. Cutler to Oliver Everett, February 24, 1790, Cutler, I, 458.

[10] Madison to Randolph, March 14, 1790.

[11] Madison to Pendleton, March 4, 1790. Madison to Randolph, March 14, 1790. Madison to James Madison, Sr., February 27, 1790. Abigail Adams to Cotton Tufts, March 7, 1790 (Henkels Catalog, May 13, 1937). J. Q. Adams to J. Adams, April 5, 1790. *Columbian Centinel*, February 24, 1790. *Pennsylvania Gazette*, March 24, 1790.

[12] Madison to unknown, March 14, 1790, Emmet Papers (NYPL).

[13] Maclay, February 19, 1790. "Foreigner" to Madison, February 17, 1790 (NYPL).

[14] R. King, Memorandum, December 21, 1788, King Papers.

[15] Madison to Jefferson, December 8, 1788. Jefferson to Board of Treasury, February 7, March 29, 1788. (MS of March 29 letter in Duer Papers, NYHS.) Jefferson to J. Adams, February 6, 1788.

[16] Duer-Constable contract, December 23, 1789, Constable-Pierrepont Papers, misc. (NYPL). Duer-Constable-Platt certificate account, *ibid*. William Steele to W. Duer, July 27, 1789, Duer Papers (NYHS).

[17] William Constable, Memorandum, Constable-Pierrepont Papers, misc. Constable, list of foreign holders, *ibid*.

[18] Maclay, January 18, July 17, 1790.


## CHAPTER XXIV

(Pages 306 to 318)

[1] Brant, *Madison*, II, 233.

[2] Maclay, February 22, 1790.

[3] *Annals*, February 23, 24, 25, 26, March 1, 2, 1790.

[4] Madison to Pendleton, March 4, 1790. Madison to Randolph, March 14, 1790.

[5] *Annals*, February 11, 12, March 16, 23, 1790. Madison to Randolph, March 21, 1790.

[6] *Ibid. Annals,* March 17, 19, 22, 23, 1790, January 30, 1797. F. Ames to G. Minot, March 23, 1790. Madison to R. Pleasants, October 30, 1791.

[7] *Annals,* April 22, 1790. T. L. Shippen to William Shippen, April 22, 1790, Shippen Papers (LC).

[8] D. Stuart to R. B. Lee, May 23, 1790, R. B. Lee Papers. B. Rush to Madison, February 27, May 4, 1790, Madison MSS. James Hutchinson to Albert Gallatin, June 11, 1790, Gallatin Papers (NYHS).

[9] *Annals,* May 13, 14, 17, June 29, 30, 1790. Madison to Randolph, May 19, 1790.

[10] Jefferson Account Book, August 14, 1790 (Massachusetts Historical Society). Madison to Pendleton, June 22, 1790. Madison to James Madison, Sr., May 2, 1790. Jefferson to W. Short, August 10, 1790. Jefferson to D. Humphreys, August 11, 1790. Jefferson to Gouverneur Morris, August 12, 1790.

[11] *Annals,* April 12, 22, 26, May 24, 25, June 1, 1790. Madison to Monroe, April 17, June 1, 1790. Madison to Randolph, May 19, 1790. Madison to A. Madison, May 27, 1790 (NYPL). Madison to James Madison, Sr., May 2, 1790. Ames to G. Minot, May 20, 1790.

[12] *Annals,* May 31, June 10; (Senate) June 1, 2, 7, 8, 1790. Ames to T. Dwight, June 11, 1790. Madison to Monroe, June 1, 1790. Maclay, June 1, 2, 4, 7, 8, 1790.

[13] *Annals,* June 11, 1790. Madison to James Madison, Sr., June 13, 1790.

[14] Maclay, June 14, 1790. Ames to T. Dwight, June 11, 1790. Ames to G. Minot, June 23, 1790.

[15] Jefferson, "Anas," *Writings* (Library ed.), I, 274-276. Jefferson, "Memorandum on Assumption," undated, *Writings* (Congress ed., VII, 226, where it is dated "February ? 1793." The final paragraph suggests a much later time of writing).

[16] Rives, III, 110. Madison to Monroe, June 17, 1790. Madison to Pendleton, June 22, 1790.

[17] *Annals,* July 6, 7, 8, 9, 23, 24, 26; (Senate) June 28, 29, 30, July 1, 13, 14, 16, 19, 20, 21, 1790. R. B. Lee to Theodorick Lee, June 26 (27), 1790, R. B. Lee Papers. Ames to Minot, June 23, 1790. R. King, Memorandum, June 30, 1790, King, *Rufus King,* I, 384.

[18] Madison to Monroe, July 24, 1790.


## CHAPTER XXV

### (Pages 319 to 326)

[1] Madison to James Madison, Sr., July 31, August 14, 1790. Fontaine Maury to Madison, July 20, 1790, Madison MSS. T. L. Shippen to W. Shippen, August 12, 1790, Shippen Papers.

[2] Madison to A. Rose, G. Paine, T. Underwood, G. Thomson, W. C. Nicholas, G. Gilmer, Mann Page, James Pendleton, August 13, 1790. Madison to James Madison, Sr., August 14, 1790.

[3] Jefferson Account Book, 1783-1790.

⁴ T. L. Shippen to W. Shippen, September 15, 1790, Shippen Papers. Washington's correspondence reveals that he was in Baltimore on September 9, 1790, and reached Mt. Vernon on the eleventh. Madison and Jefferson spent the night of September 8 in Wilmington, the ninth in Chestertown, the tenth in Annapolis, the eleventh at Queen Anna's, the twelfth and thirteenth in Georgetown.

⁵ T. L. Shippen to W. Shippen, September 16, 1790, Shippen Papers. Jefferson Account Book, 1783-1790.

⁶ Jefferson to Madison, September 20, 23, 1790, Coolidge-Jefferson Papers (MHS).

⁷ Jefferson to Madison, January 10, 12, 1791, Madison MSS. Jefferson Account Book, January 12, 1791. Madison, account with Jefferson, undated, but written January 11, 1791, Madison MSS, XC, 8.

⁸ Madison, "Instructions for Mordecai Collins, Lewis Collins and Sawney," Madison MSS, XIII, 74. Madison to James Madison, Sr., February 21, 1794 (notation on manuscript).

⁹ F. Maury, statement of Madison's account, July 20, 1790; James Maury to Madison, August 21, 1789, Madison MSS.

¹⁰ Jefferson to Washington, October 27, 1790.

¹¹ Annals, December 13; (Senate) December 8, 13, 1790. Jefferson to G. Morris, November 26, 1790. Washington to Madison, undated, but written immediately after a House vote of December 11, 1790. Hamilton, "Topics for President's Speech," Works (Lodge), VIII, 94.

¹² Annals, December 16, 22, 23, 24, 1790.

¹³ Annals, December 27, 1790, January 5, 6, 11, 1791.

## CHAPTER XXVI

### (Pages 327 to 333)

¹ Madison to Samuel Johnston, June 11, 1789. Madison to Pendleton, January 2, 1791.

² Annals, January 14, 1791. R. King to C. King, September 29, 1823, Farrand, III, 460.

³ Annals, February 1, 2, 4 (Sedgwick on Madison), (Senate) January 20, 1791.

⁴ Annals, February 2 (Madison), 3 (Ames), 4 (Sedgwick, Laurance, Boudinot), 5 (Smith), 7 (Giles, Gerry), 8 (Madison), 1791.

⁵ Jefferson, "Opinion against the Constitutionality of a National Bank," February 15, 1791, Works (Library ed.), III, 145. Hamilton, "Opinion," etc., Works (Lodge), III, 445.

⁶ Madison, "Detached Memoranda," William and Mary Quarterly, October 1946. Madison, draft of veto message, February 21, 1791, Writings, VI, 42n. Hamilton to Washington (February 21, 1791), Works (Lodge), III, 444. Madison to Jefferson, May 1, 1791.

⁷ Annals, April 15, 20, 1789, December 16, 1790, January 6, 28, 1791. Samuel S. Smith to Madison, March 26, 1789, Madison MSS.

## CHAPTER XXVII

### (Pages 334 to 350)

[1] Jefferson to Philip Freneau, February 28, 1791. Jefferson to Washington, September 9, 1792. C. Gore to R. King, January 18, 1789, King Papers.

[2] Madison to Randolph, September 13, 1792. Freneau to Jefferson, March 5, 1791, Jefferson Papers. Madison to Jefferson, May 1, 1791.

[3] Jefferson to Madison, July 21, 1791.

[4] Madison to Jefferson, July 24, 1791, Henkels Catalog of McGuire collection. Freneau to Madison, July 25, 1791, Madison MSS. Madison to Charles Simons and to Mann Page, August 1, 1791, Haverford College Library. Madison to James Madison, Sr., November 13, 1791.

[5] Jefferson to Madison, May 9, 1791, Madison MSS. Madison to Jefferson, May 12, 1791. T. M. Randolph to Jefferson, April 30, 1791, Coolidge-Jefferson Papers (MHS).

[6] Jefferson to Madison, March 13, 1791, *Domestic Life*, 197. Jefferson moved to the banks of the Schuylkill, near Gray's Ferry, in 1793.

[7] Madison, Memorandum of talk with Beckwith, *Letters*, I, 530. Jefferson, Memorandum on diplomatic nominations (letter to Senator Strong), January 4, 1792. Another newcomer to Madison's boardinghouse was the Italian sculptor Ceracchi, who made a bust of him in 1792. Madison sympathized strongly with his desire to create a great memorial of the American Revolution, but told him Congress would grant no funds for it and vainly advised him to rely on popular subscriptions. Madison to Professor Tucker, April 30, 1830.

[8] Jefferson Account Book, 1791-1803 (NYPL). *Domestic Life*, 194, 196, 201. Jefferson to T. M. Randolph, June 5, 1791. Madison to James Madison, Sr., July 2, 1791. Jefferson to Monroe, July 10, 1791.

[9] Jefferson Account Book, 1791-1803. Joseph Fay to Jefferson, September 20, November 29, 1791. Jefferson to Fay, November 4, 1792, Jefferson Papers.

[10] Madison to Jefferson, May 12, June 23, 27, July 10, 1791. Jefferson to Madison, July 6 (Madison MSS), August 3 (Coolidge-Jefferson Papers), 1791.

[11] J. C. Hamilton, *History of the Republic*, IV, 506. Madison to Jefferson, May 1, 1791. Jefferson Account Book, 1791-1803.

[12] Madison to Jefferson, July 26, 1788, June 23, 1791. Jefferson to Madison, June 21, 1791, Madison MSS. Jefferson to Charles Thomson, April 20, 1791.

[13] Madison to Jefferson, July 13, 1791. Jefferson to Madison, May 9, 1791, Madison MSS. Jefferson to Washington, May 8, 1791.

[14] Madison to Jefferson, May 12, June 27, 1791. Jefferson to Madison, June 28, 1791, Madison MSS.

[15] Madison to Jefferson, July 13, 1791. Jefferson to J. Adams, July 17, August 30, 1791. Adams to Jefferson, July 29, 1791.

[16] Randolph to Madison, July 21, 1791, Madison MSS. Madison to James Madison, Sr., July 2, 1791.

[17] Madison to Jefferson, July 10, 13, August 8, 1791.

[18] Madison to Jefferson, May 1, 1791. S. L. Mitchill to Mrs. Mitchill, January 3, 1802, in A. C. Clark, *Life and Letters of Dolly Madison.*

[19] Jefferson to Madison, August 26, 1791, Madison MSS. Jefferson to the D. C. commissioners, August 28, 1791. Jefferson to Washington, December 1, 1791. Washington to L'Enfant, December 2, 1791.

[20] Jefferson to unknown, August 7, 1791, Coolidge-Jefferson Papers. Madison to Jefferson, August 8, 1791. Jefferson to Mary Jefferson, August 21, 1791. Jefferson Account Book, 1791-1803.

[21] Jefferson to T. M. Randolph, October 25, 1791, *Domestic Life.* Madison to James Madison, Sr., October 30, 1791.

[22] Madison to James Madison, Sr., October 30, November 13, 1791.

[23] *Annals,* October 27; (Senate) October 25, 1791. Madison to H. Lee, January 21, 1792, Rives Papers.

[24] *Annals,* December 12, 14, 1791, January 24, 1792. Jefferson, "Anas," April 6, 1792. Madison to H. Lee, April 15, 1792.

[25] Madison to Randolph, March 21, 1790. Charles Carter to Madison, December 16, 1791, Madison MSS. Hening, XIII, 331.

[26] Madison, *Writings,* VI, 43. Madison to Jefferson, June 19, 1786.

[27] Madison, *Writings,* VI, 67-123.

[28] *Annals,* February 6, 1792. Madison to H. Lee, January 1, 1792.

[29] *Annals,* February 8, 9, 1792.

[30] Comptroller Eveleigh died on April 16, 1791. Hamilton wanted Oliver Wolcott to succeed him. Tench Coxe asked Jefferson to forward his application for the post to the President at Mt. Vernon, unless Madison saw some reason for not doing so. Jefferson sent it without recommendation. Three months later word reached Madison that Hamilton was saying he had been told of an effort by Jefferson and Madison to promote Coxe because of a "Southern antipathy" to Wolcott's Eastern descent. Meeting Hamilton in New York, Madison gave him the facts. Jefferson knew that he had them from the start, for Coxe had written in a P.S.: "It is my intention to confine my views to yourself and Mr. Hamilton, leaving it to your ideas of propriety to converse with Mr. Madison." Commented Jefferson to the latter: "Nobody could have heard of T C's application but himself, H, you and myself. Which of the four was most likely to give it out at all, and especially in such a form . . . as to excite an opinion that you and myself were hostile to everything not Southern?" Coxe to Jefferson, April 16, 1791, Jefferson Papers. (First sheet missing, sent to Washington.) Jefferson to Washington, April 17, 1791. Madison to Jefferson, July 24, 1791. Jefferson to Madison, July 27, 1791, Madison MSS.

[31] *Annals,* March 8, 1792 (Sedgwick on Madison). Madison to Pendleton, February 21, 1792. Hamilton to Carrington, May 26, 1792.

## CHAPTER XXVIII

### (Pages 351 to 370)

[1] Hamilton to Carrington, May 26, 1792.

[2] Jefferson to Madison, September 6, 1789. Madison to Jefferson, February 4, 1790.

³ Hamilton Papers, XIII, 1724.

⁴ William Steele to W. Duer, August 20-21, 1790. J. Hardy to Duer, November 30, December 9, 13, 1790. Duer-Macomb contract, December 29, 1791; W. Duer Account Book, 1791-1792, Duer Papers. Hamilton to Duer, March 14, 1792. Charles A. Beard, *Economic Origins of Jeffersonian Democracy*, 155n.

⁵ Madison to Pendleton, April 9, 1792. Hamilton to William Seton, March 25, April 4, 12, 1792. Seton to Hamilton, April 16, 1792, Hamilton Papers, XV, 2106. Ben Walker to R. King, February 19, 1795, King Papers.

⁶ Madison, Memorandum, May 5, 9, 25, 1792. Washington to Madison, May 20, 1792. Madison to Washington, June 21, 1792 (with draft of address). Jefferson to Washington, May 23, 1792.

⁷ Memorandum, Hubbard Taylor to Madison, August 9, 1795; Richard Taylor, receipt, Madison MSS, XVII, 64, XCI, 114.

⁸ G. Mason, Observations on caveats; Panther Creek plat and surveyor's memorandum; Madison MSS, XCI, 77, 130. *Mason* v. *Wilson*, 1 Cranch 44. J. H. Daveiss to Madison, November 4, 1801. H. Taylor to Madison, January 16, 1803, Madison MSS.

⁹ Jefferson to Madison, May 13, June 1, 4, 1792. Jefferson to Hammond (draft with notes by Jefferson and Hamilton), May 29, 1792, Jefferson, *Writings* (Congress ed.), VII, 3n, 4n. Madison to Jefferson, June 12, 1792.

¹⁰ *Ibid*. Jefferson to Madison, June 21, 1792. Madison to Jefferson, June 29, 1792.

¹¹ Hamilton, "Vindication of the Funding System," undated, *Works* (Lodge), III, 3. Lodge dated this conjecturally 1791, but parts of its language are common to the letter to Carrington, May 26, 1792, and to a memorandum to Washington, August 18, 1792 (*Works*, III, 427).

¹² Hamilton, *Works* (Lodge), VII, 229-303.

¹³ Hamilton to Elisha Boudinot, August 13, 1792. Boudinot to Hamilton, August 16, 1792.

¹⁴ *Gazette of the United States*, July 25, August 1, 4, 11, 1792. *National Gazette*, July 28, 1792. Hamilton's editors (J. C. Hamilton, H. C. Lodge) omit the damaging "T. L." letters of August 1 and 11.

¹⁵ Hamilton Papers, XVIII, 2793, 2794, 2795. The part quoted is crossed out after the word "purpose."

¹⁶ Madison to Randolph, September 13, 1792. Monroe to Madison, September 18, October 9, 1792. Jefferson to Madison, October 1, 1792, Rives Papers. Madison to Jefferson, October 9, 1792, Madison MSS. Jefferson to Washington, October 17, 1792. Philip Marsh, "Madison's Defense of Freneau," *William and Mary Quarterly*, April 1946.

¹⁷ Hamilton, *Works* (Lodge), VII, 274, 261. Quoting a letter from Jefferson to Foreign Secretary Jay (September 26, 1786) on a Dutch proposal to Finance Minister Calonne, Hamilton inserted the words "I submit whether," thus making it a proposal by Jefferson. Jefferson's letter, badly garbled through misreading and attempting to edit his letterpress copy, is in his writings edited by H. A. Washington. Ford published accurate extracts sent by Jefferson to George Washington on October 17, 1792, but (presumably relying on the accuracy of the H. A. Washington edition)

erroneously accused Jefferson of offsetting Hamilton's doctoring by some of his own.

[18] *American Daily Advertiser,* October 20, 1792.

[19] Jefferson to Washington, October 17, 1792.

[20] Monroe to Madison, October 9, 1792. Madison to Monroe, October 11, 1792, Madison MSS. Madison and Monroe to M. Smith and M. Willet, October 19, 1792, Monroe Papers (LC). John Nicholson to Madison, October 3, 1792, Monroe, *Writings,* I, 242*n.*

[21] John Beckley to Madison, September 2, 10, October 17, 1792 (NYPL).

[22] Madison to James Madison, Sr., November 6, 1792. Madison to Pendleton, November 16, December 6, 1792, February 23, 1793. James Hutchinson to Gallatin, October 24, 1792 (NYHS). Madison, "Outline of Answer," Rives Papers.

[23] Jefferson, "Anas," December 17, 1792. (Initials "JM" are erroneously interpreted "James Monroe," "Webb" appears as "Webr" and "testibus" is rendered "testifies" in Jefferson *Writings* edited by Ford.)

[24] Madison to Pendleton, November 16, 1792, February 23, 1793.

[25] *Annals,* November 7, 10; (Senate) November 6, 1792. Madison to Pendleton, November 16, 1792.

[26] *Annals,* November 7, 13, 14, 1792, February 15, 26, 1793. The two reports on St. Clair are in *Annals,* III, 1052, 1106.

[27] *Annals,* November 19, 20, 21, 1792. Madison to Pendleton, December 10, 1792.

[28] *Annals,* December 24, 26, 1792. Hamilton to Washington, November 19, 1792.

[29] *Annals,* December 27, 1792, January 23, 1793.

[30] *Annals,* January 10, 12, 21-25, 1793. Maclay, July 16, 1790. F. Ames to T. Dwight, January 1793.

[31] *Annals,* January 25, 1793. Madison to Pendleton, February 23, 1793.

[32] *Annals,* February 27, 28, March 1, 1793. Jefferson, "Anas," March 2, 1793.

## CHAPTER XXIX

### (Pages 371 to 388)

[1] Madison to Pendleton, March 4, 1790. Robert Beverly to A. Stuart, February 11, 1790, A. H. H. Stuart Papers (LC).

[2] Madison to Randolph, March 21, 1790. Madison to James Madison, Sr., January 21, 1791. Madison to Jefferson, May 12, 1791. Madison to Pendleton, December 18, 1791.

[3] Madison to Pendleton, December 6, 1792. Jefferson to Madison, March 1793. Madison to Jefferson, April 12, 1793. News of the king's death was published in Philadelphia newspapers on March 16. Madison probably left about the twentieth, as he reached Alexandria on the twenty-fourth. Jefferson's letter dated March 1793 treats the execution as something already known to Madison.

[4] *Journal des Débats, Assemblée Nationale*, August 24, 1792. *Lois et Décrets, Assemblée Nationale*, August 26, 1792. Those given honorary citizenship were Priestley, Paine, Bentham, Wilberforce and Clarkson (enemies of the slave trade), Mackintosh, David Williams, Gorani (called Gorain), Cloots, Pauw (the geographer), Campe, Pestalozzi, Washington, Hamilton, Madison, Klopstock, Kosciusko, Gille (German publicist). Madison was listed as "N. Madisson"—N. for Nommé instead of Monsieur.

[5] Madison to J. M. Roland, French Minister of the Interior, April 1793.

[6] Madison to Jefferson, May 29 (Madison MSS), June 13, 1793. Jefferson to Madison, June 9, 1793.

[7] Madison to Jefferson, May 8, June 19, 1793.

[8] Madison to Jefferson, May 8, 27, June 13, 17, July 22, 30, 1793.

[9] Jefferson to Madison, June 30 (postscript to 29), July 7, 1793. Madison to Jefferson, July 18, 22, 30, 1793. Hamilton, *Works* (Lodge), IV, 432-489. Madison, "Letters of Helvidius," *Writings*, VI, 138-188.

[10] Madison to Jefferson, June 13, 17, 19, 29, July 18, 30, August 11, 20, 1793, Madison MSS (published in part). Jefferson to Madison, August 3, 1793 (Madison MSS for cipher).

[11] Madison to Jefferson, May 27, June 17, July 30, 1793. Jefferson Account Book, August 24, 1793. Madison to James Madison, Sr., December 27, 1795, Madison MSS.

[12] John Taylor to Madison, May 11, June 20, August 5, 1793, Madison MSS. Madison to Jefferson, August 11, 20, 1793.

[13] Madison to Jefferson, May 27, August 27, 1793.

[14] *Ibid*. Jefferson to Madison, August 11, 1793, Madison MSS. Jefferson wrote twice to Madison on this day. His editors (H. A. Washington, Ford, Lipscomb and Bergh) published the one written first, omitting the one which was too important to be trusted to the mails.

[15] Madison to Jefferson, June 17, September 2, 1793. Madison, draft of resolutions, *Writings*, VI, 192. Madison to A. Stuart, September 1, 1793.

[16] Madison to Jefferson, September 2, 1793.

[17] Jefferson to Madison, August 25, September 1, 8, 1793. Madison to Monroe, September 15, 1793.

[18] *Ibid*. W. Smith to Hamilton, August 22, 1793, Hamilton Papers.

[19] Jefferson to Madison, September 8, 15, 1793, Madison MSS. Madison to J. Taylor, September 20, 1793, Madison MSS.

[20] Jefferson Account Book, September 25, October 25, 1793. Madison to Monroe, October 29, 1793. Madison to Jefferson, July 24, 1788. Madison to James Madison, Sr., June 13, 1790, November 25, 1793, Madison MSS.

[21] Washington to Madison, October 14, 1793. Madison to Washington, October 24, 1793.

[22] Jefferson to Madison, November 2, 9, 17, 1793. Madison to Jefferson, November 24, 1793; Madison to James Madison, Sr., November 25, 1793, Madison MSS. F. Ames to G. Minot, December 6, 1793.

[23] *Annals*, December 5, 6; (Senate) December 5, 1793.

[24] Jefferson to Madison, June 9, 1793. Herman Le Roy to R. King, February 23, 1794, King Papers.

[25] Madison to Jefferson, April 12, 1793. W. Smith to Hamilton, April 24, 1793, Hamilton Papers.

## CHAPTER XXX

(Pages 389 to 400)

[1] *Annals*, February 14, 21, 23, 1791, December 16, 1793. Jefferson to E. Rutledge, August 25, 1791. Jefferson, "Circular to Foreign Ministers," February 13, 1793. Jefferson, "Report on Commerce," *Annals*, IV, 1288. Madison, Memoranda on ship clearances, imports and exports, British laws, war insurance, Madison MSS, XIII, 25. T. Coxe, various reports in Jefferson Papers, 1791. Coxe to Jefferson, February 5, 1793 (returning Jefferson's report with suggested revisions).

[2] *Annals*, January 1, 10, 28, 1794, and Appendix, 1417.

[3] *Annals*, January 13, 14, 1794.

[4] *Annals*, January 16, 21, 1794.

[5] *Annals*, January 29, 1794 (includes speech of the 30th).

[6] *Annals*, February 6, 7, March 12, 1794. Madison to Jefferson, March 2, 9, 12, 1794. Fauchet to the Minister of Foreign Relations, June 4, 1794, A.H.A. *Report* 1903, II, 373.

[7] Madison to Jefferson, March 14, 1794. *Annals*, March 24, 27, 1794.

[8] Madison to Jefferson, March 14, 24, 26, 1794. *Annals*, March 25, 1794.

[9] Pierce Butler to Madison, February 4, 1794. Horatio Gates to Madison, March 13, 1794. Joshua Barney and twenty-one other ship captains to Madison, March 9, 1794. Charleston Republican Society, resolutions, March 12, 1794. All in Madison MSS. Madison to Jefferson, March 26, 1794.

[10] *Annals*, February 24, 1794. *American State Papers, Finance*, I, 290-291. Madison to Jefferson, March 26, April 14, 1794. Hamilton to Washington, April 10, 14, 1791. Washington to Hamilton, May 7, 1791, April 8, 1794. Randolph to Madison, August 8, 1811, Rives, III, 301.

[11] Madison to Jefferson, April 14, 28, 1794. R. King, Memorandum, *King*, I, 519, 521. *Annals*, April 7, 18, 21, 25, 1794.

[12] Madison to Jefferson, April 28, May 11, 1794.

[13] F. Ames to C. Gore, May 2, 1794. Madison to Jefferson, May 11, June 1, 1794.

[14] *Ibid. Annals*, June 2, 1794.

[15] Madison to Jefferson, May 25, 1794. Monroe to Madison, May 26, 1794. Monroe to Jefferson, May 26, 27, 1794. Madison to James Madison, Sr., June 6, 1794, Madison MSS.

## CHAPTER XXXI

(Pages 401 to 414)

[1] Virginia Magazine of History, VI, 314, VII, 79, 200. New Garden, N. C., Records in William W. Hinshaw, *Encyclopedia of American Quaker Genealogy*.

[2] John H. I. Browere to James and Dolley Madison, May 20, June 26, 1826, Madison MSS. New Garden Record Book, Guilford College Library. (Wherever the spelling "Dolly" is used in the title of a book, it is followed in these notes.)

[3] Dolley Madison to Margaret B. Smith, August 31, 1834, published in Smith, *First Forty Years of Washington Society,* 351.

[4] Elizabeth Drinker, *Journal,* March 5, 1781, July 9, 1783, July 7, 10, August 12, 1784, October 19, November 24, 1785; footnotes on pages 18, 20, 168.

[5] Hinshaw, *op. cit.,* II, 460, 527, 617, 668, 691. Dolley Payne to Eliza Brooke, published in Katherine Anthony, *Dolly Madison, Her Life and Times,* 32.

[6] *Ibid.,* 35. Minutes, Philadelphia Southern District, November 25, December 23, 1789, Friends Mission Board, Philadelphia.

[7] George Washington to John A. Washington, January 16, 1783.

[8] Will of John Todd, Jr., in Maud Goodwin, *Dolly Madison,* 46.

[9] Lucia B. Cutts, *Memoirs and Letters of Dolly Madison,* 12-13. Drinker, *op. cit.,* August 27, 1793.

[10] Dolley Madison wrote to Margaret B. Smith on August 31, 1834: "In the year '91, and after the death of my father, my mother received into her house some gentlemen as boarders—and in '93 she left Philadelphia to reside with her daughter Washington." Departure in 1793 is further indicated by the disappearance, from the 1794 Philadelphia directory, of the 1793 entry, "Payne, widow, boarding house, 96 North Third." It may be assumed that Anna stayed with her sister at the Todd home (51 South Fourth) because there was more reason to do so than to live with her—as she did—after Dolley's remarriage.

[11] Cutts, *op. cit.,* 15. Summary of Dolley P. Todd's will, dated May 13, 1794, in Henkels Catalog 1478. Nathan Schachner, *Aaron Burr,* 129, 130. Mrs. Drinker's journal records five visits by Burr to her home.

[12] Abigail Adams to John Todd, Henkels Catalog 1478. A. White to Madison, November 2, 1794, Madison MSS.

[13] Madison to Dolley Todd, August 18, 1794. Joseph Jones to Madison, August 14, 1794 (about "poor Antoine's situation").

[14] William W. Wilkins to Dolley P. Todd, August 22, 1794, in Allen C. Clark, *Life and Letters of Dolly Madison,* 22. MS in Dolley Madison Papers (LC).

[15] Dolley Madison to Eliza Lee, September 15, 1794, Dolley Madison Papers. The incorrect figure 16 is written over the 15. The second "Alass" has been torn off, but appears in a copy. Tradition has the Madison-Todd wedding a big affair, with merry bridesmaids cutting off Madison's Mechlin lace ruffles for souvenirs. Dolley, expressing her regret that Eliza and Mr. and Mrs. L. Lee were away, referred to the latter as "the only family invited except *his* sister and Brother Washington."

[16] Goodwin, *op. cit.,* 60. Madison to James Madison, Sr., October 5, 1794, in Clark, *op. cit.,* 24; Anthony, *op. cit.,* 90. Some months before, Madison agreed rather unwillingly to send his sister Frances a pianoforte. The choice was between an ordinary instrument's economy of space and "the superior swell of the notes" of a grand piano, but unless Fanny had extraordinary talent for music he doubted the advantage of bestowing much time on it. Madison to James Madison, Sr., March 10, April 21, 1794.

[17] Madison to James Madison, Sr., May 4, 19, December 14, 1794, De-

cember 25, 1796 (last two in Madison MSS). J. Jones to Madison, November 4, 16, 19, 21, 1794; Madison to Monroe (memo), March 26, 1795, Madison MSS. Madison to Monroe, April 7, 1796.

[18] Hinshaw, *op. cit.*, II, 491, 617, 668. Records, Monthly Meeting of the Friends of Philadelphia, November 28 (appointment of committee on Dolley), December 26 (expulsion), 1794.

[19] H. Lee to Madison, September 23, 1794; P. Freneau to Madison, May 20, 1795; the Reverend J. Madison to Madison, November 2, 1794; Horatio Gates to Madison, December 27, 1794; Jefferson to Madison, October 30, 1794; J. F. Mercer to Madison, February 11, 1795, Madison MSS. On January 15, 1797, Madison wrote to R. R. Livingston (letter in NYPL) asking him to patronize Freneau in the establishment of a daily newspaper in New York.

[20] C. Pinckney to Madison, October 26, 1800, Madison MSS. Jefferson to Madison, December 28, 1794. Madison to James Madison, Sr., February 23, 1795.

## CHAPTER XXXII

### (Pages 415 to 430)

[1] Hamilton to Washington, November 8, 1794. William Findley, *History of the Insurrection*, etc. (1796). Rives, III, 459-461. Claude G. Bowers, *Jefferson and Hamilton*, 255-256.

[2] Madison to Jefferson, November 16, 1794. Madison to Monroe, December 4, 1794. Hamilton to R. King, October 30, 1794.

[3] Madison to Jefferson, November 30, 1794. Madison to Monroe, December 4, 1794. William Cobbett, *Porcupine's Works*, II, 45. *Annals*, November 20, 28; (Senate) November 19, 20, 21, 22, 1794.

[4] *Annals*, November 24, 25, 26, 27, 28, 1794.

[5] Letters of note 3. *Annals*, November 29, 1794.

[6] Ames to T. Dwight, November 29, December 12, 1794, February 28, 1795. Ames to Gore, December 17, 1794.

[7] Madison to Jefferson, November 16, 30, December 21, 1794. Madison to Monroe, December 4, 1794. William Giles to Madison, April 12, 1795, Rives Papers.

[8] Pierce Butler to Madison, January 23, June 12, 1795. Madison MSS. Samuel Dexter to Madison, February 3, 5, 1795; Madison to Dexter, February 5, 1795, Rives, III 482-483.

[9] *Annals*, December 15, 22, 26, 31, 1794, January 1, 2, 1795. Madison to Pendleton, January 8, 1795.

[10] Madison to Jefferson, December 21, 1794, February 15, 1795. Ames to G. Minot, January 20, 1795.

[11] Jefferson to Madison, December 28, 1794, April 27, 1795. Madison to Jefferson, March 23, 1795.

[12] Madison to William Madison, March 1, 1795; Madison to James Madison, Sr., March 13, 1796; Madison to Jefferson, March 23, June 14, 1795, Madison MSS. Will of Isaac Zane, June 17 (probated September 2), 1795, copy in Madison MSS. Jacob Rinker to Sarah Zane, July 1, 1803, Zane

Papers (Historical Society of Pennsylvania). H. Taylor to Madison, January 16, February 3, August 9, 1795, undated (1796), May 1, 1797, Madison MSS. F. Taylor diary, August 5, 7, 1795.

[13] Madison to Monroe, December 4, 1794, March 11, 26, 1795. Madison to Jefferson, January 11, February 15, 1795. P. Butler to Madison, June 12, 1795, Madison MSS. Madison to R. R. Livingston, February 8 (NYPL), August 10, 1795. Livingston to Madison, January 30, 1795, Madison MSS.

[14] *Ibid.* Livingston to Madison, July 6, 1795 (NYPL). Madison to Monroe, December 20, 1795. Washington to Randolph, July 22, 1795.

[15] Hammond to Grenville, July 27, 1795, F. O. 5, v. 9. Fauchet to the Minister of Foreign Relations, June 4, September 5, October 31, 1794, French text in A.H.A., 1903, II, 372, 414, 451. Madison to Monroe, January 26, 1796. Pickering to Hamilton, December 14, 1795, Hamilton Papers. Pickering's translation is in Hamilton Papers, October 31, 1794.

[16] P. Butler to Madison, August 21, 1795. Randolph to Madison, November 1, 1795, Madison MSS. R. R. Livingston to Madison, November 6, 1795, Rives Papers. Madison to Jefferson, January 10, 1796. Madison to Monroe, January 26, 1796. Irving Brant, "Edmund Randolph, Not Guilty," *William and Mary Quarterly,* April 1950.

[17] Madison to James Madison, Sr., November 8, 1795. J. Swanwick to Madison, June 14, July 26, 1795.

[18] Madison to (A. J. Dallas, identified by Rives), August 23, 1795. Jefferson to Madison, September 21, 1795. Noah Webster was "Curtius."

[19] Madison to Monroe, December 20, 1795.

## CHAPTER XXXIII
### (Pages 431 to 451)

[1] Madison to Jefferson, December 6, 1795. James Jackson to Madison, November 17, 1795, Madison MSS.

[2] Madison to Jefferson, December 6, 13, 1795. R. King to Hamilton, December 16, 1795 (accompanied in Hamilton Papers by underlined draft referred to). W. W. Henry, *Character and Public Career of Patrick Henry.*

[3] Jefferson to Madison, December 3, 1795. Ames to Dwight, December 30, 1795. Madison to Monroe, December 20, 1795. Madison to Jefferson, December 27, 1795.

[4] Madison to Jefferson, January 10, 1796. *Annals,* see Randall and Whitney in Index to v. 5.

[5] Madison to Jefferson, February 7, 1796. Madison to Monroe, February 26, 1796.

[6] *Ibid.* Madison to Jefferson, February 29, 1796.

[7] *Annals,* March 1, 7, 10, 11 (Assembled treaty debates, March 7-April 6) 1796. Ames to Gore, March 11, 1796.

[8] *Annals,* March 24, 30, 1796. Madison to Jefferson, March 13, April 4, 1796.

[9] *Annals,* April 6, 1796. J. Beckley to Monroe, April 2, 1796 (NYPL). Madison to J. G. Jackson, December 27, 1821.

[10] *Annals*, April 14, 15, 1796.

[11] Madison to Monroe, April 18, 1796. Madison to Jefferson, April 23, May 1, 1796.

[12] *Annals*, April 29, 30, 1796. Madison to Jefferson, May 1, 9, 22, 1796. Madison to Monroe, April 19, May 14, 1796. Hamilton to King, April 20, 1796. The anti-treaty men who went over to the other side were Christie, Crabb, Dent and Smith of Maryland, Bailey and Van Cortlandt of New York, Muhlenberg of Pennsylvania, Gilman of New Hampshire, Grove of North Carolina. The "wrongheads" (anti-treaty extremists) who spoiled Madison's strategy were Parker, Claiborne and Heath of Virginia, Bryan of North Carolina and Sprigg of Maryland.

[13] Madison to Monroe, May 14, 1796. Hamilton to King, May 4, 1796, King, *Rufus King*, II, 47. Beckley to Madison, June 20, 1796 (NYPL).

[14] Washington, draft of address, in V. H. Paltsits, *Washington's Farewell Address*, published by NYPL.

[15] Washington to Hamilton, May 15, 1796, and draft of same date. Hamilton's elimination of Madison's indorsement of rotation in the presidency has caused unwarranted controversy as to Washington's views. Washington suggested the passage to Madison in 1792 and specifically consented to Hamilton's removal of it in 1796. Presumably it did not seem fitting to use, at the end of his second term, a passage which logically pointed to his retirement four years earlier.

[16] John Jay, combating a claim that Hamilton composed the Farewell Address, wrote to Richard Peters on March 29, 1811, that he and Hamilton, together, revised Washington's own draft. What they revised was Washington's revision of Hamilton's revision of Washington's enlargement of Madison's draft of Washington's ideas. No man whom Washington esteemed, Jay asserted, would have dared write the passage about his "very fallible judgment." Actually, this was taken verbatim from Madison's 1792 draft, and is an exact reflection of Washington's remarks about himself on May 5. Madison, *Writings*, VI, 108*n*.

[17] Madison to Monroe, September 29, 1796, Madison MSS. The code errors were caused by writing 147 instead of 1470 and 878 instead of 879.

[18] Madison to Monroe, March 26, December 20, 1795, January 26, April 18, September 29, 1796. Wolcott to Hamilton, June 14, 17, 1796. Hamilton to Wolcott, June 15, 1796. Hamilton to Washington, June 1796. Pickering, Wolcott and McHenry to Washington, July 2, 1796. George Gibbs, *Oliver Wolcott*, I, 359, 360, 366.

[19] Madison to Monroe, April 7, 1796. Fulwar Skipwith to Madison, July 1, 26, 1796 and accompanying papers, Madison MSS, XIX, 76-81.

[20] T. Pickering to Madison, August 19, 1796; Philip Mazzei to Madison, March 24, 1796, Madison MSS. Madison to Jefferson, February 7, April 4, 1796. Arthur H. Dohrman to Madison, February 26, March 11, 1796 (NYPL).

[21] Madison to James Madison, Sr., August 10, 1796, January 22, 29, 1797, Madison MSS. James Madison, Sr., to Joseph Chew, January 15, 1797 (NYHS).

[22] J. Taylor to Madison, November 16, 1796, Rives Papers. Madison to

James Madison, Sr., November 27, 1796, Madison MSS. Beckley to Madison, October 15, 1796 (NYPL).

[23] Madison to Jefferson, December 5, 10, 19, 1796, January 15, 1797.

[24] Jefferson to John Adams (unsent), December 28, 1796. Jefferson to Madison, January 1, 30, 1797. Madison to Jefferson, January 15, 1797.

[25] *Annals*, December 7, 8, 14, 16, 1796. Madison to Jefferson, December 10, 19, 1796, January 15, 1797.

[26] *Annals*, December 12, 21, 26, 27, 1796. A. White to Madison, September 26, December 2, 1796, Madison MSS.

[27] *Annals*, January 12, 20, February 10, 11, 1797. Madison to Jefferson, January 15, 22, 1797.

[28] *Annals*, January 19, 1796, and Appendix, 2713-2769. Madison to Jefferson, January 22, 29, February 5, 1797. Robert Liston to Lord Grenville, April 18, 1797, F. O. 5:18.

[29] Jefferson "Anas," March 2, 1797 (but written after 1800). John Adams, "Letters to the Boston *Patriot*," 1809, *Works*, IX, 286. Randall, *Life of Jefferson*, II, 344.

[30] Thomas Paine to F. Skipwith, April 24, 1797; Paine to Madison (retained by Skipwith), April 27, 1797 (Pennsylvania Historical Society).

[31] Madison to James Madison, Sr., February 13, 19, March 12, 1797. Madison shipping list, April 27, 1797, Madison MSS.


## CHAPTER XXXIV

### (Pagees 452 to 471)

[1] John Dawson to Madison, May 18, 1797, Madison MSS. Jefferson to Madison, May 18, June 1, 15, 22, 1797. Hamilton to Wolcott, March 30, April 5, 1797. Wolcott to Hamilton, March 31, 1797.

[2] Jefferson to Madison, August 3, 1797. Jefferson to Mazzei, April 24, 1796. Monroe to Jefferson, July 12, 1797. Madison to Jefferson, August 5, 1797. Richard Hildreth, *History of the United States*, V, 54.

[3] Madison to Monroe, December 17, 1797. Madison to Jefferson, January 21, February 12, (19?), 1798. Jefferson to Madison, January 24, 1798.

[4] Jefferson to Madison, April 6, 1798. Madison to Jefferson, April 2, 15, 22, 1798.

[5] Jefferson to Madison, April 26, 1798. Madison to Jefferson, May 5, 13, 20, 1798.

[6] Madison to Jefferson, June 10, 1798. Madison to Monroe, June 9, 1798.

[7] Madison to Jefferson, December 25, 1797, March 4, April 29, October 31, 1798; Madison to James Madison, Sr., June 9, 1798; Madison to Monroe, December 11, 1798, Madison MSS. Jefferson to Madison, November 17, 1798. F. Taylor diary, April 7, 1798.

[8] Mrs. William Thornton, diaries, September 5, 1802, September 25-29, 1806 (LC). Augustus J. Foster, "Notes on the U. S. A.," II, 82 (LC). Mrs. Thornton described Madison's house in 1802 as "built by his father, but added to by himself," which might suggest that the wings were of earlier date. However, she gave the length as "upwards of eighty feet,"

instead of its 150 feet with the wings, and Madison wrote to Margaret Smith in September 1830 that "the only drawing of our house is that by Dr. Thornton, and is without the wings now making part of it."

[9] Madison to Jefferson, October 15, 1794, Madison MSS. Jefferson, *Writings* (Ford), VII, 288-309. Madison, *Writings*, VI, 326-331. Jefferson to Madison, October 26, 1798. Jefferson's Account Book shows that he paid Madison $26 on July 2, 1798, for Congressman Dawson, and gave half a dollar to a Madison valet next day.

[10] Samuel Chase to J. McHenry, December 4, 1796 (NYPL). Madison to Jefferson, August 5, 1797 (partially published). Jefferson, jury petitions, August 1797 and October 1798.

[11] W. C. Nicholas to Jefferson, October 4, 1798, Jefferson Papers. Jefferson to Nicholas, October 5, 1798. Nicholas to John Breckenridge, October 10, 1798, Breckenridge Family Papers (LC). Jefferson to Madison, October 26, November 17, 1798. Further evidence of two-state planning is found in Jefferson's comment to Senator Mason on October 11, 1798, that "some of the state legislatures" would probably take a strong stand.

[12] Adrienne Koch and Harry Ammon, "The Virginia and Kentucky Resolutions: an Episode in Jefferson's and Madison's Defense of Civil Liberties," *William and Mary Quarterly*, April 1948. (All earlier accounts have serious factual errors or omissions.)

[13] *Ibid.* Jefferson to Madison, November 17, 1798. Jefferson to W. C. Nicholas, November 29, 1798.

[14] D. R. Anderson, *William Branch Giles*, 63, 67. Madison to James Robertson, March 27, 1831. Madison to Jefferson, December 29, 1798.

[15] Address of the General Assembly, Madison, *Writings*, VI, 332-340.

[16] Jefferson to J. Taylor, November 26, 1798. Hamilton to Speaker Jonathan Dayton, undated, *Works* (Lodge), X, 329. Anderson, *op. cit.*, 69.

[17] Jefferson to Madison, February 5, 1799. Representatives Jones, Nicholas, Harrison, Eggleston, Venable and Brent to Madison, February 7, 1799, Madison, *Writings*, VI, 341n. J. Taylor to Madison, March 18, 1798, March 4, 1799, Rives Papers.

[18] J. F. Mercer to Madison, November 14, December 20, 1799, January 6, 1800, Madison MSS. Monroe to Madison, July 13, 1799. Madison to Monroe, December 4, 1794. Jefferson to Madison, January 16, 1799. Madison to Jefferson, February 8, 1799.

[19] *Ibid.* Moving Adams toward peace (though he would have denied it) was the friendly reception France gave to the private "peace mission" of the much-traduced Dr. George Logan (Madison's plow-maker).

[20] Jefferson to Madison, January 3, February 26, 1800. Hamilton to J. McHenry, June 27, 1799 (NYPL).

[21] Jefferson to Madison, August 23, 1799, *William and Mary Quarterly*, April 1948, 165. Jefferson to W. C. Nicholas, August 26, September 5, 1799.

[22] Jefferson to Madison, Monroe to Madison, November 22, 1799.

[23] Madison, "Report on the Resolutions of 1798," *Writings*, VI, 341-406. Madison to Jefferson, December 29, 1799; January 4, 9, 12, 1800.

# INDEX